HITLER'S WAR POETS

Jay W. Baird comes to grips with a theme that has been generally avoided by more than two generations of scholars and literary critics. He argues that German literature did not end with the advent of Hitler in 1933 only to be reborn after the fall of the Third Reich in 1945. Baird demonstrates how poets and writers responded enthusiastically to Hitler's summons to artists to create a cultural revolution commensurate with the political radicalism of the new state, thereby affirming the centrality of renewed German culture.

Hitler's War Poets focuses on the lives and the works of six leading conservative, anticommunist, yet revolutionary authors who articulated the dream of World War I veterans to form a socially just national community. Tradition was redrawn by Rudolf G. Binding, whereas Josef Magnus Wehner dramatized the link from Flanders Fields and Verdun to the Third Reich. Hans Zöberlein exalted anti-Semitism, the Free Corps, and Nazi violence, providing the counterpoint to Edwin Erich Dwinger, who launched an unrelenting assault against "Jewish-Bolshevism." The torch was passed to Eberhard Wolfgang Möller, the leading bard of the revolutionary young generation. But it was Kurt Eggers, a tank commander in the Fifth SS Panzer Division "Viking," who delighted Hitler as he appeared as a prophet bearing the testament of Nietzsche's Zarathustra. Taken together, these authors offered the regime significant support. More important, theirs was a tragic legacy because they provided aesthetic accompaniment to Nazi barbarism and ultimately to the Holocaust.

Jay W. Baird is Professor of History Emeritus at Miami University in Ohio. He has also taught at Stanford University and Pomona College and was a visiting Fellow at the University of Cambridge in 1997 and 2004. His previous books include *To Die for Germany* (1990), *The Mythical World of Nazi War Propaganda, 1939–1945* (1977), and the edited volume *From Nuremberg to My Lai* (1974). He served as president of the German Studies Association from 1993 to 1995 and was recognized by the Holocaust Educational Foundation for distinguished contributions to Holocaust education in 2006.

Hitler's War Poets

Literature and Politics in the Third Reich

JAY W. BAIRD

Miami University (Ohio)

 CAMBRIDGE
UNIVERSITY PRESS

CAMBRIDGE UNIVERSITY PRESS
Cambridge, New York, Melbourne, Madrid, Cape Town, Singapore, São Paulo, Delhi

Cambridge University Press
32 Avenue of the Americas, New York, NY 10013-2473, USA

www.cambridge.org
Information on this title: www.cambridge.org/9780521876896

First published 2008

Printed in the United States of America

A catalog record for this publication is available from the British Library.

Library of Congress Cataloging in Publication Data
Baird, Jay W.
Hitler's war poets : literature and politics in the Third Reich / Jay W. Baird.
p. cm.
Includes bibliographical references.
ISBN-13: 978-0-521-87689-6 (hardback)
ISBN-10: 0-521-87689-3 (hardback)
1. German poetry – 20th century – History and criticism. 2. National socialism and
literature. 3. German poetry – Themes, motives. 4. World War, 1914–1918 – Influence.
5. Heroes in literature. 6. Nationalism in literature. 7. Antisemitism in literature.
I. Title.
PT553.B35 2007
831'.91409358–dc22 2007020893

ISBN 978-0-521-87689-6 hardback

To the memory of my beloved sister, Nancy Baird Rudolp (1933–2001), and for my brother, Jeffrey Ross Baird, one of the world's most generous men

Contents

List of Illustrations

Acknowledgments

Many individuals have been generous with their counsel and assistance during the research and writing of this book. The Fellows of Clare Hall, University of Cambridge, kindly elected me to a visiting fellowship and provided a grand environment in which to work. My thanks go to Michael O'Brien of Jesus College for making this possible and to Richard J. Eden for his many personal kindnesses. Jonathan Steinberg, Richard J. Evans, and Brendan Simms all shared with me the best Cambridge has to offer.

Horst Möller and Udo Wengst of the Institute for Contemporary History in Munich graciously facilitated my extended research visits there, and Hermann Graml, Hans Woller, Klaus Lankheit, Christian Hartmann, and Johannes Hürter made me feel very much at home as well. I would like to thank Hartmut Lehmann of the German Historical Institute, Washington, D.C., as well as Anselm Doering-Manteuffel of Tübingen University for offering me a platform on which to test my views on literature in the Third Reich. The Alexander von Humboldt Foundation awarded Walter Schmitz of the Technische Hochschule Dresden and me a generous Transcoop Program grant to finance a research project and an international conference on the theme of culture and dictatorship held in 1999 at Dresden.

It is proper here to salute Theodore Z. Weiss, president of the Holocaust Educational Foundation (Chicago), a survivor of Auschwitz. For many years Zev, a wonderful human being and friend, has supported my work. His prudence in sending me to study at Yad Vashem, the Holocaust Martyrs' and Heroes' Remembrance Authority, has not only deepened my knowledge of this tragic era but made me acutely aware of the dangers inherent in the marriage of power and culture in the totalitarian state.

Many of the strengths this work might have are attributable in no small way to the influence my mentors have had on me over many decades. I wish to salute here Fritz Stern, Guy Stern, George Mosse, and Gordon A. Craig, whose intellectual leadership and kindness shown to me will never be forgotten.

I would also like to thank my general editor at Cambridge University Press, Lewis Bateman, for his belief in this project and Eric Crahan, who skillfully directed it through the editorial and production process. Konrad Jarausch helped me by offering conceptual and methodological advice as well. I am grateful to both Geoffrey J. Giles and Michael H. Kater for their critical reading of the manuscript for this book. Together they have improved it significantly. The *German Studies Review*, George Mason University Press, Böhlau Verlag, and Thelem Universitätsverlag have all graciously granted permission to reprint materials that originally appeared in their publications.

Without the technical computer support of both Paula Fogt and Bonnie Fannin of Miami University, the book might well have never come to fruition. Finally, words could never express the depth of my gratitude to my wife, Sally Eshelman Baird, for her enduring love and loyalty demonstrated over fifty years. She represents all that is laudable in the Midwestern heartland.

Abbreviations

BAB	Bundesarchiv Berlin
BHSA	Bayerisches Hauptstaatsarchiv
BDM	Bund deutscher Mädel
DLAM	Deutsches Literaturarchiv (Marbach)
IfZ	Institut für Zeitgeschichte
NSDAP	Nationalsozialistische deutsche Arbeiterpartei
OKW	Oberkommando der Wehrmacht
RKK	Reichskulturkammer
SD	Sicherheitsdienst

HITLER'S WAR POETS

Heroic Imagery in the Literature of the Third Reich

In 1914, during the first months of the Great War, the worker poet Heinrich Lersch took pen in hand as he was deployed on the western front and struck up a rhapsodic heroic motif in his poem "Soldier's Goodbye" (*"Soldatenabschied"*). Its words reflect the fiery intensity of those heady days of late summer when naïve youth, like their mythical Greek forbearer Icarus, seduced by the golden beauty of the sun, launched their own flight to death:

> Let me go, Mother, let me go!
> It is no use crying anymore,
> Because we are leaving, to protect the Fatherland!
> Let me go, Mother, let me go.
> I want to take your last goodbye with a kiss.
> Germany must live, even if we must die!
> Lass mich gehn, Mutter, lass mich gehn!
> All das Weinen kann jetzt nichts mehr nützen,
> Denn wir gehn, das Vaterland zu schützen!
> Lass mich gehn, Mutter, lass mich gehn.
> Deinen letzten Gruss will ich vom Mund dir küssen,
> Deutschland muss leben, und wenn wir sterben müssen.[1]

This euphoric death motif set the tone for most of the war generation, as well as for the youth too young to fight in the war but not too young to dream the dream of glory on distant battlefields. After the trauma of 1918, the myth of heroic death became a central theme in the monuments devoted to the Great War. Its most dramatic embodiment was at Langemarck, the heart of the embattled terrain on the Ypres front in Flanders. There, upon entering the sacred grove of heroes, in the German memorial

---

[1] *Kampfgedichte der Zeitenwende. Eine Sammlung aus deutscher Dichtung seit Nietzsche,* "Die junge Reihe. Kampfgedichte der Zeitenwende" (München: Langen-Müller, undated), p. 20.

cemetery where the graves of the fallen are embraced by the same stone and cement bunkers that they once had manned, one sees the lines of Lersch's poem inscribed on the gate.

It is also revealing to walk through the storied Invaliden Cemetery in Berlin, founded by Frederick the Great and thereafter celebrated as the cemetery of national heroes. Much of it was destroyed by the ravages of World War II, as well as by German Democratic Republic building crews who devastated much of it while building the Berlin Wall in the early 1960s. Nevertheless, this mutilated and melancholy reminder of lost German honor has its own historic tales to tell. Among the tombstones there, lying in the shadow of the graves of Scharnhorst and von Moltke and the esteemed holders of the Pour le Mèrite, one can discern the following poem, written for his own epitaph by Major Guido von Gillhaussen, commander of the Light Infantry Battalion in the Prussian Grenadier Guards Regiment Nr. 5, holder of the Iron Cross First and Second Class, and Knight of the Order of St. John of Jerusalem. In April 1918, as Gillhaussen lay dying at the age of forty-eight – he had but a week to live after having been wounded in action at Villers-Brettoneux on the Somme front – he mused on his fate:

> I know why I am suffering,
> And have shed my blood . . .
> I fought in the German Army
> For German sacredness,
> As a shield bearer for German honor
> For the glory of the German future!
>
> Therefore despite terrible pain,
> And despite the excruciating agony of my wounds
> There lives in my German heart
> Only gratefulness and the warm rays of the sun.
>
> Ich weiss wofür ich leide,
> Mein Blut vergossen habe . . .
> Ich stritt im deutschen Heere
> Für deutsches Heiligtum,
> Als Schildknapp deutscher Ehre
> Für deutscher Zukunft Ruhm!
>
> Drum lebt trotz grimmig Schmerzen,
> Trotz wundenheisse Qual
> In meinem deutschen Herzen
> Nur Dank und Sonnenstrahl.[2]

[2] Jay W. Baird, Berlin diary, June 7, 1992. Major von Gillhaussen was born May 12, 1870 and died in a military hospital in Aachen, May 2, 1918. At his death he was a member of the Third Garde-Grenadier-Regiment zu Fuss. See *Ehrentafel des reichsdeutschen Adels 1914–1919* (Gotha: Justus Perthes), p. 76.

In earlier centuries, such innocent rapture was directed to Christ and the Church, but in the modern era the secular state took on the aura of the divine. In Hitler's words, "We want no other God except Germany."[3] The lyric joy in death for Germany that so many professed in the Great War soon enough would give way to the celebration of death for the new trinity of Führer, Volk, and Fatherland. Ultimately a distorted concept of heroism found Germans ascending a mountain whose grand peaks were crowned by a union of the virtues of strength, race, and intellect. The long road from Flanders and the Somme would lead to Stalingrad high above the Volga, and from Stalingrad to the acid terrain of Auschwitz. It is my hope in this work to demonstrate how the muses of poetry and literary creativity were employed to offer aesthetic accompaniment to this tragic and vainglorious quest for greatness.[4]

The agony of defeat and communist insurgency, of the postwar shame, humiliation, and hunger found its poet in Dietrich Eckart, who had a profound influence on the thinking of Hitler, Rosenberg, and Goebbels and the future course of Nazi ideology. His hard-hitting style pulled no punches and gave his assault on Bolshevism and world Jewry a resounding force and a primitive yet seductively influential attraction. The greatest attraction was to Hitler himself, however, who acknowledged his personal debt to Eckart in the development of his own political convictions. Eckart's admonition, "Germany awake!," was to be found on every National Socialist Party standard, and his frightful poem was to become a fighting song of the movement:

> Storm, Storm, Storm!
> Ring the bells from tower to tower!
> Ring, so that sparks begin to fly,
> Jewry has appeared to take over the Reich...
> Ring out the storm, so that the world rises up
> Amidst the thunder in avenging salvation.
> Woe be to the Volk, that dreams on today,
> Germany, awake!

[3] Hans Müller, "Der pseudoreligiöse Charakter der nationalsozialistischen Weltanschauung," *Geschichte in Wissenschaft und Unterricht*, Heft 6/1961, pp. 337–52. According to Müller, this Hitler quotation was reported only in one newspaper, the *Bayerischer Kurier* Nr. 142, May 25, 1923.

[4] One could not ask for better commentary on this theme than that offered in George L. Mosse, *Fallen Soldiers: Reshaping the Memory of the World Wars* (New York/Oxford: Oxford University Press, 1990). See also Claus-Ekkehard Bärsch, *Die politische Religion des Nationalsozialismus* (München: Fink, 2002); Konrad H. Jarausch and Michael Geyer, *Shattered Past. Reconstructing German Histories* (Princeton: Princeton University Press, 2003), pp. 111–48.

Sturm, Sturm, Sturm!
Läutet die Glocken von Turm zu Turm!
Läutet, dass die Funken zu sprühen beginnen,
Judas erscheint, das Reich zu gewinnen...
Läutet Sturm, dass die Erde sich bäumt
Unter dem Donner der rettenden Rache.
Wehe dem Volk, das heute noch träumt,
Deutschland, erwache![5]

For more than two generations, leading scholars and writers representing virtually every discipline have grappled with the problems posed
by Germany's tragic history in the twentieth century. However, there is
a serious gap in this scholarship, which until recently has almost totally
ignored the literary aesthetics of the German nationalist experience. Many
German and Austrian scholars, as well as the international community of
Germanists – understandably longing for political and cultural transformation – have shunned the era as if there were no continuity whatsoever
between the Weimar Republic, the Third Reich, the Federal Republic
of Germany, and the German Democratic Republic.[6] Richie Robertson,
writing in *The Cambridge History of German Literature*, edited by Helen
Watanabe-O'Kelly of Oxford University, devotes all of six pages to the
entire era of the Third Reich in a work spanning over six hundred pages.
Seldom in the history of literary criticism has a more poorly informed
analysis been published by a writer who has quite obviously never read
the works he is discussing.[7]

Ingo Roland Stoehr, in his survey of German literature in the twentieth,
century asserts that National Socialism is insignificant in the history of literary movements.[8] However, it is much more illuminating to understand
that the poetry and literature of the Third Reich were not written with
abstract beauty and universal absolutes in mind. What was significant was
its political importance and the writers of the period quite consciously

---

[5] Bärsch, pp. 60–98.
[6] There have been some notable exceptions to this rule. See, for example, Uwe-K. Ketelsen, *Literatur und Drittes Reich* (Schernfeld: SH-Verlag, 1992); Horst Denkler and Karl Prümm, eds., *Die deutsche Literatur im Dritten Reich* (Stuttgart: Reclam, 1976); Ralf Schnell, *Dichtung in finsteren Zeiten* (Reinbek bei Hamburg: Rowohlt, 1998); Günter Hartung, *Literatur und Ästhetik des deutschen Faschismus* (Berlin: Akademie Verlag, 1983).
[7] Helen Watanabe-O'Kelly, *The Cambridge History of German Literature* (Cambridge: Cambridge University Press, 1997).
[8] Ingo R. Stoehr, *German Literature of the Twentieth Century*, Camden House History of German Literature, no. 10 (Rochester, NY: Camden House, 2001), pp. 137–92.

endeavored to further the goals of Hitler and the National Socialist program. Their writers knew just how important literature, poetry, drama, and music were in the assault on modernity. These purveyors of Nazi lyricism saw life in terms of a warrior ideal on the Homeric model, and many gave poetic expression to their belief in a *völkisch* racism and the superiority of the Germanic racial ideal. Theirs was a new historical reality, often inspired by romanticism and love for great historical figures and eras. They heard songs that others did not hear and worshipped at the altar of unchanging organic principles. The eternal German oak was their mantra. Theirs was the world of nature and Alpine beauty, of field and stream, of dense forests, of fresh snow adorning majestic pine trees. They clung to a hopeless idealization of harmonious German family life that existed only in their imagination. Many lived in a historic world peopled by long-dead heroes. They marched with the Germanic tribes under Hermann the Cherusker to victory over the legions of Caesar Augustus in the Teutoburger Forest, they heard the trumpets of Roland calling them to sacrifice against the Moors, and they joined the forces of Frederick II, Hohenstaufen, and stood witness to his glorious court at Monreale, high above Palermo in bone-dry Sicily. They formed a guard around Martin Luther against the forces of evil and rode with Frederick the Great against the enemies of Prussia. For these writers, it was only natural that they would crown the mythical edifice of the Third Reich and its leader with the laurel leaves of poetry and song.

Taken together, National Socialist poets and writers drew variations on the mystic vision of the youthful songwriter Hans Baumann, composer of the most popular political songs of the era, when, pointing to the heavens, he intoned:

> Now the cathedral is standing, it's standing squarely in the light. . . .
> The suffering is gone, that tore our Volk apart . . .
> And our song makes us strong and sure. . . .
> The cathedral is standing, it's standing squarely in the light.
>
> Nun steht der Dom, nun steht er ganz im Licht . . .
>
> Die Not verging, die unser Volk zerriss . . .
> Und unser Lied macht sicher und gewiss . . .
> So steht der Dom, so steht er ganz im Licht.[9]

[9] Jay W. Baird, *To Die For Germany. Heroes in the Nazi Pantheon* (Bloomington: Indiana University Press, 1990), p. 161.

Baumann's words offered an eloquent – if naïve – expression of the belief
that they were the heralds of a new era, indeed prophets of Germanic fate.
As Arthur Zweininger has observed, National Socialists saw themselves
as victims of history, and they were determined to overcome the shame
of defeat, communist insurrection, and the humiliation of Versailles.[10]
Their writers became Hitler's poets, validating their dreams of a brilliant
future for the German Reich. Their contributions were in harmony with
the movement's ideology, which at the core was based on the irrational.
They were as certain of victory as their Marxist adversaries, and their
belief that race was the central determinant for historical change paralleled
the communist faith that dialectical materialism held all the answers to
historical development.

The cultural and intellectual rebellion against modernity had roots in
Central Europe going back to the French Revolution, and its enemies
stood foursquare against liberalism in all its forms. They hated the city
and its culture, and they loathed democracy. They were absolutely certain that "parasitical world Jewry" stood behind not only the treachery
that led to defeat in the Great War but also for the culture of Weimar,
which mocked traditional German values. Millions of German soldiers,
they asserted, had not been killed and wounded so that the Jews could
turn Berlin into a decadent, materialistic, and cosmopolitan playground,
host to capitalist excess and communist putrefaction alike. When Hitler
wrote in *Mein Kampf* that race was the dominant factor not only in historical development but also in the formation of culture and values and
that Jewry, "the bearer of a culture-destroying parasitical bacillus," must
be eradicated, he did not stand alone. Rather, his was the most radical
reaction to the incendiary cultural milieu of the era. Hitler called for not
only a total political transformation of the nation but a complete cultural
transformation as well.

Goebbels established the ground rules for this endeavor in an address
he gave at the ceremonial opening of the Reich Culture Chamber in the
Berlin Philharmonic in November 1933. Hitler himself looked on as his
propaganda minister addressed the theme of a new beginning for German
culture. In this speech, Goebbels both established guidelines for future cultural policy and appointed the leaders of a new cultural administration,
which in fact turned out to be a vast and unwieldy bureaucracy intent on

---

[10] Bernhard Weyergraf, ed., *Literatur der Weimarer Republik 1918–1933*, Vol. 8: *Hansers
Sozialgeschichte der deutschen Literatur vom 16. Jahrhundert bis zur Gegenwart*
(München/Wien: Carl Hanser Verlag, 1995), p. 30.

achieving the Führer's goal of a revolution in culture commensurate with the dramatic changes in the political life of the nation.[11] In his grandiose Ciceronian style, Goebbels boasted that after enduring a tortured period in their history, the German people had finally found themselves through National Socialism. The shackles of liberalism and parliamentary democracy, foreign to the nature of the Germanic Volk, had been overthrown. The time had now come to reconfigure German culture with artistic forms organically rooted in the soul of the people. The decadence of the Weimar Republic demonstrated that art does not and cannot stand alone as an absolute. Rather, he claimed, "from this day forward the life-threatening crisis of artists and writers has come to an end. Culture is the highest expression of the creative impulses of a people. Should the artistic man ever lose his firm grounding in the folk community on which he must depend to withstand the struggles of life, then he has delivered himself over to the enemies of civilization, and sooner or later they will destroy him." The future of Germany and its culture would be firmly grounded in a new romanticism, a "romanticism of steel," at once heroic, realistic, and aggressive. German culture needed new blood, he claimed. Leadership could only come from the young, brave artists, who were in harmony with the nation's breakout to the future, individuals who stood fearlessly on the precipice between yesterday and tomorrow, totally rejecting the failed values of the reactionary past. The way to the future lay open, he intoned. In a grandiose flourish, he invoked the words of Ulrich von Hutten to grace the proclaimed union of power and intellect in the Third Reich, saying, "What a period we live in, oh arts and sciences, what a wonderful time to be alive!"[12]

It did not take long for Germans to discover what Goebbels's visionary proclamation of a new era of fascist aesthetics based on political realities would actually mean. More often than not, pedantic dilettantism ruled the day, as most literary works had to pass the litmus test as to whether they emanated from and reflected the Aryan Volk soul. A complicated situation was made even worse through the machinations of Alfred Rosenberg, who endeavored to extend his powers as the official Nazi Party ideologist into areas involving censorship of literary and artistic endeavors, and who proceeded to establish his own Byzantine bureaucracy with a gaggle

---

[11] See Alan E. Steinweis, *Art, Ideology, and Economics in Nazi Germany. The Reich Chambers of Music, Theater, and the Visual Arts* (Chapel Hill: University of North Carolina Press, 1993).

[12] "Feierliche Eröffnung der Reichskulturkammer," *Börsenblatt für den deutschen Buchhandel*, Nr. 269, November 18, 1933.

of offices dealing in cultural red tape.[13] Three years later, Rosenberg's bureaucratic minion, *Reichskunstwart* Franz Moraller, proudly reviewed the accomplishments of the Reich Culture Chamber in an address to the leaders of the publishing industry in Berlin. The book was truly the "sword of the spirit," he claimed, and how splendid it was that once and for all the "Jewish-Bolshevik cultural anarchy" and its inciters had been swept away. No exceptions had been made, he claimed, to the overarching obligation of every single artist to fight and to write for the Volk in the Nationalist Socialist spirit. The artist of the future, he submitted, the writer of the Third Reich, comes from the marching columns of the Sturmabteilungen (SA), and he, too, is ready to fight and die for the people. The "blood-red flags of the Movement" link the past and the future and inspire the artist to conceive of and to create the new National Socialist man.[14]

Many right wing intellectuals and cultural conservatives demanded the destruction of liberal institutions and the political culture which they fostered. Many conservative literary figures had joined in the assault on Weimar Germany and taken together, their ideas formed the basis for the breathtaking changes to come in the Third Reich. Many of them believed firmly in the idea that race determined culture, and their cultural criticism was in harmony with the parameters Hitler, Goebbels, and Rosenberg had established. The novelist and critic, Erwin Guido Kolbenheyer, was a leading herald for the Germanic cause, calling on the nation's writers to think heroically and to write heroically. They were obliged to form a united cultural front in the sacred struggle for freedom. "Creativity rests on the foundation of race," he posited, and the muses must enter the struggle against the Americanization and Bolshevization of German culture. The nation was not in a cancerous Spenglerian decline, he affirmed. Quite the contrary, it was engaged in a life or death struggle against the forces of mediocrity. Greatness, he was certain, was assured if only the muses would return the national gaze toward the stars.[15] The critic Ludwig Friedrich

[13] See Ernst Piper, *Alfred Rosenberg. Hitlers Chefideologe* (Munich: Karl Blessing, 2005), pp. 323–99.

[14] Reichskunstwart Franz Moraller, "Buch und Volk," *Der deutsche Schriftsteller. Zeitschrift für die Schriftsteller in der Reichsschriftumskammer*: 5 (May 1936), pp. 97–8. See also Franz Moraller, personnel file, Reichsschriftumskammer, Bundesarchiv Berlin-Lichterfelde (herein after cited as BAB).

[15] E. G. Kolbenheyer, *Die volksbiologischen Grundlagen der Freiheitsbewegung* (München: Langen/Müller 1933). See also Ulrike Hass, "Vom Aufstand der Landschaft gegen Berlin," in *Literatur der Weimarer Republik 1918–1933*, pp. 358–9.

Barthel struck the same motif when he proclaimed that "where our blood ends, Germany ends as well."[16]

The writer Wilhelm Schäfer parodied foreign and Jewish assaults on the Third Reich in an address he delivered in Berlin titled "The German Return to the Middle Ages." In a highly articulate, rhetorically eloquent style, he launched into an attack on European culture since the Enlightenment. Like so many conservatives of the era, his critique of modern culture was based on his admiration for the medieval world. He interpreted that era as an integrated, class-based, God-centered, absolutist culture grounded in battle and struggle, the antithesis of what he assayed to be a modern concern for the popular welfare. Such a world had colonized the East, when the Cross, united with the Sword, formed the dual columns of sovereignty. This, Schäfer noted, led to a heroic worldview whereby "all of life was grounded in the mystery of eternity."[17] This grand edifice has been replaced with the shallow and superficial modern concept of progress, in a world in which bravery, loyalty, pride, and naturalness had no place. Greed and the endless, stultifying chase after material wealth and the new idolatry of technology made modern man think he was the ruler of the earth. Gradually, the self-satisfaction of modern man with his toys became a way of life, and ultimately he would choke on technology. Modern man had even learned to fly. Yet curiously, Schäfer observed, his soul could not fly with him into the heavens. It had become so besotted with sensational new discoveries that it simply could not take off and instead remained earthbound, mired in vacuous mediocrity. Even knowledge could not feed the soul, hanging as it was on the tree of progress. All this stopped abruptly, however, in 1914, when all the old leaves blew down in one rush of wind. Those who returned in 1918 knew only one thing: "man, his duty, and Germany." Henceforth, "only the Volk can give meaning to history." This was the true meaning of the birth of the Third Reich, Schäfer proclaimed. This was a "return" not to medieval depravity – as Germany's enemies would have it – but rather a return to the Germanic peoples' true heroic nature.[18]

The academic literary critic Heinz Kindermann, a professor of literature at the University of Münster, drew variations on these themes in a work that summarized the central motifs of what he considered to be a

---

[16] Ludwig Friedrich Barthel, *Vom Eigentum der Seele* (Jena: Eugen Diederichs, 1941).
[17] Wilhelm Schäfer, *Der deutsche Rückfall ins Mittelalter* (München: Langen/Müller, 1934).
[18] Ibid.

reborn German culture. Literary values had been completely transformed in the new era, he proclaimed, as the perverted literary movements of Expressionism and New Reality faded into the dustbin of history. "Show me your view of the past, and I will show you what kind of a future you are worthy of," he wrote. German letters, he argued, clearly had been as decadent as the Weimar Republic, whose leaders did everything possible to foster and cultivate its weak, cosmopolitan literary effusions. Man and nature would be joined, as the "I" gave way to the "we" of the folk community, where the individual found true freedom by surrendering to the racial whole. Henceforth, Kindermann argued, a noble, tragic-heroic worldview would be joined with an organic-biological racial consciousness, resulting in the flowering of a grand literary culture. The "rhythm of immortality" would flow spontaneously from its source deep in the spring of the eternal Germanic life source as cosmic beauty replaced decrepit, craven and materialistic democratic values.[19]

The glory of the new era was that once more – as in the great days of Hölderlin and Schiller – the literary arts would chart the way to a Germanic golden age. The road to this future had, however, been paved in the blood of Flanders Fields, Verdun, and the Somme. The German spirit had been reborn in that tragic struggle. "Comradeship became the ruling standard for life," he submitted, offering consolation in defeat and an eternally renewing confidence in the final victory. Comradeship was the new blood of life, offering what the lettered front writer Paul Alverdes called the grace of the "eternal truth" that replaced reason and all concerns of self-interest. Duty and love of the flag ruled over all other considerations. Mass death at the front had brought the rebirth of the soul and returned the German vision back to what was real. In the simple but profound words of Ernst Jünger, "We had gotten to know the earth once more."[20]

The educator and literary critic Arno Mulot put a sinister twist on the front experience in his essay "The Soldier in German Literature of Our Era." The comradeship demonstrated by German soldiers was unique, he claimed, a world apart from the perfidious defeatist values celebrated in Weimar war literature. In no way could its alienating and world-weary pacifism be compared to the beauty of the unifying inner spirit of the real German soldiers. Mulot wasted no words in describing the reason

---

[19] Heinz Kindermann, *Die deutsche Gegenwartsdichtung im Kampf um die deutsche Lebensform* (Wien: Wienerverlagsgesellschaft, 1942).

[20] The poet Herybert Menzel believed in this primal truth as well, as demonstrated when he wrote the memorable line, "Earth, we belong to you." Ibid., pp. 23–4.

for this when he claimed that the authors of these works "were never blood of our blood and nature of our nature." Rather, they acted as a bacillus that was able to cast the Germanic body politic temporarily into a serious fever but that eventually was overcome when the nation cast them out of its blood-based community once and for all. Thus, in the future, Mulot argued, these outcasts would have nothing whatsoever to do with the Germanic cultural community. The poisonous spirit and writing emanating from their smoky and decadent spiritual headquarters, the Romanisches Café on Berlin's Kurfürstendamm, had passed into history. From now on, German culture would be rooted in the monumental spirit of the German front soldier and his sacrifice, a spirit that had engendered the rebirth of an entire people. Adolf Hitler, the incarnation of that spirit, would show the way.[21]

The critic Hermann Pongs grounded his influential work *War as Folk Destiny in German Literature* in the belief that the front experience set the stage for a transformation that would lead Germany to a spiritual rebirth. He noted that one had to look no further than the works of Paul Alverdes, most notably *Reinhold im Dienst*, to discover that true creativity and poetic insight occurs only when fundamental images of the soul take on immortal form, that is, when word and Gestalt are united.[22] The protagonist, Reinhold, was to experience the beauty of learning personally that comradeship was the source of grace, a grace that enabled a young bourgeois volunteer to become united in spirit with the common man. This miraculous blessing in tragedy amid the carnage of the Great War enabled him to become transfigured as he became one with the peoples' destiny. Mortally wounded, Reinhold did not want to be transferred to a field hospital, only to die alone. Rather, he requested to be returned to the men of his battery, and he passed away there surrounded by his comrades, all of whom understood the divine gravity of the moment. He had achieved immortality and would remain safe and secure among his brothers forever. As Reinhold was transfigured, "he felt the eyes of the Fatherland directed at him, and all saw this." According to Hermann Pongs, death in this manner was a thing of beauty, and "those present were confident that men who passed away like this never die."[23] Loyalty, goodness, and depth of character had accompanied

[21] Arno Mulot, *Der Soldat in der deutschen Dichtung unserer Zeit* (Stuttgart: J.B. Metzlersche Verlagsbuchhandlung, 1938), pp. 85–6.

[22] Paul Alverdes, *Reinhold oder die Verwandelten* (München: G. Müller, 1931).

[23] Hermann Pongs, *Krieg als Volkschicksal im deutschen Schrifttum* (Stuttgart: J.B. Metzlersche Verlagsbuchhandlung, 1934), pp. 47–49. See also Bernhard Weyergraf,

his transfiguration. Through the grace of comradeship, class had given way to the national community, as a bourgeois was thrust into the heroic role of Everyman. According to Pongs, it was only Stefan George who reached greater heights of eloquence, most notably in his poem "To the Dead."[24]

The poetry and literature of the National Socialists was written by the young generation. As Peter Loewenberg demonstrated in his seminal article, "The Psycho-historical Origins of the Nazi Youth Cohort," the youth of Germany had a special burden to bear in this era. Their shared experiences, including hunger, malnutrition, longing for their absent fathers, loneliness, and defeat – led them to outrageous wish-fulfilling fantasies and to the maintenance of infantile attitudes as adults. This situation was exacerbated by economic need and career hopelessness. Their longing for a Führer, for a Volk community, for the security of hierarchy, for shared danger, for mutual love, and for power were all components of this fantasy. Loewenberg was on the mark when he observed that the young generation made a political program of the longings of their deprived childhoods, resulting in a "regressive illusion of Nazism which ended in a repetition of misery at the front and starvation at home made worse by destroyed cities, irremediable guilt, and millions of new orphans."[25] It is impossible to recreate the past, and to deny this basic fact of historical reality leads inevitably to disaster.

Myth is a seductive siren, calling the vulnerable to their destruction, and Germans in the twentieth century were particularly susceptible to its sinister enticements. The classic hero Odysseus, on the long journey home from Troy, understood the danger posed to his mariners by the haunting beauty of the songs of the sirens. He had the good sense to fill the ears of his sailors with wax and to tie himself to the mast of his ship to avoid certain destruction. How different it would be for German youth in the

---

"Konservative Wandlungen" in *Literatur der Weimarer Republik 1918–1933* (München/Wien: Carl Hanser, 1995), pp. 266–73.

[24] He considered especially the lines of George that pointed to the immortality of heroes, saying, "dann flattert im Frühwind mit wahrhaftem Zeichen die Königsstandarte und grüsst sich verneigend die Hehren, die Helden!" Ibid., pp. 85–7. See also Robert E. Norton, *Secret Germany. Stefan George and His Circle* (Ithaca, New York: Cornell University Press, 2002), pp. 481–2.

[25] See Peter Loewenberg, "The Psychohistorical Origins of the Nazi Youth Cohort," *American Historical Review* 76 (1971), pp. 1457–1502. See also Michael H. Kater, "Generationskonflikt als Entwicklungsfaktor in der NS-Bewegung vor 1933," *Geschichte und Gesellschaft* 11 (1985), pp. 217–43.

first half of the century, whose search for wholeness only appeared to be purifying and ennobling but in fact featured a continuous interplay with death. The Nazi obsession with lyric beauty, which was found in their poetry and songs of death, lends credulity to the contention of the Vichyite Robert Brasillach that fascism was poetry, the poetry of the twentieth century.[26]

The German romance with death was nothing new, having flowered in the Romantic period in the works of Novalis (Friedrich von Hardenberg), who set a standard for longing for death. Wagner wove variations on this motif, and the youth of the war generation found Rainer Maria Rilke's *Die Weise vom Leben und Tod des Cornets Christoph Rilke* a welcome antidote to fin de siècle cultural malaise. Yet no matter how far afield the National Socialists might roam, they invariably returned to the killing fields of their fathers and brothers in World War I. Battle was where they found their soul, as had the young recruit Ernst Jünger, for whom the storm of steel and the excitement of combat was an adventurous life experience second to none. For Jünger, full-scale battle was something grand, akin to riding a thunderbolt through cosmic space, thrusting man ever closer into the realm of the gods. For Walter Flex, however, the gifted poet who would be killed on the eastern front in 1917, to serve the Fatherland presented the young soldier with the rare opportunity to receive the elements in a feast of national communion. Death became a blood sacrifice and was to be welcomed. "Death is the greatest experience for great souls," he wrote in his sensitive book, *The Wanderer between Two Worlds*, noting that

> When your days on earth are over and the windows of the soul,
> the colorful human eyes, darken like church windows in the twilight,
> the soul embraced in the dimming temple of God in your dying body
> blossoms forth in a darkened glow like the All Holy at the altar under the
> everlasting light and fills with the deep splendor of eternity.[27]

After burying his dear friend Lieutenant Ernst Wursche, Flex felt the pain of separation, a pain that would find no end. In his suffering, Flex

---

[26] David Carroll, *French Literary Fascism: Nationalism, Anti-Semitism, and the Ideology of Culture* (Princeton: Princeton University Press, 1995), pp. 122–3. On the fascist death motif, see also Saul Friedländer, *Reflections of Nazism: An Essay on Kitsch and Death* (New York: Harper & Roe, 1984).

[27] Walter Flex, *Der Wanderer zwischen beiden Welten* (Munich: Beck 1918), p. 82. See Scott D. Denham, *Visions of War* (Bern: Peter Lang, 1992), pp. 55–69.

turned within to find the answer, the better to discern meaning in the death. And he wrote:

> The sword, so often gazed at with joy
> Glows silently in its own brightness.
> It covers the breast of the sun youth...
> The golden lance of flowers.

> Das Schwert, so oft beschaut mit Lust,
> Glüht still in eig'nem Glanze.
> Es deckt des Sonnenjünglings Brust...
> Der gold'nen Blumenlanze.

The fallen were now fulfilled. No longer were they among those striving to find meaning in a materialistic society that seemed to be devoid of honor. Flex admonished those left behind to cease grieving for their loved ones but instead to affirm the nobility of their sacrifice. "Don't you know about the eternal youth of the dead?" he queried.[28]

Throughout the 1920s, countless novels and poetic works were devoted to the hopeless endeavor of somehow making sense of the tragedy of the Great War. The antiwar literature produced by the Expressionists, pacifists, and communists after the defeat in 1918 was given a great deal of attention and enjoyed a wide following. Caustic critics such as Kurt Tucholsky and an entire stable of left-wing writers waged an endless assault on both the Weimar Republic and the nationalists. Erich Maria Remarque enjoyed a spectacular success with his pacifist novel *All Quiet on the Western Front*. In the event, the conservatives and National Socialists launched a deadly barrage of their own, offering a cultural accompaniment to parallel the increasing political success of the right wing. Ernst Jünger was brilliantly seductive in his eloquent yet troubling works that found something beautiful, and even transcendent, in the violence and death he encountered at the front. For his part, Rittmeister Rudolf Binding clung to the past, lauding the values of bravery and individualism in a manner that can only be referred to as an atavistic, neo-romantic longing for the values of an era that had in reality passed into history and was based on the nobility of the horseman and cavalry. For the time being, the future lay with lesser talents, men who shared both the front experience and a vision of future greatness for Germany under totally new leadership. They all agreed that Germany had fallen short at the

---

[28] Flex, pp. 88–9, 98. Flex used the word *Heimrecht* in this connection, in effect claiming that his immortal soul had the right to return home and to live forever among his loved ones.

moment of destiny not because of weaknesses in men and materiel, but simply because of incompetent leadership. This corps of writers included Hans Zöberlein, Josef Magnus Wehner, Edwin Erich Dwinger, Richard Euringer, Heinz Steguweit, and Franz Schauwecker, all of whom published novels firmly grounded in German nationalism. Individuals such as these were very much in vogue and taken together sold staggering numbers of books.

Tedious Nazi novelists such as the Berlin-Wedding Sturmführer Otto Paust entered the lists as well. Paust numbered among the influential journalists on the staff of Goebbels's daily newspaper *Der Angriff*, and he went to great lengths to create the definitive saga glorifying the street fighters without whose bravery and sacrifice, he was certain, the creation of the Third Reich was inconceivable. Paust mythologized the nation's agony with titles that barely concealed the banality of the writing: *Volk in the Firestorm* for the war, *Nation in Agony* featuring the deployment of the Free Corps in the liquidation of the communist-led Spartacist revolution, and finally the last work in the trilogy, *Land in Light*, which detailed the euphoria and optimism of the early years of the Third Reich.[29]

Poetry and song were very inspiring to the young generation who were only boys during the war but who longed to take part nevertheless. They idolized their fathers, uncles, and older brothers who served at the front, and glorified the exploits of their favorite war heroes such as the fighter aces.[30] However, they themselves, a different generation, would form a new wave of poets and writers who formed the elite corps of the National Socialist literary guard. They were drawn to Reich Youth Leader Baldur von Schirach, a melodramatic troubadour with a burning death wish, whose rhapsodic lyrics fired their youthful imaginations into heights of ecstasy. Schirach had an uncanny ability to give poetic expression to the National Socialist movement, as the myths of Langemarck and the Somme gave way to the often macabre lyricism which accompanied the Party's breathless "period of struggle." One poem of his in this genre stood out above all others, lending a baroque luster to the abortive Munich Beer Hall Putsch of November 1923. In this work, Schirach borrowed the central redemptive motif of Christianity when he likened the blood shed by the

---

[29] See Otto Paust, *Volk im Feuer* (Berlin: F. Eher, 1938), *Nation im Not* (Berlin: W. Limpert, 1936) and *Land im Licht* (Berlin: W. Limpert, 1941).

[30] For an outstanding example of this, see "The Image of the War Ace," in Peter Fritzsche, *A Nation of Flyers. German Aviation and the Popular Imagination* (Cambridge: Harvard University Press 1992), pp. 59–101.

National Socialist "immortals" to that of Christ on the Good Friday hill
of Calvary:

> God isn't showing himself
> In the old ways
> But you can feel his presence
> Where the flags
> Of our faith wave: on the scaffold.

> There, where the devils cry out:
> "Recant, you dog, or die!"
> That for which they once built cathedrals,
> For us the steps of the Feldherrnhalle
> Are an altar.

> Nicht in alten Bahnen
> Ist Gott
> Du kannst ihn ahnen,
> wo die Fahnen
> des Glaubens wehen: am Schafott.

> Dort wo die Teufel rufen:
> "Schwör' ab, Hund, oder falle!"
> Was sie auch Dome schufen,
> Uns sind Altar die Stufen
> Der Feldherrnhalle.[31]

The postwar instability and shame left the young generation very confused. The loss of the war, the fall of the monarchy, the threat of communism, and the rejection of familiar institutions and values exacerbated
their instability. It was not only that the politics of the day was chaotic;
rather, it was the fact that a chaos reigned deep in their souls as well.
They suffered not only the loss of their fathers and older brothers in the
war, but many had lost their homelands to Poland or Czechoslovakia.
Such was the case with Hans Jürgen Nierentz, a native of Poznan (Posen),
whom Goebbels later was to call to the Propaganda Ministry in the division of cultural affairs. Nierentz expressed the agony of his generation in
the poem, "We are Germany":

> As Germany collapsed, we were still only boys,
> We were young and had no banners of our own.
> Victory lay buried out there at the feet of the enemy.
> Germany was night. And we were Germany.

---

[31] Baldur von Schirach, "Am 9. November vor der Feldherrnhalle zu München," *Die Fahne
der Verfolgten* (Berlin: Zeitgeschichte Verlag, n.d.), p. 32.

> We too died from the pain of the swift fall,
> We too were destroyed and shattered,
> And loved Germany, Germany above all,
> And loved nothing more than this in the world.

> Als Deutschland stürtzte, waren wir noch Knaben,
> wir waren jung und hatten kein Panier.
> Der Sieg lag draussen vor dem Feind begraben.
> Deutschland war Nacht. Und Deutschland waren wir.

> Wir fielen mit im Schmerz des jähen Falles,
> Wir waren mit zertrümmert und zerschellt,
> Und liebten Deutschland, Deutschland über alles,
> Und hatten nichts mehr lieber in der Welt.[32]

Many of the young were drawn to what they considered the sacrificial majesty of death, and they were ready to lay down their lives for Germany and for Hitler. It was not by chance that the lyrics of the Hitler Youth anthem – written by Baldur von Schirach – were dedicated not to life but to the search for eternal life in death. They sang their song with great enthusiasm not only at Nuremberg, but at weekly meetings in their lairs, on city streets, and on country paths. Only misplaced idealism could have inspired their hymn of praise to death, which concluded with the lines:

> And our flag leads us into eternity,
> Yes, our flag means more than death!

> Und die Fahne führt uns in die Ewigkeit,
> Ja, die Fahne ist mehr als der Tod![33]

In their joy, others could not resist casting a contrasting gaze back to the terrible days of their boyhood in the Weimar Republic, never doubting for a moment that the Jews were to blame for their unhappiness. Life was so different now in the Third Reich, but lest they forget how they had suffered, young Gerd Gaiser wrote in his poem, "Der Führer":

> And so we were created in poverty and hardship.
> But we learned even as boys that hunger does not
> Make one dishonorable. We never sold out our
> Ideals for the good life. We aren't beguiled by you over
> There with your cozy warm stoves. The eyelashes

---

[32] Hans Jürgen Nierentz, "Deutschland sind wir," *Kampfgedichte der Zeitenwende. Die Heldische Dichtung von Langemarck bis zur Gegenwart* (Berlin: Junge Generation Verlag, 1934), p. 36.

[33] Baldur von Schirach, "Unsere Fahne flattert uns voran!", in *Rufe in das Reich*, ed. Herbert Böhme (Berlin: Junge Generation Verlag, 1934), p. 360.

Of your shallow women have lost their charm.
Your dances seem empty to us,
Your noise empty.
A Hebrew leads the way to this:
One day the life of a butcher sow will be your lot,
Sticky and fat.

Und so auch schuf uns die Not.
Wir lernten
Schon als Knaben, dass Hunger nicht ehrlos macht.
Nie kaufte ein üppiger Tisch uns die hohen
Hoffnungen ab.
Wir neiden euch nicht, ihr drüben, eurer Kamine
Schläferndes Warm. Die Wimper eurer
Flachen entzauberten Weiber betört uns nicht.
Leer heissen uns eure Tänze,
Leer euer Lärm.
Die ein Hebräer anführt:
Einer Schlachtsau Leben wird einstmals das eure gelten,
Stickig und fett.[34]

This cruel poem no doubt referred to the Nazi epithet, "Jewish-capitalist swine," which often appeared in Nazi propaganda.

The National Socialists made every effort to demonstrate that they were creating a beautiful world. Artists and propagandists knew that the immediacy and aesthetic potential of cinema was particularly well suited to convey the theme of lyric Nazism. Joined to poetry and song, action and sport, it made the attraction of the Hitler Youth and the *Bund deutscher Mädel* nearly irresistible to most young boys and girls.[35] Long before Leni Riefenstahl employed her directorial genius on the fields of the Nuremberg Party Rally for her classic film *Triumph of the Will*, Party cinéastes had turned to the theme of youth in their work. The result was the remarkable recruitment film *Hochland Hitlerjugend* in which the healthy and spirited activities of the Bavarian Hitler Youth are juxtaposed in remarkable contrast to the dank, diseased, and dark world of Weimar Germany. Well fed and bathed in sunlight, the Hitler Youth are presented as a joyous and confident lot. Their happiness is fueled by fast-paced, healthy activities and sport of every kind. Viewers see them hiking, sailing, racing

---

[34] Gerd Gaiser, *Reiter am Himmel* (München: Langen/Müller, 1941), pp. 58–9. I am indebted to Professor Fritz Hackert, Deutsches Seminar, Universität Tübingen, for this reference.

[35] On this important motif, refer to David Welch, "Educational Film Propaganda and the Nazi Youth," in *Nazi Propaganda*, ed. David Welch (London: Croom Helm, 1983), pp. 65–85.

boats, participating in track and field, as well as skiing and riding horses. Trim and fit bodies, drenched in sunlight, frolic euphorically in Alpine lakes. Boys' dreams come true as they fly gliders over windswept hills and race motorcycles over upland terrain. Music accompanies their activities, conveying a contagious excitement. Following long and strenuous hikes, they muse by night over crackling campfires, marveling at the beauty of falling stars while reciting heroic poetry. The mood becomes positively lyrical as columns of boys climb Alpine peaks, seemingly oblivious to danger, pressing on ever higher and higher, passing even eagles' nests in their metaphoric surge toward personal heroism. At last, having reached a towering summit, the boys mount the swastika flag, announcing the birth of a new era.

The youth are nourished by gorgeous scenes of their homeland. Mountains are seen glorious in the white blanket of winter and abloom in spring's awakening. Boys and girls cavort on the veranda of a newly built youth hostel, a beautiful river valley looming in the distance. The virginal glow of the girls of the *Bund deutscher Mädel* radiates over the idyllic scene. Beaming with joy in their reawakened Germany, they join the boys in rhapsodic songs of the Volk, of the homeland and nature, and of the movement. The commentator proudly affirms that this was a "brave youth, ready for battle."[36]

Great numbers of boys and girls responded to the excitement of the period in this fashion, and their youthful naïveté reached a fever pitch on summer camp outings. They felt deliriously free far from the oversight and discipline of their parents, sentiments they shared with their English cousins in the Boy Scouts and the Youth Movement. Thilo Scheller was one such boy, and the lines he wrote home from summer camp were ecstatic:

> Mother, I just love the camp flag.
> In the morning, when the sun rises over the pine trees,
> We raise it up the pole and it waves and waves.
> But it is most beautiful when the storm winds howl,
> Then it bends the mast until you think it will break.
> In the afternoon, when the air hangs heavy over the heath,
> And when it gets dark and there are storms in the
> Distance, then it hangs dead on the mast;
> But suddenly it springs to life and shines and shines,
> And glimmers and waves and snaps!

---

[36] *Hochland Hitlerjugend, Wochenschauen und Dokumentarfilme 1895–1950 im Bundesarchiv-Filmarchiv*, Band 8 (Bundesarchiv: Koblenz, 1984), p. 345.

And it is doing that right now and I am sitting in the
Woods and writing to you, because your boy hasn't
Forgotten you and because our camp flag is so glorious.[37]

Many young girls dreamed of carrying out the childbearing role to
which Hitler assigned them. One Austrian girl – sadly we do not know
her name – expressed this longing in the period before the *Anschluss*,
in the poem "Die Deutschen Mädchen dem Führer." Revealing genuine
youthful innocence, she promised to bless Adolf Hitler with the gift of
children. Seduced by Hitler's gift for imagery, which had the effect of an
aphrodisiac on her, she gushed forth these lines:

> We are the gateway, that leads to the future,
> we are the tree, on which the fruit ripens,
> what enraptures us, what becomes sacred to us,
> is planted for generations, strong and intact,
> no one can take that from our souls.
>
> In our hearts we bear the glow
> of the light, that you kindled for your people,
> we want to be its faithful guardians
> so that it once more, unchanged and pure,
> flows through our body into new life.
>
> Wir sind das Tor, das in die Zukunft führt,
> Wir sind der Baum, an dem die Früchte reifen,
> Was uns begeistert, was uns heilig wird,
> Das pflanzt sich weiter, stark und unberührt,
> Das kann uns niemand von der Seele streifen.
>
> In unsern Herzen tragen wir den Schein
> Des Lichtes, das du deinem Volk entzündet,
> Wir wollen ihm getreue Hüter sein,
> So dass er wieder, unverändert rein,
> Durch unsern Leib in neues Leben mündet.[38]

Such idealism contrasts markedly with the licentious conduct engaged in
by countless BDM girls and Hitler Youths.[39]

---

37 Thilo Scheller, "Die Fahne im Lager," in *Mütter und Männer*, ed. V. A. Frey (Stuttgart/
   Berlin: Truckenmüller, n.d.), p. 80.
38 "Die Deutschen Mädchen dem Führer," in *Das Lied der Getreuen, Verse ungenannter
   österreichischer Hitler-Jugend aus den Jahren der Verfolgung 1933–1937*, ed. Baldur von
   Schirach (Leipzig: Philipp Reclam jun., 1938), p. 21.
39 See Michael H. Kater, *Hitler Youth* (Cambridge: Harvard University Press, 2004), pp. 70–
   112.

If many young German girls dreamt of motherhood, most boys had visions of adventure and heroism. Their imaginations raced as they responded to the popular songs of Hans Baumann, the troubadour of the Hitler Youth. Baumann called the young to their deaths like moths to the flames with such songs as "Let the Banners Wave," which offered the young the choice of either victory or heroic death. They were certain that they bore the future of the Reich on their shoulders.[40]

It was the adulation of Adolf Hitler that led to such fatuous, self-destructive dreams of heroism. For so many people, Hitler did seem to be the great healer, a balm for the wounds of a tortured nation. It is hardly surprising that many of the leading National Socialist and conservative intellectuals – not to mention the pedantic, opportunistic bards of blood, soil, and dung who dotted the landscape in great numbers, to the great chagrin of Goebbels – competed in their literary works for the most fitting expression of their love for the Führer. For Eberhard Wolfgang Möller – prominent playwright and the leading figure in the Third Reich's literary young guard – Hitler was a figure of godlike proportions who in his person unified power, intellect, and culture. Möller was convinced that Hitler offered Europe its greatest opportunity since Charlemagne to recreate the unity of Greco-Roman-Germanic culture in a new trinity. His poem, "Der Führer," reflected Möller's infatuation with Hitler as a universal symbol:

> You great gardener, who in his garden
> sees fulfilled what he so diligently began.
> The street resounds with the storm of standards,
> yet the era evolves in silence.
>
> And your trees become large and spread
> their high crowns over your head.
> Centuries may pass, but eternities
> will still believe in that which you believed.
>
> Then you will be sitting deep in their shadow
> and realize that everything that you planted lives,
> while the sun of immortality towers
> high over their green peaks.
>
> Du grosser Gärtner, der in seinem Garten
> Vollenden sieht, was er mit Fleiss began.
> Die Strasse braust vom Sturme der Standarten,
> Doch in der Stille wächst die Zeit heran.

---

[40] Kulturamt der Reichsjugendführung, *Liederblatt der Hitlerjugend* (Wolfenbüttel/Berlin: Georg Kallmeyer, 1936), p. 52.

Und deine Bäume werden gross und breiten
die hohen Kronen über deinem Haupt.
Jahrhunderte vergehn, doch Ewigkeiten
Noch werden glauben, woran du geglaubt.

Dann wirst du tief in ihrem Schatten sitzen
und wissen: alles was du pflanztest, lebt,
indes über den begrünten Spitzen
die Sonne der Unsterblichkeit erhebt.[41]

Compared with Möller's poetry, most adulation to Hitler was on a more mundane level, typified by the childish yet popular rhymed couplets of Heinrich Anacker, whose works in effect were political editorials of rather low poetic accomplishment. Women also vied with one another in demonstrating their love for Hitler. Anne Marie Koeppen, a young West Prussian writer, journalist, and political activist who had joined the Party in 1928, simply could not contain her enthusiasm for the Third Reich. Her poem "To Hitler" was typical of this genre. Although testing the outer limits of kitsch, it nevertheless reflected a troubling death wish. Anne Marie stood ready to trade shallow individualism for the beauty of a possible love death with Adolf Hitler:

We do not ask anymore, where the road is leading
That you are leading us down, whether or not the way is stormy.
We ask but one thing alone, where you are,
And will go with you unto death.

Wir fragen nicht mehr, welch ein Weg es ist,
Den du uns führst, ob Stürme ihn umwehen.
Wir fragen nur noch eines: Wo du bist,
Und wollen bis zum Tode mit dir gehen.[42]

The opportunities for death were not long in coming, and with the onset of the war in 1939, National Socialist poetry and literature took a radical turn.[43] No longer did the bards long for death, because death would soon enough be ever-present, both at the fighting fronts and at home in the Reich. Nevertheless, the joy of astounding Blitzkrieg successes brought

[41] Eberhard Wolfgang Möller, "Der Führer," *Das brüderliche Jahr* (Wien: Wienerverlags-gesellschaft, 1941), p. 73.

[42] Anne Marie Koeppen, "An Hitler," *Wir trugen die Fahne* (Leipzig: Hesse & Becker, 1938), pp. 78–9.

[43] See Uwe-Karsten Ketelsen's outstanding chapter, "Lyrik der 30er und 40er Jahre in Deutschland," *Literatur und Drittes Reich* (Vierow bei Greifswald: SH-Verlag, 1994), pp. 305–74.

with it unbounded exuberance, no more deeply felt than with the humiliation of France in 1940, as evidenced in the lines of Heinrich Anacker:

> Greater Germany, young and strong,
> Won the victory in spring's splendor,
> And brings in the harvest of the dead
> At Ypres and Langemarck!
>
> Den Sieg erkämpft im Frühlingsschein
> Grossdeutschland, jung und stark,
> Und bringt der Toten Ernte ein
> Bei Ypres und Langemarck![44]

The World War veteran and worker poet Karl Bröger spoke for many in
his poem, "Verdun 1940," lauding the Wehrmacht's victory that took a
matter of days in contrast to the titanic lost campaign of 1916 in which
defeat was purchased at the cost of hundreds of thousands of lives. It
was indicative of the euphoria of those halcyon days when Hitler was at
the apex of his power that Friedrich Hölderlin was cited anew in praise
of victory married to noble heroic death: "We have won the battle! Live
on high, O Fatherland, and do not count the dead! For you, sweet one,
not one too many has died."[45] During the Battle of Britain, Herybert
Menzel conjured up once more the spirit of the idolized air ace Freiherr
Manfred von Richthofen, the "Red Baron," in his poem "To the Young
Dead Hero," which he published in Goebbels's weekly newspaper *Das
Reich*.[46]

The road to the future was analyzed by the uncompromising Nazi
critic and cultural functionary Hans W. Hagen in *German Literature
and Today's Epochal Decision Making*. In this work, which appeared
in 1938, Hagen was in effect calling for a profound literary accompaniment for the new radical world in which Hitler and the SS were leading
the nation. Today's creative writers must cast aside all considerations of
individualistic aesthetic creativity, he submitted. They are either with us
or against us, because the "idea of the Movement is an organic whole."
Good writing is political writing, that which strengthens our nation at
its moment of destiny, and helps lead the nation on to victory. All the

---

[44] Heinrich Anacker, *Über die Maas, über Schelde und Rhein. Gedichte vom Feldzug im
Westen* (Munich: Franz Eher, 1940), p. 12.

[45] Friedrich Hölderlin, "Der Tod furs Vaterland," in *Den Gefallenen. Ein Buch des
Gedenkens und des Trostes*, ed. Volksbund Deutsche Kriegsgräberfürsorge e.V.
(München/Salzburg: Akademischer Gemeinschaftsverlag, 1952), p. 17.

[46] Herybert Menzel, "Auf einen Frühvollendeten: Dem Freiherrn von Richthofen," *Das
Reich*, August 18, 1940, p. 17.

rest, he submitted, was "cultural Bolshevism." Because now, "once more, war is the father of all things for us." The Enlightenment and its Jewish adherents had faded away into the nation's dark history. Yesterday's supercilious "enlightened" were today's émigrés, he boasted. The duty of German writers "to synthesize and to configure the eternal mission of Germany" was of world-historic importance.

Knowing what we now know about the "Final Solution of the Jewish Question," Hagen's praise of the Germanic *Ordnung der Sippe* (clan) and *Ordnung der Gefolgschaft* (those who have pledged allegiance to a leader) was prophetic. Very soon the SS would cultivate these Germanic tribal motifs in the most frightening way. The future, he observed, would belong to the brave who master danger in battle, who demonstrate honor and deliver the German ideal of freedom. Therefore, the function of writers in the future was not to report on reality but rather abstractly to reflect the ideals of the *Gefolgschaft*. In this way they could correctly mirror the spirit that lay at the heart of the heroism that motivated heroes in their noble actions. Henceforth, authors were to think of themselves as muses, not unlike those who once had written and sung the aesthetic praises of their Germanic-Nordic ancestors, whose songs and poems strengthened the future heroes as they faced the often superhuman tests that fate had cast on them. Only in this way could they respond to the challenges of recreating the historic and aesthetic setting that had once motivated the Nibelungen in their saga of greatness. The times called for "lyricism of action" rather than "lyricism of ideas." Such poets as Baldur von Schirach and Gerhard Schumann had served their historic situation well by writing in the former genre, but the way to victory in the future lay with National Socialist lyricism of action. Hagen offered Kurt Eggers as a model for this project, pointing to his *The German Demon* as a work that beautifully embraced the Germanic idea of freedom as well as the greatness and strength of Germanic man.[47] Hagen was calling for nothing less than lyric Nazism, the National Socialist ideology in literary form.

In the final analysis, Nazism was based on a dialectical struggle between love and hate, a dualism that had the most profound consequences. In this worldview featuring the struggle between Aryan man and world Jewry, Hitler continually employed suggestive images of beauty, harmony, and health, juxtaposing them to depictions of hatred, ugliness, and disease. On

---

[47] Hans W. Hagen, *Deutsche Dichtung in der Entscheidung der Gegenwart* (Berlin/Dortmund: Volkschaft Verlag, 1938).

one hand, images were presented of Alpine mountains and the tranquility of German cottages tucked away in pleasant hills and valleys, accompanied by moving selections from Wagner, Mozart, or Schubert. This harmonious world was engaged in a brutal battle to the death against modernity, symbolized by the Jews, Bolshevism, and capitalist materialism. Honor versus materialism, light against darkness, purity versus impurity, the heroic and the craven, Aryan and Jew – any child could understand this dichotomy. Ironically, both components are necessary to the whole. As Saul Friedländer pointed out in his *Reflections on Kitsch and Death*, "This coexistence gives the totality its significance." Reflections on the Third Reich's apocalyptic reveries and hypnotic repetition of the leitmotifs of good and evil in literature, poetry, and song will enable us to understand the tragic phenomenon of National Socialist totalitarianism more clearly.[48]

This work focuses on the lives and writings of individuals who played a major role in building the Nazi literary Pantheon. Each essay could stand alone, yet taken together the chapters form a tapestry reflecting the two-faced Janus that Nazism represented. The book begins with analysis of the troubled career of Rudolf G. Binding, who stands as a figure with links to traditional bourgeois nationalist norms of the nineteenth century, was shaken by the tumult of the Great War, and answered the revolutionary changes of the Weimar Republic by retreating to his roots in the classical-romantic past. Binding remained an upper bourgeois horseman and cavalry officer who had outlived his time. The humiliation and sting of Versailles never left him, and the joy in Germany's renewed position of strength in the Third Reich cast him into the uncomfortable role of defending Hitler from his prestigious position as head of the literature section of the Prussian Academy of Arts. Although his basic decency never really allowed him to fit into the Third Reich, Binding's poetry and conservative literary works were nevertheless an inspiration to many young people who were lost souls after World War I and who found a home in the German nation.

Josef Magnus Wehner also serves as a link to the cultural conservatism of the past, yet the author was every inch a product of the trenches on the Western front. The success of his best-selling novel, *Seven at Verdun*, the nationalist alternative to Remarque's *All Quiet on the Western Front*,

---

[48] Saul Friedländer, *Reflections of Nazism: An Essay on Kitsch and Death* (New York: Avon Books, 1986), p. 131.

placed him in the vanguard of those to whom conservatives and right-wing radicals turned as they sought solace for their spiritual wounds.[49] Wehner was also an incense burner for the front generation who shared his vision of the Reich, shrouding the German war dead in the assured glory of national resurrection. The fallen had not died in vain; rather they formed the advance guard of those marching out of their graves at Langemarck, Verdun, Tannenberg, and the Somme, standing ready to storm the walls of the Weimar Republic and to root out and destroy every vestige of decadence that it allegedly inspired.

Wehner was extremely useful to the National Socialists at a critical juncture in their history and his dream of the Third Reich suited them well. He was one of the most effective propagandists for their cause in the period from 1930 through the founding years of the Third Reich. Just before Hitler took power, Wehner passed the torch from the hands of the fallen youth of the war to the future National Socialist leadership at the dedication ceremonies of the Langemarck (Battle of Ypres) National Memorial. If Ernst Jünger could not be won for the Nazi cause – and that greatest of the front writers firmly rejected their solicitations – Josef Magnus Wehner would serve their purposes quite well for the time being. As time went on, however, Wehner no longer fit in with the increasingly radical Nazi regime.

Such was decidedly not the case with the next writer to be considered, Hans Zöberlein, the leading figure of the literary front generation to be recognized and honored by Hitler. Zöberlein served as a model Nazi writer-activist. His career began as a brave young front fighter, and his novel *The Belief in Germany* so accurately reflected the smoke and fire, death and destruction of the front experience that Hitler himself wrote the introduction to the work. Zöberlein also served as a member of the Free Corps Epp in Bavaria. His book *The Command of Conscience* was also a best-seller, mirroring the murderous activities of the front fighters turned street-fighting counterrevolutionaries in their defeat of the violent forces of the "Jewish-Bolshevik" communist revolution.[50]

Zöberlein, a decidedly lesser intellect, was a bold Brown Shirt leader whose exploits in Munich street fighting became legendary, lending exciting subjects for the many songs and poems that celebrated the SA. Zöberlein was present at the Creation, Hitler's famous abortive "March

---

[49] Josef Magnus Wehner, *Sieben vor Verdun* (Munich: Langen/Müller, 1930).
[50] Hans Zöberlein, *Der Glaube an Deutschland* (Munich: Franz Eher, 1931); *Der Befehl des Gewisswens* (Munich: Franz Eher 1936).

to the Feldherrnhalle," the Nazi Calvary experience that claimed the lives of the "Sixteen Immortals." This enabled him to wear the Blood Order Medallion and thereafter to take part in the annual march with the Führer, who returned each November 9 thereafter to recreate their march into eternity. Zöberlein became a Brigadeführer in the SA, received numerous literary prizes in the Third Reich, and was an active Nazi propagandist throughout the 1930s. During World War II, he volunteered for duty and served at the front in the Luftwaffe. Zöberlein never veered from his radicalism, holding firmly to his unspeakably crude racial delusions and remaining loyal to Hitler his entire life. Even when the Third Reich had collapsed and burned to ashes, he became a leader of a notorious Werewolf action unit, engaging in the slaughter of communist civilians at Penzburg in Bavaria. Zöberlein faded from history just as he had entered it, with the spirit of the trenches and the blood of the ruthless Free Corps counterinsurgency on his hands.

Edwin Erich Dwinger, the fourth representative figure from the Great War to be considered here, became an example that proves the rule. He demonstrated that facts, properly presented, can take on artistic form and that an historical chronicle with the proper subject matter can reach a higher level in the proper hands. So it was with Dwinger, for whom the epic struggle between communism and Western values became the leitmotif of his entire life. For Dwinger, whose works taken together sold in the millions, *Weltanschauung* and the German spirit and love of nation were merged, whereas *völkisch* racism played a minor role.

Dwinger's best-selling trilogy commenced with *An Army behind Barbed Wire*, mirroring the young cavalry officer's passionate memories of the agony he suffered in disease-ridden prisoner of war camps in Siberia. The work was based on his fiery conviction that the prisoner of war experience was a spiritual war, albeit fought on another front, and as challenging and harrowing as it might become, victims could reach the realm of transcendence despite their anguish. Dwinger demonstrated that even in the worst circumstances, a brave German soldier could hold firm to what was right and die like a man for his country. In the novel *Between Red and White*, Dwinger took the story into the Russian Civil War, detailing his dramatic adventures while serving with the counterrevolutionary army commanded by Admiral Kolchak. One senses a passionate love for the Russian people here – Dwinger's mother was Russian after all – and the conviction that the forces of Lenin and Trotsky were bearers of cultural destruction. He was certain that their ultimate victory could mean the end of civilization itself. In the final volume, *We Call Germany*, the author takes the story to an East Prussian estate after the war. There many of the prisoners who survived the Siberian camps gather to heal their wounds and to forge their strength for the coming showdown against communist insurgency. They loathed the Weimar Republic, certain that it was an unorganic democratic governmental form, supporting all that was wicked in the postwar world.[51]

Dwinger became a well-known figure during the Third Reich. He was politically well connected as a member of both the Nazi Party and the SS. Honorary commander of the 15th Reiterstandarte in Munich, he delighted in sporting about in his uniform, with the rank of Obersturmführer. Dwinger would publish two more novels based on his own experiences, but his propaganda tracts in support of the Nazi regime gained him considerably more attention. His works on the Spanish Civil War and the campaigns in Poland and France were major components of the Nazi propaganda offensive in those years. Both were written in the aggressive yet authoritative style so characteristic of Dwinger. It was his background as an officer with significant knowledge and experience in the Soviet Union, however, that increased his fame. *Return to Soviet Russia. Diary of the Eastern Campaign* was a major historical chronicle, written while Dwinger was attached to the personal staff of the Reichsführer SS, Heinrich Himmler.[52] This was vintage Nazi propaganda and delighted Goebbels.

The fact that Dwinger hated the Soviet rulers yet loved the Russian people came to haunt him. He went so far as to circulate a memorandum criticizing Nazi Eastern policies and calling for radical changes in them, a latitudinarianism that veered widely from Hitler's "subhuman" ideology. He came under Gestapo surveillance and in 1943 was placed under house arrest, forbidden either to publish or meddle in politics. It made matters worse that Dwinger frequently met with and encouraged General Andres Vlasov, the Soviet officer who had changed sides after the Battle of Moscow and hoped to lead an anti-Soviet Russian military force at the side of the Wehrmacht on the Eastern front. Ironically, although thereafter he was persona non grata with the Nazis, after the war Dwinger energetically launched his second successful career as a writer after his rehabilitation. History, as it often does, had come full circle. As the Cold

---

[51] Edwin Erich Dwinger, *Die Armee Hinter Stacheldraht* (Jena: Eugen Diederichs, 1929); *Zwischen Weiss und Rot* (Jena: Eugen Diederichs 1930); *Wir rufen Deutschland* (Jena: Eugen Diederichs, 1932).
[52] Edwin Erich Dwinger, *Wiedersehen mit Sowjetrussland* (Jena: Eugen Diederichs, 1942).

War broke out and the Federal Republic of Germany aligned itself to the anti-Soviet NATO alliance system led by the United States, Dwinger once again became a best-selling author. Anticommunism wore many coats in the twentieth century, and the author exploited this theme with skill.

The career of Eberhard Wolfgang Möller was perhaps the most problematic of all the authors considered here. Möller dreamt of a renewal of German intellect and power, centering on Adolf Hitler, and despite his youth he longed to play a major role in this development. Winner of the National Prize for Literature in 1935 for *The Letters of the Fallen*, he was also celebrated for his dramas *Douaumont, Rothschild Victorious at Waterloo*, and *The Frankenburg Dice Game*, the last of which was featured at the Berlin Olympic Games of 1936. Möller, deeply anti-Semitic, was also involved in the writing of the film script for Veit Harlan's highly successful – yet notorious – *Jud Süss*. It is quite possible that in another era, his undeniable lyrical gifts would have ensured him a lasting place in German letters. But it was Möller's fate to be a National Socialist idealist in a period of both spiritual and moral corruption. In 1938, he dealt with this theme in the play *The Fall of Carthage*, an assault on National Socialist leaders by one of their own. The performances of this drama became a cause célèbre in Party circles when several members of Hitler's inner circle, including Goebbels, took personal offense because they were the obvious targets of Möller's attack.

Möller's problems were just beginning. His biography of Hitler, commissioned by Baldur von Schirach as a gift to the Hitler Youth, was brutally assaulted by Alfred Rosenberg, who began a personal vendetta against him that lasted for years. This paled in comparison to what Möller would suffer at the hands of his enemies within the circles of the SS cultural elite, however. When Kurt Eggers and Hans W. Hagen stamped him as a "cultural Bolshevik" and "aesthetic desecrator of the heroic war dead" for his sensitive poetry on the motif of death in wartime, Möller was in for real trouble. As a result, he joined the Waffen SS as a war reporter and was assigned to the Fifth SS Panzer Division "Viking." Barely surviving the war, he had seen his dream for a renewal of German tragedy absolutely shattered.

The final writer to be considered in this book is Kurt Eggers, self-appointed propagator and protector of SS ideology. His career represented at once the apogee and fiery denouement of his dream for a Thousand Year Reich led by the Black Order. Eggers was by nature a desperado and was only a boy when he first saw action in a Free Corps unit fighting Polish forces for the contested regions of Upper Silesia. Upon returning home, he was a misfit in the Weimar Republic, which he loathed. Eggers for varying periods of time was a high school and university student, a recruit in the Reichswehr, an agricultural intern on a Junker estate in Mecklenberg, and an ordained evangelical minister. None of these pursuits, however, could answer the longing in his soul for comradeship, hierarchy and authority, national greatness, and Nordic elitism. Quite alone and on the edge of poverty, he found solace in writing historical dramas and nationalist poetry on heroic motifs. Kurt Eggers restlessly awaited a personal and German hero.

For Kurt Eggers, Adolf Hitler was heaven sent. Enthusiasm, hope, and renewed creativity welled up in him and he published work after work on martial and heroic themes. He saw enemies of the new order on all sides but focused his energies on a relentless assault on what he conceived to be the devilish trinity of communism, Jewry, and the church. Having joined the SS, he published a catechism for the renewal of the Nordic race, ultimately drawing the favorable attention of both Hitler and Himmler. Ultimately, he assumed the mantle of Zarathustra, as philosophy, racism, and a call for a radical new order were all fused in his work. The future of Nazism lay with the radicals, and Eggers was one of their number.

With the coming of the Battle of Russia and the Holocaust, Kurt Eggers was in his element. When Hitler looked to the SS to fulfill his goals at Germany's hour of destiny, Eggers took the center literary stage as the murderous Black Order set out on its mission. Lieutenant Eggers became a protégé of Himmler and even received favorable notices from Hitler for his vicious attacks on Christianity, the bourgeoisie, Jewry, and the Bolshevism. His book, *On the Freedom of the Warrior*, published in 1940, offered a Nietzschean orgy of irrationalism and symbolism and should be seen as a literary prelude to the actual twilight of the gods played out in the Führer bunker in Berlin in 1945.[53] In this major work of World War II propaganda, Eggers celebrates the warrior who, never seeing the tears of those left behind, leaves the comfort of the green valley to ascend what he calls the "mountain in midnight," the gateway to the sun that was bathed in the light of the stars. Eggers's warrior figure glows like a torch in the glory of his mission, to light the fire uniting heaven and earth in the luminous glow of eternity. It goes without saying that the final destination of the soldier's road to freedom lay in heroic death.

True to his mission, in the summer of 1943 Eggers died a warrior's death on the Russian front in command of a tank unit of the Fifth SS Panzer

---

[53] Kurt Eggers, *Von der Freiheit des Kriegers* (Berlin: Nordland, 1940).

Division. In his own person, Eggers reflected the macabre union of myth and reality that characterized Hitler's Third Reich in both its climb to the summit of power and its ultimate destruction. He had been at odds with many of the writers analyzed in this book, but he reserved his hatred for only one of them, Eberhard Wolfgang Möller, whose aestheticism and antiheroic poetry repelled him. In the end, they all were destroyed by Hitler's megalomania and determination to win absolute control of the continent.

Rudolf G. Binding and the Memory of the Great War

The life of the author Rudolf G. Binding, which stretched from 1867 to 1938, was problematic. A sensitive, narcissistic gentleman living on inherited money and totally in the shadow of his father – the esteemed professor of international law at Leipzig, Karl Binding – he was well into his forties before writing a line. Yet he gradually emerged as a best-selling author of neo-Romantic novellas, blending themes of love, sacrifice, and heroism, which caught the imagination of both fin-de-siècle readers, as well as many unfulfilled youths of the Weimar era. Service as a cavalry officer in World War I was the inspiration for the publication of both his diaries, published under the title *On the War*, and the collection of war poetry, titled *Pride and Mourning*, which established his credentials as a literary exponent of the conservative cause. Binding was in demand not only on the literary lecture circuit but also as a nationalist bard for anniversary services of commemoration for the fallen of the Great War. He received many awards, including a Silver Medal at the 1928 Amsterdam Olympic Games for his book on horsemanship, *Riding Instructions for a Lover*, the Goethe Medal in 1932, as well as an honorary doctorate from the University of Frankfurt. He was called to membership in the Prussian Academy of Arts, when fellow members included such luminaries as Thomas Mann, Heinrich Mann, and Lion Feuchtwanger.[1]

Real trouble began for Binding with Hitler's ascent to power in 1933, when the author had reached the age of sixty-six. Binding, who was vice president of the Section for Literature of the Prussian Academy of Arts,

---

[1] Rudolf G. Binding, *Aus dem Kriege* (Potsdam: Rütten & Loening, 1937), and *Stolz und Trauer*, in Rudolf G. Binding, *Gedichten um den Krieg. Ausgewählte und Neue Gedichte* (Frankfurt: Rütten & Loening, 1930). For biographical materials on Binding, see Franz Lennartz, *Die Dichter unserer Zeit* (Stuttgart: Alfred Kröner, 1938); and Ludwig Friedrich Barthel, ed., *Das war Binding* (Wien/Berlin/Stuttgart: Paul Neff, 1955), pp. 9–50.

1. Rudolf G. Binding on His 70th Birthday, 1937. Courtesy of Bayerisches Hauptstaatsarchiv.

remained in Germany when many writers of deeper conscience emigrated. Even though, as a conservative, he preferred Hitler to many other alternatives on the political horizon, he only reluctantly assented to the regulation of writers in the Academy. Binding published a notorious defense of the Hitler regime in the *Kölnische Zeitung*, which received wide circulation in pamphlet form under the title *Six Declarations of Loyalty to the New Germany*.[2] This branded him as a proponent of Nazism and ever afterward cast a shadow over his career. Despite his growing disappointment with the regime, Binding nevertheless steered a troubled course during the first years of the Third Reich. Even though he was appalled by the crudity of the Nazi gangsters, he continued to view himself as a non-Party witness for the regime. Summing up the first year of the revolution, he noted in a letter to Gerhart Hauptmann in December 1933 that "The year was a serious one and a troubled time for the arts."[3]

The middle road chosen by the author came at a great cost to his reputation, and it proved to be disappointing to him personally. He found himself increasingly under attack from leading Nazi figures such as Baldur von Schirach, as well as rank-and-file functionaries. In the last years of his life, he made appearances at Hans Grimm's Lippoldsberg Writers Forum, an annual summer retreat for inner opposition figures. Having withdrawn to his Starnberger Lake home near Munich with his Jewish mistress, Elisabeth Jungmann, he died in August 1938, virtually ignored in international literary circles, scorned by Party radicals, alienated, and nearly forgotten.

It is clear that Binding attributed Germany's tragic fate to the fact that the generation of 1914 who survived the war did not answer the call of destiny. It had been incumbent on them to remake the nation in their own image after the defeat, and they had failed in the attempt. The Hitlerites, on the other hand, were certain that traditional conservatives such as Binding were pathetically devoid of will and had missed their historic opportunity to change the course of history by not aligning themselves with the National Socialist movement. It was alleged that they were mired in upper-bourgeois elitism, preferring to allow their class instincts to dominate them at a time when radical solutions to the problems of the day were called for. The SS organ, *Das Schwarze Korps*, noted with regret in

[2] Rudolf G. Binding, *Sechs Bekenntnisse zum neuen Deutschland* (Hamburg: Hanseatische Verlagsanstalt, 1933), pp. 14–21.
[3] Binding to Gerhart Hauptmann, December 19, 1933, in Rudolf G. Binding, *Die Briefe*, ed., Ludwig Friedrich Barthel (Hamburg: Hans Dulk, 1957), pp. 233–4.

its obituary that for Binding, "classical values were more important than blood." As a result, he fell in the "tragic middle between the hopeless leaders of 1918 and the really determined leaders of 1933."[4] In contrast, Rudolf Kreutzer, writing in the Nazi Party organ, *Völkischer Beobachter*, was kinder to Binding, noting that he was a true son of classical Greece, a man who joined mass, form, and intellect, which placed him in the tradition of Goethe and Winckelmann, Schiller and Hölderlin. Kreutzer found him to be a chivalrous figure with an undying love for Germany, whose writings on the war had greatly inspired the young. Binding had an enduring faith in youth, and he encouraged the young generation to keep their spirits high, let years to come do what they may. He trusted them, they knew it, and thus they were drawn to him as well.[5]

International literary critics, reflecting Germany's tortured political history in the twentieth century, have concentrated more on the political than the literary Binding. As a result, his standing among them has been problematic. There is no question that before Hitler, Binding enjoyed a much better press than would be the case thereafter. Even though he was viewed as a cultural icon of the conservative right, Stefan Zweig, himself a Jew, referred to Binding as one of the masters of German letters, among the few who "have formed and fulfilled the poetic vision as a manly, ethically responsible mission."[6] Binding's political engagement evoked bitter criticism from many quarters, and he was sensitive to attacks from the German exile community. For Klaus Mann, he was among those who wrote their beautiful sonnets, surrounded by their comforts, preferring not to hear the screams from Hitler's concentration camps. Writing from his agonizing exile in Paris, he referred to him as "Herrenreiter Binding, the literary von Papen."[7] Binding was incensed and went to the trouble of writing two letters to Klaus Mann defending himself, asserting that

---

[4] "Für einen toten Soldaten," *Das Schwarze Korps*, September 8, 1938.

[5] Rudolf Kreutzer, *Völkischer Beobachter*, August 6, 1938. Binding fits the model for the German cultural obsession with Greece analyzed by Suzanne L. Marchand in *Down from Olympus. Archeology and Philhellenism in Germany, 1750–1970* (Princeton: Princeton University Press, 1996), pp. 3–35.

[6] Letter from Stefan Zweig to Rudolf Binding, August 10, 1927, Barthel, *Das war Binding*, pp. 100–1.

[7] See Klaus Mann, "Am Pranger," in *Mit dem Blick nach Deutschland. Der Schriftsteller und das politische Engagement*, ed. Michael Grunewald (Munich: Ellermann, 1985), pp. 88–91. See also Klaus Mann, "An die Schriftsteller im Dritten Reich," in *Heute und Morgen*, ed. Martin Gregor-Dellin (Munich: Nymphenburger, 1969), pp. 224–64. Binding to Klaus Mann, *Die Sammlung*, Amsterdam, November 9 and November 13, 1933, Sammlung Klaus Mann, Münchener Stadtbibliothek, Monacensia Literaturarchiv.

he had never signed the list of German writers who swore allegiance to Hitler in late October 1933.

Hellmuth Langenbucher, a prominent Third Reich literary critic, found Binding much more concerned with the fate of the individual than with the needs of the racial community, the overarching consideration of the fascist era. Nevertheless, the value Binding placed on heroic behavior appealed to Langenbucher. According to the author's knightly ideal of honor, it did not matter whether victory or defeat was the outcome but rather whether the participant was the victor in the central moral battle of life, the struggle for character.[8] For Wolfgang Weyrauch, writing in the *Berliner Tageblatt* in 1934, Binding at his best was more European than he was German, a man whose character made him assuredly beloved by Apollo. Like a river moving in stages to the sea, Binding begins his creations with anecdotes – Weyrauch used Binding's *We Demand the Surrender of Reims* as his example – that become legends, before running out to sea in epic form. In just the same way, Weyrauch averred, Kleist had given way to Stifter before reaching the source in the epic fullness of Tieck, Hebbel, and Hauptmann.[9]

For Günter Hartung, writing in *Literature and Aesthetics of German Fascism*, a volume in a series titled "Literature and Society" sponsored by the Central Institute for the History of Literature of the German Democratic Republic, Binding was to be viewed entirely within the Marxist dialectical framework, a spokesperson for repressive late capitalism.[10] On the other hand, many of Binding's loyal colleagues idealized him. The nationalistic writer Ludwig Friedrich Barthel, a strong supporter of National Socialism with a predilection for hyperbole, in all seriousness ranked his poetic talents with Rainer Maria Rilke and Stefan George.[11] For Barthel, Binding was reminiscent of Goethe, who did not stand as a shadow behind his writing but rather lived the life reflected in his words. Paul Alverdes, author of *The Pipeman's Nook* and editor of the *Inner*

---

[8] Hellmuth Langenbucher, *Volkhafte Dichtung der Zeit* (Berlin: Junker & Dünnhaupt, 1937), pp. 77–80

[9] Weyrauch noted that "Where Binding is fulfilling and perfect, he belongs to Europe, a successor of the European Goethe, of the European "Grünen Heinrich" and Stendhal. Where Binding is less than complete and less fulfilling, he belongs to us." Written in 1934, at the height of the German culture wars, these were fighting words for radical National Socialists. Wolfgang Weyrauch: "Über Rudolf G. Binding," *Berliner Tageblatt*, November 25, 1934.

[10] Günter Hartung: *Literatur und Ästhetik des deutschen Faschismus.* Akademie der Wissenschaften der DDR. Zentralinstitut für Literaturgeschichte. *Literatur und Gesellschaft* (Berlin: Akademie Verlag, 1983).

[11] Barthel, *Das war Binding*, p. 48.

Reich, a leading journal of the inner opposition, had a high regard for Binding and was a member of the Starnberg Circle, a literary group that met at Binding's lakeside home in Bavaria in the years before his death.[12] Recent scholarship has mistakenly cast Binding in the racial-nationalist camp, a decidedly misguided assessment of a supreme individualist with no concept whatsoever of race as a component of his worldview.[13]

The chronicle of Rudolf Binding's early years is a melancholy one, offering little promise for the future. Born in Basel, he would live in Freiburg, Frankfurt, and Leipzig. Because of his father's importance, he saw many prominent intellectuals and men of affairs come and go from his boyhood homes, including the historians Theodor Mommsen and Heinrich von Treitschke. He was highly critical of imperial Germany, from the daily grooming of the emperor's mustache to society's false elegance and hypocrisy. He found little joy in people and was burdened with melancholy and depression. He undertook the study of both law and medicine but without genuine enthusiasm for either subject. He gave up each in turn. A disappointment to both himself and his family, he became increasingly cynical about life, which seemed more pretence than reality to him.[14]

Looking back on his early years, Binding was certain that he learned more about character from thoroughbred horses than he did from human beings. It wasn't just the little things, such as patience, discipline, respect, and the love of nature, that he learned from them. From horses one learns to reject vanity, smugness, and high-handedness. More important, he observed about riding, "Here I finally learned self-control, the cultivation of my body and my soul."[15] It was during the year in which he served as an officer trainee in the Fourteenth Prussian Hussars Regiment that taught him to have contempt for the social snobbery of the empire and to see through the political weaknesses of united Germany. Having been sent to serve in the Saxon cavalry – an inferior horseman of noble

[12] As early as 1924, Paul Alverdes, decrying the cultural shame of Weimar, wrote that one day Binding would be seen as "the one who in a sick period was the first to reaffirm the mythical." See his essay *Über Rudolf G. Binding* (Frankfurt am Main: Rütten & Loening, 1925), BHStA, Slg. Personen 3989.

[13] See Bernhard Martin: *Dichtung und Ideologie: Völkisch-nationales Denken im Werk Rudolf Georg Bindings* (Frankfurt am Main: Peter Lang, 1986), pp. 169–74.

[14] Binding hated Leipzig, where he remained an outsider. Further, he was deeply alienated with German society and was devastating in his assault on it. See Rudolf G. Binding, *Erlebtes Leben* (Frankfurt: Rütten & Loening, 1937), pp. 104–5.

[15] Binding, ibid., pp. 106–8. Only on a horse, he noted, did one find "complete harmony, a reconciliation, a resolution, a dance. It was the most harmonious machine a human being would ever drive."

ancestry had been retained in the Prussian Fourteenth in his place – he was personally insulted for his Prussian background by his commander, the brother of the king of Saxony and himself a future king. Long before World War I placed intolerable stress on that imperfect union, he clearly understood that "Germany was a phantom without reality, a state without a body."[16]

Binding consoled himself in the company of beautiful women, observing that he rode best when he was in love and could simply not have borne the tensions of life without communion with nature in this way. He moved to Berlin, bought a villa in Hoppegarten, and spent himself into financial ruin breeding and racing thoroughbred horses not only in Germany but in England and France as well. Idleness was to take its toll, and despite his marriage to Helena von Wirsing in 1907 – he was then forty years old – he fell into deep melancholy and suffered a complete mental breakdown two years later.

What, then, drew Binding to creative writing? Three factors joined to mold his character: the influence of Mediterranean culture, passion and love to inspire his work, and the cauldron of World War I. He acknowledged that the first of these took place in Italy while he was recovering from severe psychological trauma. Thanks to his wife Helena, who had taken him to Florence and nursed him back to health, his life took a decided turn for the better. Entirely by chance, a poem he had translated as part of his Italian language instruction was taken by his teacher to its author, the poet Gabriele d'Annunzio, who was astounded at the talents of this unknown German writer. He had found his proper métier and soon began to write himself back to emotional health.[17]

A further development in Binding's emergence as a writer was a trip he took to Greece in the company of his dear friend and fellow cavalry officer, Anton Mayer. Upon viewing the statue of Hermes by Praxiteles, he was overcome by the beauty of the master's ability to transmit the nobility of the Greek ideal in marble. Binding's determination to emulate the Greek model on German soil – to render the grace of the sculptors of classical Greece into poetry and prose – placed him within a revered

---

[16] Ibid., p. 131.

[17] The poem by d'Annunzio was "Der Tod des Hirsch." Binding, ibid., pp. 179–88, and Barthel, *Das war Binding*, pp. 9–50. Binding described his breakthrough to mental health as a form of creative writing therapy, commenting that "From now on I did not waver. I created. I was secure and took leave of my cares. I could create day and night with my words and communicated with death. I discovered a very lively spirit within me and let it come to light" (ibid., p. 219).

German tradition. He would never lose sight of the beauty of the light of Greece, even to the end of his days.[18]

Binding repaid the devotion of his wife Helena with disloyalty, falling in love with Eva Annecke Connstein (1877–1942) and using her as his poetic muse for more than a decade thereafter. Rudolf called her Joie, because of the joy with which she approached life and for the joy she brought to him. Binding used both women as the central characters in his novella *The Sacrifice*, published in 1911, a best seller that created a sensation in a period of overripe bourgeois culture. Perhaps because she understood his complex psychological needs better than anyone ever would, his wife Helena became the model for the character Octavia in that work, representing a woman who sacrificed herself for her husband during a typhus epidemic in Hamburg. In a strange twist of fate, during the last years of the Third Reich, Binding's novella came to life once again when Veit Harlan directed the color film *Opfergang*, starring the Swedish actress Kristina von Söderbaum, who as the lover of the horseman and patrician, Albrecht, joined him in death.[19]

World War I was the final, if not overriding, factor in the development of Binding's character. His was an idiosyncratic view of the war, totally out of step with the brassy nationalism of the period. It is remarkable to observe that for him, war was the ultimate test of personal, not national, character, offering fertile ground for the cultivation of the individual. Indeed, it was a natural extension of his concept of the gentleman, which focused on the ideal of the moral cultivation of the sovereign individual. It is important to note that the author's gentlemanly ideal was entirely independent of Christian dogma.[20]

Binding's beliefs were tested in the fire, and he emerged from the war with a matured concept of the individual in the era of the nation state. He never yielded to the temptation of finding his identity in the German nation or the Germanic race. Rather, he interpreted war as a transcendent

---

[18] See Anton Mayer, *Der Göttergleiche* (Potsdam: Rütten & Loening, 1939).

[19] Rudolf G. Binding: *Der Opfergang* (Leipzig: Inselverlag, 1912). Eric Rentschler, *The Ministry of Illusion. Nazi Cinema and Its Afterlife* (Cambridge: Harvard University Press, 1996), pp. 143–4, 167.

[20] It makes strange reading today to learn that King Edward VII was Binding's model gentleman, as he described it in his autobiography, *Erlebtes Leben*, p. 235. Above all, he wrote, a gentleman should be self-composed, unconcerned about his image or possessions, unsentimental, unromantic, and a fearless realist. He is a man of few words and is in fact exactly what he appears to be – an integrated personality. He is clean-shaven and always correctly attired. A gentleman does not make a fuss about this and that but holds the line for what seems right, when this is called for.

experience. If battle evoked visions of Dionysian ecstasy for Ernst Jünger, or thrilled the heart of Hans Zöberlein, it meant something entirely different to Rudolf Binding. He was convinced that those who had experienced the war came out of it as human beings far different from nonparticipants. They had seen men as they really were, with the veil removed. The war generation took a different measure of life than the others. They drank from a different source and saw the future from a different perspective. Those who had been in the field of battle had seen mankind in the raw, and they were not pleased with the experience.[21]

As he rode off to command a cavalry unit of the Young Germany Division in the late summer of 1914, Binding felt liberated. Immune to traditional patriotism, he rejected the war euphoria of many of his comrades-in-arms. He sensed that many people were carried away more by the ecstasy of the upheaval itself than for the pursuit of any particular goals. He had a terrible foreboding about the ultimate consequences of the war, predicting to a fellow officer in the fall of 1914 that the conflict might well last seven years.

Nevertheless, a total break from the tedium of bourgeois existence held its attractions for him. Eager to test his strength against the challenges of fate, he later observed: "I longed for this with reasoned yet feverish determination and circumspection, not with trust in the strength of our arms and our power. The homeland sank behind me." It was indicative of Binding's sincerity that upon taking command of the 52nd Reserve Cavalry Detachment, he addressed his officers and men, admonishing all those who could not truly detach themselves from their earlier lives – from their families, possessions, and the homeland itself – should fall out. Nor did he put credence in the myth of heroic death, observing in his diary that "I did not believe that it was more beautiful to die for the Fatherland than it was to prove one's own worth in the fire."[22] Nor did Binding succumb to the male bonding craze of the war experience, the comradeship that the infantryman, journalist, and SA novelist Otto Paust would later refer to as being "sweeter than mother's milk." Rather, he found more comfort in the company of good horses, when a man could really unite with nature.

---

[21] Binding, ibid., p. 469. Wm. K. Pfeiler noted that "Binding's individualism is not egotism. On the contrary, firmly centered in the knowledge of his own worth, conscious of his actual and potential strength, the creative – and therefore superior – individual acts on the ground of his own moral nature, and is willing and ready for sacrifice." See Wm. K. Pfeiler, *War and the German Mind* (New York: Columbia University Press, 1941), pp. 122–3.

[22] Binding: *Erlebtes Leben*, pp. 258, 264–65.

In a poem published in the *Frankfurter Zeitung* on August 16, 1914, Binding wrote:

> I leave for a sacred war,
> seeking neither fame nor fortune.
> I am a sacred rider.
> I do not seek the Cross or Grail
> but nevertheless am blessed a thousand times
> as a warrior of righteousness.
>
> Ich zieh in einen heiligen Krieg,
> frag nicht nach Lohn, frag nicht nach Sieg.
> Ich bin ein heiliger Reiter.
> Kein Kreuz such ich und keinen Gral
> und bin doch heilig tausendmal
> als meiner Sache Streiter.[23]

Freed of longing for success and from the temptations of beautiful women, nothing could get to him now, for he had no other needs. He reveled in the contentment that comes when an individual finds himself quite good company.

Although this would change in time, at the outset of the war Binding extoled the conflict as a call from the beyond to recognize the universal truths that it unleashed. Indeed, he celebrated its meaning in *Pride and Mourning*, published after the war. In the poem "Breakout," he claimed that the "eternal stars" would never forget those days, which called men to "greatness and freedom" as unto a sacred flame. In the poem "Battle," he lauded military engagement in a remarkable way.[24] Where, he queried, would one ever again discover the "wondrous shock" of battle, which freed men from all their inadequacies:

> Internal chaos was shaken out of the men,
> Memory faded away like a children's toy from our hands,
> The relief of longing was torn from its innermost depths,
> All hope was ripped out root and branch.

"Our souls were naked," he observed. "Expectantly we stood face to face with death."[25]

Engaged on the Ypres front, war enthusiasm soon gave way to disgust as losses mounted and the war of movement ground to a halt. It was

---

[23] Ibid., p. 265. Despite his protestations, Binding's weakness for the romantic interpretation of life is certainly evident here.

[24] "Ausbruch," in Binding, *Ausgewählte und Neue Gedichte*, p. 82.

[25] "Schlacht," ibid., p. 88.

unbelievable that a month into the war, losses of 50 percent for infantry divisions and as high as 75 percent for storm-troop units were not uncommon. He longed for the genius of Field Marshal Helmuth von Moltke, whose boldness had won victory over France in a matter of months in 1870. Lesser men had taken the helm, and the result was the agonizing stalemate of trench warfare. Idiotic newspaper correspondents got it all wrong in their reports, he complained, which more often than not were larded with rhapsodic tales of false heroism. The real problem, he submitted, was lack of willpower and insight at the top of the command structure. He wrote in desperation, "One can only hold out if one knows there is a plan that makes sense. Instead of this there is no plan at all; and we do not know how to make the next move." Writing from the front in December 1914, he complained that "There is no sense to this anymore." After a long, cold, and damp winter in the trenches had taken its toll on his spirit, he seemed totally alienated with the leadership, observing bitterly that "Everything stinks here just like a swamp."[26]

Were it left to him, Binding would have cancelled Christmas for the duration of the war. Its celebration was enough to make one nauseous. "The enemy, death, and a lighted Christmas tree. All this cannot exist in such close proximity," he observed. He felt it much more honest to be engaged in the front line on Christmas Eve than to have to stomach the "half untruth of the Christmas tree." It would be an accomplishment if the war were to sweep away all the holiday wreckage, "if peace-on-earth could be expressed otherwise than in terms of sausages and paté de foie!" What made it worse were the propaganda stunts featuring "love gifts" from home, often including bad cigars and indifferent chocolate, delivered directly to the troops by insensitive prestige seekers from the warmth of their cars. Civilians visiting the front, just like they were on holiday, thought that they had the right to have the war shown to them like tourists viewing a leather factory, he complained.[27]

Binding was critical of the nationalist excesses set loose by the war. Rather, he praised the war's deeper reality in such poems as "Battle: The Measure," coming to the conclusion that war was the ultimate measure of all things.[28] He went so far as to claim in "Widows' Contentment" that heroes never really could love their wives; instead, they belonged to the

---

[26] Binding, *Aus dem Kriege*, pp. 48, 79. The latter quotation was taken from his entry of March 19, 1915.

[27] Entries of December 20–2, 1914, ibid., p. 51.

[28] "Stolz und Trauer," *Ausgewählte und Neue Gedichte*, pp. 89–90.

ages. In this work, a widow who lost her beloved at the front comes to the realization that he could only belong to her in death. Were he to have returned home victoriously from the field of battle, she would never really possess him. His soul would always be out there, on horseback far from her. As a result, she averred, "I shall love him in death." As for mothers who had lost their sons, they were admonished not to cry but to take solace in the knowledge revealed in this poetic query, written as a balm for their wounds:

"What would victories be without the death of heroes?"[29]

For the warrior himself, death was liberating, he claimed. Last thoughts flew away like butterflies as death snatched its sons from the earth. A peace that passed all understanding came over the dying, who were freed forever from the siren songs of longing.[30] Binding's concept of heroism was characteristically linked not to nation or race but rather flowed from the individual's own private struggle to act nobly in the face of fate. Yet he offered little to those who enjoyed traditional family relationships based on love. Woe to the forlorn person who dared seek solace in his cold and patrician prose. Surely their longing would go unfulfilled. What were they to make of a poet who on one hand praised dying heroes in the style of Homer and on the other made it plain in his diary that the war was devoid of all grandeur?[31]

There was a marked contrast between Binding's idealized hero and the reality of the war that he himself experienced. As it was becoming certain that the war was lost, he noted in late July 1918:

Mankind has always made war on one another for something stupid. In the Trojan War it was for an evil woman; in other wars it was because one god was supposed to be better than another. In the Middle Ages the manhood of the West went to its death for the sake of an empty tomb which the Turks controlled. And now the whole world of our enemies pretends that they have to liberate us. From what and from whom?[32]

Binding had nothing but contempt for both Allied and German war propaganda, not sensing his own distortion of the truth in his poetic works. He mocked the German claim that the Reich was fighting for *Kultur* against enemies who stood for cultural decadence and shopkeeper mediocrity, noting that, "What is the sense of saying that one fights for culture?" No thinking person can argue that by killing Englishmen, who

[29] "Beweinung," ibid., pp. 107–8.
[30] See "Schlacht-Abend-Gewölk," ibid., p. 94.
[31] *Aus dem Kriege*, pp. 219–23.   [32] *Aus dem Kriege*, p. 358.

have done me no harm, one serves German culture, Kaiser, and Reich. Let's face it, the ideals for which we are supposed to be fighting renders the war meaningless."[33]

Binding was brutally frank in his diary concerning the lack of discipline and outrageous destruction of property by German troops, especially during the final year of the war. But his sharpest condemnation was reserved for the caprice of the German officer corps in its generous awarding of undeserved medals to its own. A feverish competition among units had become widespread, and the distinction of winning a medal had become lost. He dismissed the whole practice, claiming that the honors bestowed merely concealed humankind's inner depravity. "It simply makes me sick to see certain people chasing after medals and decorations," he noted. What made it worse was that every little principality began to find ways to strike new medals, which only compounded the corruption. People who really understood the ways of the front would only recognize the Iron Cross, First Class, worn by captains, subalterns, non-commissioned officers and privates. Binding himself, it should be noted, was awarded both the Iron Cross, First and Second Class.[34]

Binding had great respect for those officers who performed bravely in the war, the majority of whom were killed in action. He delighted in the brilliance of certain officers of the General Staff as well, men of the stature of General Hans von Seeckt, whose patronage in August 1916 secured him a staff position as quartermaster of the 199th Infantry Division attached to Archduke Karl's Army Group, the South Army. He was, however, repulsed by such individuals as the Prussian Crown Prince, who kept a monkey as a pet at headquarters as well as a personal stable of twelve thoroughbred horses with the best provisions, at a time when Binding often could not procure proper fodder for an entire division. Such behavior led him to the observation that once the war was over, after all the trials and sacrifices they had experienced came to an end, the officers and men of the front would never sink back into the same swamp in which they once had lived.[35]

Considering the controversy that would arise late in Binding's career, one must assess his attitude toward the Jews during the Great War. There is no question that the author shared the anti-Semitism that was widespread

---

[33] West Flanders, October 25, 1915, *Aus dem Kriege*, pp. 113–15.
[34] Binding noted that "Das ist bitter für die welche ihr Kreuz wirklich im Feuer und in Heldenhaftigkeit errungen haben." Entry of December 27, 1914, ibid., p. 57.
[35] Entry of February 17, 1915, ibid., pp. 73–4.

in the empire, and his attitude on this score was entirely consonant with traditional German conservatism. Observing that a number of incidents had shown Jews to be unsuitable to become officers, he attributed the situation to the fact that it was not in their nature to devote themselves to the military life. Nevertheless, he admitted that there were exceptions to this rule. One such case involved a Jewish aide-de-camp on the staff of his commanding general. The person in question had won the Iron Cross and had performed brilliantly. As a result, Binding placed him on a list of candidates for promotion, only to see him initially rejected on prejudicial grounds. Binding stood firm, however, and the Jewish subaltern was placed on the list for advancement forwarded to the Kaiser. Ultimately the promotion went through.[36]

Four years at the front had crippled Binding's imagination and stifled his intellect. Late in the war, he had been sent to a military hospital in Baden-Baden after a severe bout with fever and dysentery. He continued to fight an inner battle about the meaning of it all, sometimes giving way to pessimism but always returning to a classical idealization of the titanic struggle. Of one thing he was certain – that the best had died and would not return home to lead the nation to its necessary renewal.[37]

Time would heal the wounds of Binding's soul, and the spirit within him would flower once more. Over the coming twenty years – he was fifty-one years old when all was lost – he would return again and again in the twilight of his imagination to the thoughts reflected in the poem he wrote in August 1916, which was inspired by the Battle of the Somme. Although memorializing the fallen and lamenting their sacrifice, it makes no mention whatsoever of the Fatherland, heroic death, God's presence, or other nationalistic clichés. The hell of those days stands naked before the reader, and the author's fatalistic message would have to wait for another day for its transformation into myth:

> The ultimate battle arises
> from the many hundred battles.
> The last night appears
> Among the moons under which we stood guard.
>
> Honor is no more, nor disgrace,
> We are all alone here,
> Abandoned and banished:
> The enemy tramples over us...

[36] Entry of March 24, 1915, West Flanders, ibid., pp. 79–84.
[37] Entry of August 12, 1918, ibid., p. 363.

Death toasts us goodbye
In dreadful celebrations.
War beats us into pulp
In horrible clouds of smoke.

It was as if it spit us all
Out at once:
For here our whole company
Lies dead.

Aus vielen hundert Schlachten
hebt sich die letzte Schlacht.
Aus Monden die wir wachten
steht auf die letzte Nacht.

Kein Ehr' ist mehr, kein Schande.
Hier sind wir ganz allein,
Verlassne und verbannte:
der Feind trommelt uns ein. . . .

In ungeheuern Feiern
trinkt uns hinweg der Tod.
In ungeheuren Schleiern
stampft uns der Krieg in Kot. . . .

Und wär' es dass von allen
einen es von sich spie:
Hier ist ja doch gefallen
die ganze Kompanie. . . . [38]

    The hurt was so great, the ache so deep, that only a mythical interpretation on the Greek model could lend meaning to it all. Long after the war was over, Binding proceeded to follow the example of the classical sculptors he admired, artists whom he perceived could hew nobility in death from naked marble. He was determined to cast in words what they created in stone, and he endeavored to do this in his poem titled "Legacy." In this work, the army of surviving comrades exhorts the army of the dead to arise once more, the nation needing them so desperately in its struggle for rebirth. The army of the dead answers the call, and turning to the survivors, claim that they had been transformed beyond recognition and had never really returned home. Their spirits had remained at the front, with their comrades. The only hope for the future lay with their sons, who would carry their banner proudly in the storms of the times, remembering the noble deeds of their fathers. This was the true legacy of the front.[39]

---

[38] Entry of August 15, 1916, ibid., p. 175.
[39] "Vermächtnis" ("Anrufung" and "Antwort der Toten"), *Stolz und Trauer*, pp. 120–21.

Three years into the Weimar Republic, Binding returned to the novella form that had given him such great commercial success before the war. The result was *Immortality* (*Unsterblichkeit*), a union of the erotic and heroic genres that was greeted with sales of 150,000 copies and praise from the nationalist right.[40] In this work, the barely camouflaged "Red Baron" – the German ace fighter pilot Manfred von Richthofen – takes on super-human qualities. Seemingly part man and part God, the fighter squadron commander establishes his headquarters in Flanders on the estate of the young, beautiful, and unmarried noblewoman, Demeter van Beveren. Like many of Binding's heroes, Richthofen was not of this world but rather stood apart from it, his eyes on the heavens from whence he had come. His time on earth was short, because those whom the gods love are called home at a young age. On first meeting the commander, Demeter swooned, realizing that she was in the presence of a godlike figure of rare beauty and strength. She was immediately overcome with an obsessive infatua-tion that would never leave her. Press reports of the Baron's exploits in air battles only intensified the deep love she felt for him. According to one account:

The battle squadron won honor after honor. Wherever it appeared, the skies over the German armies were calm for a couple of hours. Here and there, everywhere, one could hardly follow it, the metallic humming and shuddering of the strained wings fell silent, flames shot out of the sides of the planes and the enemy nose dived to the earth. The fighters formed up anew and pressed the attack elsewhere. The squadron leader dominated the heavens as far as the eye could see. Like an angel of death he pursued the enemy and sent him to destruction. None escaped whom he pursued through the clouds, and none were permitted to reach the ground alive.[41]

News of the death of Manfred von Richthofen only magnified her love for this godlike figure. Even nature herself responded to the commander, and it was said that the ocean took on an eerie stillness as it received the Baron's fiery-red coffin. Demeter's grief knew no end, and despite marrying a man whom she pretended she loved and with whom she had two children, her intense longing only worsened. Her unrequited love could simply not be stilled. Heartbroken, she returned again and again to the shore of the North Sea, which lay near her chateau, certain that the Red Baron was present in the waves that bathed her body in salty

---

[40] Paul Alverdes praised the mythic qualities of *Unsterblichkeit* and found Binding to be a master writer in the novella form. See Paul Alverdes, *Über Rudolf G. Binding* (Frankfurt: Rütten & Loening, 1925).

[41] Rudolf G. Binding, *Unsterblichkeit*, (Frankfurt am Main: Rütten & Loening, 1928), pp. 35–6.

foam. Demeter gave herself up to one mighty wave, which shredded her clothing and wounded her, at once bloodying and caressing her before calmly returning her to the shore. Demeter was absolutely certain that the son to which she gave birth after this seemingly miraculous event was the result of the seed of the hero planted in her womb by the wave that bore his spirit. Consumed by her mental illness – no doctor could help her now – she felt absolutely hopeless. Finally, desperate with grief, Demeter in a fit of passion took the son – born of the waves – with her in a joint suicide, drowning in the ocean. Free at last, death liberated her from the torment of having loved, but not possessed, her hero.

In this work, Binding tested the limits of his readers' credulity, while giving full rein to his predilection for decadent erotic motifs. Classical mythology once more had served as the backdrop for his ethos of heroism, which featured Demeter, goddess of the earth and fields, uniting with the sky, in the form of the flying ace.[42] Without question, this work exudes the perfume of decay so characteristic of the period of late neoclassicism.

In the years following the war, Binding suffered not only from the disappointment of defeat but from the psychological turmoil of the postwar era as well. Hunger, inflation, communist insurgency, and Weimar democracy all converged to drive him to ever more strident polemical writings. He was convinced that Germany had become overrun not only by foreign political doctrines – most notably in the form of Marxist revolutionary insurgency – but also by foreign manners and fashions, customs, and ways of thinking. His reactions to Germany's political crisis were mild compared with those of his father, Professor Karl Binding, who had retired as an eminent scholar of international law but continued his work in Freiburg in retirement. Just before his death in 1920, the elder Binding – paired with the psychiatrist and psychopathologist Alfred Hoche – published a sinister study with the most profound implications for the future of eugenics. The work, titled *Permitting the Destruction of Life Unworthy of Life*, would become notorious.[43] Addressing the German crisis, Karl Binding affirmed that

When one thinks of a battlefield covered with thousands of dead youth and contrasts this with our institutions for the feebleminded with their solicitude for their living patients, then one would be deeply shocked by the glaring disjuncture

---

[42] See Bernhard Martin, *Dichtung und Ideologie*. Binding would write two other novellas dealing with the war, *Die Wingult* (Potsdam: Rütten & Loening, 1938) and *Wir fordern Reims zur Übergabe auf* (Potsdam: Rütten & Loening, 1934).

[43] Karl Binding and Alfred Hoche, *Die Freigabe der Vernichtung lebensunwerten Lebens. Ihr Mass und Ihre Form* (Leipzig: Felix Meiner, 1920).

between the sacrifice of the most valuable possession of humanity on the one side and on the other the greatest care given to creatures who are not only worthless but even of manifestly negative value.[44]

The implication was clear. The state must be empowered to practice euthanasia because the needs of the community must transcend those of the individual. Persons whose lives were without purpose and who imposed a burden on their families and the state must be liquidated. National wealth was being squandered, as was the huge medical establishment needed to support this scandalous situation. There is but a short leap from euthanasia practiced on the incurably ill to the murder of those considered "unworthy of life" for reasons of alleged racial inferiority. In effect, Professor Karl Binding offered the prestige of his position to support the racial hygiene movement, which was embraced enthusiastically by the National Socialist medical establishment and later put into practice in the Holocaust. Although there is no evidence that his son Rudolf and he had communicated about these ideas, this connection is extremely disturbing.[45] Curiously, Rudolf Binding never referred to this issue in his copious writings and he had died before euthanasia became an approved, if covert, state policy in September 1939.

The German crisis inspired Rudolf Binding to move from poetry to political engagement, and the influence of his work on the postwar conservative revolution was significant, overlapping with National Socialist ideology at critical points. He supported the conservative right, as was evidenced by his manifesto to the German nation titled "The Ethical Foundations of a People." In this work, published in 1920, he admonished Germans to establish their own ethos and to discard all foreign influences. Under the stress of the national crisis, they had been all too naïve in accepting Russian-Marxist, Jewish, and other international ideas. Many people had begun to equate their national identity with economic market forces, falling prey to the illness of modern industrial society. Germans were instructed to put aside their fascination with technology, democracy, progress, and relentless haste.[46] They were instead to embrace the German idea of freedom, to hold firm to the traditional values of the Fatherland,

---

[44] Ibid., p. 27. See also Henry Friedländer, *The Origins of Genocide* (Chapel Hill: University of North Carolina Press, 1995), pp. 14–16.

[45] This father-son relationship was a troubled one indeed. Rudolf, then fifty-three years old, wrote shortly after his father's death: "Thus the man died who would have loved me more than any other person had I not been his son" (*Erlebtes Leben*, p. 309).

[46] Rudolf G. Binding, "Ethische Grundlagen eines Volkes," *Rufe und Reden* (Frankfurt am Main: Rütten & Loening, 1928), pp. 119–38.

and to replace Christianity – "a Greco-Jewish implant on German soil" – with an indigenous German religion.[47]

Binding's lamentation against modernity became ever more strident. In the essay "Ecce Europa," published in 1925, he lashed out at the Americanization of the culture of Europe, which threatened to destroy any remaining humanistic impulses. Claiming that materialism cannot bring happiness to a people, he submitted that it would ultimately prove to be destructive. The genuine spirit of youth must show the way rather than the false values of the bankers, lawyers, engineers, and shallow thinkers who dominated the period. Physiognomy alone revealed the sad truth that Weimar Germans were vacuous, unsettled, and muddled. Binding also pointed to the threat posed to humanity should Europe continue to waver from its ethical foundations, a development that would have frightening repercussions. Like Jacob Burckhardt before him, he warned of the ominous revolutionary currents stalking Europe from both the political left and right.

Like so many veterans of the front generation, Binding criticized the German revolution of 1918, finding it wanting at the core. "Many cheered," he noted, "but those of us who felt that we were the bearers of the true revolution did not cheer. How we would have applauded a revolution with real ethical principles, a revolution of the spirit!"[48] As a result, Binding devoted much of the rest of his life to educating youth to his ideals. His background as a squadron commander with the Fourteenth Prussian Hussars attached to the *Jungdeutschland Division* gave him added credibility with the young, who were most impressed with his appearances at their conclaves. The author's description of his visit to an encampment of two thousand German boys from various youth groups gathered to honor the dead in the high Rhön country on the tenth anniversary of the battle of Langemarck (Ypres) in 1924 was a classic embodiment of neo-romanticism and secular nationalism.

Although based in mysticism – Langemarck, he said, had transcended history and had the force of a mythos, eternally rejuvenating the nation – nevertheless Binding's love of country was a far cry from venomous Nazi racism. Instead, it reflected his idealism, grounded on classical Greek models, which he was certain were pure in form and spirit. Here no attention was given to creed, gender, race, or class. The climb itself through the misty moorland into the foggy higher realm – the pilgrims made their

---

[47] Ibid., pp. 119–38. See also Martin, pp. 141–9.
[48] Rudolf G. Binding, "Ecce Europa," *Rufe und Reden*, pp. 139–48.

way to the peak of the Heidelstein in a metaphoric ascent reminiscent of Petrarch's musings on Mount Ventoux – was itself an act of grace, preparing the young knights to receive the miraculous healing transmitted by the spirits of the dead. Heroic poetry of Hölderlin was recited:

> You come, oh battle! . . .
> Approach the souls of the youth,
> Because the righteous strike like the possessed
> And their patriotic songs
> Bring the dishonorable to their knees.   ʼ
>
> Du kommst, o Schlacht! . . .
> Kommt über sie die Seele der Jünglinge,
> Denn die Gerechten schlagen wie Zauberer,
> Und ihre Vaterlandsgesänge
> Lähmen die Knieen der Ehrelosen.

Nietzsche's "Pride of the Last Will" was read as well, in an effort to inspire the young to "die, like I once saw him die, joyfully and soulfully." They, too, were admonished to enter battle like dancers, "shouting for joy that they died as victors," enabling them to sing, like their brothers before them in Flanders Fields, the sacred strains of that most German of songs, "Deutschland, Deutschland über alles."[49]

It was evident that the desperation and pessimism that Binding felt at the war's end had been healed and that once more he was ready to return to the spirit of 1914. However, he went to great lengths not to romanticize the deeds of his comrades, observing that although the front generation had an insight into the true spirit of humanity, what they saw upon returning from the war was horrifying. "We who were out there and really experienced the war," he observed, "have a different entitlement, a different source for our being, a different future than those who did not serve." Above all, he noted, "we had become honest."[50] As a result, Binding had contempt for the trendy *Kriegsliteraten*, the opportunists who wrote about the war only to make money. Those who had really experienced that hell, he noted, could not write about it: "We smothered the poems we had taken with us to the front and out there all songs died among the shell fragments just like everything that was living died."[51] The true meaning of the sacrifice was the chance for a new beginning it offered the nation. Herein lay the hope for the future. A new ethos, a

---

[49] Rudolf G. Binding, *Deutsche Jugend vor den Toten des Krieges* (Dessau: Karl Rausch, 1924). See also Baird, *To Die for Germany*, pp. 4–5.
[50] Binding, *Erlebtes Leben*, p. 269.   [51] Ibid., p. 298.

new pathos had been born in the hearts of the men at the front, and it was this shining torch of truth and spirit that they now passed to the new generation. Monuments, mausoleums, and official days of mourning and remembrance paled in comparison with this living spiritual legacy.[52]

In an address delivered on Memorial Day (*Volkstrauertag*) in 1927, Binding wove variations on this theme. He was determined that memory did not wither and decay, becoming yet another perfunctory ritual of the Weimar Republic. The dead, he affirmed, had been reborn and opened the way to the realization of a more pure humanity. There was now life where death had once ruled and hope where grief and loss had held sway. Germany's two million dead were bathed in the grand light of a new dawn. Despite the wonder of this gift – of transforming defeat into a moral victory – everything in real life went on just as before. Fearful politicians sat around green tables, ruling halfheartedly, while diplomats, meeting in pleasant hotels on blue Swiss lakes, earnestly discussed ways of bringing all the nations of the world together. The old generation simply did not see the new light of the dawn! All the more was it incumbent on the young to show the way to the future, to transcend the shackles of the past.[53]

Binding was appalled when Erich Maria Remarque's *All Quiet on the Western Front* was published in 1929. Highly critical of the war, the book had sold three million copies by the summer of 1930 and would be translated into twelve languages. It was released as a film in the same year and had become the subject of intense political debate in the Weimar Republic.[54] It was attacked from both the right and the left, but nowhere with more vehemence than by the Nazis, who made it a cause célèbre in their assault on the republic. Whereas the National Socialists were offended by the work's desecration of their cherished heroic mythology, Binding found fault with it for other reasons. Not only did it contrast markedly with his idealized interpretation of the conflict, he was also incensed that Remarque had so little personal experience of the war he described in such intimate detail. In a review ironically titled "War for Armchair Loungers," Binding attacked *All Quiet on the Western Front* in an uncharacteristically caustic tone:

Even hell can be sacred to those who have gone through it. And we have truly experienced the war. I am sorry, Herr Comrade Remarque! You are in error. You

---

[52] Binding, "Vermächtnis," *Rufe und Reden*, pp. 29–47.

[53] Ibid., pp. 39–47.

[54] See Modris Eksteins, *Rites of Spring. The Great War and the Birth of the Modern Age* (Boston: Houghton Mifflin, 1989), pp. 275–99.

will not be able to tear away the reality of this from the lives of those who have experienced it with your hundreds of thousands of copies and the hundreds of thousands of insults found in your war for – armchair loungers – which is what it really is.[55]

Binding's views paralleled those of the National Socialists on many issues, and he welcomed their assault on the Weimar Republic. On a personal level, he found Hitler to be rather inelegant by his standards as a cavalry officer of the old school. Binding did not seek to gain personal influence with Hitler, and when offered the chance to meet the Führer during the last years on the road to power, he agreed only on the condition that Hitler should visit him because he was the younger man. The author did not believe that Hitler was either a savior or a prophet. Furthermore, he resented the claim of certain Nazi functionaries that only adherents of the movement were in a position to render the front experience in properly conceived poetry and prose. Sadly, Binding was to make far too many compromises with the regime, and his letters written during the Third Reich make unsavory reading indeed. They chart a course that was initially positive, gradually embarrassed, and finally appalled by the leadership.[56]

One cannot fault Binding for cowardice, however. Ludwig Friedrich Barthel recorded an incident in which the author made a loudly audible protest at an outrageous comment made by a highly placed Nazi in Goebbels's Reich Culture Chamber. Before a crowd of prominent Nazis and authors gathered at a conclave devoted to the literature of World War I, the speaker made the offensive remark that although Great War writers had published this and that work, their efforts nevertheless did not amount to much of significance. Truly significant writing was yet to come, he asserted, and it would be literature inspired by the National Socialist movement. Speaking for all the writers in the audience, and in memory of the fallen soldier poets, Binding yelled out, "What do you mean by that!" which caused considerable consternation in the hall, embarrassing and flustering the speaker. Such an incident could have had serious repercussions for a person of lesser stature than Rudolf G. Binding.[57]

---

[55] Binding: "Krieg für genügsame Leute," *Die Literatur* 31 (June 1929), pp. 505–6. See also Anton Kaes, ed., *Weimarer Republik. Manifeste und Dokumente zur deutschen Literatur 1918–1933* (Stuttgart: Metzler, 1983), p. 516.

[56] Binding, *Die Briefe*.

[57] "Ein politischer Zwischenruf," Barthel, *Das war Binding*, pp. 213–14.

Binding's support of the government as Goebbels restructured the literary section of the Prussian Academy of Arts clearly distanced him from
the opposition authors, many of whom emigrated within weeks of Hitler's
takeover. The Academy had been a political minefield throughout the late
1920s, a showcase for the confrontation between fascist and communist sympathizers as well as adherents of traditional conservative and liberal worldviews. Indeed, in January 1931, the right–wing authors Erwin
Guido Kolbenheyer and Wilhelm Schäfer had resigned from the Academy
of Arts in protest against what they considered the provocative activities
of Heinrich Mann and Alfred Döblin in support of the writers of what
they termed left-wing "asphalt literature."[58] Soon after Hitler took power,
Heinrich Mann and Käthe Kollwitz signed a public declaration calling for
the Social Democrats to join with the communists in a united front against
Hitler. Both had resigned from the Academy, and a major crisis occurred
in the organization, which was completely restructured with the addition
of several new Nazi and extremely conservative members.

During the period of reorganization, Binding served as vice president of
the Section for Literature of the Academy of Arts, clearly seeing himself
as a protector of traditional values in a period when decency was being
assaulted on all sides. He attempted to hold the middle ground, not really
understanding that this was impossible in an era of increasing radicalism.
His inability to view the new political situation clearly would lead him to
make many serious mistakes in judgment.

The first miscalculation occurred with Binding's appalling response to
Romain Rolland's attack on the crimes of the Third Reich. Following the
notorious burning of books in Berlin and throughout the Reich, Rolland
had written a vehement letter, published on May 14, 1933, in the *Kölnische
Zeitung*. Roland called the regime the "enemy of the true Germany," and
lamented its racism and abuse of the rights of the "free spirits, Europeans,
pacifists, Jews, socialists and communists." Within a week, Binding had
written a response to the same newspaper, which in a matter of months
received wide circulation in pamphlet form under the title *Six Declarations
of Loyalty to the New Germany*. In his counterattack, Binding labeled
France the most nationalistic of all countries. Germany, he said, had not
been permitted to be a nation but had been ruled by the "Dictated Peace
of Versailles," not the constitution of the Weimar Republic. By writing
an end to the unjust Versailles system, the new regime had fulfilled the

---

[58] Jochen Meyer, ed., *Berlin. Provinz. Literarische Kontroversen um 1930* (Marbach:
Deutsche Schillergesellschaft, 1985).

longing of its people to be German again. "The world cannot conceive of the spiritual depth of this revolution," he noted. This accounted for the martyrs and fanaticism, rallies, standards, and flags, which, he admitted, descended at times into kitsch. "The world has not experienced what we have experienced," he observed. "Everything is new. A people which did not believe in itself now has that belief. And this faith is something beautiful to behold."[59]

The Old Fighter, Hans Hinkel – at the time a state commissar and a man who would later be influential in Goebbels's restructuring of German culture – was delighted with Binding's "Answer of a German to the World." In September 1933, he wrote a laudatory letter to him stating that "I am gratified with your willingness to pitch in like a good comrade in the great struggle which has been forced upon us today."[60] However, positive reactions by the government to Binding's initiatives would not last long.

At a time when the Brown Shirts were abusing people in the streets and civil liberties were being assaulted, Binding withdrew into his ivory tower. This was graphically illustrated when, at the height of the national crisis in the spring of 1933, he chose the topic "On the Power of the German Language to Represent the Nation" for a speech he delivered before the newly structured Academy of Arts. The address could have been delivered in the eighteenth century, focusing as it did on the meaning and nuance of language. However, Binding's insistence that language was the reflection of the character of a people was timely in the historical milieu of the early Third Reich.[61] The correspondent of the *Berliner Börsenzeitung* gave a glowing review of the address, noting how gratifying it was in the new era that German intellectuals were actually addressing matters of importance to the people. He delighted in the speaker's ideas and put a Nazi gloss on them, declaring that language was the creative expression of the Volk soul. "Today," he asserted, "as the national revolution begins, it is the

---

[59] Binding, *Sechs Bekenntnisse zum neuen Deutschland*, pp. 14–21. A falsified version of Binding's defense of the Third Reich was circulated, and contention about the genuineness of his answer to Romain Rolland in 1933 lasted well into the postwar era. See "Falsch, aber nicht verfälscht. Was Rudolf G. Binding gesagt hat," *Frankfurter Rundschau*, July 1, 1950.

[60] Hans Hinkel, Personnel File, BAB.

[61] In this address, delivered in Berlin on April 28, 1933, Binding noted that "Die Sprache ist das untrügbare vollständige, unwillkürlich alle Züge enthaltene Bild des Characters jedes Volkes: die wahre Gestalt seines Innern und die Stimme seines Herzens." See Rudolf G. Binding, *Von der Kraft Deutschen Wortes als Ausdruck der Nation* (Mainz: Werkstadt für Buchdruck, 1936).

right time for such a speech. The writer is indeed the herald of truth. The word of the poet is the word of the nation."[62]

Binding initially supported the Third Reich, believing that traditional German conservatism and National Socialism could somehow be integrated. As he wrote to Ludwig Friedrich Barthel, "You and I know that real poets and writers always stand behind their nations."[63] On another occasion he submitted that it was the duty of the Academy of Arts to support the state, because "art cannot be anything but the highest expression of the nation."[64] In a letter to Alfons Paquet, the acclaimed writer for the *Frankfurter Zeitung* who had resigned from the Academy on March 15, 1933, he argued that "the Academy must guarantee freedom of artistic creativity but not freedom of political expression."[65]

Binding sometimes made a subtle distinction between support for the nation and support for the regime. Without question, the criminal acts and crudity of the Nazis embarrassed him deeply. He was appalled that his name had been erroneously included on the list of writers signing an oath of loyalty to Adolf Hitler, a manifesto widely publicized in October 1933. Embarrassed, he went so far as to write a letter of protest to the Reich Association of German Writers, upbraiding them for their grievous error. He wrote an identical letter to the members of the Academy of Arts, having assured his colleagues at their October meeting that he had refused to have his name appear on the list.[66]

Binding's relationship to Thomas Mann was a troubled one, inasmuch as he considered him to be the greatest novelist of the twentieth century. Early in April 1933, he wrote to Mann, urging him to reconsider his resignation from the Academy of Arts. Unable to comprehend the magnitude of the role he was playing as an apologist for the Third Reich, Binding wrote these ill-considered lines: "You are leaving us. You leave

---

[62] "Das Wort und die Nation: Akademierede Rudolf G. Bindings," *Berliner Börsenzeitung*, April 29, 1933.

[63] Binding to Barthel, October 1933, Binding, *Die Briefe*, pp. 213–16. Binding's letter to Gertrud Hessenberg, an émigré in England, dated November 2, 1933, contained the observation that it was outrageous that an official German government body could be called the "Propaganda Ministry." Ibid., p. 219.

[64] Binding to "die Preussische Akademie der Künste, Abt. für Dichtung," March 3, 1933, ibid., pp. 174–5.

[65] Binding to Alfons Paquet, April 6, 1933, ibid., p. 182.

[66] Binding to the Reichsverband Deutscher Schriftsteller, Berlin, October 30, 1933. It is ironic to note that Binding signed this letter with the designation, "with our national greeting" (Binding, ibid., pp. 216–17). For his letter to the members of the Academy of Arts dated October 30, 1933, see Nachlass Rudolf G. Binding, DLAM.

us without considering how you are weakening your colleagues by doing so."[67] Thomas Mann responded sarcastically, observing that "it must be a pleasure to belong to the Academy when one has the right appreciation for brute strength."[68] This wounded Binding deeply, and he hastened to reply. By remaining in Germany under the new regime, he insisted, the writers in the Academy of Arts were fulfilling a difficult duty for their country. He noted cruelly that had Mann served at the front in the Great War, he, too, would probably have decided to remain.[69]

The matter did not rest here, however. Binding was naïve enough in May 1935 to propose in a letter to Minister of the Interior Wilhelm Frick that the Academy of Arts honor Thomas Mann on his sixtieth birthday by sending an official delegation abroad to congratulate him. When permission for such a gesture was denied, Binding personally paid Mann a visit in Zürich to offer him his best wishes anyway.[70] This behavior contributed in no small way to Binding's difficulties with the regime.

In October 1933, in connection with the fall meeting of the German Academy of Arts, Binding published an apologia for the restructuring of the organization titled "Duties of a German Academy of Arts," a document that received wide press coverage. In this manifesto, he claimed that "the Academy is the instrument of the Volk in its entirety" and must fulfill its function – to honor the German spirit by cultivating German letters. Their cause was noble, he posited, because "literature and poetry are the most visible and distinguished expressions of the nation, whose nature is reflected in its literature and language, where it becomes a part of history and enters the cosmic realm of the stars."[71]

Binding also commented on the departure of some of the members, observing that collegiality was a requisite for membership in the Academy. Genius alone would simply not do. Certain figures had continuously been guilty of unproductive sarcasm and belligerence and as a result could no longer be retained as members of that august body. With or without them, it was the duty of the Academy to continue to honor the German spirit

[67] Binding, April 6, 1933, *Die Briefe*, pp. 185–6.
[68] Thomas Mann to Binding, June 3, 1933, ibid., pp. 194–5.
[69] Binding to Thomas Mann, June 8, 1933, ibid., pp. 195–9.
[70] Binding, "An den Reichsminister des Innern Dr. Frick," May 23, 1935, ibid., pp. 290–1. See letters from Binding to Thomas Mann, dated August 8 and August 10, 1935, ibid., pp. 296–8. Thomas Mann related the anecdote about this visit in a letter dated January 22, 1955. See Barthel, *Das war Binding*, pp. 171–2.
[71] Rudolf G. Binding, "Aufgaben einer deutschen Dichterakademie," BHStA, Sammlung Personen 3989.

in its singular brilliance.[72] It seems strange indeed that Binding could continue to remain a member of the Academy when it included such notorious National Socialist authors as Hans-Friedrich Blunck and Hanns Johst.

Believing firmly in many of the policies of the Third Reich, Binding often willingly lent his prestige in its support. He was gratified to be able to help his country, noting that "in this very influential position I am permitted to act as an unsuspicious witness *for* National Socialism and the New Germany."[73] Yet there were occasions when materials he published might easily have been written in the propaganda ministry. For example, during the campaign for the plebiscite over the future of the Saar in 1934, he wrote:

Saar land, Saar people – German land, German people, German territory, German life, German past and German future – all this is endangered in the battle forced on us in this anxious time. The world knows – and no one denies it – that devilish forces are at work in this situation, they know that foreign elements in the territory stirred things up considerably there, that foreign elements are playing with the life and fate of eight hundred thousand German people. The question is: "Will they be successful in tearing this German land out of the body of the German nation?"[74]

From time to time, he found himself praising Hitler, even deeming the Führer's rhetoric to be extraordinary because of its simplicity, daring, and clarity.[75] Political success came at a price, however, and he complained that an embarrassing crudity in cultural matters had spread across the nation like an epidemic.[76]

Binding's posture on the Jews was problematic. On one hand, Rütten & Loening Verlag of Frankfurt, a Jewish firm, had been his publisher for decades. Further, his last lover, Elizabeth Jungmann, was Jewish. He had met her among the circle around Gerhart Hauptmann, and had lived with her for years on Lake Starnberg.[77] Nevertheless, despite these connections, he was willing to go along with the regime's gradual removal of Jews from

---

[72] Ibid.

[73] Binding to Staatsrat von Stauss, Präsident des Deutsch-Europäischen Kulturbundes, December 19, 1933, Binding, *Die Briefe*, pp. 230–2.

[74] "Ruf an die Saar," *National-Blatt*, August 25, 1934.

[75] Binding to Elisabeth von Bonnet, Klingenburg, March 13, 1935, Binding , *Die Briefe*, pp. 286–7.

[76] Binding to Adolf von Hatzfeld, January 31, 1934, Binding, *Die Briefe*, pp. 241–3.

[77] See the author's numerous adoring letters to Elizabeth Jungmann, Nachlass Rudolf G. Binding, DLAM.

public life. Indeed, in November 1933, he withdrew the prize nomination of Robert Musil for *The Man without Qualities* after a bureaucrat in the Prussian Ministry of Education claimed – mistakenly as it turned out – that Musil was Jewish. He opted instead for an inferior work by Ina Seidel.[78] Further, he observed in 1936 that "I can understand a statesman who says: 'I do not want to deal with Jews.' My standpoint is that National Socialism will be realized because in fact it comes closest to what I expect and demand from a state as a living reality: namely the fulfillment of life through it."[79]

Binding was among the few conservative authors of the period who were determined to maintain their own identity, a group that included Hans Grimm, Walther von Molo, and Paul Alverdes, and as a result he fell out with the radical elite of the Third Reich. It was a cardinal error for him to believe that he could somehow stand aloof from the powers that be, maintaining his characteristically dignified yet Olympian attitudes. His disagreements with the regime became acute only in the wake of Goebbels's radical cultural realignment in 1935. He was appalled that the authorities tried to control writers and artists, whose mission was to reflect national ideals and to act as the conscience of the people. In his opinion, Party spokesmen, bureaucrats, and puritanical ideological overseers simply had no business meddling in the affairs of the mind. He observed that the role of the intellectual had absolutely nothing to do with public enlightenment or propaganda, much less their being herded into its credentialed professional chambers.[80]

Binding only gradually came to realize that his view of the world could not coexist with National Socialist radicalism. He had refused to be included in Heinz Kindermann's *The Mission of the German Writer Today* at a time when so many nationalist authors felt an obligation to propagandize for the nation.[81] Furthermore, he had disappointed the popular military writer Werner Beumelburg by refusing to be included

---

[78] Binding to Preussische Ministerium für Wissenschaft, Kunst, und Volksbildung, "Betrifft: Harry Kreismann-Stiftung," November 29, 1933, Binding, *Die Briefe*, pp. 222–3.

[79] Binding to Rütten und Loening Verlag, Frankfurt, May 29, 1936, ibid., p. 319.

[80] Binding to "Stellvertretenden Präsidenten der Preussischen Akademie der Künste," March 5, 1935, Binding, *Die Briefe*, pp. 278–80. See also Alan E. Steinweis: *Art, Ideology, and Economics in Nazi Germany. The Reich Chambers of Music, Theater, and the Visual Arts* (Chapel Hill: University of North Carolina, 1993), pp. 103–46, and Jonathan Petropoulos: *The Faustian Bargain. The Art World in Nazi Germany* (New York: Oxford University Press, 2000), pp. 215–16.

[81] Binding to Prof. Dr. Kindermann, Deutsche Seminar der Technischen Hochschule Danzig, October 27, 1932, ibid., pp. 169–71.

in *Writings of the Nation*, a series clearly aligned with the Third Reich.[82] The patrician cavalry officer simply could not go along with Goebbels's expectation that all writers and publications must fall into line with the National Socialist cause. It unnerved him to be subjected to continuous requests to fill out the irritating obligatory forms that streamed from the Reich Literature Chamber. As if dealing with Berlin were not enough, local Party bureaucrats with swollen heads – often young enough to be his grandson – were constantly demanding that writers prove their ideological purity. It is not surprising that self-important Party officials, so sensitive to position and privilege, were offended by an aging author who dared question their authority. Ultimately, his behavior was bound to backfire.

Long simmering agitation between Binding and leading Nazi cultural officials broke into the open in 1935, resulting from the author's repeated attempts to win recognition for writers considered beyond the pale by the new guard. These included not only Thomas Mann but also Carl Zuckmayer and Paul Neubauer, all of whom had long before been blacklisted as *Asphaltliteraten* and attacked by Alfred Rosenberg, the Combat League for German Culture, and officials of Goebbels's Reich Literature Chamber. Binding engaged in ongoing disagreements with Reich Minister of the Interior Wilhelm Frick, and he infuriated Reich Theater Dramaturgist Rainer Schlösser when he nominated Carl Zuckmayer for the Schiller Prize.

Binding caused a scandal when, as head of the German jury acting as judge for the World Novel Competition, he forwarded the name of Paul Neubauer for *The Last Chapter*. The problem was that Neubauer was a Jew, then residing in Hungary. Binding's enemies saw to it that the case received widespread newspaper coverage, an assault led by the *National Zeitung* of Essen.[83] One representative article, headlined "Excuse me, Binding...!" offers the flavor of the biting sarcasm that followed. What kind of a world were we in, the critic opined, when an esteemed author who enjoyed all the privileges of the Third Reich and who had just pledged his support for National Socialist ideology at the recent Berlin conclave of World War I writers hosted by Goebbels, could support a Jew for the prize? The matter was made more outrageous, the article continued, when the

---

[82] Binding to Werner Beumelburg, Berlin, January 9, 1935, ibid., pp. 268–70.
[83] See Binding's letter of complaint to Reichstheaterdramaturg Rainer Schlösser regarding the work of the Kommission für Verleihung des Schillerpreises, dated March 9, 1935, ibid., pp. 283–6.

Jewish-owned Warner Brothers of Hollywood purchased the film rights to Neubauer's *The Last Chapter*.[84] Clearly, Binding had crossed the Rubicon and would have to take the consequences.

Late in 1935, the Gestapo became interested in Binding because of his liaison with Elizabeth Jungmann. Hanns Johst, at the time president of both the Reich Literature Chamber and the German Academy of Literature, found it appropriate to write a caustic letter to Binding, stating that "I would like to inform you today that I have received a letter from the Secret State Police, notifying me that you are employing a Jewess as your private secretary. Please let me know if this is the case. Heil Hitler!"[85] Johst even corresponded with Himmler about the matter, but no specific action was taken to deal with his complaint.[86]

Binding was essentially blacklisted by the Propaganda Ministry in 1936 when his name was excluded from the list of representative German authors showcased by the government in connection with the Berlin Olympic Games. He complained bitterly about this affront in a letter to Dr. Heinz Wisman, deputy president of the Reich Literature Chamber, noting that his name alone was missing among the members of the German Academy of Literature. He observed that it was doubly insulting because he would be attending the games as the guest of the International Olympic Committee, having won a silver medal for his book *Riding Instructions for a Lover* at the 1928 Olympiade held in Amsterdam.[87]

Binding's problems were to worsen in the coming months and continued until his death. In October 1936, he protested to Goebbels about the banning of the journal *The Inner Reich*, edited by Paul Alverdes and Benno von Mechow. *Das Schwarze Korps*, the press organ of the SS, claimed that an article in the August 1936 issue of the journal, written by Frank Thiel, had besmirched the memory of Frederick the Great. Günther d'Alquen, enfant terrible and editor of the newspaper, was a Cromwellian firebrand in the ranks of the SS, who often took radical positions in his search for a purified Third Reich. Binding defended the editors to Goebbels in the strongest possible terms, claiming that they were distinguished members of the literary front generation, known for their loyalty. He urgently requested that the ban be overturned, arguing that the article in question

---

[84] *Rheinische Landeszeitung*, October 22, 1936.

[85] Rolf Düsterberg: *Hanns Johst: "Der Barde der SS"* (Paderborn: Schöningh, 2004), p. 250.

[86] Ibid., p. 250.

[87] See Binding's letters to Dr. Heinz Wismann, Stellvertretender Präsident der Reichsschriftumskammer, July 9 and July 16, 1936, Binding, *Die Briefe*, pp. 326–33.

was nothing more than an academic treatise on the storied king. Binding made a point of not attacking d'Alquen personally, whom he credited with proven missionary zeal. "Because we, the war writers, want National Socialism to be *realized*. Certainly in that pure form in which we find it embodied in every word of the Fuhrer."[88] The ban on *The Inner Reich* was lifted, although there is no evidence concerning the influence Binding's letter played in this change of course.

Obviously offended by Binding's criticism and always on the hunt for new prey, Gunter d'Alquen counterattacked, assaulting his ideological views in *Das Schwarze Korps*. Binding complained to d'Alquen directly, querying: "Why would someone like me be attacked who is completely on your side regarding the minefield of Christianity?"[89] For d'Alquen's edification, Binding included a copy of a speech he had recently delivered, titled "The Future of German and Humanist Thought." In this address, Binding, now in the twilight of his life, praised the luminaries of the German Enlightenment, including Winckelmann, Goethe, Schiller, and Hölderlin, for their humanistic love of ancient Greece. According to Binding, the German vision of the Greek ideal had since become blurred, ceasing to inspire the nation. However, that vision had taken form once more in the Berlin Olympic Games in the summer of 1936, when a German youth, a herald of gods and men, entered the stadium bearing a torch to light the eternal flame. At that point, Binding swooned:

An entire nation stood with us in the immense oval stadium, with outstretched arms, bated breath and rushing pulse. Absolutely silent and still in the passion of the moment. The Volk was not greeting a German youth in Greek form, but instead was coming face to face with its own image.[90]

Besides graphically illustrating the many inconsistencies in Binding's worldview, this was a curious selection to send a leading SS ideologue and

---

[88] Binding to Goebbels (Entwurf), October 1936, ibid., pp. 340–2. See also Marion Mallmann, *Das Innere Reich. Analyse einer konservativen Kulturzeitschrift im Dritten Reich* (Bonn: Bouvier Verlag, 1978), pp. 138–51.

[89] Binding to Gunter d'Alquen, Berlin, January 17, 1937, *Die Briefe*, pp. 349–50.

[90] Rudolf G. Binding, "Der deutsche und der humanistische Gedanke im Angesicht der Zukunft," *Das Innere Reich* 10 (January 1937). On the other hand, Binding was contemptuous of Eberhard Wolfgang Möller's *Das Frankenburger Würfelspiel*, which was showcased at the Olympic games and staged at the Dietrich Eckart Bühne in the Olympic complex. He complained that it was devoid of ideas and bored the packed outdoor theater the night he attended. See Binding's letter to Carl Zuckmayer, Henndorf bei Salzburg, September 18, 1936, Binding, *Die Briefe*, pp. 337–9.

activist. Furthermore, it had been reprinted in *Das Innere Reich*, the very journal which d'Alquen had caused to be banned. Its call for a renewal of Greek values in the Third Reich, blending elitism with a humanistic model, was anathema to Gunter d'Alquen, a crusader for the realization of a pure National Socialist state. It contained not a single word about the Führer and was a far cry from the Nazi obsession with heroism and the warrior ideal.

Binding was now considered fair game for attack as a representative of an outdated period in German cultural life, and the radicals had a field day with him. Reich Youth Leader Baldur von Schirach was personally offended by the author's contempt for rallies, marches, and what he termed other manifestations of "nationalistic excess" – Schirach's stock in trade – and he felt compelled to do something about it. Choosing the prestigious forum of the Weimar Festival of German Youth staged at the National Theater in that symbolic capital of classic German culture, von Schirach attacked Binding by name in a speech on June 14, 1937, referring to him as an irresponsible representative of the intellectual elite of the Weimar Republic, completely out of touch with youth in the new era. Schirach went so far as to accuse Binding of "juvenile pranks" in his Goethe memorial address delivered in 1929, a degrading remark indeed considering that when Binding rode off to war in 1914, little Baldur was but a seven year old boy playing with toy soldiers. There is no question about the vast difference in style between these two men as they addressed the young people of Germany, representing as they did two clearly distinct historical eras. Binding was deeply offended and sought an apology, but von Schirarch refused to take back his words.[91]

The sun had clearly set for Rudolf G. Binding, whose political and literary activity had been scaled back to a minimum. He continued to read from his works at Hans Grimm's Lippoldsberg Writers Forum and made his last appearance at this venue for the inner opposition, which lay in a bucolic setting high above the Weser River in Lower Saxony, in the summer of 1938.[92] In August 1938, at the age of seventy-one, he died at his villa above Lake Starnberg. His mistress, Elizabeth Jungmann, soon emigrated to London, thus escaping the Holocaust. Devastated with the

---

[91] See "Reichsjugendpressedienst Nr. 132," Berlin, June 16, 1937, as well as letters from Binding to von Schirach, dated June 17 and July 2, 1937, Binding, *Die Briefe*, pp. 359–62.

[92] See *Die Lippoldsberger Dichtertage*, Klosterhaus zum Dichtertag (Bielefeld: Klosterhaus Verlag Lippoldsberg, 1960), pp. 13–16.

loss of her beloved Rudolf, she wrote: "Now it is really all over, all our hopes and plans have given way to a terrible deep sadness which I cannot shake off nor will I ever be able to in this life!"[93]

Burial ceremonies in the East Cemetery in Munich offered mourners an opportunity for quiet reflection about a man who may have outlived his time politically but nevertheless was the object of intense loyalty among his devoted friends. Rudolf Alexander Schröder spoke at graveside, quoting verses from Goethe's "Achilleis" on themes of eternal youth, grand poetic expression, and fulfillment in life and death.[94] Ludwig Friedrich Barthel spoke movingly for the members of the Binding circle, which included Paul Alverdes, Georg Britting, Edwin Erich Dwinger, Karl Benno von Mechow, Ernst Penzoldt, W. E. Süskind, and Heinrich Zillich.[95]

Although Rudolf Binding remained true to himself to the end, nevertheless he continues to be a troubling figure. A representative of traditional conservative values, he mistakenly was willing to give Hitler the benefit of the doubt for far too long. His list of enemies was long, embracing nearly the entire political spectrum. On one hand, he had been reviled by the left-wing Weimar intelligentsia. Both Kurt Tucholsky and Alfred Döblin had been extremely caustic about him.[96] And for their part, the new National Socialist elite had declared him persona non grata in their turn. It goes without saying that few, if any, Nazi uniforms were in evidence at his burial. President of the Reich Literature Chamber, Hanns Johst, declared his absence to be due to "illness." For the time being, he appeared to be a nearly forgotten man. Yet for decades after his death, memorials to Binding continued to appear in newspapers, journals, and books.[97] As late as 2002, the Odense Orchestra (Denmark) under the

---

[93] Elisabeth Jungmann to Herr Rehkopf, Akademische Orchester-Vereinigung Göttingen, November 2, 1938, Nachlass Rudolf G. Binding, DLAM.

[94] "Köstliches hast du erwählt. Wer jung die Erde verlassen, wandelt auch ewig jung im Reich Persephoniens. Ewig jung erscheint er den Künftigen, ewig ersehnet. . . . Völlig vollendet liegt der ruhende Greis, der Sterblichen herrliches Muster." See "Rudolf Alexander Schröder: Rede am Sarge von Rudolf G. Binding," *Die neue Rundschau* 12 Jahrgang (II 1938), pp. 306–9.

[95] "Abschied von Rudolf G. Binding," *Münchener Neueste Nachrichten*, BHStA, Sammlung Personen 3989.

[96] See Kurt Tucholsky, letter to Walter Hasenclever dated May 17, 1933, in Kurt Tucholsky: *Ausgewählte Briefe 1913–1935* (Reinbek: Rowohlt, 1962). Alfred Döblin correctly placed Binding in the group of conservatives with leanings toward feudal, aristocratic, and upper-bourgeois values and who expressed themselves in nationalistic tales, pathos, and heroism.

[97] See Heinz Steguweit, "In memoriam Rudolf G. Binding," *Westdeutscher Beobachter*, August 12, 1942. On the twentieth anniversary of the author's death, Heinrich Zillich

baton of Jan Wagner performed Paul von Klenau's Symphony Nr. 7, the "Storm Symphony," composed in 1941. The alto, Susanne Resmark, sang six songs that Rudolf Binding had written in 1916, titled "Conversations with Death."[98] His works have never gone out of print.

referred to him as "der letzte Grandseigneur der deutschen Literatur" (*Mangfall-Bote*, Bad Aibling, August 5, 1958). See also the nearly devotional memorial book by Ludwig Friedrich Barthel, *Das war Binding*.

[98] Paul von Klenau, 1883–1946, *Symphony Nr. 7*, sound recording, *Gespräche mit dem Tod* (Copenhagen: DaCapo, 2002).

3

Josef Magnus Wehner and the Dream of a New Reich

When Germany lost World War I, the agony of defeat had the most profound psychological consequences on the vanquished. The pain that resulted was most acute among the generation of the young who had gone off to war and for whom the trauma experienced in the killing fields of Flanders, Verdun, and the Somme forever shattered their emotional balance. Some chose radical politics as the answer to make sense of those trying times, whereas others found their outlet in alcohol, drugs, divorce, and suicide. Still others turned to the writing of poetry and literature to lend enduring meaning to their great loss. The unrequited love of the Romantics – the search for the "blue flower" that would never be found – pales in comparison to the unfulfilled longing of some poets of the front generation. None would be more disappointed than those who longed for the rebirth of a German Reich based on Christian moral and ethical principles. Their expectation that the blood of the fallen would be redemptive – that the dream of the young generation born in the trenches would take political form – was hopeless.

Josef Magnus Wehner (1891–1973), a young volunteer who served with the prestigious Bavarian *Infanterie-Leibregiment* in France, Italy, and the Balkans, was one such poet. He clung to the illusory vision of the Reich, never realizing that it was a lost cause. Wehner's career offers melancholy testimony to the shattered dreams of the war generation.[1] Long before he became a famous right-wing figure, Wehner was a charter

---

[1] See Peter Loewenberg, "The Psychohistorical Origins of the Nazi Youth Cohort," *American Historical Review* 76 (December 1971), pp. 1457–1502. See also "Germany: The Mission of the Young Generation," in Robert Wohl, *The Generation of 1914* (Cambridge: Harvard University Press, 1979), pp. 42–84; George Mosse, *Fallen Soldiers. Reshaping the Memory of the World Wars* (New York: Oxford University Press, 1995), pp. 70–106; "War Poetry, Romanticism, and the Return of the Sacred" and "The Apocalyptic

2. Josef Magnus Wehner 1932. Author's Private Collection.

member of a Munich literary forum of like-minded authors called "The Argonauts," which staged frequent public readings by literary figures of the day, individuals determined not to let the Weimar cultural scene be dominated entirely by what they called the rootless left, composed of communists, socialists, and pacifists.[2] They were appalled by figures such as Kurt Tucholsky and Bertolt Brecht, leaders of what they were certain was a growing political and cultural cancer in the nation.

It is fair to say that Josef Magnus Wehner, seen as a writer, was a second-rate literary talent whose political ideology catapulted him into first-rate political status at a critical juncture in German history – as the Weimar Republic drew to a close and the Third Reich was being formed. How else can one explain his emergence from the obscurity of his youth? He was born in 1891 at Bermbach in the Rhön, attended the Cathedral Gymnasium at Fulda, and studied the liberal arts at the universities of Jena and Munich. He was awarded the Munich Prize for Literature in 1929 for *Seven at Verdun* by a committee that included none other than Thomas Mann.[3] With the onset of the Third Reich, he was made a member of the reconstituted Prussian Academy of Arts. Although it is impossible to document Wehner's total career book sales, it was certainly well over one million copies. His early writings did not presage this kind of success; rather, it was due to Germany's political crisis.

God's Hamlet, *First Love*, and *The Wedding Cow* were characterized by Catholic piety and the exaltation of the simple virtues of rural life, family, and childhood, whereas *The Blue Mountain* was an unremarkable addition to the tired autobiographical *Bildungsroman* genre. On the other hand, *The Country without Shadows* – reflections on the author's long study trip to classical Greece – foretold his absorption with the mythical interpretation of history and reality that was reflected in his later writings on the war. However, it was Wehner's novel, *Seven at Verdun* that made him famous, followed soon after by his role as a much-heralded moral prophet of the coming Reich. He would offer the poetic link from the trenches of World War I to the Third Reich, from Flanders Fields to the Garrison Church at Potsdam, where in March 1933 Field Marshal von Hindenburg joined with Hitler before the tomb of Frederick the Great in

Imagination in War Literature" in Jay Winter, *Sites of Memory, Sites of Mourning* (Cambridge: Cambridge University Press, 1995), pp. 178–222.

[2] Ingeborg Schuldt-Britting, *Sankt Anna Platz 10* (Munich: Buchendorfer, 1999), p. 98.

[3] See Baronin Marie Amelie von Godin, "Eidesstattliche Erklärung," appended to and cited in a letter of support for Wehner, July 17, 1946, Nachlass Josef Magnus Wehner, Münchener Stadtbibliothek, Monacensia Literaturarchiv.

a grand gesture of symbolism and unity. His would become the mystical celebration of the inner Reich, what he called the "Immortal Reich."[4]

Outraged at the success of Erich Maria Remarque's novel *All Quiet on the Western Front*, which he felt misrepresented the heroism of the individual German soldier, Wehner composed his own answer to Remarque in just a few months in 1930.[5] The result was *Seven at Verdun*, which was dedicated to the fallen ("A Memorial to Our Dead Brothers"). In this work, the author was determined to propagate his mystical vision of the meaning of the sacrifice of more than two million German men. What the patrician aesthete Rittmeister Rudolf Binding did for the officer class, what Hans Zöberlein offered the future Free Corps and SA men, what Ernst Jünger gave the nihilistic intellectuals and Karl Bröger did for the proletariat, Wehner was convinced he was accomplishing for all Germans. No individual among the seven soldiers in the novel stands out from the others. They range from the thoughtful Lieutenant Robert Buchholz, to the messenger Roppel Blank, to the noncommissioned officer Eduard Lang, who most closely mirrors the views of the author. Seldom has a literary work contrasted so radically with reality. Wehner's dream of a revived empire based on Christian principles – with Catholic Bamberg as its capital – was hopelessly romantic. Nevertheless, the interpretation that Wehner ascribed to the meaning of sacrifice in the Great War found a wide echo.

The most important message of *Seven at Verdun* represented ancient generational conflict in modern guise. Wehner posited that the German soldier faced two powerful enemies – the outward enemy, the Allies, and the inner enemy, the bankruptcy of German leadership. It went far beyond the long-standing staff versus line confrontation among officers, although clearly Wehner sided with the front officers. He severely criticizes the chief of the German General Staff, General Erich von Falkenhayn, the creator of the strategic plan for the Verdun offensive, whom he deemed to be devoid

---

[4] Josef Magnus Wehner: *Der Weiler Gottes* (Munich: Delphin Verlag, 1921); *Erste Liebe. Roman aus der Jugendzeit* (Hamburg: Hanseatische Verlangsanstalt, 1941); *Die Hochzeitskuh. Roman einer jungen Liebe* (Munich: Georg Müller, 1928); *Das Land ohne Schatten. Tagebuch einer griechischen Reise* (Munich: Georg Müller, 1930); *Sieben vor Verdun* (Munich: Langen-Müller, 1930). For Wehner's own observations on his career, reflecting what he himself understood to be an unstable preoccupation with both Christian mysticism and the apocalyptic, see *Mein Leben* (Berlin: Junker & Dünnhaupt, 1934). Compare J. M. Wehner, "Autobiographie," 15.10.1949, Nachlass A. Beuttenmüller, DLAM.

[5] For an excellent discussion on Remarque, see Modris Eksteins, *Rites of Spring: The Great War and the Birth of the Modern Age* (Boston: Houghton Mifflin, 1989), pp. 275–99.

of the will to victory. For Wehner, the young were clearly the victims in the war for the German spirit waged with their elders. The old, he charged, lacked the will to victory that knows no fear.[6] This will to triumph was evidenced, he argued, by the bold captain who on his own initiative stormed Fort Douaumont at Verdun, acting without orders and leaving his own flank threatened, thereby winning a magnificent victory against a beautifully fortified strategic position. With the Fortresses Douaumont and Vaux in German hands, determined leaders would certainly have pressed on to victory forthwith come what may, deploying all their reserves in one fell swoop. The German High Command did not possess the death-be-damned confidence the situation demanded, however. As battalion commander Robert Buchholz observed at Fleury in July 1916: "We did not have the courage to force the victory."[7]

Why was it that the German soldiers died confidently in 1914 and with such dread in 1916? What had happened to the enthusiasm Wehner himself had felt in the heady days of August 1914 when he rhapsodized that "Army life is wonderful. One becomes a different, stronger man; brighter, more self-assured, happier, and healthier. One's blood surges, the fresh air is bracing, and it is as intoxicating as wine. Time and again I am almost tempted to sing, just thinking about the historical importance of this great moment."[8] The author remembered his response to the exciting news that cascaded through his troop train in October 1914 as it headed to the Western front: the fortress of Antwerp had fallen! "The sound of an organ welled up within me. I was totally carried away with the greatness of the hour and I heard the march of my Volk into the future."[9] How grand it was to recall the observation made by a General Staff officer early in the campaign for Verdun: "If there was ever a bold, Faustian, a German thought in this war, then it was the assault on Verdun."[10] This euphoria proved to be illusory. By mid-1916, the men in the ranks began to feel that they were the victims of their own leaders, weak commanders who had enmeshed them in a war of attrition.[11]

---

[6] "And thus the young learned that victory crowns the efforts of those who make up their minds decisively to seize the initiative and to take the battle to the enemy" (Wehner, *Sieben vor Verdun*, p. 87).

[7] Ibid., p. 210. See also ibid., pp. 258–9.

[8] Josef Magnus Wehner, *Als Wir Rekruten Waren* (Hamburg: Hanseatische Verlagsanstalt, 1938), p. 33.

[9] Ibid., p. 75.   [10] *Sieben vor Verdun*, p. 19.

[11] Evidence of the justification for the lack of trust in the leadership is widely extant in the literature. Readers seeking clarification about this issue will find it in John Keegan, *The First World War* (New York: Knopf, 1999), pp. 175–203, 257–308.

Bravery cemented the bonds of comradeship during the war. Wehner recounted one telling episode that demonstrated the love shown by the men for one of their fallen commanders. It involved an artillery general who had proved brave in battle and who was among the first to occupy Fort Douaumont. Never showing fear, he seemed to be everywhere at the front, always encouraging his officers and men, who cherished his loyalty. After being mortally wounded by a shell fragment, his final words were of praise for his troops. A French cat, which had accompanied him everywhere, cried inconsolably when the train carrying his body pulled away from the station.

A deep sense of comradeship warmed the spirits of the men, a source of great spiritual strength that united them remarkably from the first days of the German attack at Verdun. Wehner saw this great spiritual force as a blessing that encouraged the soldiers as shells burst all around them, bolstering their confidence.[12] Comradeship was also a great consolation to the men who were surrounded by death on all sides. While resting with his mates on an evening after a major engagement, Sergeant Eduard Lang broke into song, striking up a motif from "Wotan's Farewell," a highlight of Wagner's *Die Walküre*. Wotan, deeply sorrowful as he bids his daughter, Brünnhilde, goodbye forever, gently closing her helmet and laying the shield over her body, intones the lines:

> Farewell, you brave
> Glorious child!
> You the most sacred pride
> Of my heart
> Farewell, farewell, farewell!
>
> Leb wohl, du kühnes,
> Herrliches Kind!
> Du meines Herzens
> Heiligister Stolz,
> Leb wohl! Leb wohl! Leb wohl!

No German soldier could remain unmoved by the beauty of this moment, which in their minds married culture and force in lyric union. This, the author noted, created a "magical moment," an unforgettable example of the comradeship of 1914.[13]

According to Wehner, this noble and sacred spirit was to fade away. Once they realized the nearly hopeless predicament that fate had presented them, the young suddenly became old. Life seemed to go out of them, and

---

[12] *Sieben vor Verdun*, pp. 51–3.   [13] Ibid, pp. 77, 102–3.

"in the course of a single day, they experienced eternity." The reason for this was easily identifiable, and they sensed that their cause was doomed. For Lieutenant Buchholz, it was a clear case of the bold fighting spirit of the young frustrated by the refusal of their leaders gallantly to force victory from the jaws of defeat. He noted bitterly that in the fall of 1916, "they swept away from our eyes the towers of the cathedrals, the very walls of Paris. They crushed our spirit. Now we only know how to die bravely, loyal to the last."[14]

Sergeant Eduard Lang wove variations on this theme, pointing out that the German fighting man lacked neither bravery nor fighting spirit. Rather, it was the High Command that did not possess the will to victory. As Lang observed:

We are soldiers, born to fight for the Fatherland. Let us be clear what we are fighting for: a growing Reich, a people on the march, a rich field, a cascading river, the sight of our friends at home and of those yet to be born. We will do our duty even though we know that the rabble does not deserve our sacrifice, nor the careless and weak, the money-hustlers and traitors. We can do nothing else. This war proves the immortality of our people. We will storm into eternity.[15]

It was this same idealism – tested in the fire – that was widespread at the front and reflected in many literary works of the war generation. Wehner has Lieutenant Buchholz express his own longings when he tells his comrades that Germany will deliver "freedom to the world" following their victory, as the new Reich spreads justice, order, and peace in its name. According to Buchholz, even thinking about the greatness of the Germanic medieval Reich on the model of Charlemagne and Frederick II (Hohenstaufen) was "like music to my ears. I would gladly die for such a Reich."[16]

Although Wehner was not anti-Semitic – the word "Jew" does not appear in the novel –there are nevertheless aspects of the work that reflect racial bias. During the course of a discussion about the future of Europe, one of his comrades affirmed that not one more drop of German blood should be wasted on "foreign peoples," as had happened in the past. Further, proponents of *völkisch* thought could take comfort in the observation

---

[14] Ibid., pp. 259–60.   [15] Ibid., pp. 143–4.

[16] Ibid., pp. 140–2. For an extensive treatment of the theme of medieval symbolism and World War I, see Stefan Goebel, *The Great War and Medieval Memory. War, Remembrance, and Medievalism in Britain and Germany, 1914–1940* (Cambridge: Cambridge University Press, 2006). For a compilation of spiritual-utopian works that appeared in Germany in this period, compare Jost Hermand, *Old Dreams of a New Reich: Völkish Utopias and National Socialism* (Bloomington: Indiana University Press, 1992), pp. 66–9.

that German soldiers represented the first wave of a new movement of peoples, a wave signaling the expansion of the Reich to the east. "Where we stand," Werner noted, "there is the German Reich."[17]

Although the author respects his French counterparts and even marvels at the chivalry shown by many enemy officers, he has nothing but contempt for the Senegalese troops deployed at Verdun. German fear of the alleged brutality and savagery of the black French forces was widespread, and it is difficult to distinguish myth from propaganda on the issue. However, Wehner's descriptions of the atrocities reported to have been perpetrated on captured German soldiers at Fort Douaumont by what he called "wild beasts" that "stank to high heaven like caged animals at the zoo" are brutal. They presaged the emotional German response to Africans among the occupying French forces west of the Rhine after the war and are reminiscent of Nazi propaganda focusing on "Jewish-Bolshevik subhumanity" as well.[18]

Wehner was much truer to his character when relating several supernatural experiences at Verdun. His Christian faith was tested in the killing fields, and the wonders of his pious boyhood passed in review before him in more than one near-death experience. Christ, Mary, and all the saints in Heaven were never more vivid and alive than on the battlefield. At one point, as he lay seriously wounded in a crater for three days and certain that he was dying, Eduard Lang had a feverish vision. All at once it was Christmas; he saw the beautiful green of fir trees, and music welled up in his ears. Suddenly there was a great light, and the Christ child appeared in the arms of his mother, bathing the wounded soldier in the rays of majestic light emanating from his little hands. The next day, a medical orderly found Eduard in the crater and carried him to Fort Vaux. Eduard was certain that he had ascended into Heaven and was dismayed to return to the bitter realities of the battlefield upon returning to consciousness.

At another point, the soldier Roppel Blank was struck by shell fragments and lay severely wounded. When the dark of night gave way to dawn, it cast the scarred battlefield into a beauteous red light. In his delirium, Roppel was born anew, baptized, and prepared for entry into heaven. Suddenly a miracle happened. Mary, Mother of God – a figure of indescribable majesty – suddenly appeared in the dawn's early light. Mary

---

[17] *Sieben vor Verdun*, p. 142.
[18] Ibid., pp. 235 and 279–82. See Sally Marks, "Black Watch on the Rhine: A Study in Propaganda, Prejudice, and Prurience," *European Studies Review* 13 (July 1983): 297–334.

spoke to Roppel in soft tones, assuring him that he had nothing to fear. He seemed to be taking wing as he arose, leaving the shattered battlefield behind as he entered the safety of the fortress once more. These passages, revealing the simple beauty of Christian mysticism as experienced in combat by some soldiers, convey the impression of authenticity.[19] This motif was graphically expressed in Wehner's war diary as well. After a night of severe shelling, the author awakened to the joyous singing of larks. The contrast between nature's beauty and the hellish world he was experiencing had a profoundly transcendent affect on him, and he was overcome with a feeling of contentment that could only be described as surreal. "I feel so pure," he observed, "that I am almost drawn to death."[20] Troops of the Allied forces were known to have similar responses to the beauty of nature. As Paul Fussell observed in his masterful book, *The Great War and Modern Memory*, "For most, the morning larks were a comfort: they were evidence that ecstasy was still an active motif in the universe."[21]

For the author, there was a short leap from Christian to secular mysticism, and the vehicle was the myth of the Reich. For Wehner, the Reich was reborn in the fraternity of the spirits of the dead at Verdun. At the conclusion of *Seven at Verdun*, the entire corps of German dead in the Great War rendezvous at Fort Vaux on All Souls Night, November 2, 1916, a matter of hours before the final German retreat:

They sit in the smoke and talk and their faces are aflame with their starry dreams of the future. They know the gift they have given to the world, the example of unparalleled sacrifice for millennia to come. They talk and all recognize the invisible German Reich, which has its roots in their wounds.

And they know that this Reich is eternal.[22]

This was the high communion of the immortals, and Wehner put his vision into poetic form, saying:

> You should not cry and do not be sad,
> because our sacrificial blood was life wine.
> God created death as a brother to life
> The heart of the world beats with the blood of heroes.

---

[19] Ibid., pp. 246–9 and 192–3.

[20] Entry May 31, 1916, Nachlass Josef Magnus Wehner, Münchener Stadtbibliothek, Monacensia Literaturarchiv.

[21] Paul Fussell, *The Great War and Modern Memory* (New York and London: Oxford University Press, 1975), p. 242.

[22] Ibid., pp. 306–7.

Ihr sollt nicht weinen und nicht traurig sein,
denn unser Opferblut ward Lebenswein.
Gott hat dem Leben Bruder Tod gesellt:
Vom Blut der Helden schlägt das Herz der Welt."[23]

Clearly the elitist circle around Stefan George, despite their pretensions, had no monopoly on the concept of the secret and inner Reich.[24]

In his second war novel, *City and Fortress Belgrade*, Wehner drew variations on these themes in an extraordinary way, at many points indulging in excessive romanticism as he relayed the experiences of his beloved *Leibregiment* in the Balkan campaign of 1915.[25] He and his comrades understood that it was the goal of the Central Powers to link up with their allies in an empire extending from Berlin to Bulgaria and Constantinople. Their imaginations ran riot, however, as they conjured up grandiose historic visions along the path of their long march. As Eduard Lang observed, the war was returning Europeans to all those places where the union of myth and history, intellect and power, had once led them. The line to the East would lead all the way back to the Holy Land, to the fortresses of the Crusaders:

Did you know that our Gothic ancestors passed over these very same steppes? Over this ancient sacred land? Just like us they marched southward from the same direction and headed down the Danube to the Black Sea. And when I think of the Turkish Empire, I think of the loyal field-gray front of the Anatolian farmers in the Syrian desert, of Christ in Jerusalem, the lush gardens of Damascus and Baghdad, the oil fields of Mesopotamia, past the Tigris and Euphrates, over Kurdistan and Persia, all the way to the Caucasus. We'll see Macedonia, where Paul prayed. We will storm Nish, birthplace of Constantine, founder of the Byzantine Empire.[26]

Eduard completed his starry-eyed musings with the observation that in their era, the Goths had moved on from their positions in the southeast, spreading Christianity as they headed over the Mediterranean into Italy,

---

[23] Cited in *Der Gute Kamerad*, "Die 'Grauen Hefte' der Armee Busch," Schriftenreihe zur Truppenbetreuung, Heft 21, p. 71.

[24] See Robert E. Norton, *Secret Germany. Stefan George and His Circle* (Ithaca: Cornell University Press, 2002).

[25] Josef Magnus Wehner, *Stadt und Festung Belgerad* (Hamburg: Hanseatische Verlagsanstalt, 1936).

[26] Ibid., pp. 28–9. This historical fantasy was of a piece with the growing imperialist designs of the German war planners in Berlin. From the tone of Wehner's account, it is obvious that many officers and men in the German army shared this dream of *Lebensraum*. See Woodruff D. Smith, *The Ideological Origins of Nazi Imperialism* (New York: Oxford University Press, 1986), pp. 166–95.

Spain, and France, where the road lay open for the great Theodoric and later the Holy Roman Empire of Charlemagne.

Yes, answered Paul Lang, the young intellectual and volunteer, their mission had world-historic significance because they were building the Reich once more. Their excitement ended with a salute to the immortal German Reich, which would be founded anew, as well as to the "inner Reich," which had been reborn in their souls. Together they gave a fiery affirmation to the myths they loved so much. They hailed "the victorious Field Marshals of the West" and offered an enthusiastic "Heil!" to the German armies on the western front, "from the sea to the mountains" as well as to the entire "eastern front," from the icy seas of the north to Jerusalem. The *Leibregiment* burst into song, and their excitement spread like a wildfire, igniting the spirits of the 200,000 German and Austrian troops marching toward Belgrade, led by the legendary cavalry commander, August von Mackensen.[27]

City and Fortress Belgrade reflects Wehner's fascination with Serbia and the Balkans. He described it as a scene of mountains and mystery, of gypsies and strange customs, impenetrable secrets and lurking dangers, in representations of isolated and remote people of southeastern Europe that later found its parallel in Leni Riefenstahl's film *The Blue Light* (Bela Balazs 1932). Wehner's account of the German soldiers crossing the Danube and storming Fortress Belgrade in the dead of night in October 1915 is unforgettable precisely because of the mystery he conveys about the Serbian theater of war. "I know what I am talking about," one veteran soldier explained. "I've known this land and its people for years. We are in Tibet or a preserved village of the Middle Ages with all its magic and mystery."[28]

The author shows great respect for the Serbian enemy, whom he deems to be brave and honorable. His description of the rout and nearly total destruction of the Serbian army in the snow and ice of the winter of 1915 – they had crossed the mountains into Albania and Macedonia along with great numbers of refugees – was extraordinarily poignant and graphic. All but forgotten today, Wehner's novel ranks with some of the best campaign literature of the entire war.

The variations the author drew on the comradeship motif were striking. Kolb, an enlisted man, observed that "in battle we are all equal." It was this sentiment that emboldened Kolb to confront his superior, Lieutenant

---

[27] Wehner, *Stadt und Festung Belgerad*, pp. 30–2.
[28] Ibid., p. 42.

von Au, for engaging in sexual misconduct with a camp follower in the hours before a major battle. He admonished him sharply, saying: "Lieutenant, comradeship is as sacred as Holy Communion."[29] The nearer the onset of an attack, the more intense the men felt this bond to be. One night before a German assault, Paul Lang, listening attentively to hundreds of his fellow soldiers nervously rambling through the tall grass, turned to Kolb, and said: "We all feel near to death. But we wander about. This is the hour of sacrifice. That's why everyone is so quiet."[30]

For Wehner, the blood of fallen comrades represented an enduring link to the Reich. He venerated their memory in solemn wonder. This obsession, which he shared with the National Socialists, cast him into the vortex of the political storms in the final years of the Weimar Republic. Several months before Hitler took power, on the occasion of the dedication of the German national cemetery at Langemarck (Ypres) in Flanders, Wehner passed the torch from the hands of the fallen youth of the war to the leaders of the future Reich. His address, which many people found profoundly moving, was read simultaneously at memorial ceremonies at all the German universities, and its tone was that of a grand Te Deum mass, celebrating national deliverance from defeat and dishonor, from Versailles and Marxist turmoil. Like a high priest standing guard at the doors of heaven, Wehner united the living with the dead:

German students, at this hour you now assume the guard of honor before the nameless graves of German youths of the Great War. The transfigured spirits of these grand heroes arise gleaming and unite with you, person to person and hand to hand and faith to faith and honor to honor and loyalty unto death. Storming and dying they are the bearers of the last will of the Reich.

Once more they arise and heroically storm the hills around Messines and Dixmude, Passchendaele and Langemarck. They see again the destroyed St. Martin's Church and the burning Cloth Hall of Ypres. Transfigured, they die singing "Deutschland, Deutschland über alles," giving their lives enduring meaning. They merge with the nation, knowing that they are the living Reich. Wehner reached heights of mystical ecstasy as he affirmed that even as he spoke, the dead were reborn, reflecting the glow of immortality:

They are already beginning to shine, those tender shadows. Happiness wells up on their young faces, the eternal happiness of the immortal. They come and greet

---

[29] Ibid., pp. 42–4.   [30] Ibid., pp. 133–4.

us, the survivors, we who are in the twilight, the doubters, the despairing. Now
they are more alive than we and joyfully sing:

> Build the columns of the Reich
> over the corruption of the world!

The chorus of men in field gray becomes louder. The Reich is everywhere and
its blood witnesses are everywhere. Its heaven glows and its dead shine like the
stars.[31]

For Wehner, the fallen reflected the German idea of freedom. They had
been resurrected, their sacrificial blood forming a divine arch joining the
Reich of the dead with the future Reich of the living. According to the popular nationalist writer, Franz Schauwecker, they were a living testament
to his belief that "Germany had to lose the war, to win the nation."[32]
The Nazis were drawn to Wehner and several individuals who would
assume important roles in the cultural establishment of the Third Reich
took note of him. Alfred Rosenberg recruited him for service in the Kampf-
bund für deutsche Kultur before the ink had dried on *Seven at Verdun*, and
he soon was speaking on nationalist programs in Munich.[33] Hanns Johst,
who would later become president of the German Academy of Arts and
direct the Reich Literature Chamber for Goebbels, commended Wehner
for his Langemarck address, observing that his greatest gift was forever
burying the pacifist lament – born in the murderous Bolshevik chaos in
1918 – that German youth had died in vain in the Great War. Instead,
he argued, their sacrifice affirmed the cause of the Volk. Accordingly,
German cemeteries had become sacrificial altars, symbols of the eternally
creative Aryan people. Celebrating Wehner's union of politics and religion, Johst asserted that the fallen shone like bright stars in the dark skies
of Weimar, witnesses of eternal glory, heralds of the coming Third Reich.
They gave enduring meaning to the affirmation of Field Marshal August

---

[31] "Langemarck. Ein Vermächtnis," "Worte von Josef Magnus Wehner, am 10. Juli 1932, zur
Stunde der Übernahme des Gefallenen-Friedhofs in Langemarck, durch die Deutsche Stu-
dentenschaft, gesprochen an allen deutschen Hochschulen," in Wehner, *Das unsterbliche
Reich* (Munich: Langen-Müller, 1933), pp. 64–71.

[32] Paul Fechter, *Geschichte der deutschen Literatur* (Berlin: Th. Knaur Nachf., 1941),
p. 754. Heinz Steguweit became well known for his novels dealing with the difficulties suffered by returning veterans on the home front, most notably, *Der Jüngling im
Feuerofen* (Hamburg: Hanseatische Verlagsanstalt, 1932). See also Kurt Sontheimer,
Antidemokratisches Denken in der Weimarer Republik (Munich: Nymphenburger Ver-
lagshandlung, 1962), pp. 115–16.

[33] *Mitteilungen des Kampfbundes für deutsche Kultur*, cited in Rolf Düsterberg, *Hanns
Johst: "Der Barde der SS"* (Paderborn: Schöningh, 2004), p. 126.

von Mackensen that "nothing was in vain that was done for Germany."[34] However, by grafting Nazi racist ideology to the author's romantic Reich musings, Johst set a precedent that would haunt Wehner to the end of his life.

Just as the sun was setting on the Weimar Republic, the political spotlight shone on Wehner in a very dramatic way. On January 18, 1933 – two weeks before Hitler was named chancellor – Wehner delivered the speech of his life at the Berlin Philharmonic Hall on the occasion of the anniversary celebration of the founding of the Reich in 1871. In his address titled "The Eternal Reich," Wehner summarized all his longings for spiritual and political change. Any number of other alienated writers might have been chosen for this role, including Friedrich Hielscher, another adherent of extremely mystical concepts of nation who had published *Das Reich*, which drew variations on these nationalist themes. Further, neither the esoteric aesthete Stefan George nor the Olympian Ernst Jünger would have been appropriate for this performance. Rather, it was Wehner who, as a former student and warrior, was ideally suited for the occasion. There is no question that he had gained a following among many in the country who longed for change in that turbulent era.

"The Eternal Reich" was in essence an exercise in secular religion. Wehner's assault on modernity was brutal and unrelenting, embracing attacks on both capitalism and communism. In this address, echoes of the deep spirituality of his pious Catholic boyhood in the Rhön – bordering on superstition and animism – could be heard, as well as the nationalism of the front soldier. He submitted that the state must become the outward manifestation of the pure inner Reich. Remarkably, Wehner was certain that he was connected in a miraculous way with the spirit of the Hohenstaufen Emperor Frederick II, buried in Sicily high over Palermo at Monreale, after Charlemagne the most evocative symbol of universal empire. This fantasy, more than any other aspect of the address, epitomized the author's hopelessly romantic worldview.[35]

Although the Nazis laid claim to Wehner, ironically his goals differed dramatically from theirs. Without question, he addressed the nation like a priest, calling it back to its better self. It was not the drums and trumpets of Nuremberg rallies that he sought, nor racial hatred, nor was it power

---

[34] Hanns Johst, "Langemarck: Bekenntnis zu Josef Magnus Wehners Rede," August 1, 1932, Sammlung Personen, 4747 Josef Magnus Wehner, BHStA. Wehner, "Werner Beumelburg," Nachlass J. M. Wehner, Münchener Stadtbibliothek, Literaturarchiv Monacensia.

[35] Josef Magnus Wehner, *Das unsterbliche Reich. Reden und Aufsätze* (Munich: Langen-Müller, 1933).

and armed might for its own sake. His dream took him far from the outward trappings of empire; rather he called for the spiritual rebirth of the German soul, the establishment of a Reich from within. He yearned for the creation of a German spiritual cathedral, the proverbial "world tree" (*Weltbaum*). Come home, he cried, come home to your great mother, German idealism.

He claimed that the Versailles system represented the victory of Antichrist in the twentieth century, the tyranny of perfumed effeminacy over the manly German spirit, of technology over heart, of materialism over idealism, of capitalism and Bolshevism over the German who united the roles of warrior, priest, and artist in a new trinity. Begun in the "Franco-English Enlightenment," taking form in the French Revolution, the forces that united at Versailles guaranteed the emergence of a crass civilization and intellectual mediocrity. Hypocrisy crowned the entire edifice, which was concocted in intrigue in the name of democracy and humanity. In Germany, he argued, it resulted in the victory of "subhumanity," the weak and eternally doubting, whereas the rationalist and materialistic lawyer class suddenly was ennobled, thereby becoming the princes of the day. Versailles guaranteed the victory of modernity, the spirit of commerce and soulless reason, and the spread of the cancerous metropolis – home of mass man, criminality, and disease. Versailles brought the victory of technology over mind. To make it worse, it paved the way for the superior white races to be raped and enslaved by inferior peoples. The twin pillars of Western civilization, the Cross and the Sword, had given way to a heinous betrayal. The result was the political, social, and cultural chaos that characterized the era.

In its place the new German must emerge, freeing its people from the tyranny of Mammon. A new creativity would accompany this revolution of the spirit, opening the way for the domination of heart over calculating intellect, of the organic whole over disparate parts. Wehner's Reich was a metaphysical idea, not a call for any particular form of government. Youth would form the vanguard of the surge toward the Reich, one eye focused on the ideal, the other on its earthly mission. The new German would be knightly, lucid of mind, and devout, informed by that magical space where German genius meets world spirit. Predictably, this starry realm was peopled by fallen heroes and emperors, who formed a heavenly arch as a protective shield for the godhead. Those Germans prepared to receive the Reich would offer to humanity what the Parthenon gave to Greek and world culture – victory over chaos through cosmic form, transmitted in the glory of art. And what Roman genius delivered in the form of law, the Germans would transmit through the idea of the Reich, the key to universal truth. Germans were "born in the Reich" and can be "reborn in the Reich" when they dedicate themselves to its majestic vision. For when one speaks of God, one speaks of the Reich, he submitted.[36]

When discussing the nature of the Reich, Wehner stretches one's credulity, so mystical is his vision. The Reich was the home of order and hierarchy and must be distinguished from the state, which represented a lesser creation. Indeed, the Reich forms the godhead. Whereas states come and go, the Reich is eternal. The German spirit rests securely in the majesty of the Reich, untouched by the ephemeral rise and fall of its incarnation in the nation state. The Reich thus has no fate or goal (*schicksallos*). According to Wehner, it is the home of the archetypes of all that is good and beautiful, the abode of all German spiritual form, the life source of the German nature. The Reich hosts cosmic moral value – primal virtue – and the state is the servant of the Reich. The state is the sum of its parts, whereas the Reich is immeasurably more, the fullness of eternity in endless space. Crown, Sword, and Cross are embraced in the sacred union of the Reich, which reached its summit in the Holy Roman Empire of the German Nation. The Reich represents a grand cultural synthesis, embracing the East and West in a line including Old Testament Jerusalem, Greece, Rome, and Byzantium.

According to Wehner, virtue was one with the mystical life source of the Reich, which had its origin when God created man. Accordingly, the storied medieval German emperors were direct descendants of Adam, models of the German Reich spirit that inspired the great Christian medieval orders. When Germans were virtuous, brave, loyal, selfless, and pure, they were drawing on the inner Reich, just as the Teutonic knights did in a more glorious era. Heroism is the model within the context of the state, a heroism immortalized in God's special gift of the German language, transmitted in epic poetry based on myth. Nevertheless, the German does not die for the state, much less the Volk. Instead, he dies for the Reich. Wehner wove what to him was a majestic tapestry, praying to the saints of his Reich, a colorful display indeed featuring the great figures of the medieval empire. It was this Reich spirit, he submitted, which inspired a German soldier in Alsace, who, suffering in deep fever as he lay dying of war wounds, sang the words "O Strassburg, o Strassburg." It was this same Reich spirit that reassured a grieving German mother during the war, upon receiving the news of the heroic death of her son. Desperate,

[36] Ibid., pp. 11–19.

she tore the clothing from her body, stood naked before God, and uttered the words, "Take him." This proverbial mother of men understood that her sacrifice, although it brought temporary suffering on earth, was her link to the eternal glory of the Reich. She was thus reborn and transfigured in the Reich. Wehner called on Germans to follow these examples, to turn within, change their characters, and let the grace of the Reich flow in them and through them. Cross and Sword would victoriously emerge to rule once more, thus guaranteeing a grand future for the Germanic Reich.[37]

Wehner's passionate love for his majestic Reich had its counterpoint in his hatred of industrialism and technology, a calamity that he had lamented in a defining speech in 1932, titled "On German Reality." This address was very personal, occasioned by the nervous breakdown he had suffered following the Christmas Eve radio sermon he delivered in 1931. Just as his own soul was tortured, he was convinced that the German national soul was confused, empty, and lost as well. It was the rootlessness of modern life and the attendant rejection of the traditional organic union with the Germanic landscape that in great part caused the neurosis of the twentieth century. In his idealized view of the past, a grand balance between soil, village, and intellect had guaranteed harmony and order. But this old balance between farm and village had been destroyed, leaving widespread alienation and desperation. Within this milieu, the author saw himself as a prophet of national regeneration, warning his countrymen that rebirth was the only alternative to the death of their culture.

The soldiers of the Great War, he asserted, had experienced this alienation when they came to the bitter realization that the bureaucracy and the General Staff had completely lost touch with the aggressive fighting man. Real leadership had given way to the domineering force of technology. The machine did not serve but rather drove its creators. The result was tragic. The helpless foot soldier was sacrificed to devastating artillery assaults, made worse by the fact that undefined fronts guaranteed that friend and foe were indistinguishable. Mass death at Verdun resulted when technology controlled the leadership. With the coming of peace, he argued, the situation did not improve. Instead, technology continued to control the mind, for the fundamental reason that the human spirit cannot be integrated with technology. It would destroy the human spirit just as for decades it had twisted the minds of the industrial labor force in the Ruhr Valley. There workers were no longer human beings but instead

---

[37] Ibid., p. 34. See also *Münchener Neueste Nachrichten*, January 19, 1933.

had become mechanized and lifeless Golems. Were this situation to continue unabated, the entire nation would end up looking like the horrifying landscape at Verdun, which resembled the scarred face of the moon.

Spiritual death stared the nation in the face, he contended. The November Revolution of 1918 had exacerbated the situation, as law and order, church and morality, gave way to the excesses of Weimar decadence, where pacifism and parliamentary squabbles further poisoned human relationships. The cultural world was drowned in "foreign trash," the spirit of Paris ruled as the literary establishment gave way to fashionable cosmopolitanism, and the vulnerable German Babbitt totally lost his bearings. How lamentable this was, he noted, when contrasted to Fascist Italy, where the spirit of the Renaissance and ancient Rome had taken form anew, resulting in the rebirth of the noble *Italianità*. The greatest danger to the German spirit lay in seductive Messianic Bolshevism, with its promise of salvation through the chosen working class. Bolshevism went hand in hand with the victory of godless materialism and technology, offering itself in the camouflage of the collective. This collective was murderous, committing atrocities against people, families, and the church. It was of a piece with the putrefaction of modern mass civilization, a blight on the West since the Enlightenment.

The great seducer of the modern German was language, behind which cowered another curse of the century, the emancipated woman. These liberal women, he warned, were distinguishable by their hysteria and whining egoism, and they employed a language and phraseology all their own. When challenged, they hid behind shallow rhetoric, quoting Freud and blaming their parents for their own misconduct. The Weimar Republic was their proper milieu, and its leaders catered to their fantasies. Poor creatures, they were constantly being "misunderstood." They were always in a hurry, running to political meetings, to the theater, to the office – wherever they could avoid responsibilities to their families. Their worst fear, he noted, was an unassuming glance from a man, which devastates them. They are relativists, pacifists, and generally at home with all the "isms." These emancipated women know everything and speak out thoughtlessly on every conceivable subject, while in fact saying little of substance. They can do anything except really live. But their glory days were fading fast as a new era in German politics was dawning.

Wehner submitted that in the inorganic chaos of twentieth-century Germany, there was only one route to salvation – the return to "German reality." This involved rejecting materialism and greed and embracing the eternal verities. Neither the secular state nor its leaders were to be exalted.

Accordingly, Bolshevism and even the Italian model of state-centered existence were to be cast aside. In their place Germans were to turn to the
Reich within, their link to the heavenly realm where Christ and the emperors ruled over the cosmos, surrounded by great ancestors who have gone
home before them. Only then would they find the totality that their lives
lacked, a wholeness guaranteeing them a life of real meaning. The Germans alone had been commissioned by the eternal source of all power
and good to carry the banner forward. Ultimately they should be able to
say joyfully:

> We are fulfilled and grow undistracted by seductive phrases,
> And for us fate means: to be true to ourselves.
>
> Wir sind und wachsen, keinem Spruch verfallen,
> Und Schicksal heisst uns: selbst Geschick zu sein.

Only in that way would they be ultimately victorious over the forces of
decadent modernity. They would discover genuine freedom in obedience
to the eternal law of the Reich. They would fulfill their destiny by returning
to the greatness they had known before the French Revolution, which
Novalis had considered to be the defining event of modern history, after
which all that was sacred had been destroyed.[38]

Wehner continued to propagate his idealistic worldview during the
early days of the Third Reich, when his speeches and writings contrasted
markedly with the brutalities of the period. More and more his observations took on the tone of otherworldly sermons, delivered from above.
For some time it was impossible to distinguish his rhetoric from that of
the Nazi propaganda corps, which set to work feverishly to control the
media after Hitler was named chancellor. He lauded the leaders of the new
Germany for instituting radical cultural changes, transformations made
from the ground up. He was convinced that for the Volk to become the
nation, Germans had to be changed from within.

Initially Wehner found much to please him in the Third Reich. For one
thing, he was called to membership in the reconstituted German Academy
for Literature, and he more and more fancied himself to be a literary
spokesman for renewed national morality.[39] It was the duty of thinking
persons, he argued, to move beyond talk of blood and soil, repetitious

---

[38] Josef Magnus Wehner, "Über die deutsche Wirklichkeit," in *Das unsterbliche Reich.*
(Munich: Langen-Müller, 1933), pp. 35–64.

[39] Josef Magnus Wehner, *Mein Leben*, pp. 76–8. On Wehner's call to membership in the
Academy, see Hildegard Brenner, *Ende einer bürgerlichen Kunst-Institution.* (Stuttgart:
Deutsche Verlagsanstalt, 1972), pp. 75–85.

jargon that threatened to dull the senses. Yet he was not above employing Nazi vocabulary himself, drawing attention to the growing affirmation of the traditions of the Germanic Volk community, emanating from the alleged "eternal mythical source" that had formed and nourished the character of the Germanic people from their earliest beginnings. This "world spirit" was once again renewing the Germanic race, revitalizing its law, morality, customs and language, as well as its arts and sciences. Beauty and strength were embraced in its pure life source, enabling writers and intellectuals to shed the poisonous cultural and overly intellectual perversions of the Weimar era like the skin of a poisonous snake. The blood of this Germanic source was the indestructible taproot nourishing eternal Germanic cultural values. The battle against modernity had begun when Napoleon, at a time of German political weakness, forcefully spread the cancerous values of "Enlightenment civilization," thus polluting *Kultur*, the heart of all life. The peoples of the Reich, he submitted, were "now undergoing their struggle for an organic state as they endeavored to fulfill the sacred mission entrusted to them by the Germanic life source." This was the reason for the renewed joy people were taking everywhere in folk dances and songs, in Germanic costumes, in poetry and literature as well as in the theatrical productions staged in forests. Wherever one looked, German culture and customs had been revitalized, and it was beautiful to behold. This, Wehner contended, was the true meaning of "blood and soil." The culture of alienated, industrial mass man had given way to the traditional noble values of the countryside. The chains that bound German world spirit were broken, freeing it to cultivate a flowering of hallowed German culture.[40]

Wehner praised Hitler for winning the greatest political victory of the century by neutralizing the danger of world communism. Historians in the future, he submitted, would deem this his finest accomplishment, and should "Asiatic Bolshevism" once more dispatch its hordes against the territory of the civilized West, the Führer's National Socialist leadership corps would again rise up and destroy them. To guarantee this, Hitler must make clear that in the new Reich, power and culture were to be joined. Providence must be recognized as well, because the godhead was the source of Germanic culture. Once this great unity was achieved, nothing could hold them back. Workers, soldiers, farmers, and writers had already joined hands in a common effort to effect a common vision. The

---

[40] Josef Magnus Wehner, "Sinn und Heiligkeit des Volkstums," *Süddeutsche Sonntags Post*, July 2, 1933.

Reich had the potential to become the beacon of hope for a Europe lost in crass materialism. As a result, Germany would become the model for the world.[41]

The translation of myth into political reality is a difficult project in any historical setting, but it was beset with insurmountable problems in the Third Reich. Although the new regime was a far cry from Wehner's visionary Reich, he was in a position to take advantage of his background. He became a Nazi Party member and also belonged to the Reich Culture Chamber, an obligatory step for all those who wished to continue publishing.[42] He brought out several nationalistic works infused with mystic religiosity. On Heroes Memorial Day in March 1933, he published "The Man in the Bomb Crater," a memorial vignette to a fallen comrade at Fleury, mortally wounded in the last stages of the battle for Verdun. His description of the dying soldier was characteristically otherworldly and mysterious. Although looking death in the face, and hardly able to stand – he used two rifle butts as crutches – nevertheless, he refused help as he met the enemy. This was the same brave soldier who had said to him earlier on the Somme front that "Death is the way to the beyond." He declared in somber style:

> I still see you standing there, how you pulled
> yourself together at the last. You had helped me when
> I was weary. When I lay trapped with slime up to
> my breast, I thought of you and your last hour.
> I understand the meaning of your example and will
> pass it on and thereby show the real meaning of
> the war.[43]

Despite his political background, it is quite understandable that early on Wehner sensed that he could not continue as a political editor of the *Münchner Neueste Nachrichten*. The stress would have simply been overwhelming. This was a wise decision indeed, considering that the editor-in-chief of this prestigious newspaper was the arrogant Giselher Wirsing, whose appointment had the support of Heinrich Himmler. Wirsing was a

---

[41] See Josef Magnus Wehner, "Das Reich als Sendung und Forderung," *Berliner Börsen Zeitung*, October 1, 1933; "Deutschland hält Wacht!," *Süddeutsche Sonntags Post*, December 31, 1933; "Bemerkungen zur Kultur der Gegenwart," *Deutsche Studenten Zeitung*, June 28, 1934.

[42] Josef Magnus Wehner File, BAB. Wehner had a high Nazi Party Card Number (3,209,365) and could hardly have been considered an "Old Fighter."

[43] "Josef Magnus Wehner, "Der Mann im Trichter. Zum Gedächtnis eines Kriegers," *Münchener Neueste Nachrichten*, March 12, 1933.

former editor of the conservative journal, *Die Tat*, and was both a noted anti-Bolshevik and anti-American. An anti-Semite, he discerned Jews as the shadowy wirepullers manipulating the governments of both the Soviet Union and the United States. Wirsing had refined and reworked his ideas on world politics at Alfred Rosenberg's Institute for the Study of the Jewish Question in Berlin. An SS Sturmbannführer with connections to several high-ranking officers of the Black Corps, he worked closely with the SS espionage chief, Walter Schellenberg. As such, he was a foreign espionage enabler through the newspaper correspondents he posted at appropriate points throughout the world. Wirsing became one of the Third Reich's leading journalists and during the war Goebbels hired him to edit the prestigious glossy magazine, *Signal*. Wehner and Wirsing mixed like oil and water. As a result, Wehner withdrew to the relative safety of his new role as theater critic of the lively Munich stage scene.

It is not surprising that Wehner would soon learn cultural critics were also an endangered species in "reawakened" Germany. One Heinz Frank, a self-appointed spokesperson for Brown Shirt cultural policy, lashed out at him mercilessly early in 1934 in the Munich edition of the *Völkischer Beobachter*, the Party organ. Using Wehner's devastating review of a crass work by the Austrian playwright of mystical pastoral dramas, Richard Billinger, as a pretext, Frank accused Wehner of being a finger-pointing bourgeois moralist, murmurer, and grumbler totally out of step with the times. The young, Frank wrote, needed no fatherly advice from the pencil pushers, mere intellectuals who during the period of struggle had narcissistically pondered their navels in the quiet of their studies while the SA had gone about the dangerous business of forging a revolution. The victory won, these gentlemen – sporting the Party insignia on their lapels – now had the temerity to comment on the "intellectual firmament" of the new Reich, which they themselves did not create. It was their duty now to keep their discussions of art, religion, and morality to themselves while the revolutionaries completed what they had so honorably begun.[44] Incensed with the arrogance of the self-conscious, postadolescent new elite, within a week Wehner had filed suit against the newspaper before the Nazi Party Court in Munich, charging that his honor had been maligned by the attack. He presented letters of support as exhibits from Hans Friedrich Blunck, president of the Reich Chamber for Literature, and the noted conservative writer, Erwin Guido Kolbenheyer. In the judgment which ensued

---

[44] Heinz Frank, "Cultural-political Notices. Morality in Danger!," *Völkischer Beobachter*, January 17, 1934.

after the Party trial held later in 1934, the Nazi court came down strongly in support of Wehner.[45]

The author continued to applaud the regime at every opportunity, most notably when Germany withdrew from the League of Nations in 1933. The nation's suffering at the hands of the League, he submitted, was not unlike that endured by the early Christians abused by a decadent Roman elite. To become reborn as a nation, Germany perforce must cast aside the diplomatic shackles of the Versailles system. He praised the National Socialist leadership corps, affirming that the spirits of the war dead inspired the brave heroes who had donned the brown and black uniforms of the SA and SS. Their cause was sacred, he argued, because they were protecting the new Germany as if it were the Holy Grail of Christ. No patriotic German could question the wisdom of the country's withdrawal from the League, which, like the entire Versailles system, was structured to keep Germany weak and demoralized.[46]

Wehner continued to be active as an educator of youth, ceaseless in his efforts to inspire the young to serve the nation and to prepare themselves for self-sacrifice for the Reich. Throughout the peacetime years of the Third Reich, he made countless appearances throughout the country, often reading from his works as if he were reciting Holy Scripture. Many of his writings were excerpted in anthologies used in the schools of the period, and he published biographical works dealing with Field Marshal Paul von Hindenburg and Albert Leo Schlageter, the Nazi martyr executed by the French for guerrilla activity in the zone of French occupation in 1923.[47] Although successful as a critic and earning generous royalties for his publications, Wehner nevertheless felt unfulfilled. His goal had always been to write the model German epic war novel, but he had never accomplished this feat. By nature a complainer, he blamed his failure to do so on the necessity to support his family with a day job.

In 1938, shortly after the first conclave of writers in Weimar held in connection with Goebbels's birthday, Wehner approached Goebbels at a reception and laid bare the frustrations that burdened him. Although he had bled for the nation in the war, for years thereafter he had been forced

[45] NSDAP, Kreisgericht, München IV, three man jury chaired by Dr. Greiner, judgment dated December 22, 1934, Wehner File, BAB.

[46] Josef Magnus Wehner, "An die geistigen Deutschen," *Berliner Börsen Zeitung*, Nr. 327, 1933.

[47] Josef Magnus Wehner, *Schlageter* (Berlin: Franz Schneider, 1934) and *Hindenburg* (Berlin: Franz Schneider, 1935). For an historic vignette on Schlageter, see Baird, *To Die for Germany*, pp. 13–40.

by financial straights to engage in marginal journalistic work to support his family. As a result, he had suffered a terrible mental breakdown. Only his longing for the coming of the Third Reich had given him the strength to pull out of his deep depression, he observed. Goebbels listened intently, remembering his own problems with the Weimar literary establishment, and told Wehner that he personally would rectify the situation. Within a few days, the propaganda minister had rewarded Wehner's loyalty to the regime with a gift of ten thousand Reichsmark. In the author's effusive letter of thanks to Goebbels – he referred to it as a significant reversal of fate – he promised that an epic novel on the subject of Germany's rebirth would result from this magnificent gesture.[48] Such a work was never published.

Wehner contributed to the book of adulation presented to Hitler on his fiftieth birthday in April 1939, an elaborately bound compendium, edited by Alfred Rosenberg, containing poetry and tributes by literary figures considered to be loyal by the regime. Wehner lauded the Führer with the accolade, "He came forth from our thousand wounds and is the living spirit of his immortal people."[49] It was this same sort of conformity that irritated not only German émigré authors but many writers of the inner emigration as well and put the lie to Wehner's claim after the war that he had not really supported Hitler.

Throughout most of the Third Reich, Wehner became something of a cultural pope within the narrow yet influential world of the arts in Munich, the "Capital City of the Movement." His reviews ranged over the entire repertoire of the period, from classic Greek tragedy to Shakespeare and the master works of Goethe and Schiller, from the Romantics to the Naturalists, from Molière to Oscar Wilde and George Bernard Shaw. Wehner's commentary on the productions of works by National Socialist dramatists offers significant testimony to their belabored and unsuccessful efforts to create an entirely new school of theater in the Third Reich. They knew quite well what they hated so passionately. It was the theater of Berlin and the Weimar Republic, symbolized by Bertolt Brecht, which they considered positively decadent, even culturally poisonous.

---

[48] Wehner to Goebbels, November 3, 1938, Wehner File, BAB. The gift was paid over three years through the *Spende "Künstlerdank,"* a slush fund that Goebbels administered. See Reichsministerium für Volksaufklärung und Propaganda, *Spende "Künstlerdank,"* Der ehrenamtliche Geschäftsführer, November 25, 1938, bearing notations of gifts of RM 3600 paid during the Christmas seasons of 1938–40.

[49] Alfred Rosenberg, ed., *Festgabe deutscher Dichter für Adolf Hitler* (Berlin, 1939).

Nazi intellectuals faced almost insurmountable difficulties when they were faced with the problem of creating their own original style.[50] Unlike their innovative counterparts in the world of cinematic art, they were never successful in this endeavor in the realm of theater, where various schools of thought competed for center stage in the crowded theatrical world. Sensitive dramatists were uncomfortable with the star system that so often focused the spotlight on great individual performers rather than the works themselves. Perhaps the best example of this was Gustaf Gründgens's interpretation of Mephistopheles at the Berlin State Theater in which a single actor's brilliance clearly overshadowed the message Goethe wished to convey in Faust. As he addressed the problems of the contemporary theater, however, Wehner once again was swimming in shark-infested waters. Repercussions were not long in coming, reflecting once more how bizarre the cultural conflicts of the period could be.

The dramatist Curt Langenbeck caused quite a stir early in the war when he pompously proclaimed the theoretical foundations for a new German tragedy, principles that would inform a theatrical school commensurate with the alleged greatness of the Thousand Year Reich. Langenbeck, director of the Bavarian State Theater in Munich, was the author of the tragedy, *The Traitor* (1938) and would later write another widely played tragedy, *The Sword* (1941). In a pretentious speech delivered in Munich in November 1939 titled "Rebirth of the Theater in the Spirit of the Era," Langenbeck endeavored to propound the ground rules for German tragedy while at the same dismissing the intellectual hodge-podge of competing ideas purporting to represent theoretical approaches to the subject. However, the result was that he himself contributed to the confusion by adhering to an intellectually weak and idealized concept of tragedy based in part on the work of the neoclassicist reactionary, Paul Ernst.[51] Langenbeck was convinced that classic Greek tragedy must be reborn in modern guise. His ideas fit neither the worldview of Goebbels, for whom theater as an art form had the sole function of contributing to the Reich's mission to reorder Europe on a racially sound basis, nor that of Wehner, who attacked Langenbeck's weaknesses in a devastating series of articles in the *Münchner Neueste Nachrichten* in which he demolished Langenbeck root and branch. Whereas Goebbels at the time was far too

---

[50] For a general discussion of this problem, see Richard J. Evans, *The Third Reich in Power: 1933–1939* (New York: Penguin, 2005), pp. 120–218.

[51] Uwe-K. Ketelsen, *Völkisch-nationale und nationalsozialistische Literatur in Deutschland 1890–1945* (Stuttgart: Metzler, 1976), pp. 95–98.

preoccupied with orchestrating war propaganda to concern himself with dramatic theory, Wehner saw an opportunity to reconcile Christianity with National Socialist ideology, and he proceeded to do just that.

Langenbeck based his theoretical construct on the claim that Christianity had essentially died toward the end of the fifteenth century with the rise of individualism in the early modern era. Thereafter, only two forces informed the dramatic arts – the Christian and the tragic worldviews. God as a redeemer played no role whatsoever in Greek tragedy, he explained. Man stood alone vis-à-vis the fates. According to this theory, Shakespeare wrote no tragedies whatsoever and could not be considered a bridge to the German masters of the Enlightenment and Romantic traditions. Further, he posited, the new German drama must avoid the aestheticization of the theater and above all, cast out the idea that absolute cultural values ever have existed. In a cosmos devoid of an afterlife, it is the existential historic situation that determines whether tragic heroes can bring order out of disorder, thereby conferring heroic meaning to a world devoid of transcendence. Wehner rejected outright the idea that tragedy cannot exist in a worldview which accepts the idea of heaven or an afterlife.

Langenbeck, like the other theorists of tragedy in the Third Reich, embedded his ideas within a National Socialist framework. Accordingly, he believed that the new era was accorded the possibility of establishing an original religion that would leave Germans stronger, more devout, and purer than before the war. Just as their Greek forefathers – united in culture and race – had experienced great challenges, so now the Third Reich stood ready to face total victory or defeat, the first step toward tragedy. "Tragedy," he noted, "can serve as a model for those men who see themselves exposed to adversity, disaster, or self-destruction, and show them how one can master even the most dangerous situations, how they can hold out through the worst strengthened by their belief in the gods, knowing that ultimately they have to depend on themselves for the final victory." In a final flourish, which turned out to be prophetic, Langenbeck affirmed that it was the role of tragedy to show men how to behave in the worst of circumstances. "In that way, they can go to their destruction knowing that they are doing what is right."[52]

For his part, Wehner clung to his belief in transcendence, firm in his conviction that most great cultures have flourished with a sense of the

---

[52] Curt Langenbeck, "Wiedergeburt des Dramas aus dem Geist der Zeit," *Das Innere Reich* 10/11 (January-February 1940), pp. 923–57. See Ketelsen, *Literatur und Drittes Reich*, pp. 375–83.

afterlife. He quoted Hölderlin on this point, a poet who enjoyed a renaissance during the Third Reich:

> May the walls of this prison fall
> In the most sacred of storms,
> And more noble and free will my spirit
> Swirl to the unknown land.

> Im heiligsten der Stürme falle
> Zusammen diese Kerkerwand,
> Und herrlicher und freier walle
> Mein Geist ins unbekannte Land.

This, Wehner posited, was indeed the triumph of immortality, the same belief that inspired Goethe when he wrote, "A launching of wings and behind us the aeons." This was the identical belief, he noted, which informed not only the Egyptians, the Christian martyrs, and Germanic heroes who entered Valhalla, but the Athenians themselves as they formed their processions to Eleusis, where Demeter and the mysteries would bring them face to face with immortality.[53] It simply would not do, Wehner noted with a flourish, "arrogantly to brush all human creativity under the table, while ceremoniously serving up the dark wine of tragedy, with the single goal of fulfilling a rule of dramaturgy in an act of abstract exclusivity."[54] Wehner was skillfully using the camouflage of dramatic theory to argue the case for his enduring faith in Christ, a boldness that went unnoticed in the period of Blitzkrieg victories.

At the same time that Wehner was defending Christianity, he took to the airwaves on a national radio hookup initiated by Friedrich Castelle for the Reichssender Cologne. Week after week, in the fall of 1939 and throughout the winter of 1940, the nationalist author and frustrated priest read his messages of hope and consolation to the German people. Sources reveal that he had a wide following among churchgoers, especially in the heavily Catholic Rhineland. One of the messages, titled "On the Meaning of Suffering," could have been drawn from the sermons of Saint Paul. In it, Wehner presented death as life's natural brother. Suffering and death did not lead the warrior to Valhalla, and neither Hitler nor the mantra of the day, "heroic death," received any mention whatsoever in these homilies. Rather suffering and the "melody of death" were offered as links to God,

---

[53] Josef Magnus Wehner, *Vom Glanz und Leben deutscher Bühne. Eine Münchner Dramaturgie. Aufsätze und Kritiken 1933–1944* (Hamburg: Hanseatische Verlagsanstalt, 1944), pp. 20–38.

[54] Ibid., p. 31.

affirming the role of human beings as sons of God, in whose image they were created. It followed that the words of the thirteenth-century master, Meister Ekkehart, were cited as bearing an enduring truth: "God speaks to us through suffering. Mankind's spirit is thus freed and offered salvation through pain. That is, he suffers along with us." This was in Christian parlance, "the peace which passeth all understanding, uniting our hearts and our minds in Christ Jesus." Wehner went so far as even to reinterpret Nietzsche in this otherworldly view of reality.[55]

When the Staufen Publishing Company of Cologne rushed to publish the speeches to take advantage of the Easter and first communion gift market, it drew the unfavorable attention of the Propaganda Ministry. Rudolf Erckmann of the Ministerial Chancellery complained that Wehner simply "wallowed in suffering" and was out of tune with the heroic worldview of National Socialism. Great victories were never won with such passive emotions, he noted.[56] The head of the Reich Propaganda Office in Cologne filed a complaint as well.

Although Wehner's prestige precluded the banning of his book on this occasion, he continued to experience difficulties with Propaganda Ministry censors.[57] Manuscripts were rejected, older titles forbidden reissue, and there were even some serious concerns about the alleged "pacifist" nature of his classic, *Sieben vor Verdun*. Questions were raised repeatedly by Party members who increasingly found the incense and religiosity that suffused his works to be out of step with the times. Complaints were also heard in Party circles that Wehner was not reliable. One "G. Hagen" groused in an article published in the Nazi newspaper, *The Movement*, under the headline, "Horrifying Readers." He submitted that Wehner's book *The Great Our Father* was simply unacceptable because of its oppressive banality written in the style of a trash novel. "Did Wehner

---

55 Josef Magnus Wehner, *Bekenntnis zur Zeit* (Cologne: Staufen Verlag, 1940). Wehner's initial title for the work was *Consolation in Wartime*, but the authorities insisted that the title be changed.

56 Dr. Rudolf Erckmann, Reichsministerium für Volksaufklärung und Propaganda, May 28, 1940, to Hanns Johst, Präsident der Reichsschrifttumskammer. In the letter from Wehner to Johst explaining the controversy, he pleaded for help in coming to the aid of the wife of the Jewish author Walter Eidlitz, who faced deportation to Poland. See Wehner to Johst, April 13, 1940, Josef Magnus Wehner file, BAB. The Reich Propaganda Office in Cologne had also entered the fray, offended by the purely Christian nature of Wehner's programs.

57 See Wehner's letters of complaint to his publisher, the Albert Langen-Georg Müller Verlag dated July 23, 1941 (Herr Holm), and August 26, 1941 (Herr Fischer), Nachlass Josef Magnus Wehner, Stadtbibliothek München, Monacensia Literaturarchiv.

knowingly wish to drive readers to desperation with his endless depictions of death and useless sacrifice? Did he really want to convey the feeling of total hopelessness and pessimism in a work offending Christians and non-Christians alike and that should never have been published?" Wehner, he argued, had simply lost his bearings. Nazi Party members were thus forewarned that such works of "spiritual capitulation" boded ill for any future publications by this once-revered author of what Hagen referred to as "the most significant book on the Great War."[58]

Whether it was in response to public criticism or because he came to realize that his rather outmoded ideas did not fit well with the ever-increasing radicalization of the Nazi program, Wehner withdrew to his activities as a commentator on the Munich theatrical scene for the remainder of the war. His last book to appear in the Third Reich, *On the Glory and Life of the German Theater*, was published in 1944.[59] Considering the shortage of paper, it is remarkable that this work was published so late in the war. It remains today an important primary source for Third Reich drama. Tragically, his son Bernhard, a lieutenant and squadron commander in the Luftwaffe, was killed in action over Berlin in April 1945. To make matters worse, Wehner's modest home in Munich was destroyed in an Allied air raid in 1944.

After World War II, many of Wehner's books were banned, and because he was hopeless when it came to personal finances, this once best-selling author lived on the edge of poverty. Like several other authors who had supported National Socialism, he survived by writing Christian mystery plays and other religious works for the Catholic Church. The city of Munich came to his rescue and provided him with an apartment in the Künstlerhaus on the Saint Anna Square, a quiet and leafy enclave right off the fashionable Maximilian Strasse leading into the theater district. Through the auspices of Theodor Heuss, president of the Federal Republic of Germany, he was also supported by funds from federal welfare sources reserved for impecunious artists.

Wehner spent a great deal of time haunting the Saint Anna Church, spending hours at a time in prayer and contemplation. Understanding that his legacy was problematic, he put a great effort into arranging his personal archive for posterity as well. Knowing full well that he had things to hide regarding his behavior in the Third Reich, he removed and destroyed

58 G. Hagen, "Da graust dem Leser!," *Die Bewegung*, January 8, 1936.
59 Josef Magnus Wehner, *Vom Glanz und Leben deutscher Bühne. Aufsätze und Kritiken 1933–1945* (Hamburg: Hanseatische Verlagsanstalt, 1944).

a considerable amount of damaging material from the voluminous collection before depositing it in the Monacensia Literature Archive of the Munich City Library. He continued to write both for his own satisfaction and for posterity. Although living in the Künstlerhaus offered him an opportunity for new friendships – the poet and war veteran, Georg Britting, also lived there – he remained a loner who suffered from frequent neurotic bouts of depression. It was there that Wehner, in the company of his wife who survived him, slowly faded away, still suffering from a war wound and agoraphobia. Having long since lost his grip on reality, he died in 1971, a totally forgotten and disappointed old man.[60]

[60] See Angelika Mechtel, *Alte Schriftsteller in der Bundesrepublik* (Munich: Piper, 1972), pp. 119–25.

4

Hans Zöberlein: The Heritage of the Front as Third Reich Prophecy

World War I occasioned a right-wing postwar literary reaction in Germany that reflected the disappointment and trauma of defeat, made a case for an ennobling beauty of the life of comradeship under fire, and the determination to fulfill the dream of many common soldiers for a reborn, socially just German Reich.[1] Although Ernst Jünger became the most eloquent spokesman for the regenerative powers of the "storm of steel" at the front, he was joined by many other writers whose works became enormously popular between the wars. Among others, Franz Schauwecker, Heinrich Zerkaulen, Heinz Steguweit, and Werner Beumelburg, all contributed to the literary wave that exalted the front experience and played no small role in the seduction of the young generation. It was Hans Zöberlein, however, who drew the favorable attention of Adolf Hitler himself. Among all the war chroniclers and writers, he deemed Zöberlein's account of the experiences, hopes and, dreams of the front soldier to be the most authentic.

The career of Hans Zöberlein was representative of the generation that fought in the Great War, saw action in the Free Corps, joined the SA, and formed the vanguard of revolutionary youth that was to mold the Third Reich. Born in Nuremberg in 1895, Zöberlein came from working-class origins. He was the son of a shoemaker and was reared in modest circumstances. He was raised in a typically Frankish household – not unlike that of Julius Streicher – where anti-Semitism was as natural as

---

[1] For an excellent discussion of this genre, see Karl Prümm, "Das Erbe der Front. Der antidemokratische Kriegsroman der Weimarer Republik und seine nationalsozialistische Fortsetzung," in *Die deutsche Literatur im Dritten Reich*, Horst Denkler and Karl Prümm, eds. (Stuttgart: Philipp Reclam jun., 1976), pp. 138–64; also consult Bernd Hüppauf, ed., *Ansichten vom Krieg. Vergleichende Studien zum Ersten Weltkrieg in Literatur und Gesellschaft* (Königstein/Ts: Forum Academicum, 1984), pp. 88–91.

3. Hans Zöberlein, President, Order of the Bavarian Medal for Bravery, Speaks on Heroes Memorial Day before the Warriors Memorial, Munich, 1935. Courtesy of Stadtarchiv München.

mothers' milk and a child learned early on to distrust the Jews. He was taught that the Jews represented the Devil in human form, the beginning and end of perfidy. His wife reinforced his prejudices as well. He had married Lisl Geretzhauser, also a child of the proletariat from Munich-Giesing, who bore him four daughters and a son. Trained as a bricklayer and stonemason, Zöberlein would have spent his life as a simple worker had fate taken a different turn.

From an early age, Zöberlein was consumed with love for all things military and he responded naturally to the Germanic heroic warrior ideal. With the outbreak of the war, he enlisted in the 26th Bavarian Infantry Regiment and fought at Verdun, the Somme, in Flanders, and on the Marne. Zöberlein was an exceptionally brave soldier. He became a shock troop commander and attained outstanding proficiency in machine gun tactics. He was awarded the Iron Cross First Class and the Bavarian Gold Medal for Bravery, the highest Bavarian military distinction. As a member of the Free Corps Epp, Zöberlien took part in wresting Munich from the hands of the left wing insurgents in the spring of 1919. He joined Julius Streicher's German Socialist Party in Nuremberg in 1921. A year later, he became an SA man, and it was a source of pride to him that he was one of Hitler's earliest Brown Shirt leaders. He took part in the historic Nazi assault on Coburg and marched with Hitler to the Feldherrnhalle in the abortive Munich putsch in November 1923.[2]

Zöberlein achieved fame both as an SA man and a writer. As a result, he was promoted to high rank in the SA, moving up from Sturmführer (1928) to Standartenführer (1931) and ultimately to the generalship level of Brigadeführer (1938). With the Nazis' assumption of power, Zöberlein became a member of the City Council of Munich, led the cultural section of that body, and in 1933 was awarded the Literary Prize of the City of Munich as well.

Hitler himself wrote the introduction to Zöberlein's war memoirs, titled *The Belief in Germany*, which ultimately sold 800,000 copies. These amazing sales figures were due only in part to the popularity of the themes Zöberlein discussed – he sold briskly in bookstores and was heavily sub-scribed and widely circulated by lending libraries as well – but also because all of his works were supported and distributed by the regime well into the World War II years. His autobiographic novel, *The Command of Conscience*, detailing Germany's distress in the early years of the Weimar Republic, also enjoyed brisk sales, reaching 600,000 copies. Two short

---

[2] Zöberlein had NSDAP membership number 869 (Hans Zöberlein File, BAB).

books that drew variations on war themes, *The Easy Assignment* and *The Shrapnel Tree*, were also commercial successes, appearing in editions of 500,000 and 250,000, respectively. *The Belief in Germany* became a feature film and was released as *Stosstrupp 1917* (*Shock Troops 1917*, Arya Films 1934). *Um das Menschenrecht* (*For the Rights of Mankind*, Arya Films, 1934), was a cinematic treatment of the immediate postwar years. It was a brazenly propagandistic Nazi production that accurately reflected the Party's ideology, playing on fear and resentment of alleged "Jewish-Bolshevik" revolutionaries. As such, it was an outstanding example of the triumphant Free Corps genre in literature and film.[3]

The Belief in Germany, Zöberlein's remarkable memoirs of the Great War, is notable for many reasons. The work recounts the ardor of a young Bavarian boy who overnight became a man at the front, who fought bravely and ferociously, and indeed joyfully. He could serve as a role model for Ernst Jünger's storm-trooper ideal, a warrior who became drunk with the Dionysian ecstasy of battle, steel, and fire and for whom the smell of blood was as exciting as that experienced by a school of sharks on the hunt for prey. He was inspired by an enduring faith in German victory, even in defeat. He longed for a reborn nation grounded in social justice and crafted by soldiers. The book provided considerable support for the National Socialists' contention that the comradeship of the front was redemptive and that the war generation was baptized in the blood of the fallen and would ultimately redeem the German nation by founding the Third Reich.

Zöberlein made no attempt at the art of letters, which he considered to be effete posturing. Rather, his straightforward presentation was brutally realistic. Amid the heat of battle, after enduring weeks of thunderous artillery shelling, and suffering from hunger and thirst, he was absolutely certain that he heard the call of Germany. It was this vision that inspired

[3] Hans Zöberlein, *Der Glaube an Deutschland* (Munich: Franz Eher, 1931); *Der Befehl des Gewissens* (Munich: Franz Eher, 1936); *Der Druckposten. Eine Frontgeschichte aus des Jahres 1917* (Munich: Franz Eher, 1939); *Der Schrappnellbaum. Vom Stellungskrieg an der Somme* (Munich: Franz Eher, 1939). See Hans Zöberlein, "Eidesstattliche Erklärung zur Denkschrift Max Jüttners für IMT Nürnberg," March 20 1946, Kornwestheim, ZS 319, Institut für Zeitgeschichte, Munich. For examples of the treatment Zöberlein received by the critics in the Third Reich, see Hellmuth Langenbucher, *Volkhafte Dichtung der Zeit* (Berlin: Junker und Dünnhaupt, 1937), p. 37, and Hermann Pongs, *Krieg als Volksschicksal im deutschen Schrifttum* (Stuttgart: J. B. Metzlersche, 1934), pp. 7–10. See also Rolf Geissler, *Dekadenz und Heroismus. Zeitroman und völkisch-nationalsozialistische Literaturkritik* (Stuttgart: Deutsche Verlagsanstalt, 1964), pp. 94–8.

members of the front generation and led Hitler in 1931 to write in his introduction to Zöberlein's work:

> This is the legacy of the front! Battles
> and military engagements are accurately
> portrayed in every detail. The highs
> and lows are all here and above all the
> unwavering loyalty of comradeship. One can
> hear the heart of the front beating, the
> source of that strength which forged our
> eternal victories. The book has something
> to say to everyone: to the soldiers, to
> the politician, to the productive Germans
> of all classes. For youth now growing up
> it is the heritage of the front![4]

Zöberlein did indeed have a remarkable gift for recreating the mood of the front. As he retold his experiences as a messenger at Verdun, one can hear the staccato of the machine guns, the roar of artillery shells, the whine of mortars, and the dull thud of shrapnel. One feels pity for the soldiers – some far too old for front-line duty – as they move toward their positions at Verdun. The thousands upon thousands of crosses that had sprung up like mushrooms on those once beautiful hills now summon the men to their own deaths. One hears the curses and cries of fathers: "Nine children are waiting for me to come home!" Another yelled out: "I've got seven of them!" As the attack commences, the reader is alerted to the cries of the wounded and is horrified at the carnage. Deep in the night, flares illuminate the sky, casting an appalling glare across a devastated landscape that resembles the face of the moon.

The reader runs and crawls with Hans past trenches and craters, over bodies and mounds of mud, as he inches his way toward Fort Douaumont. His description of the fate of most messengers there is devastating. One morning, when three of them do not reappear from a night assignment, he muses:

> No one says what he really thinks! Probably
> disappeared in one of the countless craters
> out there. The fate of all messengers at
> Verdun. One goes out and does not return.
> Whoever is wounded and cannot help himself,
> bleeds to death Godforsaken and alone in a

---

[4] Zöberlein, *Der Glaube an Deutschland*, p. 5. For the war experience (*Kriegserlebnis*) as the fountainhead of the National Socialist revolution, see Sontheimer, pp. 115–16.

crater. "Help, comrade, help!" Who is going
to hear this over the roar of the battlefield?[5]

Hans himself is struck by shrapnel fire, and certain that he is about to
die, cries out, "Mother!...Mother!" As he lies wounded in the fortress
hospital, one hears the murmurs of the medical staff as they attend to
Hans. The air is fetid at Douaumont, a blend of the pungent smell of iodine
and assorted medicines, chlorinated lime, carbide, and stale tobacco.
Inside the fortress one knows neither day nor night – it is always dark
there. Candles flicker their macabre dance on the moist and mildewed
walls, piling up mounds of wax. Death on a massive scale is in evidence
everywhere.

Zöberlein is quick to praise his intrepid comrades, but it is clear that
he himself set a standard for bravery. Gazing across the parapet with his
binoculars, Hans spots a wounded man several hundred meters from the
fortress. He seems to be dead but begins to move from time to time and
calls out for water. Although it would place him in grave danger, Hans
nevertheless decides to try to save him. The conscience of a true soldier
has demanded this course of action, he affirms. Miraculously, he returns
amid crashing shells with his precious load, a young Prussian soldier who
would live to fight another day.

In the storm of steel his regiment encountered at Fleury, the furthest
point of the German advance at Verdun, Zöberlein was almost certain
that he would die during a horrible artillery barrage:

> The French artillery lay down an unbelievably
> accurate barrage in front of our trench, locking us
> in. They are shooting wildly. All around us their
> awesome, lightning blows strike home. A sandstorm
> breaks out over us. Astonished, we stare out toward
> the enemy, but couldn't see anything for the smoke
> and debris. Over there a red glow glimmers above
> the smoke; the whole front is ablaze in Bengal
> lighting, a demonic scene of the underworld. The
> world is going to its destruction at Fleury, and we
> with it.[6]

At another juncture, Hans survives for days without food or water. Mad
with thirst, he cannot bring himself to take water from the only available
source – a puddle with a dead Frenchman lying in it – even if his comrades
did.

---

[5] Ibid., p. 86.   [6] Ibid., pp. 120–1.

It was during the Battle of the Marne in the summer of 1918 that Zöberlein truly distinguished himself, winning the coveted Bavarian Gold Medal for Bravery. At a point in the action when his unit retreated unbeknownst to him, Hans held the line with his machine gun. In the course of several hours, employing four machine guns, he succeeded in killing hundreds of the French enemy. Ironically, during the course of the engagement, it was initially reported that Zöberlein had deserted because he was nowhere to be found.

Despite the honors he had won, Zöberlein was as excited as a little boy when sent to represent his unit at Kaiser Wilhelm's Christmas inspection at Solesmes in 1917. According to his account, he could hardly contain himself as fighter planes of the von Richthofen Squadron took to the air and circled the field. When the band struck up the *Präsentiermarsch*, he noted, "We felt our strength and it was a joy to see this German power. This is us, us!"[7]

Zöberlein waxed enthusiastic when discussing the subject of comradeship. It is clear that male bonding under fire offered an experience that blessed only those who underwent the front experience. For Hans, theirs was a sacred union, born in the firestorm, quickened by common danger and ever-present death. Truthfulness, readiness for self-sacrifice, and purity of spirit were its hallmarks. Shared danger had molded a new order at the front, an order that knew only loyalty, obedience, and love of nation. Out of the living hell there emerged a new man, the man of the storm, he submitted.[8]

Comradeship was an integral part of the heroic ethos. Comrades shared a mutual willingness to consider the needs of their fellows before their own interests and to undergo danger for one another. They had deep respect toward those officers who earned the esteem of the men, but they loathed the strict disciplinarians in the *Etappe* – the military organization behind the lines. There martinets played at being soldiers and often abused fighting men who had been granted rest and recreation leaves after months in battle. Shirkers, cowards, and socialists were beneath contempt. True comrades scorned the home front as well, a world that could never understand the fighting man. Real soldiers were not interested in the idle talk of politicians and swivel-chair officers who dreamed of grand annexations in the east and west. Quite the contrary;

[7] Ibid., p. 419.
[8] Robert G. L. Waite's observations on this theme remain compelling. See his *Vanguard of Nazism*, pp. 22–32; see also Michael Gollbach, *Die Wiederkehr des Weltkrieges in der Literatur* (Kronberg/Ts: Scriptor Verlag, 1978), pp. 212–16.

the real soldiers were more concerned with survival for another day or week.

Considerations of comradeship in the Great War, unlike World War II, sometimes extended even across the lines to the enemy. A case in point occurred on Christmas Eve in 1917 in the Siegfried Line. Zöberlein had opened his annual Christmas package, which contained all manner of food and other items to delight the front soldier. But the most treasured gift was a miniature Christmas tree. Hans and his comrades lit it on that Holy Night, and Schmied-Martl played his harmonica as if it were an organ in a beautiful cathedral. Just as they were singing "Silent Night," their thoughts focusing on their loved ones far away and on yearning for peace, an English patrol attacked. During the engagement, an enemy officer was severely wounded and lay trapped in barbed wire in "No Man's Land." Responding to his cry of "Help – help – comrades!" Hans and the others ventured out from their own positions, cut him loose, and carefully brought him into their bunker. As he whispered his thanks to the Germans, it was obvious that his death was near; his chest had been torn open by a hand grenade. As he caught sight of the little Christmas tree, a shadow of a smile passed over his elegant face. With that, Hans lit the tree once more, so that his enemy could die in dignity. Just as the lonely soldiers of the regiment struck up that most beautiful of Christmas carols once more, the Englishman died. As the orderlies carried him away, Hans tucked the Christmas tree under the snow-white camouflage coat which covered his body. At that, one of the soldiers, contemplating the desperation of their situation, uttered the words that expressed the hopes of them all, saying, "It is high time we had peace."[9]

Comradeship and the vision of the nation and Reich served to unify the men at the front. According to them, the real Germany marched in the field gray ranks of the Kaiser's army. As he affirmed so often during the war, what motivated the soldier to die for Germany was not duty; instead, it was this "belief in Germany" that lent meaning to the sacrifice of two million men. Zöberlein was to shed tears as his regiment was dissolved after the battle of Noyon in 1918. The ceremony signaled the breakup of what for him had become more important than his own family – the beloved company. For he had learned among the men of the company that "loyalty is Germany's soul."[10]

---

[9] Ibid., pp. 426–31. On the subject of fraternization, see also the film *Stosstrupp 1917* and Eric J. Leed, *No Man's Land. Combat and Identity in World War I* (Cambridge: Cambridge University Press, 1979), pp. 107–10.

[10] Ibid., pp. 573, 730, 818.

It is only in this context that one can understand Zöberlein's reaction
to the death of his friends. One by one they were killed. First it was Meier
Hannes and then Heine, the third son to die in his family, and finally, in
the summer of 1918, his old pal Girgl. Zöberlein described the pathetic
scene, as Girgl lay dying:

> Soon the tired heart of a soldier, the likes of
> which I have never known, will stop beating. I can
> still see him, just as he was: warmhearted and noble
> in all things. Back there, on the Somme, in the
> great battle of Villers-Bretonneux – at Noyon and
> finally on the Marne – the upright, modest comrade,
> the incarnation of selflessness and loyalty in good
> times and bad. Oh God, you are taking one of our
> best from us. For with him you are calling away the
> old Tenth Company. You will soon be seeing the
> other comrades from those days – all of them from the
> Tenth – most of them are already with you there. We'll be
> coming too, there's only a few of us left now. The light
> has gone out – the light we must carry into the world.[11]

Death for the Fatherland in the pursuit of properly conceived strategic
and tactical missions was understandable, according to Zöberlein. But
death resulting from poor leadership was intolerable. When only thirty
men of his company survived out of a total of 150 at the battle of Amiens
during the massive spring offensive of 1918, Zöberlein cursed the miserable "half effort" that had caused the unbearable loss of his men. He was
convinced that the weak leadership of the General Staff combined with
poor generalship on the Somme front had caused the disaster.

Worse was yet to come, he wrote. With defeat came dissension and
betrayal. The Red bacillus had spread from the ranks of the Leninists in
Russia, to the shirkers on the home front, to the weary fighting men in
the trenches and the sailors in the fleet. It was hard enough to have to
face the trauma of defeat after four long years of struggle, but communist
insurgency added the acid of betrayal. Anti-Semitism, which was relatively
latent during the war, suddenly spread during the revolution, when it
was learned that a disproportionately high number of the radical leaders
were Jews. At no time during the war had Zöberlein acknowledged the
presence, much less the bravery, of his Jewish fellow soldiers. Apparently
they were not considered to be comrades, and their longing to become
totally assimilated into the German body politic would remain forever
unrequited.[12]

---

[11] Ibid., pp. 718–19.   [12] See Hüppauf, pp. 71–5.

Zöberlein deplored the abuse meted out to the troops returning to the homeland. The train carrying his regiment from the front was not even allowed to stop in Munich. The Eisner regime in Bavaria justifiably feared the counterrevolutionary force of the returning German divisions. For Zöberlein, it was a bitter fate to have been honored with Bavaria's highest medal for valor, only to have to conceal it after the armistice. To have men he considered to be Red traitors tear the cockade from his uniform on the street near the Munich railway station was unthinkable. The world had been turned upside down. Zöberlein clung to the heroic ethos as consolation under the bitter conditions, declaring that

> Loyalty is always victorious, even if the
> war is lost. It is better to lose the war
> than loyalty and faithfulness. Because
> loyalty is Germany's soul. And without this
> soul Germany would surely die.[13]

He was convinced that the nation could be reborn only through the spirited efforts of the front soldiers. Zöberlein concluded his work with the affirmation: "The war is over. The battle for Germany continues! Volunteers to the front!"[14]

Although the film *All Quiet on the Western Front* had been a great success, the war film based on Zöberlein's novel, titled *Shock Troops 1917*, was a total failure. Directed by Hans Zöberlein and Ludwig Schmid-Wildy, it lacked the passionate intensity of its literary source, depending instead on episodic and unconnected scenes of endless shelling, carnage, and terror. Even the comradeship theme – the heart of the production – was not exploited in convincing form.[15]

Zöberlein did not consider himself to be a writer in the traditional sense. Rather, he wanted to be seen as the conscience of the front and a prophet of the Third Reich. Indeed he made every effort to distance himself from the other war writers of the period. Like all literary movements, the genre had taken on the proportions of a plague, attracting great numbers of imitators. The last thing such a front soldier turned chronicler wanted was to be compared with the aesthetes and careerist literary smart set that he imagined to be lounging about in the smoky Romanisches Café on the fashionable Kurfürstendamm in Berlin. Nazi writers were not expected to engage themselves in rational intellectual discussion; rather, they were to

---

[13] Ibid., p. 730.   [14] Ibid., p. 890.
[15] See Stosstrupp 1917 in Alfred Bauer, *Deutscher Spielfilm Almanach 1929–1950* (München: Filmladen Christoph Winterberg, 1976), p. 256.

celebrate the perceived beauty of the irrational spirit of the fighting front whose veterans were spreading a heroic tale of battle, blood, race, and national regeneration. As a result, the leitmotif of all of Zöberlein's books was political battle.

One can only imagine Zöberlein's embarrassment when he received a letter from Professor Artur Kutscher of the University of Munich, noted literary critic and a major figure in the nascent field of theatrical science, requesting desk copies of his works for use in his seminar. Kutscher was after all the teacher of Bertolt Brecht, the darling of the political and cultural left wing, but it seemed safe enough to answer him because the notorious Hanns Johst, president of the Reich Literature Chamber, had also sat in this seminar. Zöberlein obliged the request, and in a letter to Professor Kutscher, he observed: "I cannot imagine that my book is suitable for teaching literary criticism and good German style, because I am not a professional writer, but I am sending you two copies of it for your use nevertheless. Heil Hitler!"[16]

The Command of Conscience, Zöberlein's second historical novel, dealt with the unstable period from 1918 to 1923. In this work, the author himself is thinly concealed as the protagonist, Hans Kraft, whose experiences present variations on the epic theme of suffering Germany. Communist revolution, the trauma of defeat, the agony of Weimar politics, economic collapse, and moral putrefaction command the historical stage.[17] Was this the world for which two million German soldiers had died in the Great War, he queried? The author recounts what he calls the reawakened spirit of the front, and according to this scenario, the souls of the dead were said to inspire the German soldiers who once more answer the call of duty. The front lay neither in France nor in the East, however; instead, it was in the industrialized cities of the homeland. The Free Corps, the armed fist of the "true Germany," arose to deal the first blow to the "Jewish Republic," he claimed.

The story line followed the litany that would become so repetitious over the following years. Out of the chaos, a simple front soldier, Adolf Hitler, took up the banner and formed a fearless band of men loyal to the vision of the Reich. Hans Kraft joins the SA and commences the battle for the nation's soul in the proletarian wards of Munich. Wherever he looks, he sees the lurking hand of the Jews, whom he equated with the scourge

---

[16] Zöberlein File, DLAM.

[17] On the theme of alienation, see Robert Weldon Whalen, *Bitter Wounds. German Victims of the Great War, 1914–1939* (Ithaca: Cornell University Press, 1984), pp. 31–5.

of Bolshevism. Kraft becomes the victim of Jewish prejudice as a young architect, and hand in hand with his Aryan bride, Berta Schön, he is resolved to fight the "world pest" wherever the Jews might show their colors. The hour of decision arrives on November 9, 1923, as Hitler and his band stage their Munich coup d'état. The blood that drenched the Nazi banner at the Feldherrnhalle was redemptive, he submits, fulfilling the legacy of the fallen and showing the way for the final victory of the German nation.

Anti-Semitism is the central theme of the novel, and the Jews were accused of being the force of evil that lay behind the nation's myriad problems. Most lamentably, they were said to be responsible for the "stab in the back" that caused the loss of the war and the destruction of the German Empire. The leadership of the Soldiers and Workers Councils was composed of cowards, scribblers, and armchair soldiers whose physiognomy alone betrayed them as part of the international Jewish conspiracy. He claimed that Lenin's most important henchmen in Germany – Liebknecht and Luxemburg in Berlin, Eisner, Levi, and Levien in Munich – were all Jews, intent on destroying what was Aryan, pure, and just. In fact, Karl Liebknecht was not Jewish at all, but nevertheless this misrepresentation was a common feature of right-wing propaganda thereafter.

The worst aspect of the revolution, according to Zöberlein, was its hypocrisy and moral depravity. Whereas the leaders lustily sang the *Internationale* calling for the onset of the Soviet paradise, their own lives and activities told a wholly different story. The life of "Comrade Wilhelm Vogel" was typical of the hypocritical breed, he wrote. Hans knew the man well from his days at the front. This was the same Wilhelm Vogel who had led the Soldiers Council in his company at the front in 1918. By day, appearing in a proletarian uniform, he led Spartacist demonstrations, posing as a Red Guard. There he harangued the crowds, mouthing the same communist slogans that could be heard from Hamburg to Moscow. However, as night darkened the city, the Jewish chameleon made a radical change. Sporting a tuxedo and monocle, he appears arm in arm with a painted tart at a throbbing jazz club looking like a new-rich industrialist. For Zöberlein, the club was a symbol of Weimar Germany, revealing the true nature of the regime. This was a world where alcohol, drugs, illicit sex, and financial corruption thrived.[18]

---

[18] Fear about the loose manners and morals in postwar Germany was widespread. See Reichard Bessel's excellent chapter, "The Post-war Transition and the Moral Order," in *Germany after the First World War*, pp. 220–53.

Hans Kraft was forced to ward off several assaults on his Germanic virtue. In the Munich Old City, cocaine traders tried to hire him as a dealer when they discovered that he was an unemployed veteran. Another encounter took place when Kraft was enjoying a measure of success as a young architect. In a grand display of self-control and rectitude, Hans was put to the test of sexual temptation by a Jewish femme fatale. Mirjam, a beautiful seductress, had tricked him into appearing at her villa through a business connection. She had prepared for a night of love and reckless abandon with Hans in a palatial setting that promised all the delights of perfumed Babylon. But Hans, at the moment of destiny, rejected this haute bourgeoisie princess, cruelly condemning her Jewish machinations.

An unfortunate incident confirmed for Hans the danger Jewry posed to the purity of Germanic blood. While on a swimming outing at a Bavarian lake, Hans saves his beloved fiancé, Bertha Schön, from sexual abuse at the hands of a "Satanic gang of Jews." In the event, Hans and Bertha were themselves unjustifiably ordered off the premises for disturbing the peace. This led to a serious conversation between the young couple, meant to convey the message that even in Germany's hour of dire need, the flame of Teutonic culture would not die. Bertha observed that "It makes me sick when I see something like this happening. These Jewish pigs are ruining us, they are polluting our blood line. And our blood is the only decent thing we have left." This led Hans to muse on the Jewish question, submitting that the entire postwar German crisis revolved around the Jews. Germans always had rejected the Jews, he observed, because it was in their nature to do so. "We will be ruined, if this continues unabated," he pointed out. "Everything that was moral, honorable, and pure would be destroyed." The couple was grateful for this moment of political awakening, and they turned to nature and the Germanic landscape for encouragement. Music blessed this moment of sacred political revelation, and they blissfully sang a folksong that acted as a balm for their wounds, "Heimat, wie bist du schön."[19]

The suffering experienced by many of Kraft's comrades from the front was indescribable. He himself underwent many indignities. Upon applying for a job as a bricklayer – before the war he had been employed as a construction foreman – a bloated capitalist treated him miserably. Upon learning that Kraft had been a front soldier and did not have the proper papers to demonstrate recent work experience, the businessman threw him out of his office. Speaking for millions of other veterans, Hans said,

---

[19] Zöberlein, *Der Befehl des Gewissens*, pp. 295–301.

"What is to become of us front soldiers?" "How am I to know?" came the answer. "We don't have time for this," the boss said, flashing his corpulent fingers, heavily laden with rings. Kraft responded, "It's obvious that you never faced danger during the war, because you wouldn't treat a front soldier this way – and to think that we put our lives on the line at the front for the likes of you."[20]

One of the saddest tales involved his comrade Sergeant Michl Anreiner, who tried unsuccessfully to succeed as a farmer after the war, but depression had overtaken German agriculture. Michl's description of his hopes for a new life with his young wife in Brazil rang hollow when he considered what he was giving up. He had placed some soil of the homeland in the false bottom of a crib, so that his children, born far across the sea, would always be able to affirm their roots. The cross he had to bear, Michl submitted, was a heavy one, comparable only to the agony of four years in the trenches on the western front. How sad it was to contemplate that German farmers were being cast aside by a thankless nation.

Zöberlein, searching for a reason for the suffering, blamed the Jews for the agricultural crisis as well. He juxtaposed the emigration of German farmers with the immigration of Jews. His revolting description of the arrival of Polish Jews at the Silesian Railway Station in gritty East Berlin gave what he considered to be graphic testimony of the nation's social problem and was a frightening omen for the future:

> Across the street there suddenly comes a
> loud pack of kikey Eastern Jews with bags
> and packages. A fresh transport from Galicia
> has just rolled into the station, belching
> forth its lousy, greasy load into the city.
> The rabble moves along, happy as larks, as if
> they had always been here, with dirty, long
> caftans and pressed, round hats, from which
> long curly locks well up and dangle from the
> cheeks of their smirking faces. Slovenly,
> fat women with disheveled, black hair look
> as if they had just jumped off a gypsy wagon.
> It is horrifying and you have to be careful
> to avoid the foul smelling garlic, which comes
> from this bellowing, whirling mob.[21]

Only the blood shed by two million German heroes could redeem a nation so mired in decadence, he submitted. It was clear that the best

---

[20] Ibid., pp. 49–50.　　　　[21] Ibid., p. 313.

had perished in the war, leaving only the shirkers on the home front to lead the Weimar Republic. One day when Hans Kraft was rummaging through his war souvenirs, he had a curious vision. Anderl, the bravest man in the company, appeared in full battle gear before him, just as he looked on that sad day at Amiens when a shell tore his neck open. Anderl was appalled with the description of life in Germany after the war. He could not believe that the French were on the Rhine and "Jewish traitors" were setting the agenda in a German Republic. "Aren't we remembered anymore? Are we completely forgotten, everything that we did and went through?" Anderl appealed to Hans to protest and to fight the miserable regime tooth and nail. Hans promised his dear friend and comrade that he would continue the good fight, until the great day when Germany would once more become German.[22]

The first gleam of hope for change came in the form of the Free Corps. Zöberlein delighted in his service with the comrades of Free Corp Epp, war veterans and desperadoes united in their hatred of the republic. Morale was high among the men; how exhilarating it was to be with comrades once more. Both officers and men shared a brotherly equality, something they had never known during the war. When Hans stormed into Munich with the old boys of Free Corp Epp, meting out punishment to the "orgiastic, Jewish-Bolshevik traitors" who had taken control of the city, the sensation he felt was euphoric. It was like the good old days once more!

It was the same sense of excitement that inspired Kraft when he first heard Adolf Hitler speak, impelling him to join the nascent Party and to fall in with the marching columns of the Brown Shirts. Hitler's political program was exactly what Hans Kraft, and so many of the war veterans, had been longing for. To hear Hitler in the legendary beer halls of Munich, to march with one's comrades to the expansive Königsplatz, and to join the march on Coburg at the height of the crisis of 1923 was to be on the cutting edge of history. To be present on that bloody November morning in 1923 at the Feldherrnhalle was to have witnessed the Crucifixion. He was absolutely certain that the blood of the martyrs inspired the ranks of the fighting SA. It was this same impulse that, according to Kraft, led Dietrich Eckart to write his famous poem, "Germany Awake," at his request, as he searched for a proper song for his SA unit. For Hans, its call to attack was a direct link to his days as a storm trooper at the front.[23]

---

[22] Ibid., pp. 328–32.
[23] Ibid., pp. 782–5. Regarding the direct political line from the fighting front in France to the battles in the streets of Munich and Berlin, see Gollbach, pp. 225–31. On Dietrich Eckart's poem, see Bärsch, pp. 95–98.

For Hans Kraft, these poetic lines were sacred and they seemed to emblazon a metaphorical blood-red cast over the German sky. Out of the defeat of 1918 and the abortive Munich Putsch would come victory, and the dead would answer their final reveille on the ultimate day of fulfillment. Zöberlein ended his novel where he had begun it, focusing on his dead comrades. Kraft points out that the dead were always with the men of the Movement, pushing them onward, fortifying them for battle. With this spiritual legacy, surely the laurel leaves of victory would crown their efforts. He admonished the nation: "The Reich will come! Be ready! The battle for Germany continues! Your conscience has commanded it."[24] It was as if the blood of the fallen had become the Holy Water of the Third Reich.

The documentary record testifies to Zöberlein's bombastic career as a Brown Shirt commander in Munich. It seemed that his life was devoted to battle, and he loved the challenge of a good street fight. Describing those early days in an article published years later, he wrote:

> We were known wherever the Movement was in 1923:
> "The Giesingers are coming!" A frightening thing
> for our opponents, a badge of honor for us.
> Everybody knew our black flag with the attacking
> lion. We were the first to carry the symbol of the
> SA, the call to action "Germany Awake!", into
> battle. And we were known especially for the
> fighting cock feathers we wore on our SA caps."[25]

Zöberlein came to know and admire Hitler in the earliest days of the movement. It was a special source of pride for him to see the Führer among the men, now marching, now riding in an open car during propaganda marches and violent skirmishes with their enemies.[26]

The Munich Police took considerable note of Zöberlein's activities. He figured as a major perpetrator of the May Day brawl in 1923 at the Oberwiesenfeld, the field made famous by the October Fest staged there each autumn.[27] Zöberlein made many appearances as a speaker throughout Munich, where he was known for his hard-hitting oratory and venomous

---

[24] Ibid., p. 990.

[25] Hans Zöberlein, "Zehn Jahre S. A. Giesing," Polizei Direktion München 10179, BHStA.

[26] Hans Zöberlein, "Adolf Hitler – damals und heute," *Völkischer Beobachter*, August 18, 1934. See Peter Longerich, *Die braunen Bataillone* (Munich: Beck, 1989), pp. 59–65.

[27] Police Report VIa, 1120/23, Munich, Juni 9,1923, Polizei Direktion München 10179, BHStA.

attacks on the Jews.[28] Time and again he attacked the republic as nothing more than a hothouse for the Jews, whom he accused of controlling every other Party except the NSDAP. All this, he promised, would change in the coming Third Reich.[29] In April 1928, Zöberlein succeeded in closing down a rally of no less a figure than Gustav Stresemann, who was in Munich to address followers of the German Peoples Party. Zöberlein personally yelled anti-Semitic taunts at Stresemann, and his Brown Shirts struck up the chords of the stirring patriotic song, "Die Wacht am Rhein," which so many German soldiers in World War I had sung with gusto on the troop trains heading toward the front early in the war.[30]

The campaign for seats in the Munich city council elections in December 1929 featured several bloody street fights, giving Zöberlein even more notoriety in the city. Now an SA Standartenführer and responsible for District I – composed of Schwabing, Giesing, Haidhausen, and Inner City – he led his forces into action one night on the Edlinger Platz as if he were in an engagement on the Somme.[31] Protecting turf that had claimed the life of SA Mann Georg Hirschmann in 1927, Zöberlein's men fought a major battle, and he himself was seriously wounded in the melee.[32] The *Völkischer Beobachter* reported on the incident with characteristic invective in an article headlined "Red Murder in Giesing":

> The Red Front continues its unabated criminality
> on the public streets. These darlings of the
> local police had the nerve to scream "Get the
> hell out of Giesing, this is the Munich Wedding!"
> This jailhouse riffraff of known hoods has

---

[28] At a Nazi Party section meeting at the Franziskanerkeller in April 1926, he condemned the Rapallo accord between Germany and the Soviet Union as nothing but a Jewish plot, before calling out the troops for a rollicking good May Day provocation against the Marxists. The time was coming, he promised, when the May 1 would become a day of celebration for the entire German people. "Mitgliederversammlung der Sektion Au-Giesing der NSDAP, 27. April 1926," "Auszug aus dem P. N. D. Bericht vom 10.5.26, Nr. 538, ibid.

[29] Zöberlein, speech at the Hafnegelscher Gaststätte, Munich-Perlach, July 24, 1926, ibid.

[30] This case went to trial before the Landgericht München I, P. N. D. Bericht Nr. 535–558/28, April 25, 1928, ibid.

[31] For Zöberlein's account of the melee, in which he received a blow to the head that caused permanent hearing damage, see Zöberlein, "Eidesstattliche Erklärung zur Denkschrift Max Jüttners für IMT Nürnberg," ZSg 319, Institut für Zeitgeschichte, Munich. For the official police report, see Schutzpolizei, Wache I., Pol. Bez. 7 an die Polizei Direktion München, Nr. 6534, 4 Dezember 1929, Betreff: "Zusammenstoss zwischen uniformierten Hitlerleuten und Kommunisten vor der Gaststätte Falkenwand, Dollmannstr. 2/o bzw. Edlingerplatz," Polizei Direktion München 10179, BHStA.

[32] See Will Decker, *Kreuze am Wege zur Freiheit* (Leipzig: K. F. Koehler, 1935), p. 113.

been a plague in Giesing for a long time. It is
the same all over town. Red bandits are
protected by the police while the National
Socialists are fair game.[33]

At his trial in May 1930, Zöberlein was successfully defended by none other than Hans Frank, the young Munich attorney who was Hitler's personal lawyer and would later become governor of Occupied Poland.[34] For Zöberlein, the war on "Bolshevik subhumanity" only deepened the sweet, indescribable bond of comradeship that he found among the Brown Shirts.[35]

It was during these latter years of the "period of struggle" that Zöberlein wrote *The Belief in Germany*, often working straight through the night on the manuscript. He was appalled at the success of Erich Maria Remarque's *All Quiet on the Western Front*, which he found to be a repulsive collection of lies and a gross distortion of the experiences of the German soldier.[36] He contended that the novel was but the most successful in a series of assaults on the truth by the literary Marxists who flourished in the Weimar Republic. Zöberlein endeavored to set the record straight by writing his own book. Alfred Rosenberg gave his work high praise in the *Nationalsozialistische Monatshefte*, noting that it was the embodiment of the German ideal of loyalty to the death. "All National Socialist parents," he wrote, "should see to it that Zöberlein's book be given as a birthday present to their sons and daughters."[37]

With the Nazi assumption of power, his fortunes were on the ascendant. In November 1933, Zöberlein was awarded the Munich Prize for Literature, an honor that had been won in earlier years by such figures as Hans Carossa, Josef Magnus Wehner, and Hans Brandenburg.[38] The *Völkischer Beobachter*, in a profile on the author, praised Zöberlein highly for the accuracy and realism of his work, observing that

No arm chair literary figure is speaking
to us here, someone who spends at most

[33] *Völkischer Beobachter*, December 6, 1929.
[34] For records of the trial, see AVZ XVI Nr. 210 ff./30, Neb. Reg. II 113/30, das erweiterte Schöffengericht bei dem Amtsgerichte, München, Strafgericht, Abt. Justizpalast, Hans Zöberlein File, BAB. For trial coverage, see *Münchner Post*, May 21, 1930.
[35] See Zöberlein, "Kameraden," *Völkischer Beobachter*, April 14, 1928.
[36] See "*Im Westen nichts Neues*: Die Antwort eines Frontsoldaten auf das Buch Remarques," *Völkischer Beobachter*, August 14, 1929.
[37] Alfred Rosenberg, *Nationalsozialistische Monatshefte* 16 (July 1931), p. 335.
[38] See Dr. Hubert Ulsamer, "Hans Zöberlein: '*Der Glaube an Deutschland*'," *Völkischer Beobachter*, December 15, 1933.

a couple of months behind the lines and
then pastes together a war novel from the
tales of front fighters; unlike so many
of the others, he is no greedy speculator
of low instincts.[39]

Zöberlein became active in the political and cultural affairs of Munich
during the Third Reich. He made the most of his position as a City Coun-
cilor in the "Capital City of the Movement," and became Director of
the Cultural Section of the City of Munich as well. However, in this role
he seriously overstepped his bounds by attempting to insinuate himself
into the development of plans to rebuild Munich, thereby incurring the
displeasure of Hitler. Although his political influence may have faded,
he nevertheless continued to function as an active Nazi propagandist. As
president of the Order of the Bavarian Medal for Bravery, he cultivated
the traditional values of military elitism. As a model National Socialist,
Zöberlein also sat in the First Senate of the notorious Peoples' Court from
1936 through 1940.

The national attention given Zöberlein for his writing won him membership in the Cultural Circle of the SA (Kulturkreis der SA). He was
also a frequent speaker throughout the country, reading from his works
at what passed for cultural functions in the Third Reich. In 1937, for
example, he made appearances in both Florence and Rome.[40] Following
the publication of *The Command of Conscience*, SA Chief of Staff Viktor
Lutze, who had replaced the murdered Ernst Röhm as head of the Brown
Shirts, awarded Zöberlein the SA Cultural Prize in 1938.[41] *Der SA-Mann*,
the Brown Shirt newspaper, went so far as to compare the work to Kleist's
Prinz Friedrich von Homburg and affirmed that in the future a German
poet would craft a national epic from such a grand saga.[42]

[39] See "Hans Zöberlein erzählt . . . Der Träger des Münchener Dichterpreises über seinen
Werdegang," *Völkischer Beobachter*, November 26, 1933.
[40] See Hans Zöberlein File, BAB; "Ein Ehrenabend für Zöberlein und Adam," *Völkischer
Beobachter*, December 11, 1933; "Hans Zöberlein vor den Inhabern der bayerischen
Tapferkeitsmedaille," ibid., May 7, 1934; "Hans Zöberlein liest; Kundgebung zur Buchwoche," *Münchner Neueste Nachrichten*, October 21, 1936; "Hans Zöberlein liest vor
Feierstunde des BDM," ibid., November 18, 1937; "Hans Zöberlein liest in Italien,"
ibid., November 28, 1937.
[41] *Deutsche Allgemeine Zeitung*, February 25, 1938.
[42] "Sang als Nachhall der Tat," *Der SA-Mann*, February 5,1938. Compare Hans Grothe,
"Begegnung mit Hans Zöberlein," *Völkischer Beobachter*, February 24, 1938. Compare "Zeugnishafte Zeitchronik. Das neue Buch Hans Zöberleins," *Münchner Neueste
Nachrichten*, January 24, 1937 and "Bannerträger einer Idee," *Die Zeitschrift der
Leibbücherei*, March 10, 1938.

With the coming of the war, Zöberlein received a commission in the Luftwaffe. As a member of the vaunted Löwengeschwader, he gloried in the esprit de corps of the unit. Awarded several medals for bravery and promoted to the rank of captain, he won decorations for the campaigns in Norway, Crete, and North Africa. Following an uninterrupted period of eighteen months of military action, he was recalled from active duty at the request of the Propaganda Ministry. Zöberlein immediately went to work on another novel, which dealt with the SA during the Hitler's rise to power. Writing to Viktor Lutze in September 1941, he noted that

> As an old SA man, I feel the duty to
> create a great literary monument to our
> SA, so that the world of letters, which
> acts as if we never existed, will have
> to take notice. Now that Bolshevism is
> being destroyed once and for all, I will
> be able to write spontaneously and with
> a happy heart.[43]

Zöberlein even had plans to respond to Lutze's suggestion that he write and direct an epic film on the period stretching from the end of the Great War to the "final victory" in World War II. The boastful and vainglorious Zöberlein actually believed that he was a literary figure, a situation explainable solely by the fact that he wrote for the leaders of a totalitarian state who felt that he was one of them and supported his writing and public image at every juncture, not to mention the massive purchase of his books the regime made for purposes of propaganda.

There were to be no more "epic" books or films produced by Hans Zöberlein. Instead, his life was to take a decidedly heinous turn. Once again, just as in 1918, Germany was to be defeated in a devastating war. As the Third Reich entered its death agony, he was tortured by the fear of a second "stab in the back" at the hands of "Jewish Bolshevism" on the model of 1918. As a result, his despair soon turned to acts of criminality.

As a *Volkssturm* commander in Munich, Zöberlein was to take part in the infamous "Penzberg Murder Night" during the last week of the war. On April 28, 1945, a left-wing resistance group attempted to take power in Penzberg, an industrial town north of Munich, responding to a radio call for immediate action from "Freedom Action Bavaria." Upon being

---

[43] Hans Zöberlein, Munich, to Stabschef der SA Viktor Lutze, Berlin, September 12, 1941, Polizei Direktion München 10179, BHStA. For an example of the views he expressed during World War II, see his articles "Das Beispiel. Zum 10. Todestag Horst Wessels," *Völkischer Beobachter*, February 23, 1940; and "Denn wir fahren gegen Engelland!," *Die bayerische Tapferkeitsmedaille* 29 (January-February 1940), pp. 2–4.

informed of this, Paul Giesler, Gauleiter and Reich defense commissar of Upper Bavaria, ordered Zöberlein to restore law and order in Penzberg. Within a matter of hours, having declared his unit a Werewolf force, Zöberlein took part in a murder operation that cost the lives of sixteen people. The citizens of Penzberg awakened the next morning to find several of the victims hanging from the trees in front of the courthouse. In 1948, Zöberlein was sentenced to death by a Munich court for the murder of three individuals but was spared this ignominious fate when the German Basic Law forbade the death penalty.[44] His sentence of life imprisonment was commuted to fifteen years in 1958.[45] Zöberlein was released from prison in 1961 for reasons of health. He returned to Munich, where he died in 1964. Zöberlein was buried next to his wife in East Cemetery on the Tegernsee.[46]

Reflections on the life of Hans Zöberlein are instructive for several reasons. His career began with the celebrated literary testament of a young soldier's belief in the vision of the German Reich, a vision he shared with Adolf Hitler. This alone won for him a secure place in National Socialist literary circles, especially in postwar Munich, a veritable anti-Bolshevik hothouse teeming with Russian émigrés. His subsequent writings and activities as a Brown Shirt leader reflected an obsession with the alleged threat of world Jewry, so central to Nazi ideology and consonant with Hitler's own racial obsession and determination to deal with the problem. Zöberlein never transcended his primitive view of the world, which was based on a deep hatred of the Jews. His character was disharmonious, as was the troubled Germany in which he lived. Word and deed merged in this man of modest intellectual stature, culminating in his final criminal acts. His life thus represents a significant, if unedifying, chapter in the German problem of the twentieth century.

---

[44] Zöberlein was tried before the Oberlandesgericht München, 1. Strafsenat. For the judgment of the court, December 8, 1949, "Gegen Ohm Berthold und 8 Andere, wegen Mordes," see SZAnw München II, Gns 291/58, BHStA. For a lively account of the trial, which caused a sensation in the Penzberg vicinity, see the report by Herbert Frank, *Münchner Merkur*, June 28, 1948. See also Klaus Tenfelde, *Proletarische Provinz. Radikalisierung und Widerstand in Penzberg/Oberbayern 1900–1945* (München: R. Oldenbourg Verlag, 1981), pp. 374–82; and Karl Luberger, *Geschichte der Stadt Penzberg* (Kollwitz über Regensburg: Michael Lassleben, 1969), pp. 152–7.

[45] Staatssekretär Goppel, Gns 1174/57, Bayerisches Staatsministerium der Justiz, February 14, 1958, "Betr.: Begnadigung des Hans Zöberlein aus München, z.Zt. Strafanstalt Straubing," Gns 291/58, ibid.

[46] *Reichsruf*, February 21, 1961; *National Zeitung und Soldatenzeitung*, March 6, 1964.

5

Edwin Erich Dwinger: Germany's Iconic Literary Anti-Bolshevik

The life of Edwin Erich Dwinger (1898–1981) spanned over eighty years of Germany's tragic history in the twentieth century. Born at the turn of the century in the German Empire, he would experience a world whose protagonists included Kaiser Wilhelm II, Lenin, Trotsky, Roosevelt, Hitler, Stalin, and Adenauer. In a best-selling trilogy published during the Weimar Republic, Dwinger would make his name as an authentic chronicler of the misery of German prisoners of war in Russia during World War I, of the horrors of the Russian Civil War, and of the suffering during the Weimar Republic that led to the onset of the Third Reich.

Dwinger was well received, even by communists and pacifists, who found much to praise in his realistic portrayal of their causes.[1] Nevertheless, he viewed his own work as the antithesis to the ideas of Erich Maria Remarque, whose "flabby, limp pacifism and rootless nihilism" he found contemptible.[2] Like Ernst Jünger, he was molded in the storm of steel. Unlike Jünger, however, who grew intellectually after working through the trauma of the Great War – no other German postwar author ever reached the heights of his dizzying rhapsodic variations on violence – Dwinger did not change in spirit at all. In his career as a writer, he never took off his cavalry officer's uniform.[3] He joined the Nazi Party, became an SS officer, and gradually declined into oily mediocrity and crass materialism. He became a propagandist for the Nazi cause, egotistically delighting in his role on the colorful stage of the Third Reich, until in turn he

---

[1] Helmut Müssener, "Edwin Erich Dwingers Roman 'Zwischen Weiss und Rot – Die Russische Tragödie' als Deutsches Trauerspiel," in *Deutschsprachige Exilliteratur*, Wulf Koepke and Michael Winkler, eds. (Bonn: Bouvier, 1984), pp. 127–8.

[2] Dwinger to Hans Grimm, September 28, 1929, Nachlass Hans Grimm, DLAM.

[3] Dwinger's widow, Waltraut Wien, made quite a point of this in an interview she granted me on January 6, 1988.

4. Edwin Erich Dwinger, Circa 1934. Courtesy of Bayerisches Hauptstaatsarchiv.

himself became persona non grata with the Nazi radicals who supported the disastrous Nazi racial policies toward the Russian and Slavic peoples.

Following some lean years after World War II, Dwinger's fortunes improved again. Sensing the winds of opportunity, he trimmed his sails yet again. He was to enjoy success once more when the United States joined the Federal Republic in discovering that – now that Hitler and the Third Reich were destroyed – communism and the Soviet Union represented their most powerful enemy. When Dwinger died in 1981, Ronald Reagan was president of the United States and the Soviet Union was entering its final stages of disintegration. Dwinger had great stamina and was a survivor of breathtaking political, social, and economic turmoil. He would leave his mark where historical experience interfaced with politically significant literature.

There was nothing in the background of Edwin Erich Dwinger that presaged such a prominent future. Born in 1898, he grew up in Kiel on the Baltic Sea, the son of a German naval officer and a Russian mother, who had an interest in literature and the arts. He became fluent in Russian even as a boy, and the fact that his mother took such pains to teach him the intricacies of the language would be a great advantage to him throughout his life. With the onset of World War I, at the age of sixteen, he set aside his studies and rushed to the colors, joining the First Hanover Cavalry Regiment as a junior officer. In June 1915, Dwinger was severely wounded in an engagement with the Russians in East Prussia, was taken prisoner, and began five hellish years as a prisoner of war. His experiences in captivity became the subject of Dwinger's first best-selling work, *The Army behind Barbed Wire*, a chronicle of profound intensity that differed remarkably from the wave of novels and remembrances of the front experience that cascaded from the presses in the latter years of the Weimar Republic and during the Third Reich. Dwinger, differentiating his memoirs from the others, commented that "I dealt with the other side, the unseen war, where men died without the benefit of being mentioned in the reports from the front."[4]

In fact, Dwinger dealt with an alternate form of heroism in his book. Seldom throughout history have the voices of prisoners of war been really heard, a situation that holds true to the present day. To his credit, the author realized that his message had universal meaning, even though he was telling a singular tale of psychological strength concerning only one

4 Edwin Erich Dwinger, *Die Armee hinter Stacheldraht. Das Sibirische Tagebuch* (Jena: Eugen Diederichs, 1929).

war.[5] This emboldened him to come to grips with the enormity of the spiritual suffering endured by his subjects. Statistics on mortality rates in World War I alone are sobering enough. The odds of dying were much greater in a Russian prisoner of war camp than they were at the fighting front. Of the 2,278,146 German and Austro-Hungarian prisoners of war in Russia, a total of 401,000 would perish in captivity. Nearly 10 percent of the German prisoners were fated to die, and 18 percent of the Austro-Hungarian prisoners succumbed.[6] Dwinger was determined to become their historian, giving these victims a voice that drove *The Army behind Barbed Wire* to the top of the sales charts upon its publication.[7]

It is no mystery why Dwinger catapulted to fame so rapidly. He was a raconteur of extraordinary ability, with astounding experiences behind him, and readers were intrigued with the images he conveyed. Dwinger and his fellow prisoners from the First Hanoverian Cavalry were transported by way of Kurland and Riga, Latvia, and taken by hospital train to Moscow. Placed in a military hospital at Camp Grudetzki, a propaganda showplace for czarist Russia, he was treated with a civility that would become inconceivable in World War II, when the Third Reich waged an all out war of annihilation against the Soviet Union. Wracked by fever and hallucinations, for weeks he fought a life and death battle while an infection in his leg wound took its terrible course. Only the resolute action of an Austrian doctor saved him from an amputation. The patient's description of the tender mercies of his nurses – often beautiful young creatures from noble families whose perfumes and skin creams nearly drove him mad with desire – is unforgettable, reminding readers that Dwinger was but an impressionable lad of seventeen years. The visit at his bedside by the Czar's daughters, Princess Olga and Princess Tatiana – themselves to be brutally murdered by their Soviet captors at Yekaterinburg four

---

[5] In a letter thanking the aged right-wing prophet, Paul Ernst, Dwinger wrote, "You have made me so happy with your letter. Your recognition means so much to me, and your words come close to conveying exactly what I wanted and felt compelled to do, to lay greater stress on the spiritual than the physical, in order to transcend the facts and to really get through to the spiritual side of our experiences." Commenting further, Dwinger declared that Ernst had strengthened him in his determination to finish volume three of his trilogy, which he alleged to be writing to help the nation find its way back to health. Dwinger to Paul Ernst, Gut Tanneck, Weiler im Allgäu, February 21, 1932, DLAM.

[6] For authoritative figures of death rates, consult Alon Rachamimov, *POWS and the Great War. Captivity on the Eastern Front* (Oxford(New York: Berg, 2002), pp. 34–44. Also see "Selbstdarstellung deutscher Dichter. Edwin Erich Dwinger," *Die Literarische Welt*, April 28, 1933, pp. 1–2.

[7] Donald Ray Richards, *The German Bestseller in the 20th Century* (Berne: Herbert Lang, 1968), pp. 60, 120.

years later – caused a sensation among the patients who witnessed it.

The prisoners were transferred to the collection point, Ugrieschskaja,
to await their deportation to Siberia, where they received a foretaste of
the horrors that awaited them. On the seemingly endless train transport
to the East, they suffered random cruelty from police guards whose life
work consisted of moving convicts to Siberian camp facilities. Surrounded
as they were by the cries of the dying and lying in vomit and diarrhea,
they experienced scenes comparable to the worst nightmares endured on
transports by Holocaust victims. Disease was rampant, and the fetid smell
of cadavers was unbearable. For an entire day, they were humiliated and
paraded through Nishi-Novgorod as war trophies. Little did they know
that they were sharing the same fate that the survivors of the battle of Stalingrad would suffer some three decades later. Finally, they were marched
through the Godforsaken Orenburg Sand Steppes to enter their new winter home, the brutally unhealthy underground barracks at Totskoe. It was
Christmas 1915.

What followed was indescribable. In a matter of months, while the
battles of Verdun and the Somme were raging, 17,000 prisoners out of a
total of 24,000 were to die a miserable death at Camp Totskoe. Despite
urgent appeals to the camp commander – a crude and insensitive Cossack –
German requests for medicine, water, soap, firewood, food, blankets, and
even shovels to bury the dead went unheeded. Because there was no water
with which the men could bathe themselves, lice spread their pestilence
freely, with the result that a typhus epidemic broke out. Because clothing
could not be washed, disease spread rapidly. Filth was everywhere, and
the floors were soaked with urine, excrement, blood, and vomit. Men lay
in their own filth and waited to die, their bodies inflamed and swollen
from insect bites. Limbs went limp and were blackened with frostbite,
while the frigid temperatures – up to forty below – ensured that lung
disease became rampant. Some men broke under the pressure, shrieking
in feverish outbursts. Prisoners sat on the dead, and leaned against the
dying. The result was that on many days, more than 200 men died, and
on the worst day of all, some 350 perished.[8]

The prisoners desperately sought to lend meaning to their tragedy. For
his part, the Fähnrich Dwinger was adopted by two fellow prisoners.
One of them, Baron von Seydlitz, of the noble Prussian house, showed

---

[8] On the typhus epidemic at Totskoe, see Rachamimov, p. 80. Conditions were so miserable
at Totskoe that a ranking Austro-Hungarian official referred to it in an official report as
a death camp (*Totenlager*).

exceptional courage, telling the young cavalryman that he himself was at peace with the fate they shared. "We never have to be ashamed," he said. "There will be no Gothic Crosses over our graves, true enough, but they will look into our eyes and see that we were brave to the end. And maybe someone will whisper, 'They were in Totskoe.' Although we are not at the front, we are holding the line for Germany here. It is just a different kind of battle for our homeland."[9]

Soon Dwinger himself came down with typhus. As his condition worsened, he was sure that the end was near. "I don't have any hope of getting home again," he wrote, "but my book has to reach there, come what may. There will be many diaries of this war – but please God see to it that there does not have to be any other document more devastating than this one! My book will suffice for a millennium." His was a plea to God not only in the name of the fourteen thousand men who died a horrible death there. Rather the atrocities they suffered were an affront to God himself, he wrote. "I am tired. I cannot go on."[10] Schnarrenberg, an enlisted man and one of the best of the brave comrades there, encouraged Dwinger and nursed him in his suffering. Both of them held firmly to the belief that their tragedy had enduring meaning, just as long as Germany gained the final victory. As Dwinger fell into a high fever and was too weak to write, he suffered hallucinations. Certain that he was dying, his "last thoughts" were of his parents and the homeland. "Germany, Germany you are our last thought. We have suffered and died for you."[11] The ensign's final hour had not struck, and he survived his bout with typhus. As the brutal winter gave way to the spring thaw of 1917, and after three thousand more prisoners had died at Totskoe, he was shipped eastward, over the Urals, into Siberia.

The ride on the Trans-Siberian Railway, stretching several thousand kilometers and lasting over three weeks, seemed endless. Compared with this, the distances Napoleon's Grand Army traversed toward Moscow in 1812 seemed to Dwinger to be very short indeed. As the vast Siberian space swallowed up the prison train, he wondered if the journey would ever end. Towns that were unknown names to most Europeans passed by one after the other, as Kurgan gave way to Omsk, Novo-Nikolaevsk to Taiga, Kansk to Krasnoyarsk, Nizhneudinsk and Zima.[12] Finally, the

---

[9] Dwinger, *Die Armee hinter Stacheldraht*, pp. 110–11.
[10] Ibid., pp. 120–1.   [11] Ibid., pp. 128–9.
[12] Dwinger was making his way over territory he would become very familiar with in the future. Just a few years later, he would retrace this route again all the way westward to the Urals while advancing with the forces of the White Army under Admiral Kolchak. Then he would traverse the thousands of kilometers eastward once again, when the Kolchak

train disgorged its load of human wreckage at Irkutsk, just west of Lake Baikal, which was the site of a prisoner of war camp. There they were to suffer over 100-degree swings in the temperature, from minus 40 in the winter to over 118 degrees Fahrenheit in the fiery heat of summer.

A heavenly respite of five months awaited Dwinger, who was assigned to work as a farm laborer for the five-month Siberian growing season at Goloustnoye, on the banks of Lake Baikal. While incarcerated in the Irkutsk camp, Dwinger came into contact with Elsa Brändström, the "Angel of Siberia," whom he idolized as a blond goddess of mercy, and to whom he would later dedicate the first book of his trilogy. The daughter of the Swedish ambassador to the court of Czar Nicholas II, General Edvard Brändström, Elsa was a legendary figure among the German and Austrian prisoners of war, to whom she ministered under the aegis of the International Red Cross as well as the protection of the Swedish and Danish embassies in St. Petersburg.[13]

It was not until the fall of 1917 that a rumor reached Irkutsk that months before, in March, a revolution had broken out, the Czar had abdicated, and Alexander Kerensky headed a new government for Russia. Nor would the prisoners learn until well into 1918, many months after the event, that Lenin had staged the Bolshevik Revolution back in October. Soon thereafter, trains arrived from the west carrying Red Army units, which hurried to occupy Camp Irkutsk. This motley lot of Red soldiers seemed more like a drunken robber band than any sort of army, but they were politically astute. Almost immediately, they offered to free all prisoners who agreed to serve in the Red Army. For the time being, all ranks were abolished. Within a short time, this regime was overturned as White forces under the command of the boastful, strutting General Semionoff, a ranking Ataman of the Siberian Cossacks, counterattacked and drove the occupying Red Army units thousands of miles westward in relentless pursuit, indeed all the way across the Ural Mountains. Semionoff proceeded to occupy the entire Trans-Baikal region, operating his own White fiefdom from his capital at Chita.

The Russian Civil War had begun in earnest, and the prisoners of the Central Powers were among its chief victims. The Treaty of Brest-Litovsk, signed between the Imperial German government and the Soviet Union in

---

forces abruptly retreated. That ill-fated army was pushed to its ultimate destruction at Lake Baikal.

[13] Elsa Brändström, *Unter Kriegsgefangenen in Russland und Siberien 1914–1920* (Berlin, 1922).

March 1918, did not mean deliverance for the emaciated German prisoners of war. Indeed at Camp Irkutsk, they were to suffer worse treatment
under White domination than they did at the hands of the rather relaxed
Red regime. Melancholy and depression set in anew, as the prisoners
buried hundreds of their comrades who had wasted away with tubercu-
losis as a result of the extreme cold. Many clung to the hopeless dream of
final victory in the west in 1918.

Even before the Bolsheviks stormed the Winter Palace, Dwinger understood the meaning of American industrial might and divined that the entry
of the United States into the war might well tip the balance. In one of the
most fascinating vignettes to be found in *The Army behind Barbed Wire*,
he recounted how night after night he had heard American trains rushing
westward across the steppes from Vladivostok, heading for the Russian
front. They were heavily laden with food and military supplies for the
faltering Russian military front under Kerensky. To his credit, Dwinger
did not turn to the myth of a Jewish-Bolshevik "stab in the back" to serve
as a scapegoat for German defeat. Train whistles deep in the night had
signaled the reason for the Allied victory to him long before.

At Camp Irkutsk, hope gave way to desperation when word arrived
that the major German spring offensive on the Western front had ground
to a halt and that the Central Powers had gone over to the defensive.
Defeat now seemed certain, and the prisoners were stricken with grief on
learning that Germany had signed an armistice. Some of the men died of
broken hearts as a result of their shattered dreams of final victory.

Late in 1918, a disastrous typhus epidemic began to take its toll on the
pathetic prisoners. One by one, the men with whom the Fähnrich had
formed close relationships were sorrowfully carried up the "homeland
hill" to their final resting place. It gradually dawned on Dwinger that he
now faced life entirely alone. He was deeply wounded with the contents of
a letter from his father that had reached him at the camp, claiming that the
suffering and hunger on the home front was just as bad as he was undergoing. He took comfort in remembering the words of Elsa Brändström
who had once said that "I know, my friends, that there is no harder or
more bitter battle than captivity. But in spite of that it can lead to victory.
And this will bring you to a maturity that no everyday kind of life could
bring you!"[14] Realizing that he might yet survive, Dwinger managed to
escape imprisonment early in the spring of 1919. Even then, however, his
challenges were just beginning.

[14] Dwinger, *Die Armee Hinter Stacheldraht*, pp. 304–5.

Little did Dwinger know that he was about to witness firsthand a historic disaster of the first magnitude, the Russian Civil War. In the second volume of his trilogy, *Between White and Red*, he would offer graphic testimony detailing the dramatic events surrounding the death of nearly all of the 500,000 members of Admiral Kolchak's White Army, as well as the suffering of some 750,000 noble and bourgeois refugees accompanying them as they fled the Red Army.[15] Conditions were brutal, and neither side took prisoners. According to Dwinger, however, when it came to psychological warfare, there was no question which side held the higher ground. By offering peace, land, and bread to their suffering people, the Bolsheviks had the advantage of seeming to serve superior ideological ideals, the criminality of the Soviets notwithstanding. On the other hand, he submitted, the White Army was motivated by no such grand program but instead served as a collection point for all manner of reactionary political, social, economic, and class interests. Dwinger was also certain that the halfhearted British, French, American, and Japanese interventionists were interested in a White victory only insofar as it would guarantee their access to the vast mineral resources and strategic bases of the fallen Russian Empire. Finally, their deplorable behavior set the stage for the outrageous conduct of the Czech Legion, which held the White Army at ransom and was responsible in the last instance for the downfall of Admiral Kolchak.

Never in his wildest dreams would Dwinger have imagined that he would one day wear the uniform of a lieutenant in the forces of Admiral Kolchak. He had no choice in the matter because a firing squad was the only alternative he had to volunteering for the anti-Soviet cause after having been discovered soon after his escape. Dwinger was much better off than many of the German and Austro-Hungarian prisoners of war in Russia, men who, unlike their brothers on the western front, could not go home but instead faced an uncertain and often tragic fate as they found themselves caught up in the revolutionary turmoil. They were trapped between the armies of the Whites, who controlled Siberia and parts of the Ukraine from their capital at Omsk, and the Reds, who had the great advantage of operating from central lines, based in the new capital they had established at Moscow. Had the prisoners been set free, they might well have cast their lot with the quarter of a million of their fellow prisoners who had joined the international Red brigades after their liberation by

---

[15] Edwin Erich Dwinger, *Zwischen Weiss und Rot. Die Russische Tragödie* (Jena: Eugen Diederichs, 1930).

the forces of Trotsky. Further complicating the situation was the fact that the Czech Legion – a band of mercenaries by any definition – held the balance of power. The Trans-Siberian Railroad was in their hands, an advantage that gave them control over all transportation between Vladivostok and the Urals, a situation they exploited mercilessly to enrich themselves.

As Dwinger looked into the mirror, he hardly recognized himself. There stood a twenty-year-old lieutenant in a spanking new green military uniform, with tall boots made of the best leather, straps over his breast, and a Cossack saber hanging at his side. "The world never looked so strange to me as it did on this day," he admitted.[16] Dwinger had the benefit of serving under an honorable figure, Colonel Vereniki, a former Czarist cavalry officer whom he had met in the camps, a man who softened the crudity of Ataman Semionoff, to whom he reported. Vereniki, Seydlitz, and Dwinger were received personally by Admiral Kolchak at his headquarters, a commander who impressed them with his dignity, integrity, and determination. All three secured an assignment on the staff of General Kappell at the front.

The situation faced by German officers and men in the Russian Civil War was deplorable and brought with it serious ethical and moral problems. Service in the German Imperial Army, with its long-standing Prussian traditions and a strict code of honor, was worlds apart from what they now experienced. Atrocities were commonplace in both the White and Red Armies, and the Geneva Convention on the treatment of prisoners was entirely disregarded. Dwinger wrote that "This is no longer a war, it is mass murder, a sadistic orgy, a return to barbarism."[17] Drunkenness, whoring, corruption, rape, and pillage became a way of life on both sides of the conflict. This situation depressed his comrade von Seydlitz deeply. He was certain that the same brutal lawlessness was taking place in Germany where the Free Corps were engaged in a civil war against the communists. Seydlitz remarked that "Our best have died at the front, just like here. The war has swallowed them up, just like here. The scum has risen to the top and the worst elements think their day has arrived. And here we are in this country – which means nothing to us – acting merely as mercenaries."[18]

In March 1919, the White Army in Siberia, employing all their reserves, began a decisive offensive. With Moscow the ultimate goal, Kolchak initially enjoyed success, driving almost to the Volga River and capturing

---

[16] Ibid., p. 68.   [17] Ibid., pp. 158–9.
[18] Ibid., pp. 70–1.

several towns west of the Urals, raising White morale considerably. The Whites celebrated Easter in nearly euphoric enthusiasm, certain that final victory would be theirs. Their expectations turned out to be chimerical, however. Although they butchered captured Red Guards mercilessly, they nevertheless could not shatter the spirit of the Soviets. As Kolchak stormed westward, invariably his troops came across strange mounds of chains at the entrances to the towns he was occupying. These were actual historic relics often taken from museums, chains that had been used by the authorities in the days of the repressive czarist regime, offering dramatic testimony to the peasantry that Lenin was indeed fulfilling the promise of Karl Marx to free them from their chains. This was a remarkable contrast to the often aged, medal-bedecked White generals, who rode their grand white horses westward in the forlorn hope of capturing Moscow and destroying Soviet power forever. They acted as if the privileges they enjoyed under Czar Nicholas II had never been curtailed and refused to admit that history had taken a major turn. They would learn soon enough that Leon Trotsky's hour had struck.

Kolchak was opposing forces of the Red Army commanded by the legendary General Tukachevsky, who set about firming up his faltering troops. Unlike the Whites, his army was composed entirely of volunteers. White units, on the other hand, often mutinied, executed their officers, and crossed over the line to serve in the Red Army. Far too many of the White officers and men were summertime soldiers, wobbling when they should have been holding the line. Trotsky was wise enough to free the peasants whom he captured, while murdering bourgeois and noble officers. All this would take its toll, and in May and June 1919, Tukachevsky – with bold thrusts at the exposed flanks of the enemy – commenced a counteroffensive that succeeded in recapturing the main strategic points west of the Ural Mountains. Then, breaking out from recaptured Ufa, he commenced an offensive that would decide the entire campaign. By winning the battle of Chelyabinsk east of the Urals in July and early August 1919, the Red Army turned the tide with a major victory.

Thereafter, having lost 20,000 men between the Tobol and Ischim Rivers, the White Army began to fall apart, In Dwinger's opinion, they had stopped being soldiers and became instead criminal "Soldteska" on a rampage. Reacting furiously to the blows of Red partisans who ambushed their supply trains and harried their flanks with great stealth, the Whites engaged in merciless reprisals of rape, fire, and pillage. After a successful counterattack, in October 1919, Kolchak's armies began their retreat once more. The White capital, Omsk – teeming with hundreds of thousands of bewildered, cold, and hungry refugees – was in chaos and fell to the Red Army in November. This event signaled the beginning of the sorrowful death march over the ice and snow of the windswept steppes that would last for months, and end only with the total destruction of Admiral Kolchak's forces. Dwinger's only solace during the coming bitter months was that he was able to link up with a detachment of German prisoners with whom he had shared the horrors of confinement in the POW camps in earlier years.

The Soviets began to employ instruments of terror and torture that would later characterize the Stalinist regime. Dwinger went to great lengths to describe how the Red Deployment Groups went about their bloody tasks, often with a repertoire of new songs celebrating the victory of the proletariat on their lips. They intoned:

> Free the way! Now we're on the move!
> The masses have awakened and attack!
> The world is changed for good!
> The slaves have taken power![19]

Summary execution was much preferable to being systematically tortured in one of the medieval chambers attached to six armored trains controlled by the White General Semionoff. In these railway torture cars, sadists employing pikes and balls with metal prongs flailed away at their victims until they died, sometimes reviving them with water before finishing them off. The blood of their victims rolled down specially prepared canalization tracks, just like those found in slaughterhouses.[20] It pained Dwinger deeply to be fighting in a civil war where such atrocities had become commonplace.

The author recounted that the Soviets continued to win the propaganda war, repeatedly emphasizing that their cause was pure and just. What did the Whites have, he asked, to counter a Soviet poster showing the Russian homeland being sold out to the English, French, American, Czech, and Japanese "interventionist hyenas"? What did they have to counter the simplicity of the Red mantra, "Peace, Land, and Bread!"? Certainly not the ragtag collection of often corrupt anti-Leninist interest groups that compared unfavorably in the propaganda wars against a regime that wrapped itself in the flag of social justice and internationalism with such skill.

Under these conditions, it was difficult to make any sense of life. Dwinger judged that in the historic situation in which he and his comrades

---

[19] Ibid., p. 478.   [20] Ibid., pp. 126–8.

found themselves, they had observed the best and the worst side of humanity. He observed: "We have seen like few others the depravity of which humans are capable – and of their nearly sacred good deeds. I just don't know anymore who is right – Red or White. I am just a human being."[21] He was even bereft of the comfort of friendship and was totally alone now that von Seydlitz had opted to escape and take his chances making it back to Germany. As he departed, Seydlitz kissed him in the name of all their dead comrades from the camps. A man whose strength and nobility of character had impressed Dwinger so deeply – in good days and bad – was gone from him forever. Seydlitz was to be captured and executed by a detachment of Red Guards within a matter of weeks.

A drama began to unfold that in the intensity of suffering, hunger, cold, and disease would find its historical parallel only in the demise of the German Sixth Army at Stalingrad in 1943. On Russian Christmas Day, January 6, 1920, the Red Army secured its decisive victory of annihilation near Tomsk, where the enemy's entire military supply train and artillery were captured. Kolchak's general staff was taken captive as well, and 100,000 fleeing refugees were cut off and would face immediate liquidation. Soon thereafter, Kolchak's personal armored command train was captured by the Czech Legion. In an act of desperation – he was certain he had no other choice – Admiral Kolchak turned himself and the State Treasury over to the tender mercies of the notorious Legionaries under General Janin, many of whom were indistinguishable from common marauders. He had been promised protection under the flags of the interventionist powers. But to save their own skins, the Czech Legionaries surrendered Kolchak to the enemy after an uprising of Mensheviks and Social Revolutionaries blocked their escape route eastward over the Trans-Siberian Railway. Bolshevik factions, as they invariably did, quickly gained control over the rebels, and the White commander was soon executed by the communists. His body was thrown into a hole in the ice of the frozen Angara River.[22]

What followed in the snowy and barren Eastern wastes to the men of the White armies, as well as the thousands of refugees, almost defies description. Dwinger, however, was at his best as he looked tragedy in the face. This was attested to by no less a figure than Adolf Frisé, the noted critic and publisher of Robert Musil, who wrote that "the chronicler Edwin Erich Dwinger reached eloquent poetic heights in his descriptions of suffering which was conveyed with scenic density and with great artistic

[21] Ibid., p. 247.   [22] Ibid., pp. 390–1, 420–1.

effect." Although they had already retreated over 3,700 miles, worse was yet to come:

We drag ourselves gradually through the snow whose blowing seemed like white sand. Our horses are dead tired, our bodies swollen with bitter cold. One doesn't hear the hooves of the horses anymore, one hears no sound whatsoever. This shrouded mass moves eastward – like ghosts, as quiet as a column of the dead. Our stomachs have been gnawing with hunger for weeks. Every so often someone breaks down, and before long snow covers him. The whole way is covered with these figures which resemble mole hills, like warts on skin. The massive snow covered spaces are so unbearably quiet that sometimes you want to scream.

The suffering of the animals would have been lamentable for anyone to observe, but it had a special sting for a cavalryman, for whom horses often had a greater significance than human beings. Dwinger noted that

Continually horses simply stop in their tracks. You could whip it or burn it, but it is not going to move. Someone comes along and strips its harness away, leaving it naked there. After standing motionless for an hour or so, it lies down, to form another mole hill in the snow. Or some men will come along and slit its throat to warm themselves in its blood or dig their teeth into its raw flesh.

Still the scenes in which the chronicler describes the suffering of the helpless refugees, so many of whom were accustomed to a life of privilege in the Old Regime, are unforgettable:

I see many sleds on which high-born ladies are lying, young girls from Imperial institutes, infants with blue lumpy hands. When such women are wearing really costly furs, people don't leave them undisturbed for long, but every passerby grabs a piece. Until finally they are lying there on their sleds naked in their silk slips, with frozen thighs, whose skin and coloring have taken on a resemblance to egg shells.[23]

With the railroad in enemy hands, the only escape for the remnants of the White armies was over the great expanses of Lake Baikal. It was there that they made their last stand, overcome with hunger and the severity of the elements. Captain Vereniki, Dwinger's commander, lay wounded on the ice and could go no farther. He insisted that his loyal lieutenants put him behind the barrel of a machine gun pointed westward, in the direction of the pursuing Red Guards. There he fought to the end, lying frozen on Lake Baikal with thousands of other White soldiers and refugees. Only with the onset of the spring thaw would Vereniki and his dead comrades

---

[23] Cited by Adolf Frisé, "Edwin Erich Dwinger," *Die Neue Rundschau* 44 (1933), pp. 840–50.

sink to the bottom of the lake, forming an eternal guard in remembrance of their lost cause.

As fate would have it, Dwinger was captured by the Bolshevik forces, but he would be saved once more by his quick wit. Claiming excitedly in Russian that he had been dragooned in a German prisoner-of-war camp by White officers into serving in their army – a common situation the year before – he was rushed back over the lake to safety in a Red Army sled. Once again, he passed the long columns of the dead, noting tellingly: "We review the parade! The last parade of the last army of the last Czar of All-Russia."[24] Within weeks, Dwinger had boarded a train heading westward, westward toward home. The memories of what he had endured near the stations where the train passed on its long journey moved him deeply, and words could not describe the joy he felt upon setting foot on German soil once again. After what he had endured, the journey of nearly two months passed by swiftly. He had left the country as a boy and was returning with experience far beyond his twenty-one years. He was now at a critical turning point in his own psychological development. One would have hoped with the enormity of this experience, the young chronicler would have undergone a character development in the direction of humanist cosmopolitanism. His musings on the bestiality of the Civil War pointed to this outcome. But sadly, quite the opposite was the case. It is quite evident that in a few short years Dwinger was to evolve into a hardline, anti-Semitic German nationalist.

The final volume of Dwinger's "German Passion" trilogy, *We Call Germany*, commences one year later, in 1921, when the protagonist appears at quayside in a northern German port. There he awaits his comrades from the POW camps and White Army legions who are returning from Asia, via Vladivostok, aboard a Japanese freighter.[25] Dwinger has established himself as a manager on an East Prussian latifundia near Tressin. There over the coming years, he was able to support many of the men with jobs as farm workers and with critical psychological assistance to enable them to get their lives in order and face the instability of the early years of the Weimar Republic. The dreams of home that helped to sustain them over their long period of captivity would prove to be illusory however. These fantasies were to be shattered immediately upon their return at a ceremony in their honor given by officials of the new German Republic. The speech delivered to them by a representative of the Weimar regime,

---

[24] Ibid., p. 473.
[25] Edwin Erich Dwinger, *Wir rufen Deutschland* (Jena: Eugen Diederichs, 1932).

flanked by a strangely unfamiliar black-red-gold flag, was pompous and cliché-ridden. The traumatized prisoners, still quite cheerless and bleary-eyed as they peeked out from their odious, tattered camp clothing, were exhausted and deeply offended by what seemed to them to be nothing more than propaganda in support of the new democratic political system. Nor were they prepared for a brazen demonstration led by a shadowy, "dark-haired" communist figure of obscure East European ancestry – an obviously anti-Semitic reference – bemoaning the injustices of loathsome international capitalism and bourgeois tyranny. A serious scuffle ensued, in which a right-wing band of Free Corps sympathizers unfurled the flag of the empire and taunted the crowd of communists with raised clinched fists, which answered with the singing of the *Internationale*, while others bellowed out the repeated cry, "Red Front!" The former prisoners had returned home to a nation in the throes of what seemed to them to be a civil war, not unlike the one in Russia that they had just barely survived. One of their flabbergasted number spoke for them all, when he cried out: "Where, then, is Germany?"[26] One disillusioned and enraged former imperial officer, Captain von Marwitz, suffered a nervous breakdown, so deep was his disappointment.

They repaired to an estate, where good food, clean air, the beauty of the countryside, physical work, and the joys of comradeship all contributed to the gradual recovery of many of the veterans. But it would take years for them to recuperate from the physical deterioration and psychological torment that they had undergone. One thing was certain: they hardly recognized the Germany to which they had returned. So much seemed foreign to them, and they only gradually learned the truth of what had happened in their country since their departure early in the war. Many of them knew little about the reasons for the German collapse in 1918, the agony of the Sparticist Revolution and the excesses of the Free Corps, the Allied blockade, the disease and hunger, and the injustices of the Versailles Peace Treaty. Continuous social unrest and the instability brought on by runaway inflation profoundly disturbed them.

The benefit of living in a supportive community acted as a balm for the men, where human weakness of all kinds was met with tolerance. This did not happen by chance. Dwinger and a medical doctor with whom he had made his successful escape from captivity had promised each other that they would create a sanitarium to nurse their comrades back to health. Having learned in Russia that moral truth was the property of

---

[26] Ibid., pp. 8–14.

neither Red nor White factions, they even allowed communists to join them.

The secret strength of their community spirit was revealed dramatically when Baron von Zirrwitz, a neighboring Junker landlord, conspired to deploy the group as an anti-Bolshevik storm brigade to "settle the accounts with the communists once and for all." In an impassioned and eloquent response, Schulenburg, one of the leading members of the group, summarized the political commitment of the men whose strength had been forged in the ice of Siberia. "We are not reactionaries," he said, "but one hundred per cent revolutionaries! We have not come to overturn the revolution, but to drive it forward." He made clear that the men did not support capitalism, because they had seen it in its worst form among the interventionists, who sought only their own profit in oil and mineral concessions while betraying the cause they were supposed to be serving. As for the Bolsheviks, they were said to have much good in them because of their idealism and spirit of sacrifice for a larger whole. He asserted that the Weimar Republic had not fulfilled the revolution but rather had betrayed it. At the moment of destiny, the monarchy had let down the nation and its fighting men, and the emperor, who had sold out the country to the interests of industry and Junker landowners, did not have the courage to seek an honorable death at the front. The elites had lost the war because they did not realize that they were engaged in a life or death struggle that would decide the future of Europe. The claim of a Bolshevik stab in the back was simply a sham, an excuse offered by weak leaders who themselves had betrayed the country in its hour of mortal agony. Schulenburg finished his homily – and his statement truly was the creed of so many veterans – with the declaration that no political faction would ever hold their political allegiance, because their hearts belonged to the millions of war dead.[27]

The culture war of the period was a major issue and the Weimar Republic became a target of considerable alienation. This was brought into graphic relief during a Saturday night outing to a neighboring town, where the veterans happened upon a dance locale. Drunkenness, rancid smoke from hundreds of cigarettes, hazy subdued lighting, and the wild cacophony of music all combined to repulse them thoroughly. They were incredulous when they saw young girls sporting short hair, and even shorter skirts, swirling to the music of a jazz band in the arms of immature postadolescent swells and beefy, new-rich businessmen flaunting their

[27] Ibid., pp. 104–7.

wealth. Scenes of the alienation and angst that characterized the canvases of Otto Dix and Georg Grosz, usually associated with Berlin and other major cities, were mirrored that night in the little town of Bullenburg, deep in the remote East Prussian provinces. Was this the Germany so many had died for, they queried? Was this the same country that they had dreamt about for so long in the filth of the Russian death camps?

After all, the only dance they had ever known was the Imperial Waltz of 1914. What had happened in the meantime? Had the screeching and bellowing of the saxophone replaced the rattle and clatter of the machine gun? They were appalled that vulgar displays of revelry could be taking place during the Great Inflation that peaked in 1922–3 and that destroyed millions of innocent people and drove many of them to suicide.[28] To make matters worse, they considered themselves to be poorly treated by the new regime. As Lieutenant Merkel observed, "Let's face it, we're second class now!" To a man they were certain that they were not at home in the Weimar Republic.[29]

The discontent described by Dwinger in his novels fed the demand for change that would ultimately lead to the establishment of the Third Reich. He was given the gift of eloquently articulating the dreams of the men of the front for political regeneration commensurate with the greatness of their sacrifice. He submitted that the community of the front must give way to the community of the nation, where "socialism of the heart" would guarantee social justice.[30] This social justice could not be delivered by the bourgeoisie, even though it was the last bulwark against Bolshevism in Germany. Bourgeois moral values were deemed to be reprehensible. Rather than endeavoring to merge man with nature, the capitalists were said to devote themselves exclusively to self-aggrandizement rather than striving to realize the German mission.

The veterans did not know where to turn, and restlessness spread within the community. Some of their number, convinced of the chicanery of the French, departed in the spring of 1921 to join the Free Corps campaign in Upper Silesia in the ethnic struggle against the Poles. Others joined various Free Corps to counter the uprisings of the communists in German cities. As a group, they found little to inspire them in the leadership of

---

[28] See Gerald D. Feldman, *The Great Disorder. Politics, Economics, and Society in the German Inflation, 1914–1924* (New York/Oxford: Oxford University Press, 1993), pp. 513–75.

[29] Dwinger, *Wir rufen Deutschland*, pp. 161–5. See also Bessel, pp. 220–3.

[30] See Jeffery Verhey, *The Spirit of 1914. Militarism, Myth and Mobilization in Germany* (Cambridge: Cambridge University Press, 2000), pp. 227–38.

the Weimar Republic. There was a feeling that Germany had not only sold out its sovereignty in the Versailles Treaty but that the nation had become a plaything in the hands of the Allies. The injustice of the Polish Corridor, which uprooted Germans in West Prussia from the ancestral homes and farms where their families had lived for hundreds of years, burned in their souls and was made worse by the perceived hypocrisy of Woodrow Wilson's Fourteen Points. They were desperately ashamed of German weakness. All this explains why some of the former prisoners, men who had seen quite enough of death in their lifetime, could applaud the murder of German national leaders, such as the minister of economics, Matthias Erzberger, and the foreign minister, Walther Rathenau. The restlessness in their hearts, all of which they blamed on the Weimar Republic, would one day boil over into revolution.

Dwinger, the youngest of them, cautioned the men: "After Siberia we can never fight for petty goals, but our souls forged in steel must find something that is a worthy legacy for our dead, so that the whole world isn't destroyed like the Bolsheviks have done in Russia." Germany, he said, must create a synthesis of the best of the East and West, and funnel its nationalism along a healthy path. Liberal chatter about personal rights and individualism must cease, giving way to considerations of duty and the common good, he argued. Parties, doctrines, programs, interest groups, and political clichés – all born in the putrefaction of the French Revolution – must give way to the organic whole. Nationalism and socialism must be joined in a state governed by a leader who would transcend parties and rule with a strong hand.[31]

Their situation became critical with the onset of the crisis of 1923, the worst year since the German collapse of 1918, when the Great Inflation spun out of control. According to rumors reaching their East Prussian enclave, it would take over 100 million marks to buy one dollar. The price of milk increased in a matter of months from 1,500 marks to 1 million marks. Paper money had incrementally less value, and as a result, moral principles had totally broken down. Other rumors made the rounds of the estate. Champagne, it was said, had become like mineral water for speculators and the new rich, who grew fat and sassy on the backs of veterans, many of whom now were reduced to suffering in the legions of the impoverished. Parlor communism was spreading like the plague, and one heard that society ladies were competing with one another for the appearance at their parties of the most fashionable spokesmen for

[31] Ibid., pp. 303–9.

Bolshevism. One even heard that the fantasy-ridden intelligentsia and children of the rich were seen to be lounging about in overstuffed chairs in posh urban clubs, proclaiming their support for the "Soviet paradise."

All of these complaints infuriated the "Siberians," but worse was yet to come. French arrogance reached a new high when President Raymond Poincaré dispatched five divisions into the Ruhr and the Rhineland, endeavoring to teach the Germans a lesson and to extract overdue war reparations. The result was passive resistance supported by the German government, which led to the murder of fourteen workers at the Krupp Steel Works in Essen and subsequently to propaganda show trials. The French occupiers created a new German martyr, Albert Leo Schlageter, who had been arrested for guerilla resistance activities. He was tied to a stake and executed at dawn on the bleak Golzheimer Heath outside Düsseldorf in May 1923, inciting an international cause célèbre and providing the German right wing with a rallying cry. Racism raised its ugly head as well, when the French deployed colonial units in the Rhineland, leading to all manner of rumor mongering about "Rhineland bastards" being born to ravished German girls. It was also alleged that French agents had bribed German traitors in their effort to separate several western German states from Berlin. Matters took a turn for the worse when communist insurgents struck in Saxony and Hitler staged his abortive putsch in Munich in November 1923. Some of the veterans began to think that Hitler might be the leader to deliver the nation from its desperate situation.

The plot of Dwinger's *We Call Germany* concludes in 1924, with the monetary reform in place and considerable improvement in the political and economic situation of the country. He and his confidant, Dr. Berger, had done what they had promised upon leaving the Soviet Union – to shepherd as many of their comrades back from the brink as humanly possible. Some of the men had already left the farm, married, and begun to live relatively normal lives, considering the weight of their experiences in captivity. Others, unable to make sense of it all, faded away into insanity and would never recover. Two of the Marxists in the community had been cured of their political fantasies, one of them having returned from a sojourn in the "Soviet paradise" a considerably more experienced and wise man. As one of them reported about his life in the Soviet Union, the ruling clique may have changed after the overthrow of the monarchy, but the misery of the working man continued. Workers were exploited just as they always had been, and the right to strike did not exist. Secret police were everywhere, and he was certain that thousands of innocent people had disappeared mysteriously. Families had turned against families, and children were being taken from their fathers and mothers. A selfish and brazen new elite had replaced the old, and in this revolutionary system Party bureaucrats, the Red Army, and the secret police were all well cared for.

The last weeks that the men spent together were especially meaningful. They were determined that their old comradeship would never die and that they would always be united in spirit along with the souls of the many thousands lost in the camps and the Civil War. Captain von Marwitz, eaten alive with third-stage syphilis, could not bear to live in a world without his comrades who had nursed him so loyally and had so graciously endured his endless reveries about the superiority of the world before 1914. He committed suicide and was buried in the little church at Tressin, a symbol of the Prussian military caste system that was fading into history. There was not a dry eye among the camp survivors as they bid their comrade – and their own past – a final goodbye.

Dwinger concluded his trilogy by reasserting his goal of acting as a witness to the victims of a tormented period in history. At the same time, he offered the hope that the dreams of the living and the dead might be realized in the coming of the Third Reich. A remark by von Roenninghoff – the officer who had gone over to the communists after his return from the front in 1918 and in turn was disillusioned by Marxism – could be read as an augury for the future. About to leave the Tressin farm forever, Roenninghoff turned to Dwinger and said, "I have a lot to thank you for. You saved me from going down a bad path – you and my time here and our comrades! We, not the Russian people, will revolutionize the world! I am convinced that we will meet again, we will be together in a true community of the folk."[32] And so it was to be, with tragic consequences.

Critical reception to Dwinger's trilogy was positive indeed. Remarkably, contemporary Bolshevik critics and writers found much to praise in his works. *Rote Fahne*, the organ of the German Communist Party, lauded *Between White and Red* highly, finding the work to be a compelling description of the Red Army's struggle to overturn the reactionary world of the czarist past. On every page, the reviewer noted, Dwinger mirrored the superiority of the Marxist worldview.[33] No less a figure than the communist literary icon Johannes R. Becher enthusiastically praised Dwinger, who he asserted had accurately described the genius and idealism of the

---

[32] Ibid., p. 533.
[33] See Helmut Müssener, "Becher und Dwinger," *Kürbiskern. Literatur, Kritik, Klassenkampf* (München: Damnitz Verlag), February 1982, pp. 125–33.

Red Army in its world-historic struggle. His book was at once objective, factual, and grandly presented. Even at the height of World War II, when Becher belonged to the coterie of German communist writers in the Soviet Union, he did not retreat from his earlier praise of the trilogy. In a major article titled "An Open Letter to E. E. Dwinger," published in 1941, Becher attacked Dwinger for his betrayal, castigating him severely for his role as a major propagandist of the Third Reich in its life or death struggle against the Soviet Union. The leading chronicler of the Great Civil War had missed the point of his own work, forgetting the words uttered by one White officer as he lay dying, "I fought for the wrong side."[34] Becher charged that it was Dwinger himself who was now fighting for the wrong side, although it was a matter of record that he knew international socialism to be superior to Nazism. By choosing not to answer the call of destiny, the author had turned his back on the most just cause in the world.

Reaction to the trilogy from the right was universally positive. Ernst Jünger, the most prestigious figure of all, wrote that

Dwinger's work is not only of historical significance, but speaks meaningfully to the present day. Those battles between White and Red reflect accurately the political realities we face today. It mirrors the present conflict between the West and East, where Germany plays the role between the two.[35]

The Austrian writer Bruno Brehm, who had received favorable treatment in *The Army behind Barbed Wire*, praised Dwinger's work lavishly in *Die Neue Literatur*. Dwinger was certain that it was Brehm, an incarcerated Austrian artillery lieutenant serving as a medical doctor, who had saved his life in CampTotskoe when he lay so close to death. Brehm observed that Dwinger had written with such sincerity and depth of meaning about their days in the camps that he could now address his own experiences there without fear. Dwinger had set a personal example for him by demonstrating that to attain the truth, an author had to work through a great deal of personal suffering.[36]

The nationalist literary establishment, entirely overlooking the objectivity that Dwinger demonstrated in his first two volumes, was also convinced that they had discovered a prophet in him. Will Vesper, the

---

[34] Ibid.

[35] Cited in an advertising flyer published by the Eugen Diederichs Verlag, Jena, 1932.

[36] Bruno Brehm, *Die Neue Literatur* 32 (1931), pp. 426–30. Brehm, the author of a trilogy on the fall of the Hapsburg monarchy, later became a pillar of the Third Reich literary establishment.

conservative zealot who had been a prominent voice on the right for decades and a key figure in Alfred Rosenberg's ideological camp, went over the top when he claimed that the German trilogy was "a truly grandiose work. It will endure and last like Xenophon's *Anabasis*."[37] The legendary Hans Grimm, the cantankerous author of the best-selling *Volk ohne Raum*, also wrote approvingly about Dwinger, whom he perceived to be an inspired missionary for the German cause.[38] The literary historian Arno Mulot remarked that Dwinger realized that neither the "subhuman" machinations of the Red Guards nor the heinous corruption of the Whites held the key to the future. Writing in the racist jargon so dear to the National Socialists, Mulot claimed that it was the genius of Dwinger "to make the killing fields of Russia the birth place of a new national and racial will to power." Moreover, the author had made himself a major voice for renewal by joining the greatness of the front soldier with a worldview based on race. Although entirely overlooking Dwinger's appeal to the Bolsheviks, Mulot claimed that the author's trilogy placed him squarely in the ranks of the Third Reich's ideological vanguard.[39]

Adolf Frisé offered the most balanced reading of Dwinger's significance. Dwinger's greatest asset, he observed, was his ability to transcend the diary genre to deliver a document of world historic importance. Frisé made the astute observation that Dwinger was not a creative writer nor should he even be viewed as one. Historical truth was his proper métier, and the power of his books lay in their simplicity of language. Profound ideas were allowed to speak for themselves. The result differs fundamentally from Ernst Jünger, in whose works violence takes on mythical form, and from Hans Carossa, whose memoirs rise to glorious aesthetic expression. With an economy of words, Frisé submitted, Dwinger presented the human experience in all its greatness and in all its horror, linking the past with the present and transmitting it to the future.[40]

Dwinger did not always appeal to the young hotheads of the Nazi movement. He was, after all, nearly forty years old, he had not been a Brown

---

[37] Cited in an advertising flyer published by the Eugen Diederichs Verlag, Jena, 1932.

[38] Although Hans Grimm did not publish reviews during this period, he nevertheless let Dwinger know his feelings in a voluminous correspondence with the much younger author. See Nachlass Grimm, DLAM. Dwinger wrote to Grimm as early as December 4, 1926, extending to him the highest praise for *Volk ohne Raum*, and asserting that he identified personally with the suffering of Grimm's protagonist, Cornelius Friebott.

[39] Arno Mulot, *Der Soldat in der deutschen Dichtung unserer Zeit* (Stuttgart: J. B. Metzlersche Verlagsbuchhandlung, 1938), pp. 72–6.

[40] Adolf Frisé, *Die Neue Rundschau* 44 (Berlin/Leipzig: S. Fisher, 1933), pp. 844–50.

Shirt or a street fighter, and his reminiscences concerned events now seemingly far in the past. One reporter for the *Völkischer Beobachter* went so far as to headline his report on Dwinger's appearance before students of Munich University in June 1935 as "Frozen Literature." The students, he charged, had appeared that evening to hear tales of greatness in World War I but instead were given a stilted, technically impressive, yet emotionally icy performance by a man whose time was past. How disappointing it all was, the author declared, because "we the young generation expect poets to speak about the unspeakable, to provide us with the emotional strength to face as yet unknown superhuman tasks, and to lend some meaning to our existence as human beings." Instead the students were fed a cold theoretical smorgasbord based on an ideological mish-mash. Dwinger's monotone delivery made his dated material seem even more irrelevant to the demands of the day. The world of 1935 was vastly different and had moved beyond consideration of the psychological suffering endured by a generation of cavalrymen forced to say goodbye forever to their horses![41]

Despite such criticism, with the onset of the Third Reich Dwinger was in a position to capitalize on the fame his trilogy had brought him. The royalties he received from the brisk sales of his works had enabled him to purchase the Hedwigshof, a 400-acre farm near Seeg in the beautiful Allgäu district of Bavaria. He settled in with his wife, Waltraut Wien, the daughter of Professor Wilhelm Wien (1864–1928), a physicist who had won the Nobel Prize in 1911 for his work in radiation. There the author played the role of a patrician farmer, where he oversaw a staff of peasants, raised two sons and a daughter, collected and rode fine Arabian horses, and raised cattle and other animals.[42]

Dwinger would celebrate his love of the land in a rhapsodic book detailing one year of life at the Hedwigshof, titled *Ancestral Farm in the Allgäu* (*Ein Erbhof im Allgäu*).[43] This brief work, illustrated with many black-and-white photographs, reveals a developing narcissistic side to Dwinger's

---

[41] Dwinger's talk was given to the Munich University students in their series, "Deutsches Volk – Deutsche Dichtung." One "gst." signed the review, *Völkischer Beobachter*, June 24, 1935.

[42] Professor Wilhelm Wien was a researcher at the Physikalisch-Technische Reichsanstalt, Berlin and was later named a professor at the University of Munich. Max Planck would revise Wien's work in the development of his path breaking quantum theory of radiation.

[43] Edwin Erich Dwinger, *Ein Erbhof im Allgäu* (Munich: F. Bruckmann, 1937). According to the advertising flyer for the book, Dwinger celebrated "work, building for the future and the joy of God's beautiful nature."

character. He began the book with a quotation from Frederick the Great, continually referred to himself in the third person as an "ancestral farmer," and assumed a heroic pose on his favorite Arabian stud horse. On the other hand, his wife, a beautiful and elegant lady, was relegated to just one photograph in the book, and that tending the children and weeding the garden. Clearly, Dwinger had begun to believe his own press releases.

Dwinger delighted in his fame and basked in the adulation it brought him. He was often seen swanning about in the company of his family in Munich's famed Regina Palast Hotel and in the finest restaurants of the "capital city of the movement."[44] Dwinger's newly acquired affluence did not flatter him, and he became increasingly more vain after Goebbels named him a Reich culture senator in 1935, the same year in which he was awarded the Dietrich Eckart Prize.[45] Yet he continued to enjoy favorable mention in the press. For example, Hilde Fürstenberg, reporting in the *Völkischer Beobachter* about her visit to the Hedwigshof on the occasion of the author's fortieth birthday, commented that she was impressed with her host's "deep appreciation for the rhythm of nature and the sense of responsibility he felt for the land, which for him was a sacred trust."[46]

During the peacetime years of the Third Reich, Dwinger, playing on the success his trilogy enjoyed, proceeded to write two novels dealing with the notorious Free Corps counterinsurgency paramilitary forces. However the content and format of both *The Last Riders* and *Half Way There* signaled that Dwinger had finished the serious work he had commenced as a chronicler of historic reality. Having decided to present himself as a creative writer, he simply did not comprehend that he was unsuited for this role.[47] Unlike the Russian trilogy, these works were clearly not the result of the author's own experiences. They seldom rise above the level of

---

[44] See the somewhat bitter reminiscences of his son, Norwin Dwinger, born in 1934, under the title, "Zwischen Lanzen und Perschings" in *Väter Unser. Reflexionen von Töchtern und Söhnen* Susanne Feigl/Elisabeth Pable, eds., (Wien: Österreichische Staatsdrückerei, 1988), pp. 179–210.

[45] See E. E. Dwinger, "Mein Lebenslauf," undated, Dwinger File, BAB. See also Edwin Erich Dwinger, "Deutsche Dichter unserer Zeit," *Völkischer Beobachter*, March 22, 1939.

[46] Hilde Fürstenberg, *Völkischer Beobachter*, April 23, 1938. Fürstenberg was struck with the beauty of a Russian painted Easter egg she found in Dwinger's home, which once allegedly belonged to Czar Nicholas II.

[47] Edwin Erich Dwinger, *Die letzten Reiter* (Jena: Eugen Diederichs, 1935) and *Auf halbem Wege* (Jena: Eugen Diederichs, 1939). See Vejas Gabriel Liulevicius, *War Land on the Eastern Front. Culture, National Identity, and German Occupation in World War I* (Cambridge: Cambridge University Press, 2000), pp. 227–46.

historical adventure tales, resembling rather journalistic accounts awash
in the National Socialist clichés of the period.[48]

Artistic subtlety of any kind was cast overboard in *The Last Riders*,
which dealt with the violent history of the Free Corps Mannsfeld in the
Baltic region after World War I.[49] Dwinger endeavored to simplify an
extraordinarily complex set of circumstances, conjuring up the black-and-
white images beloved by his readers. Good was represented by the Free
Corps, whose black flag bore a skull and crossbones in white, embla-
zoned with the motto "Trotzdem" ("In Spite of Everything"). Western
civilization itself was at stake, because Asia had declared war on cultured
Europe and was determined to destroy it. Certain that they were engaged
in a great racial war, their goal was to neutralize the Bolshevik threat,
reconquer the legendary lands of their forefathers, the Teutonic Knights,
and guarantee a Germanic Baltic for centuries to come. They were certain
that they represented the second historic wave of German warriors, storming eastward not toward death but rather toward life. When the united
Free Corps reconquered Riga, the capital of Latvia, in May 1919, they
were at the high tide of their success. But it was not to last. They alarmed
both their erstwhile backers in Berlin and the Allied powers whom they
served as surrogate anti-Bolshevik warriors, not to mention the Latvians
whom they were allegedly saving. Before being forcefully disbanded and
disgraced, they had engaged in notorious escapades and acts of criminality as cruel as those perpetrated by the Soviet and Latvian armies they
were fighting.

In August 1919, the Free Corps Mannsfeld joined the mutiny against
the Weimar regime headed by the notorious commander of the "Iron
Division," Major Joseph Bischoff, a career military desperado. In union
with all the German Free Corps operating in the Baltic, the Mannsfelders
staged a dramatic torchlight parade and rally before Bischoff's residence in
Mitau, absolutely operatic in its celebration of the traditions of the Imperial past. Bischoff urged his troops to rebel against the newly proclaimed
Weimar Republic and subordinated his units to the hopelessly romantic
General Prince Pawel Michaelovich Awaloff-Bermondt, commander of

---

[48] On the Free Corps novel as a fiction genre, see Karl Prümm, "Das Erbe der Front. Der
antidemokratische Kriegsroman der Weimarer Republik und seine nationalsozialistische
Fortsetzung," Horst Denkler and Karl Prümm, eds., *Die deutsche Literatur im Dritten
Reich* (Stuttgart: Reclam, 1976), pp. 138–64.

[49] See the chapter titled "The Baltic Adventure," Robert G. L. Waite, *Vanguard of Nazism.
The Free Corps Movement In Postwar Germany, 1918–1923* (Cambridge: Harvard University Press, 1952), pp. 94–139.

the "Russian Army of the West." Henceforth the Free Corps were to fight under the colors of a beleaguered foreign power, which only delayed their return as outlaws to the republic they loathed.

Over the subsequent months, the members of Free Corps Mannsfeld engaged in a hopeless campaign in which neither side took prisoners and where rape, murder, and pillage took place on an astounding scale. Dwinger, never at a loss for pungent rhetoric, used terrifying imagery in *The Last Riders*. The *Flintenweib* Marjam – at once a criminal in a skirt and an erotic plaything for her Bolshevik masters – is juxtaposed to the ethereal military nurse, Countess Sandra Fermor, whose angelic qualities seem saintly when compared with her dark and oily Bolshevik counterpart. Her platonic love affair with the cavalryman Lieutenant Gerhart Willmut takes on the features of the stock characterization one finds in Free Corps fiction.

The theme of Bolshevik perfidy fit Nazi stereotypes perfectly. Torture carried out by Soviet officials was commonplace, and mass executions and deportations set the stage for what would later become state policy in both the Leninist and Stalinist totalitarian systems. "Bolshevik subhumanity" was said to have shown itself as the Soviets even desecrated the coffins of the dead. Dwinger related the details of a scene of great horror when it was discovered that Red Army men had broken into the sacred family burial crypts of the dukes of Kurland, mutilating their bodies and hanging them from the walls in dreadful displays of mock crucifixion. Seldom in history had the forces of good and evil been so graphically juxtaposed as in the Baltic.

Free Corps forces were presented as invariably sensitive, brave, and resolute in their readiness for self-sacrifice for their cause. Comradeship was their mantra. The men of the corps realized that they could never be at home in the Weimar Republic, dressed in bourgeois attire and engaged in the endless, unfulfilling pursuit of money. They were certain that historic role models – heroes of legendary Prussian military families – such as Lützow, Yorck, Manteuffel, and Petersdorff – were fighting at their side. Kurland, they proudly announced, was now and would forever remain German territory. But deep down, they knew they were fighting for a lost cause.

Dwinger's portrayal of the last cavalrymen, cognizant of their historic role as horsemen in an era giving way to the new weaponry of total war, offered a romantic image of their significance in history and their appreciation of the nobility of the horse. This led to scenes that bordered on the macabre. As the protagonist, Reimers, lay dying of typhus, his last words were addressed not to God but to his horse. "Our great day is over," he whispered, "a period that had begun with Genghis Khan. When the horse gives way to horsepower, everything will change. True enough, people will race faster across the earth than we ever did on your back, but in their haste they will never appreciate the land like we did."[50] The two of them were witnesses to the end of an era.

Alas, the riders were able to saddle up yet again in Dwinger's *Half Way There*, a work published in 1939 that was heavy laden with Nazi symbolism. Nevertheless the title of the book was apt, because the Free Corps were indeed one of the links between the Great War and the establishment of the Third Reich. Although the power brokers of the Weimar Republic needed them to deal with the communist threat, they were soon forcibly disbanded. The novel's only strength was that it demonstrated the precarious situation of the Free Corps in that violent period.

In March 1920, Free Corps Mannsfeld participated in a failed coup against the Weimar Republic under Wolfgang Kapp, the "Lion of East Prussia," taking up positions in the government center near the Brandenburg Gate in Berlin. Although this aborted putsch was put down within a week by the general strike that ensued, it incited the communists to action once more, and Spartacist insurgents took to the streets throughout the country. In the heavily industrialized Ruhr area, they amassed some 80,000 workers in a revolt against the Ebert regime, proclaiming the birth of a Soviet state on the Russian model. This turn of events meant that yesterday's enemy was today's friend. As a result the Mannsfelders, along with every available Free Corps and units of the Reichswehr placed under the command of General von Watter, were immediately deployed to retake the "Red Ruhr" for the Berlin government. They were a formidable force, and early in April, within a matter of weeks, they had accomplished their goal of pacifying all the contested areas in western Germany. Nevertheless, fighting was fierce, and unspeakable atrocities were perpetrated on both sides. Having accomplished the goals for the authorities in Berlin, the Free Corps were unceremoniously disbanded once again. By the summer of 1920, Free Corps Mannsfeld had passed into history, once and for all. Henceforth they would either be celebrated or reviled, the trying role that fate had cast upon them.[51]

The heated emotions of those days offered Dwinger many opportunities to employ his characteristic hyperbole, and he made the most of the circumstances. Throughout the novel, there are repeated references

[50] Dwinger, *Die letzten Reiter*, pp. 420–2.   [51] Waite, pp. 140–82.

to the need for a strong man to govern Germany, a leader to speak for the entire people, a fighting man who would return law and order to the nation. The Mannsfelders thought they recognized these qualities in Wolfgang Kapp, who with General Paul von Lettow-Vorbeck at his side was determined to govern the country on the Spartan model. Under the new regime, the nation's Socialist leaders, alleged to be drowning in theory and without a clue as to what really worked in the world, would be cast aside. "Jewish wire-pullers and confidence men," who exercised so much control from behind the scenes and bankrolled the communist apparatus, would have to be dealt with as well. Communism would be turfed out root and branch, and German culture would be returned to German soil. The bourgeoisie, whose acquisitive values were said to be rotten, would have to change radically under the new regime. Henceforth, they would be obligated to think about what they could do for their country, not their bank accounts. Where necessary, traitors would be executed, their bodies displayed publicly as a warning to others.

Under the revolutionary circumstances of those years, a curious collection of desperadoes gathered under the flags of the Free Corps. It was gratifying for the men to know that Captain Waldemar Pabst, on whose watch the Spartacist leaders Karl Liebknecht and Rosa Luxemburg were murdered in Berlin in January 1919, had returned to fight alongside them once more. All their comrades from the Baltic campaign were present as well, and when they attacked with the men of Captain Ehrhardt's Marine Brigade, Dwinger wrote that the "symphony of war" was ringing in their ears![52]

The author stretched the literary license normally afforded writers to the limit in a dramatic account of the last hours of the Kapp Putsch. In a colorful vignette, Dwinger has Dietrich Eckart flying to Berlin with Hitler to offer their services to the cause and pledging that the National Socialists stood ready to deliver Bavaria in support of the new government. In fact, Eckart and Hitler did fly to Berlin and appeared at the revolutionary headquarters at the Hotel Adlon, but were terribly disappointed with what they found there and soon returned to Munich.[53] At many other points in the work, one is reminded that it was published in 1939 and represented the type of propaganda expected in the Third Reich. This also explains why Dwinger identified the Jews as Germany's sinister

---

[52] Dwinger, *Auf halbem Wege*, p. 99.
[53] See Margarete Plewnia, *Auf dem Weg zu Hitler. Der "völkische Publizist" Dietrich Eckart* (Bremen: Schünemann Universitätsverlag, 1970), pp. 64–6.

enemy in this novel, which drew frightening images of their alleged perfidy. Whereas the crimes committed by various Free Corps units were excused as unavoidable reactions to historic conditions, Spartacist atrocities were said to demonstrate the perverted nature of "Jewish Bolshevism." Jews were beastly adherents of a foreign doctrine, and their very nature was criminal. They were said to be rootless at the core, and asphalt was their natural element. Jewish "parliamentary hamsters" were to be seen waving their arms on the street corners of central Berlin, with long hair and dark Semitic eyes peering out from their wizened faces, doing what Jews do best – spewing forth provocative, hateful, revolutionary invective.

Dwinger's account of the heartless slaughter of the Free Corps leader, Captain Rudolf Berthold, commander of the "Iron Legion," was shattering. An air ace with forty-four kills to his credit and holder of the Pour le Mérite, the nation's highest award for valor, Berthold was a major war hero. Although his entire Free Corps was surrounded and liquidated by Red sailors in Harburg, Berthold himself was the great prize. He was trampled to death, stripped, strangled, and finally beheaded, his destroyed "Blue Max" thrown over his mangled body.

Dwinger concluded *Half Way There* as he began it, with extravagant praise for the men of the Free Corps, who were presented as selfless defenders of their country in its darkest hour. They had remained loyal to the nation, even when being wrongfully attacked as a brazen horde of Viking marauders. Their fate was to be forced to endure political purgatory for years to come, to be only "half way there" while understanding full well that many members of their band would not live to see the founding of the Reich to come.

Dwinger struck this leitmotif of Nazi ideology in a revelatory scene of redemption. A major sacrifice of Free Corps Mannsfeld involved the death of four men representing four classes, all of whom were determined to play a part in the founding of the Third Reich. A soldier, a student, a bourgeois, and a worker were murdered by a small band of communists returning home after their defeat in the Ruhr. The message was clear enough. If these four could love one another and die as noble comrades in an act of exemplary sacrifice, surely in the future Third Reich people of all classes would be motivated to transcend their origins and merge into a united peoples' community. What further evidence was necessary to prove the fallacy of the Marxist theory of class struggle, Dwinger queried?

It only remained to integrate the aristocracy in the Reich to come. The author dealt with this problem with the death and mutilation of Rittmeister von Truchs, whose sacrifice was pregnant with meaning. Truchs traced his lineage to a field marshall under Friedrich Wilhelm, the Great Elector, founder of the Prussian military state. The dramatic burial of the Rittmeister in the family crypt on his estate in Mark Brandenburg united all classes and charted the course for the future greatness of Germany. Noblemen and peasants, owners and workers, and henceforth all Germans would be joined in an enduring and united Reich. The Cross and Knight's Sword adorning the mausoleum were symbols of a bygone era and were about to give way to the National Socialist swastika, the twisted cross. At the funeral, Captain Mannsfeld solemnly bore the baron's medals on blue velvet and lay them over the body. The sharp report of rifle salvos signaled at once the death and rebirth of the spirit of the corps, which was to be born anew when Hitler took power.

Dwinger's expertise on the Soviet Union would become useful during the Third Reich, when his services were employed by the Propaganda Ministry. Because he was a member of the Party and an SS Untersturmführer in the 15th SS Reiterstandarte based in Munich, his influence was immensely strengthened. As the Nazi propaganda campaign against Bolshevism increased in intensity, Dwinger began publishing a series of works that dealt with this theme. Brief and to the point, they were devastating attacks on the Soviet regime. The first of these, appearing under the title, *Und Gott schweigt . . .? (And God Is Silent . . .?)*, was released as a weapon in the coming struggle that, he claimed "would decide the future of our century."[54] Purported to be based on the experiences of a disillusioned German communist who remained anonymous, the protagonist was a well-connected member of a commercial family whose firm had engaged in extensive business in the export trade with the Soviet Union. Like so many idealists of the day, this wealthy bourgeois was convinced that the capitalist system was corrupt at the core, and the only route to social justice lay with Bolshevism. As a result, in the summer of 1933, he emigrated to the Soviet Union to help construct the "workers' paradise," certain that it was the greatest social experiment of all time.

The result was not at all what he expected, forever shattering his illusions about life in the communist state. The inequalities of the czarist regime had given way to the inequalities of the Soviet state, and the pervasive system of hierarchical rank and privilege disturbed him greatly. He found that essentially five classes were represented there, all receiving

---

[54] Edwin Erich Dwinger, *Und Gott schweigt. .?* (Jena: Eugen Diederichs, 1936), p. 3. See also Hermann Gerstner and Karl Schworm, eds., *Deutsche Dichter unserer Zeit* (München: Franz Eher, 1939), pp. 91–100.

food, housing, income, and privileges commensurate with their station. First came the Party apparatchiks, then the GPU, the secret police, and next came the Red Army. The urban proletariat came fourth and below them, the rural peasantry. Standing below these groups were society's castoffs, the political prisoners, the kulaks, and other "asocial elements," slated to perish either in the Gulag or in their unsightly hovels. He was appalled with the opulence and luxury reserved for the elite who enjoyed access to beautifully stocked stores that only the privileged could frequent. He saw them prancing about in the glittering Hotel Metropol and traveling on special trains, where they cavorted drunkenly with their perfumed lascivious women late into the night. For their part, the undernourished working masses were poorly clothed and had to wait for hours in long lines to purchase inferior food. It soon dawned on him that Jewish influence in the Soviet Union was widespread.[55] Jewish intellectuals were claimed to be master propagandists, manipulative and mendacious schemers who were training cadres of activists in Marxist ideology and practice and dispatching them throughout the world to proselytize for the Bolshevik cause. According to Dwinger, his protagonist was only beginning to see the truth.

Taken by rail to the massive Dnjeprostroj hydroelectric power plant, purported to produce 900,000 horsepower and 4 billion kilowatts of electricity per year, he was flabbergasted. Only in a command economy could such an expensive effort be utilized to produce power for such little purpose, he claimed. For hundreds of miles outside this industrial plant, which existed only for show, lay nothing but unpopulated Ukrainian steppes. Dwinger's worst judgments, however, were reserved for the disastrous results of the forced collectivization of agriculture. Under this program, he noted, production of foodstuffs had fallen by some 80 percent, and as a result, the peasantry was starving. The secret police roamed the countryside, forcing the peasants to move to collective farms, while shipping off the most successful of their number, the kulaks, to Siberian work camps. While Party members, the GPU, and the Red Army were eating well, the peasantry starved to death. Because the government requisitioned all their crops, there was no incentive to produce grain efficiently. Further, rather than surrender all their livestock, they simply slaughtered their animals. It was obvious that the noble dreams and idealism of the founders of

---

[55] For an analysis of the not inconsiderable Jewish participation in the Bolshevik movement and in the Soviet Union, see the chapter titled "Babel's First Love: The Jews and the Russian Revolution," in Yuri Slezkine, *The Jewish Century* (Princeton: Princeton University Press, 2004), pp. 105–203.

Bolshevism had been betrayed by Stalin, he asserted. Instead of the land, bread, and social justice that they had been promised, the majority of Russians were the subjected to a merciless, even brutal life under their Soviet masters.[56]

An especially poignant vignette featured a vivid description of the horrors suffered by the peasantry. He was deeply moved by what he witnessed on a visit to Gottswort, a settlement of pious and industrious German immigrants that traced its roots to the days of Catherine the Great. He found nothing but killing fields and virtually deserted towns and villages in what was once the breadbasket of the nation. He knew how prosperous these farmers had once been, because he had worked there as a German prisoner of war. It was heartbreaking to observe their suffering and to hear the morbid details of their treatment by the GPU, the Soviet secret police. The survivors were dressed in nothing but rags. Mothers, producing no milk to feed their babies, were forced to watch their offspring slowly die of starvation. There was no God in Gottswort, no spiritual balm for their wounds. All the churches had been destroyed and the priests deported. Surviving children either joined gangs of murderers or the Komsomol, the communist youth organization, where they were taught to inform on their own parents. The hopeless victims of Bolshevik barbarity simply waited to die, a marked contrast to the vulgar, fat, and drunken apparatchiks he observed feasting in the dining car on the return trip to Moscow. Soviet reality made him sick in heart and in body.

Thoroughly disillusioned, and with his Bolshevik dreams in tatters, "the young German" returned home with his communist past behind him for good. Certain that he would be exonerated and treated fairly, upon reaching German soil he turned himself over to the police with the words, "Arrest me! I was a communist."[57] Henceforth, he would spread the truth about the criminality of the Soviet Union and help strengthen the Third Reich as it prepared for the coming life or death struggle with world communism.

---

[56] Leading authorities estimate that more than two millions peasants were deported and six million people died of starvation as a result of the forced collectivization and dekulakization program. See Stéphane Courtois, Nicolas Werth, Jean-Louis Panné, Andrzej Paczkowski, Karel Bartosek, and Jean-Louis Margolin, *The Black Book of Communism. Crimes, Terror, Repression* (Cambridge/London: Harvard University Press, 1999), pp. 146–68. For a full account of this criminal program, see Robert Conquest, *The Harvest of Sorrow: Soviet Collectivization and the Terror-Famine* (New York: Oxford University Press, 1986).

[57] Ibid., p. 154.

It was quite evident that Dwinger himself was on the identical warpath as the protagonist of his book. According to Hitler and Himmler, a great future lay ahead for the Germanic peoples of Volkswort and all the *Volksdeutsche* in the East. Those among them who were fortunate enough to survive the Great Famine resulting from the Soviet forced collectivization and dekulakization programs were to be embraced in the wildly delusional resettlement programs that the Nazi radicals planned and proceeded to establish after the invasion of the Soviet Union. For a time, the National Socialists were to replace one form of criminality with another, as the alleged Jewish enemy replaced the kulaks and small holders as the victims of ideologically based genocidal terror on a mass scale.[58]

The Spanish Civil War, which broke out in 1936, was perfectly suited for Dwinger's talents. Claiming that Spain was the springboard for the Bolshevik assault on the entire continent of Europe, the veteran chronicler of the Russian Civil War came to life once more as a war reporter. He now donned the uniform of an SS officer, having been assigned to the staff of the 15th SS Reiterstandarte based in Munich at the personal request of Himmler. In October 1936, he informed the SS personnel office in Berlin that he was traveling to Spain as a special war reporter.[59] The result was *Spanish Silhouettes*, a colorful report of his experiences covering the Civil War, which was rushed into print in 1937.[60]

Dwinger delighted in wearing a uniform once more, leaving his estate, and shipping out on the SS *Ancona* for Spain. His breathless description of meeting with General Francisco Franco at his headquarters in Salamanca was not without operatic grandeur, as was his description of General José Enrique Varela, the flamboyant victor of the legendary siege of Fortress Alcazar at Toledo. The images he drew of aristocratic refugees streaming through the lobby of the Grand Hotel in Salamanca were unforgettable. As an old soldier, he was fascinated with the colorful uniforms of the Caudillo's diverse military units, especially the blue of the Falange and the

---

[58] For an analysis of how this was actually to take place, see Wendy Lower, *Nazi Empire-Building and the Holocaust in Ukraine* (Chapel Hill: University of North Carolina Press, 2005).

[59] Dwinger to Personalkanzlei des RFSS, October 14, 1936, Dwinger File, BAB. See also SS *Sturmbannführer* (name illegible), Reichsführer SS, Chef Adutantur, Tgb. Nr. A/6743, October 7, 1936, "Da Dwinger mit Leib und Seele Reiter ist, bittet der Reichsführer ihn einer Reiterstandarte zu überweisen.," ibid.

[60] Edwin Erich Dwinger, *Spanische Silhouetten. Tagebuch einer Frontreise* (Jena: Eugen Diederichs, 1937).

rainbow bursts worn by the Moroccans, proudly signaling their curious role as Islamic protectors of the Christian West.

Dwinger regaled his readers with tales of atrocities committed by the Bolsheviks, horrifying descriptions of the mutilation of prisoners, the destruction of churches and monasteries, and the rape of nuns. The Red Army and the power brokers of international communism were by nature criminal and brutal, he charged, asserting that should the Bolsheviks conquer Spain, their next target would be the German Reich. A victory by the forces of General Franco, on the other hand, would parallel in significance the summary defeat meted out to the Moors at the gates of Europe in the eighth century, thus saving Europe for Western civilization. However, Dwinger's own encounter with Spain was more prosaic. He returned to Europe aboard the *Monte Pasqual* in November 1936 after a painful flare-up of his ongoing duodenal ulcer condition.[61]

With the onset of World War II, Dwinger put himself at the disposal of the regime. Commissioned a lieutenant in the Wehrmacht, he was given the position of "officer on special assignment" (*Sonderführer*), enabling him to pull strings to become temporarily attached to the headquarters of armies of his choice among those forming the vanguard of the German Blitzkrieg. To the author's dismay, however, the worm turned in a most curious way, leading to a propaganda assignment that he simply could not refuse. In the fall of 1939, soon after the end of the campaign in Poland, Dwinger received a call from Goebbels requesting that he write an anti-Polish propaganda tract to justify German policies in Poland. Dwinger agreed, resulting in the publication of the notorious *Death in Poland* in 1940.[62] Specifically, he was to report on Polish crimes against ethnic Germans in the so-called Bloody Sunday massacres at Bromberg. Bromberg was the center of German culture in the Polish Corridor, which had been transferred from German sovereignty in the Versailles Treaty. The disputed question of what exactly happened to the German minority in the Corridor during the first week of the war has never been clarified.[63]

---

[61] Ibid., pp. 100–101. See Prof. Dr. Med. W. H. Veil, Direktor der Universitätsklinik Jena, March 4, 1938, attesting that he had been treating E. E. Dwinger for years for chronic duodenal ulcers. Dwinger File, BAB.

[62] Edwin Erich Dwinger, *Der Tod in Polen. Die volksdeutsche Passion* (Jena: Eugen Diederichs, 1940). Dwinger told his son, Norwin, about Goebbels's telephone call long after World War II. See Feigl/Pable, *Väter Unser*, pp. 204–5.

[63] See the documentary film *Der Bromberger Blutsonntag. Eine Legende in Polen und Deutschland*, Zebra Film, TVP Gdansk/Südwest 3/1996, Buch und Regie, Ute Boennen and Gerald Endres, which deals in a balanced matter with the disputed facts of the issue.

But the facts seemed very clear to Dwinger, who had the audacity to compare the events of "Bloody Sunday" with Lucius Cornelius Sulla's execution of the followers of Marius in 82 B.C. and even with Catherine de Medici's conspiracy, which led to the murder of twenty thousand Huguenots on the "Night of Saint Bartholomew" in 1572. Dwinger claimed that over the course of a week's time, sixty thousand Germans had been butchered in Bromberg.[64]

Death in Poland represented a gross distortion of the historical facts. According to the author, the Polish authorities in Warsaw ordered the army to begin the pogrom against the German minority, which had been planned long before the onset of hostilities. A murderous assault began in Bromberg, through which retreating Polish units were already passing. Smelling blood, Polish civilians joined the murder squads in what Dwinger claimed to be ruthless acts of sadistic criminality on a scale not seen since the days of Genghis Khan. Over the coming week, columns of prisoners were herded eastward in a death march. Offered neither food nor water, they were assaulted by Polish bystanders, and as they approached the suburbs of Warsaw, Jews in caftans spit on them and struck them with their umbrellas. Dwinger's descriptions were extraordinarily graphic, and he insisted that his reports were truthful and were based on the sworn testimonies of survivors. "This book," he claimed with characteristic immodesty, "presented me with the most difficult task I have ever faced as the chronicler of our era."[65]

It is not surprising that Dwinger would claim that the reason for the tragedy lay in the racial substance of the Polish people. The entire nation was guilty of the crimes, he observed. "It was the typical reaction of those of inferior character," he declared, "and they have removed Poland forever from the community of cultured nations."[66] Poland, he submitted, had perpetrated a cultural crime of the first magnitude, and therefore the world must understand that they deserved everything that later befell them, no matter how severe. With claims such as these, Dwinger had clearly gone over the top. There was no question that this polemical work was an attempt to rationalize the harshness of German rule in occupied Poland. Bruno Brehm, Dwinger's friend from the harsh years in the camps and a fellow nationalist writer not known for his humanitarian opinions, castigated him for the racism on which this work was based. But for his part,

---

[64] Dwinger, *Der Tod in Polen*, pp. 7–8.　　[65] Ibid., p. 5.
[66] Ibid., p. 30.

Goebbels was very pleased with *Death in Poland*, calling it a "shocking and deeply moving" chronicle of the "martyrdom of Germanic people" that would have its desired affect in his propaganda vis à vis Poland.[67]

In 1940, Dwinger was attached to the staff of a Panzer division in the Battle of France, with direct access to its commanding general and staff. Certain that he was about to be a firsthand witness to revolutionary breakthroughs in strategy and tactics, he took advantage of every opportunity the position offered him. Further, he was determined to become the Third Reich's leading chronicler of a war that would decide the future of Europe for hundreds of years. The result was some of the most fascinating front reporting of the entire war, parts of which he published in abbreviated form in the book *Panzer Leader*.[68]

In *Panzer Leader*, Dwinger returned to his old form once more. He had always been a soldier and was in the milieu he knew best. Although it was never mentioned specifically, there is every indication that Dwinger was attached to the headquarters of the illustrious tank commander, General Heinz Guderian. He reported memorably on the headlong Panzer dash westward to the French coast – the breakthrough to Calais and Amiens – which opened the way to victory. Dwinger's account of tank commanders passing over the Somme battlefields was dramatic and not without an overhang of melancholy and regret. These, after all, were the fields soaked in the blood of their fathers. Their longing for victory had been realized at last, he wrote, and their sacrifice avenged. Perched in the citadel high above Calais with his commanding general, he observed that "They did not get the chance to experience the greatness of this hour. Far on the horizon a bright land mass arose out of the sea – these were the Cliffs of Dover, this was the white coast of Great Britain."[69] "If we reach Calais, then we have England!," was now the battlecry.

The assault on the Soviet Union in June 1941 offered Dwinger the opportunity once again to witness history in the making. He would publish a section of his experiences in the East in the war diary titled *Return to Soviet Russia*, which captured the dramatic intensity of the German

[67] Goebbels, diary entry, April 25, 1940, Elke Fröhlich, *Die Tagebücher von Joseph Goebbels* 4 (München: Saur, 1987), p. 127.

[68] Edwin Erich Dwinger, *Panzerführer* (Jena: Eugen Diederichs, 1941). In his introduction, the author noted that "These diaries are excerpts from the extensive campaign report which the author intends to publish after the war." For obvious reasons, this work was never published.

[69] Ibid., p. 21.

victories of 1941.[70] When Himmler learned that Dwinger was attached to an Army Panzer division, he endeavored to cherry pick the author away from his competitors and invited him to join an SS staff in the field for a time. "I would be very gratified," the Reichsführer SS wrote, "when after the first four weeks of your new deployment you would come to my headquarters, because I have assignments to carry out which are entirely in your realm of expertise. It would be of great value, if you were able to witness the final act of this revolution in an appropriately chosen place."[71] In the event, early in September 1941, Dwinger was attached to the staff of SS Gruppenführer von dem Bach-Zelewski, commander of the SD on the central front, notorious for his organization of the murder of Jews in his sector.[72] Hitler himself was particularly fond of von dem Bach-Zalewski, who, he said, could "wade through blood" with more courage and zeal than even Reinhard Heydrich. Dwinger, in a letter thanking Himmler for making this deployment possible, reported that he had visited Warsaw where the SS Security Service commander briefed him thoroughly on affairs there. He had also visited Bialystok, where he learned about the policies pursued in connection with its annexation to the East Prussian realm before proceeding to Minsk, to familiarize himself with problems in White Russia.[73] As the author would later report to his family, he was witness to extermination operations carried out by the Einsatzgruppen.

When Dwinger published his diary of the Russian campaign, there was no mention of his experience with the SS. Rather, in this work he dramatized the breathtakingly swift victories of the Wehrmacht in the Soviet Union in the summer of 1941. He returned home in early October, thus missing the rainy season entirely, the onset of winter, and the Battle of Moscow. What characterized *Return to Soviet Russia* was its relentless

---

[70] Edwin Erich Dwinger, *Wiedersehen mit Sowjetrussland. Tagebuch vom Ostfeldzug* (Jena: Eugen Diederichs, 1942).

[71] Reichsführer SS Heinrich Himmler to "Lieber Parteigenosse Dwinger," June 18, 1941, Dwinger File, BAB.

[72] Standartenführer u. Stabsführer des. Pers.Stabes RFSS Ullmann to SS Gruppenführer von dem Bach, September 2, 1941, ibid. Ullmann noted in his letter that it was Himmler's intention to take Dwinger with him to the Führer Headquarters but that it was rather quiet there at the moment. It was better to send him to Erich von dem Bach-Zelewski to see how a higher SS and police leader went about his business and the latter was instructed to extend every courtesy to him as he carried out this function. On the role of Bach-Zelewski as an organizer of mass shootings in his sector of the front, see Christopher R. Browning, *The Origins of the Final Solution* (Lincoln, Nebraska/Jerusalem: University of Nebraska Press and Yad Vashem, 2004), pp. 281, 288–9, 303.

[73] Dwinger to Himmler, October 5, 1941, Dwinger File, BAB.

and devastating assault on the Bolshevik masters of the Soviet Union. Visiting with Russian prisoners of war and observing their behavior, he soon came to the conclusion that they were no longer Russians at all. One knew immediately that a major change had come about because of the odor they emitted, not unlike the smell of a herd of deer or the stench of gypsies and Mongols. He clearly remembered these smells from his days in the Siberian camps, a mixture of old leather and sour bread. How shocking and displeasing the new Soviet herd-man was, he submitted, what a miserable and emaciated people they had become:

I felt as if I had happened upon a nest of horrible termites. There was absolutely no doubt about it, these men had been subjected to such devastating totalitarian propaganda that they could no longer think for themselves. There were none of the traditional blond Great Russian types among them. Instead those with Mongolian characteristics predominated. The Soviets had bastardized the entire nation.[74]

Dwinger made much of these themes in the speech he gave to the annual meeting of writers that Goebbels hosted in October 1942 in Weimar.[75] This racist worldview seemed to indicate that Dwinger had fallen in line completely with the "subhuman" ideology propagated by Himmler and the SS, whereby the Soviet population of all national groups only appeared to be human but in reality formed an inferior genus of swamp peoples. For Dwinger, such was not the case and could not have been, given that his own mother was Russian. The fundamental difference was that Dwinger supported the destruction of the Soviet system, not the Russian people, whereas Hitler and Himmler truly believed that all Russian national groups were inferior, fit only for enslavement. For Hitler and the hard-line Nazis, the epithet "Jewish-Bolshevik" embraced all Russian national groups and the war in Russia was one of conquest and colonization, pure and simple. According to this policy, thirty million Russians were slated to die during the war of annihilation in Russia alone.[76] He even held to this line after the Soviet General Andrei Vlasov was captured, that offered the possibility of forming a Russian army of hundreds of thousands of men to fight at the side of the Wehrmacht, thus joining

---

[74] *Wiedersehen mit Sowjetrussland*, pp. 57–9.

[75] Dwinger, "Der Bolshewismus als Bedrohung der Weltkultur," *Dichter und Krieger. Weimarer Reden 1942*, ed. Dr. Rudolf Erckmann, Oberregierungsrat im Reichsministerium für Volksaufklärung und Propaganda (Hamburg: Hanseatische Verlagsanstalt, 1943). Compare to *Deutsche Soldaten sehen die Sowjetunion. Feldpostbriefe aus dem Osten*, ed. Wolfgang Diewerge (Berlin: Wilhelm Limpert, 1941).

[76] Christian Gerlach, *Kalkulierte Morde. Die deutsche Wirtschafts-und Vernichtungspolitik in Weissrussland 1941 bis 1944* (Hamburg: Hamburger Edition, 1999).

with the Germans in their joint goal of overthrowing Stalin and the entire Bolshevik system.

With remarkable boldness, in 1942 Dwinger began a very public and often recklessly dangerous attack on Hitler's policies vis-à-vis the Soviet Union. With characteristic vanity, he was convinced that there was no more significant authority on the Soviet Union than he. In fact, his goal of winning the Russian peoples over to the German side by treating them as allies in their common goal of destroying the Soviet apparatus had many significant supporters. These included several important members of the army General Staff and as well as line officers, including Henning von Tresckow, Chief of Operations, Army Group Center, and Claus von Stauffenberg, chief of staff to the commander of the Home Army, both of whom would form the heart of the anti-Hitler resistance movement. Other adherents of this position included significant experts on Russia, including Wilfried Strik-Strikfeldt and Nikolas von Grote of the Wehrmacht's Propaganda Section; Gerhard von Mende of Rosenberg's Ministry for the Occupied Eastern Territories; Peter Kleist and Otto Bräutigam of the Foreign Ministry; and finally the leading journalist Giselher Wirsing, as well as Professor Theodor Oberländer.[77]

Throughout 1942, but with increasing urgency after the fall of Stalingrad in the winter of 1943, Dwinger capitalized on the protection that his SS officer's uniform afforded him to pursue his dissenting policies. He wrote one memorandum after the other, bearing such titles as "What Must Be Urgently Done to Topple Stalin" and circulated them among ranking figures in the regime.[78] A complete dossier on Dwinger, including these memoranda, was found in the safe of the Führer Headquarters Berchtesgaden compound, marked "ad acta Adolf Hitler," proving that his strikingly bold and dangerous criticisms of the "subhuman" ideology and the resulting murderous policies in Russia had reached Hitler himself through SS channels critical of Dwinger.[79] His memoranda also reached General Heinz Guderian, with whom he became reacquainted during his

---

[77] Alexander Dallin, *German Rule in Russia 1941–1945. A Study of Occupation Policies* (London: Macmillan, 1981), 2nd ed., pp. 511–32.

[78] Dallin, pp. 512, 584–5.

[79] Dr. med. Heinrich Junkermann to Dwinger, February 12, 1969, Personal Archive Ellen Dwinger, original letter in possession of the author. In this document, Junkermann relates details of his visit in August 1944 with his old school comrade Ringsdorf, at the Berchtesgaden compound, where his friend was a communications officer at the Führer Headquarters. At that time Ringsdorf showed Junkermann this file, which had been signed and filed "ad acta Adolf Hitler."

deployment with Panzer armies on the Russian front. He was able to win over Field Marshal Ernst von Busch as well, with the result that in his area of the Central Front, hundreds of thousands of copies of a flyer instructing German soldiers how to behave toward the Russian people were distributed.

In the spring of 1943, he had the courage to publish "The Russian Man" in the organ of the Hitler Youth, *Will and Power*. In this essay, Dwinger argued that the Russian was of good genetic stock and the damage done by the Soviets to his spirit could be healed, if only German attitudes and behavior were changed. To this end, German soldiers must be directed to handle the Russians with respect, to be correct in their deportment, and never to be abusive toward their women. They were advised to treat them like human beings, and even to show photographs of their own children to Russian families. If this were to happen, Dwinger argued, Russians would stop joining the partisan units that were growing by leaps and bounds. Such a political reversal would soon give the Germans the upper hand. What, then, must be done without delay, he queried? The answer was to "win the Russians over to the European family of peoples." Russians can be outmaneuvered, he argued, but they are very hard to defeat. They are masters at forming a united front of the masses, inspired by the conviction that they are the most progressive nation on earth. Victories against the Red Army are not victories at all, he argued, as the Wehrmacht had learned in the battles of encirclement early in the campaign. "We can only defeat the Soviets if we crush their head," he submitted, and "that head is the revolutionary idea which inspires the masses and drives them to renewed effort. Treat the Russian like a beast, and he will treat you that way in return." Nothing can be accomplished through force, he said, because there is no way that Germans could compete in that arena with the GPU. Further, the "subhuman" theory was totally wrong and should be done away with immediately. We can only lead by example, he argued, not by brutality or the arrogant and ill-conceived concept of the *Herrenvolk*. "The East cannot be defeated with Western methods," he argued. "Only a radical psychological reversal can bring about a German victory."[80]

Dwinger continued his efforts well into 1943, when he traveled to Vienna with General Vlasov to lobby with Gauleiter Baldur von Schirach, who promised that he would take the matter up with Hitler. This, of

---

[80] Edwin Erich Dwinger, "Der russische Mensch. Der Weg zur Überwindung des Bolschewismus," *Wille und Macht* 11 (April–June 1943), p. 8.

course, was hopeless, because von Schirach himself had fallen into disfavor at the Führer Headquarters. Dwinger had simply gone too far, and the hammer was about to come down on him. Returning from Vienna, he was summoned to the offices of the head of the SS Reich Central Security Office, Gottlob Berger, who ordered him to return to his home where he was put under house arrest, forbidden to write or utter another word publicly on the Eastern question. His telephone was bugged, his mail was read by the authorities, and his ulcers were acting up horribly. Word reached Dwinger that a complaint about his essay in *Will and Power* had been made to Hitler, and Himmler became disillusioned with his former protégé as well.[81]

The Reichsführer SS had become so fed up with Dwinger's machinations that he criticized him in his notorious speech to the Higher SS and Police Leadership Corps at Poznan in October 1943. Without naming Dwinger, he sarcastically dismissed "the Baltic and Eastern dreamers, some of whom have written very good books and had a Russian mother too." "Russians, they believe," he continued, "can only be defeated by Russians. So give Vlasov 500,000 or 1,000,000 Russians, arm them with good equipment, give them good German military training, and Vlasov is so gifted that he will lead a campaign against the Russians and kill them for us."[82]

There is no question that Dwinger was correct all along about the Russian question, and within a matter of months, the desperation of the military situation was such that Himmler was forced to consider supporting the use of General Vlasov's Russian Army of Liberation after all. In the end, this, too, was a hopeless endeavor and a missed opportunity. Once again Dwinger entered the political arena, carrying out missions abroad for both the Foreign Ministry and the Propaganda Ministry.[83] As

[81] See Dwinger to Hans Grimm, October 23, 1943, Nachlass Hans Grimm, DLAM.

[82] Reichsführer SS Heinrich Himmler, Posen, October 4, 1943, Document No. 1919-PS, Nuremberg Trial Records. Dwinger remained problematic for higher SS officers until the end of the war. For further correspondence about the Dwinger problem at the highest levels, see SS Obersturmbannführer von Kielpinski, Reichssicherheitshauptamt, Abt. II C4-PA, January 29, 1945, letter of complaint to SS Standartenführer Dr. Brandt, Persönlicher Stab, Reichsführer SS, Feld-Kommandostelle, Dwinger File, BAB; Brandt to von Kielpinski, Feld-Kommandostelle, February 9, 1945, ibid. In this missive, Brandt directed von Kielpinski to contact Dwinger, advising him that his personal opinions should not be expressed while wearing his SS uniform.

[83] A postcard from Waltraut Dwinger to the SS Personal-Hauptamt, dated March 7, 1944, noted that because her husband was "abroad most of the time on missions for the Foreign Ministry and the Propaganda Ministry," it would be best if the SS authorities would address correspondence to him in the future at his home address. Dwinger File, BAB.

late as March 13, 1945, Dwinger received a request from an officer on Himmler's personal staff to schedule a meeting where he could share his expertise on Russia with them.[84]

When all was lost for Vlasov in the final weeks of the war, he came to the Hedwigshof and discussed a hopeless plan to avoid surrendering to the Red Army, certain that death and dishonor would be the result. Vlasov's hope was to enlist Dwinger as an emissary to gain a promise from the Americans that his forces would not be returned to the Soviet Union.[85] But the fate of the Vlasov's army was sealed. One final chapter remained in the Dwinger-Vlasov relationship however. Norwin Dwinger, then but a ten-year-old boy, reported that he was witness to what may well have been his father's betrayal of Vlasov in the last days of the war. Vlasov, gaunt and stretched to the limit, made a dash to the Dwinger estate in his command car, certain that his famous patron would hold true to his pledge to hide him should that ever become necessary. Pretending that he was not at home, Dwinger concealed himself in his villa, while Vlasov dashed off with his guards as quickly as he had come.[86] Later captured by the Americans, Vlasov and what remained of his forces were indeed delivered over to the Soviets. He would be hanged as a traitor in Moscow in August 1946, and the entire Army of Liberation would be liquidated.

With the war over, Dwinger lay low on his estate. Several weeks later, he was arrested and incarcerated for more than six months in a prison at Ludwigsburg, not far from Stuttgart. He and his first wife, Waltraut Wien, were divorced and he married Ellen Dwinger, the former wife of the journalist, Giselher Wirsing. Certain that the Allied coalition with the Soviet Union would soon be shattered, Dwinger made every effort to have his trial postponed as long as possible. In fact, he would not have to face trial before the denazification court at Füssen until 1948, which was certainly to his advantage. By that time, Russia had long since been declared the enemy in Washington and the Berlin Airlift was in full swing. German-American friendship was beginning to blossom, and within a year

---

[84] SS Sturmbannführer (illegible) to Dwinger, Feld-Kommandostelle, March 13, 1945, Dwinger File, BAB.

[85] Jürgen Thorwald, *The Illusion. Soviet Soldiers in Hitler's Armies* (New York: Harcourt Brace, 1974), pp. 281–4.

[86] Norbert Dwinger in Feigl and Pable, *Väter Unser*, pp. 198–9. Dwinger detailed his version of the events surrounding his final meetings with Vlasov in his novel, *General Wlassow* (Frankfurt: Otto Dikreiter, 1951), pp. 341–50. As Alexander Dallin noted years ago, Dwinger's novel on Vlasov, while offering much vivid background material, cannot be used as documentary evidence by serious historians.

the Federal Republic of Germany was established. The conditions were excellent for his acquittal, and Dwinger hoped to begin his voluminous publication activity once more.

The Dwinger trial proceeded favorably for the defendant, and the procedures lasted for only two days. The accused was so confident that he claimed before the court that the onset of the Cold War had caused American authorities to engage him because of his acknowledged expertise and balanced judgment on the Soviet Union. He went so far as to question the court quite impishly: "Would someone want to punish me after the fact for highlighting the Soviet danger? This is exactly what America is doing all over the world today." The court deemed the prosecution's case to be weak, and the inexperienced state prosecutor assigned to his case was able to win only a paltry 1,500 mark fine and the designation of the author as a "supporter" of the Nazi regime. Under the conditions, this was a very light sentence indeed.

There are many reasons why Dwinger was able to do well before the denazification court, most notably because the strategy for his defense was soundly conceived. Generally the proceedings of the denazification courts were terribly flawed and a great deal of evidence presented to support the case of defendants was fabricated. However, in Dwinger's case, there was no need to contrive evidence, but instead it would suffice to stretch the truth. His attorneys based their case on the contention that their client was but a chronicler of historical events. To prove their contention, they pointed to the author's book, *Between White and Red*, which had been so fair to the Soviet cause that a Russian edition of the work had been published, and as a result, their client had been invited to visit the Soviet Union to be their guest to witness the "workers' paradise" at first hand. The defense team also contended that Dwinger was perceived to be an enemy of the Third Reich very early on, as evidenced by the fact that some volumes of his trilogy were burned in the notorious night of book burning staged by Nazi students in Berlin in May 1933. Furthermore, in 1934 the Gestapo had forced the closing of his play *The Prisoners* because this allegedly defeatist and pacifist work was out of step in reawakened Germany. He was denounced by the Munich SS, who placed him on their watch list, and because he was blacklisted, he was unable to write for the press in the Bavarian capital. To buttress the case that Dwinger had internationalist leanings, it was noted that Aurélien Lugné-Poe, editor of the journal, *Oeuvres*, in Paris and a member of the selection committee for the Nobel Peace Prize, informed him that he had been nominated for that honor. Further, Third Reich court records revealed that in 1936, the

Gauleiter of Munich warned him to stop his clandestine meetings with émigrés and also suggested that it was high time that he join the Nazi Party. The defense also charged that Göring had Dwinger's telephone bugged by his notorious *Sonderdienst Seehaus* intelligence operation, and this was confirmed under oath by a former government official.

Evidence of Dwinger's "extensive interventions" concerning the Russian question was placed into the record. As early as 1942, it was noted, he had met clandestinely with Fritz-Dietlof Graf von der Schulenburg, a major figure in German resistance circles. It was also claimed that Dwinger was recruited by army resistance figures close to Count Claus von Stauffenberg to join an editing and production team for a film sponsored by the Wehrmacht High Command that would be used by the resistance at the appropriate time.[87] It is difficult to support Dwinger's contention that this assignment had anything remotely to do with resistance against Hitler. After all, this allegedly took place at the same time that he was engaged in writing the very pro-Nazi account of his experiences on the Eastern front, sponsored in part by Himmler. The defense also claimed that their client had hosted several meetings of the resistance at his Hedwigshof estate and remained active in Füssen opposition circles until the end of the war. Even a local Catholic priest was trotted out, claiming that Dwinger was known in the neighborhood as a resistance figure.

It remained for the defense to call several witnesses to present further evidence that Dwinger was at heart an enemy of National Socialist ideology – a thoroughly false claim – and that he was never an anti-Semite, did not support Hitler, and even had been heard to call the Führer a "bandit." The writers Hans Grimm, Paul Alverdes, and Rudolf Alexander Schröder, and the widow of a noted historian whom the regime had defamed, Hermann Oncken, were all called as witnesses to attest to Dwinger's innocence. It was also noted that during the last months of the regime, when many of the highest-ranking members of the SS officer corps met at Plassenburg Castle in Bavaria, hardliners were still talking of doing away with Dwinger once and for all.[88]

---

[87] It is of interest to note that in Dwinger's letter to Himmler of October 5, 1941 (Dwinger File, BAB), he reported that his work for the Reichsführer in the East had to be interrupted because he had been ordered back to Berlin to take part in the production of a film on the war in Russia for the Wehrmacht High Command (OKW).

[88] See Dr. Wunderlich, "Auszüge aus dem Urteil der Spruchkammer Füssen vom 28. Juli 1948 über den Schriftsteller Edwin Erich Dwinger," Archive Ellen Dwinger, original in possession of the author.

The announcement of Dwinger's light sentence was attacked in much of the German press, which was not surprising. Since the end of the war the media, which hitherto had been singing the Nazi tune in grand harmony, now turned against their former orchestrators with a vengeance. Long before the trial took place, Rudolf T. Spitz had written a devastating attack on Dwinger in the *Hochland Bote*, judging that he significantly furthered the Nazi cause and demanding that he be properly punished. The claim that Dwinger resisted the regime was ludicrous, Spitz charged. His nefarious militaristic propaganda was read to the last days of the Third Reich by the misled youth of Nazi Germany, earning the author RM 45,000 in 1945 alone.[89] The *Berliner Tagespiegel* observed caustically that Dwinger was one of "those militant mystics who had prepared the way for Rosenberg. It was said of *The Last Riders* at the time it appeared that the book 'mirrored the myth of eternal Germanness'. The Bavarian court seems to have fallen for the same myth."[90] The *Abendzeitung* of Munich offered a balanced report of the proceedings, coming to the conclusion that although a case could not be made that Dwinger was a convinced Nazi, nevertheless he had had the effect of one.[91]

The communist and left-wing press had a field day with the Dwinger sentence. *Neues Deutschland*, the organ of the German Democratic Republic, attacked Dwinger as an opportunist who always followed popular trends because that was where the money was. From the communist point of view, Dwinger was nothing but a literary arsonist for militarist causes and their writers' association called the judgment shocking.[92] Angelus Hartkopf wrote a brutal critique of the affair in *Aufbau*, the influential Socialist Unity Party's literary journal, which was the intellectual mouthpiece of the communist Central Committee in East Berlin. She charged that the sentence was yet more proof that the fascist restoration, led by greedy upper bourgeois financiers and industrial capitalists, was under way in the Western zones of occupation. When would her fellow countrymen learn, she questioned, that a fundamental and radical social change had to be instituted to reform the German spirit, to purge the nation of the specter of fascism, and to embrace true freedom? The proceedings of the Denazification Commission were said to be an insult to German intelligence. Dwinger, Hartkopf charged, had been a leading

---

[89] Rudolf T. Spitz, "Edwin Erich Dwinger – gestern und heute," *Hochland Bote*, November 8, 1946.
[90] *Tagespiegel*, Berlin, July 29, 1948.   [91] *Abendzeitung*, Munich, July 29, 1948.
[92] *Neues Deutschland*, August 1 and August 3, 1948.

member of the arrogant Nazi literary establishment, whose "elegantly barbaric heroic writings" led German youth down the path of criminality. It should have been evident to all parties that Dwinger was at the forefront among those setting the intellectual and cultural stage for the National Socialists, whose Bacchanalian orgy set the entire continent afire, destroying the cultural legacy of hundreds of years.[93]

Unlike most National Socialist authors, Dwinger did not disappear into shadowy obscurity in the Federal Republic of Germany. Indeed, just as he had throughout his life, he proved adept at tacking his sails skillfully to conform to the shifting political winds while remaining what he always was, a convinced critic of the policies of the Stalinist Soviet Union. He took a cynical pleasure in exploiting the fact that the United States and the entire NATO bloc had now joined him as convinced enemies of the Kremlin. Although he would never again reach the prominence he had earlier enjoyed, Dwinger once more began to publish voluminously. His trilogy was reissued, and he brought out two new works devoted to the theme of Vlasov and Germany's failed Russian policies, among them *General Vlasov: A Tragedy of Our Times* and *Twelve Discussions*.[94] The latter works were autobiographical, and Dwinger himself appears in both of them in his characteristically vain and hyperbolic form. *Twelve Discussions* is a reconstruction of meetings the author held during the war with, among others, Generals Guderian, Arnim, and Vlasov as well as with Himmler, Darré, and von Schirach.[95] His novel on the postwar German tragedy in the East, *When the Dams Break – The Downfall of East Prussia*, dealt with Russian atrocities that had not received the attention they deserved, an understandable situation considering the enormity of the Nazi crimes. In 1967, Dwinger's reminiscences about his personal experiences at the time of the Bolshevik Revolution were published in a special edition of the journal *Eastern Europe*, edited by the specialist on Soviet affairs Professor Klaus Mehnert.[96] Although some eyebrows were raised about this, no major repercussions ensued as a result.

---

[93] Angelus Hartkopf, "'Mitläufer' Edwin Erich Dwinger'," *Aufbau* 8: 1948, pp. 807–8. See also W. Storman, "Nur ein harmloser Mitläufer," *Heute und Morgen. Literarische Monatsschrift* 8: 1948.

[94] Edwin Erich Dwinger, *General Wlassow. Eine Tragödie Unserer Zeit* (Frankfurt: Dikreiter, 1951) and *Zwölf Gespräche* (Essen: Verlag Blick & Bild, 1967).

[95] Georg Böse reviewed *Zwölf Gespräche* under the headline "Zwischen den Fronten" in the *Berliner Tagesspiegel*, February 5, 1967, noting that historical events had overtaken Dwinger long before he wrote his recent books.

[96] Edwin Erich Dwinger, "Wie ich die Revolution erlebte," *Osteuropa*: 9 (July 1967), "Sonderheft: Erlebter Roter Oktober. Augenzeugenberichten," pp. 606–24.

Although he himself never realized it, Edwin Erich Dwinger simply did not count for much anymore. Postwar critics were devastating in their attacks on the German nationalists and militarists of his era, and in general they either ignored or mocked the entire stable of writers whose literary publications overlapped in any way with National Socialist ideology.[97] Such major figures as Dwinger did not even appear in most of the standard reference works devoted to twentieth century literature published in the Federal Republic of Germany. This development was lamentable and an assault on historical truth, even if it was understandable considering German sensitivities about the Third Reich and the place of their nation in history. Except for an occasional birthday notice, Edwin Erich Dwinger was nearly totally forgotten. He died in 1981 at the age of eighty-three in Gmund on the Tegernsee.

---

[97] For an example of this, see Christian Ferber, "Märtyrerkronen ohne Köpfe. Ein deutliches Wort zu einer Literatur, die keine ist," *Die Neue Zeitung*, September 27, 1952, Dwinger File, BHSA, Personensammlung 4643.

6

Hitler's Muse: The Political Aesthetics of the Poet and Playwright Eberhard Wolfgang Möller

The career of Eberhard Wolfgang Möller (1906–1972), which paralleled the rise and fall of the Third Reich, was at once brilliant and problematic. Poetry and the poetic vision, as well as the medium of theater, were well suited to complement film, music, art, and literature in the formation of the Fascist aesthetic. A neo-Romantic, blood-based world of illusion was at the core of National Socialism and in the Third Reich art and politics were joined as seldom before in history.[1] For Hitler, the state was a work of art, where political theater was the order of the day. A radical political movement that purported to represent the spirit of the young was in great need of youthful writers to give aesthetic justification to brutal political reality. Möller fit this role remarkably well because he was a true believer and as a result was to become a leading figure in the young National Socialist literary guard.

Möller grew up in Berlin-Charlottenburg. He was the son of the Berlin sculptor Hermann Möller, whose roots lay in rural Thuringia, and his wife, the intellectually gifted Margarete Genschmer, who traced her background to Salzburg settlers in the Warthe River area. After taking his *Abitur* at the Schiller Gymnasium, he studied philosophy and aesthetics at Berlin University under Max Dessoir, a leading Jewish scholar. Möller's prose writings were influenced by E. T. A. Hoffman and Schiller, while his models for poetry included Rilke, Werfel, Rimbaud, and Verlaine. Richard Wagner and especially Gustav Mahler – despite the fact that Mahler was a converted Jew – were enduring musical influences on the

---

[1] For observations on Fascist aesthetics, see Walter Benjamin, *Gesammelte Schriften*, vol. 3 (Frankfurt: Suhrkamp, 1977); Ernst Bloch, *Erbschaft dieser Zeit* (Frankfurt: Suhrkamp, 1962); Saul Friedländer, *Reflections of Nazism. An Essay on Kitsch and Death* (New York: Avon Books, 1982), George L. Mosse, *Masses and Man. Nationalist and Fascist Perceptions of Reality* (Detroit: Wayne State University Press, 1987).

5. Eberhard Wolfgang Möller, at the Height of His Prestige, Berlin 1935. Author's Private Collection.

poet. Möller's innate talent for the writing of drama was traceable to a fascination for Büchner, Hauptmann, Strindberg, Wedekind and Fritz von Unruh. Leading Expressionists – including Georg Kaiser, Reinhard Goering, and Hanns Johst – served as models for him as well, as did the early works by Brecht.

Like so many young intellectuals of the era, Möller passed through a decidedly left-wing phase. Although he was a critic of Karl Marx, nevertheless he became totally absorbed with the writings of the leading founder of anarchism, Mikhail Bakunin. The overriding intellectual influence on Möller, however, was the neoclassicism of Paul Ernst, and he often met with the writer in the latter's twilight years. Möller was drawn not only to the aesthetic principles of Ernst but also to his belief that Germany must be the culture bearer for Europe and the world. Möller's debut directing a production of Ernst's *Chriemhild* at the Prussian State Theater – he was only twenty years old, wrote the accompanying music, and mounted the entire production with a cast of other ambitious student amateurs – cemented their relationship.[2] Upon the death of Ernst in 1933, Möller gave the memorial speech in his honor at the State Theater in Berlin, referring to him extravagantly as the "German Tolstoy." Möller thus assured Paul Ernst, an obscure writer who had been totally overshadowed and mocked by the brilliant panoply of Jewish writers in the liberal golden age of Weimar literature, a place in the National Socialist literary and cultural canon.[3]

Möller's poems, plays, and literary works often lent strangely seductive intellectual accompaniment to National Socialist ideology. He won the National Prize for Literature in 1935 (Stefan George Prize) and was lauded for his play *The Frankenburg Dice Game*, which premiered at the Berlin Olympic Games in 1936. Eleven of his plays were staged in more than two hundred theaters across the Reich in a period of some fifteen years, a remarkable record of success.[4] Yet this reveals only a part of the story. Möller was an uncompromising purist, a modern Icarus who flew far

---

[2] "Kurzer Abriss der Lebensdaten Eberhard Wolfgang Möller," Privatarchiv Eberhard Wolfgang Möller, Bietigheim. See also E. W. Möller to Renate Mouchard, March 17, 1967, ibid.

[3] See, for example, the special issue of the Hitler Youth house organ, *Wille und Macht*, dated May 1938, which was devoted to the memory of Paul Ernst. Möller's nearly reverent attitude toward Ernst was enduring and he continued to publish memorials to him well into the war years. See *Völkischer Beobachter*, May 9, 1943, in which Möller compared Ernst's influence on German culture to that of Goethe.

[4] This information was included in the playbill to Möller's *Das Opfer* (Munich: Langen-Müller, 1941).

too close to the sun. Although regarded as something of a genius by many other writers in the young guard of fascist writers, he was viewed by some in Party and SS circles as an enfant terrible.[5] Although he had reached meteoric heights of success almost overnight, nevertheless over time he was to become persona non grata in Nazi Germany, rejected by the threatened radicals in the political and cultural establishment. After a certain point, his protectors – to some degree Goebbels; Hitler Youth Leader and later Gauleiter of Vienna, Baldur von Schirach; and Rainer Schlösser, who headed the Theater Section of the Propaganda Ministry – could do nothing more for him. Although the documentary record is clouded, there is every reason to believe that determined SS radicals wished to have him done away with during the war. As a result, following the example of others who had made influential enemies, he sought refuge in the Waffen SS as a war reporter. Yet even the field-gray uniform of the SS military elite offered little protection for the fallen angel. An official if erroneous announcement informing the nation of his death was made in September 1944:

> In the fighting on the Western front the young poet
> Eberhard Wolfgang Möller died while serving as an
> SS war reporter. His heroic death came while
> covering the exploits of the 12th Waffen SS Division
> "Hitler Jugend" on the invasion front in Normandy.[6]

Although the details of his life make for fascinating reading, they offer a cautionary tale to gifted cultural figures who are tempted to offer their talents to totalitarian regimes.

Möller's works were diverse in regard to time, place, and historical situation. They ranged from the age of the Roman Republic in *The Fall of Carthage* (1938) to the seventeenth century in *The Frankenburg Dice Game* (1936), from the Struensee saga of the eighteenth century in *The Fall of the Minister* to the Napoleonic era in *Rothschild Victorious at Waterloo* (1934), from the late nineteenth century in *Panama Scandal* (1930) to the battlefields of the Great War in France in *Douaumont* (1929). Whether in

---

[5] Friedrich Wilhelm Hymmen referred to him as "almost a genius" in a personal interview conducted with the author in 1989 in Würzburg. Gerhard Schumann, winner of the National Prize for Literature in 1936, praised him to me highly as well in a series of interviews conducted at his home in Bodman/Bodensee in May 1985.

[6] Dr. Bernhard Payr, Leiter des Amtes Schriftumspflege, NSDAP Berlin, "Kurzin-formationen für die Hauptämter und Ämter," September 1944, Bundesarchiv, NS 15/72, cited in Gerd Simon, *Hitler's Hofdichter*, http://homepages.uni-tuebingen.de/gerd/ChrMoeller.pdf.

his dramatic works, poetry, or radio dramas, Möller always stressed the leitmotifs of heroic behavior within a tragic context, anti-Semitism, and anticapitalism. Above all, he was moved by an all-consuming love of the Germanic Volk, a passion fueled by his devotion to Aryan mysticism. This took the form of a heroic worldview, quite common in the period, but that took on a special cast when rendered by Möller's extraordinary gift for the lyric. Möller hated modernity, which he found symbolized in world Jewry, capitalist greed, and teeming, fetid cities. As might be expected of an artist on the far right, he had little use for reason; rather, he favored the mystic force of the irrational that guided the Germanic spirit in its quest for heroic fulfillment.

Möller was inspired by a belief in the nobility of this vision, and he earnestly desired to play a leading role in the rebirth of German drama. With the coming of the National Socialist revolution, he submitted, fate had endowed writers with a special duty in the life of the nation, which transcended all individual concerns. Henceforth, purely aesthetic considerations must give way to the aesthetics of politics. Creative works were to be written to express the highest ideals of the Nordic racial community in its struggle against all of its enemies, joining ideological beliefs with the religious and cultural longings of the Volk. The result was to be nothing less than a "Germanic confession of faith" in literary form.[7]

Just because Germany possessed a "National Theater," Möller submitted, such a theater did not represent the nation. The transition from Volk to nation required arduous cultural work. The theater must become the educator of the nation, he argued, the nearly divine link to the Germanic spirit. It could no longer remain a cultural cesspool, a stage on which Weimar aesthetes fulfilled their narcissistic longings. Inspired by the great classics, German drama must be reborn, he submitted, because "theater is one of the fundamental vehicles of the human intellect."[8] Thus it was the duty of the writer to give poetic form to the deepest longings and feelings of the German spirit, thereby enabling the masses to transcend their brutal nature and to become the Volk. In turn, the Volk, coming face to face with the higher truth transmitted by their poets, had the potential

---

[7] See Eberhard Wolfgang Möller, "Junges Schrifttum," *Das Deutsche Wort*, 1935, nr. 7. Heinz Grothe observed that "Möller tries to be decidedly political and artistic at the same time. Individuals are not the focus of attention, it is rather higher morality that concerns him. As a result, Möller's works not only have a political effect but they are in fact political" ("Der Dramatiker Eberhard Wolfgang Möller," *General-Anzeiger*, Würzburg, January 22, 1938).

[8] Möller, "Die Wiederauferstehung einer Grossmacht," *Die Bühne*, July 5, 1938.

to become the nation. Poets, like great philosophers before them, must give graphic expression to eternal and absolute truth. Anything less was simply scribbling in the minor key of Weimar – distorted, meaningless, and devoid of all moral value.

Möller's path to National Socialism, like that of many artists, followed an agonized course. There were many twists and turns until, in 1932, having put his left-wing flirtations behind him, he joined the Nazi Party at the urging of his brother, Johann Michael, signing on with the Brown Shirts in Berlin (SA Sturm 113, Standarte 29). Acquaintance with his earliest plays, *Uprising in Carinthia* (1928), *Douaumont* (1929), *California Tragedy* (1930), and *Panama Scandal* (1930), which combined themes of social injustice, capitalist greed, and national and moral weakness, offered no clue as to his future political engagement as a leading Nazi intellectual. Some of them could just as easily have been written by Bertolt Brecht, with whom he shared discussions in the storied cafés of the seductive Friedrichstrasse theater district in Berlin in the late 1920s. Indeed, his biting political satire, *The Fall of Carthage*, shares many anticapitalist themes with Brecht's *The Rise and Fall of the City Mahogany*. What really characterized him were the nearly hysterical, visionary qualities of the revolutionary fantast that he exhibited early on in his career, a zealotry shared not only with Hanns Johst but with the entire corps of pacifist and left-wing Expressionists. During Möller's youth in the 1920s, he flirted with Bakunin's anarchism as well as with modish communism. His play *Douaumont. The Return of the Soldier Odysseus* received considerable attention when it opened in 1929 at the liberal Volksbühne in Prenzlauer Berg in Berlin. Heinrich Neft, who replaced Erwin Piscator as director of the Volksbühne theater, staged *Douaumont* with considerable success. Möller was called to membership in the exclusive PEN Club in 1930 and received favorable attention abroad as a result.[9] *Douaumont* was published in London by Victor Gollancz and was one of the first German plays to be staged in England after World War I.[10]

---

[9] Exhibit 31, correspondence with Thomas Mann regarding his election to the PEN Club, "Eberhard Wolfgang Möller an die Spruchkammer der Interniertenlager," Ludwigsburg, Kornwestheim, May 2, 1948, in Spruchkammer der Interniertenlager, Verfahrensakten des Lagers 76, Hohenasperg, EL 903/4, Vorsignatur J/76/1438, hereinafter cited as Möller, Denazification Records, Staatsarchiv Ludwigsburg.

[10] Early in his career, Möller is said to have had long discussions in the storied cafés of the theater district with Bertolt Brecht and other left-wing writers concerning the state of the dramatic arts and expressionistic literature. See "Kurzer Abriss der Lebensdaten Eberhard Wolfgang Möller," and the letter dated June 6, 1974 from Dr. Heinz Schwitzke

Möller may have been perceived by some critics to be on the left at the outset of his career, but soon enough the political and cultural crisis in postwar Germany drove him into the radical nationalist camp. At a press conference early in the Third Reich, Möller offered this observation about the traumatic effect the lost war and the turmoil of the Weimar Republic had on him and his generation:

> My first psychologically devastating experience took place as
> a result of the World War. It was at a heroes' memorial ceremony
> after the collapse. I was still very young, perhaps sixteen years old.
> At the very time that a minute of silence was declared to honor
> the fallen, the hate-filled song of the *Internationale* shattered the
> sacred stillness of the moment. That was the very second that
> I became a poet, the event which defined my thinking and feeling
> ever after. When I went home very deeply moved after a wild
> pitched battle, I realized that I had to write a memorial work for
> the dead. And that is how my wish later matured, first with my
> *Douaumont* and later *The Letters of the Fallen.*[11]

Douaumont, which fulfilled Möller's need to come to grips with this trauma, represents an unbearable blend of late Expressionist excess, gratuitous nationalism, and overindulgent passion. Named after the most important fortress at Verdun, *Douaumont* was a symbol of the barbarism of the war. The soldier Odysseus returns home after ten years of wandering following the defeat. What he finds there – a decadent homeland – was devastating. After indescribable suffering, he demands the rebirth of Germany, like so many of his fellow front fighters baptized in blood had done before him. The message was clear enough: crass materialism and cultural decadence must be replaced with the heroic spirit of the front generation.

Möller demonstrated his sense for impassioned dramatic effect in the directorial notes appended to the play. He began the work with the first movement of Mahler's Third Symphony, which accompanied glaring searchlights over Fortress Douaumont and a "litany of a living hell, a deafening hurricane of resounding shells striking sandbags, cement, and

---

to Frau Alice Möller, Privatarchiv Möller, Bietigheim. See John Willett, *The Theater of the Weimar Republic* (New York 1988).

[11] See Charlotte Köhn-Behrens, *Berliner Illustrierte*, May 4, 1935, covering an interview with Möller, headlined, "Die Sekunde, da ich Dichter wurde/Der Träger des Nationalbuchpreises 1935 Eberhard Wolfgang Möller erzählt." See also Eberhard Wolfgang Möller, "*Über Douaumont oder Die Heimkehr des Soldaten Odysseus,*" Saarbrückener *Theaterblätter*, Halbmonatsschrift des Stadttheaters Saarbrücken, 1930–1931. See also Herbert Schönfeld, "Eberhard Wolfgang Möllers Dichtung im Deutschunterricht," *Zeitschrift für Deutsche Bildung* 10 (1936), pp. 503–10.

casements, the sickening sweet smell of chlorine, screaming and endless marching." Trumpets resound as a fiery parade of the godforsaken dead passes in review. "Who," Möller noted, "could forget that God held his breath at Douaumont and the pulse of the world stood still in the face of the enormity of the events?"[12]

The play that followed demonstrated that *Douaumont* was a typical example of the emotional *Zeittheater* genre of the late 1920s that was often more devoted to political propaganda than aesthetic considerations.[13] Critics were generally dissatisfied with *Douaumont*. Bernhard Diebold of the *Frankfurter Zeitung* observed that although the play's message was important, it amounted to rebaked Expressionism written by a twenty-three-year-old imitator. *Germania* called it "technically deficient but honest and gripping." On the other hand, the *Berliner Börsenzeitung* referred to it as "a typical first drama by a young writer, but the work of an author who means what he says and we have to listen to him."[14]

Nevertheless, *Douaumont* gave Möller considerable notoriety and as a result he decided to cast his lot with the Nazis. He would take his place among the vanguard of what came to be known as the "fighting poets of the Movement" (*Kampfdichter*), and his star shone brightly in the National Socialist constellation. More and more, the artistic works of radical conservative writers were cast in the spotlight, and Möller was able to ride the crest of this wave.[15] The relatively new medium of radio was particularly well suited to the works of Möller, who knew instinctively how best to blend haunting music with his mysterious works of longing and remembrance. On All Souls' Day 1932, the Deutschlandsender brought *Douaumont* in a radio version, featuring the titanic figure of Heinrich George as the soldier and Maria Koppenhöffer as his mother. This launched Möller's career as one of Germany's leading radio dramatists once the Third Reich was established.[16] Not to be outdone, on the first anniversary of Hitler's assumption of power, no less a figure than

---

[12] Eberhard Wolfgang Möller, *Douaumont oder Die Heimkehr des Soldaten Odysseus* (Berlin 1929), p. 5. See Richard Elsner, ed., *Das Deutsche Drama. Ein Jahrbuch* (Berlin 1929). Möller himself was delighted with the success his play enjoyed with the public. Möller to Hannes Küpper, Stadttheater Essen, June 5, 1929, 7617435/5, DLAM.

[13] See Arno Paul's remarks on the Berlin theater scene in Weimar in Eberhard Roters, ed., *Berlin 1910–1933* (New York: Wellfleet Press, 1982), pp. 206–66.

[14] Roters, pp. 206–66. *Die endlose Strasse*, by Sigmund Graff and Carl Ernst Hintze, enjoyed considerably more popularity than *Douaumont*.

[15] Junge nationalsozialistische Kunst: Der Dichter Eberhard Wolfgang Möller," *Völkischer Beobachter*, October 7, 1933.

[16] See Jan Berg, ed., *Sozialgeschichte der deutschen Literatur von 1918 bis zur Gegenwart* (Frankfurt: Fischer, 1981), p. 243.

Werner Krauss played the role of Bismarck in a radio play titled *The Road to the Reich*, in which Bismarck communes with the spirit of Kaiser Wilhelm I at his grave.

Above all it was Möller's heroic poetry of remembrance of the fallen that catapulted him to fame, because these works at once inspired the young generation, consoled the grieving mothers of the fallen, and gratified the conservative and radical right. Through this creative effort, Möller was able to bring peace to his own soul, so anguished by the turmoil of the postwar era. As he remarked at the time, "It was not only the visible components of our lives which were broken, but more importantly our inner being. The chaos in us young people was a hundred times worse than all the chaos in the world at the time."[17]

Möller's poetic works gave expression to his vision of the spiritual communion of the dead with the living dead. His poem, "Call and Proclamation of the Dead" (1932), announced that the sacrifice of the fallen was not in vain because the dream of the Third Reich would soon become a reality. From afar, the voice from the living shadows cries out and learns that "the great awakener" – Adolf Hitler – had delivered the nation from the nightmare of Weimar, signaling the "first news of the arrival of the Third, the sacred Reich." The dead soldiers form ranks once again in Flanders and begin to march, as the epic youth of Langemarck sing the national anthem, just as they were said to have done in 1914. From the Somme and from Verdun they rise up, from Allenstein and the Masurian Lakes, from the watery depths of the Skagerrak, their faces crowned with seaweed and snails, from the Rumanian forests to the icy Carpathians. The earth begins to quake, as Möller, in poetic outbursts reminiscent of the Romantics, conjures up images of cosmic power:

> and Heaven and Earth cry out with fear,
> as if Judgment Day had begun.

> und Himmel und Erde stöhnt
> vor Angst, als begönne der jüngste Tag zu gewittern.

It was clear that God would show mercy on them on "that day of awakened grace." The lonely mothers joined the marching columns of their dead sons, and they saw God, and God cried. Finally, answering the question of when the spirits of the dead would once again join the nation, Möller's answer was clear: when the shackles of Weimar were broken, the trumpets would sound, and the army "of the strong, the free, and

---

[17] See Möller's notes on *Douaumont* in the *Saarbrücker Theaterblätter 1930–1931*, pp. 42–3.

the heroic" would storm the heights, the fog would clear, and Germany would once more return to herself as the Third Reich was born.[18]

Möller drew variations on the motifs of death and redemption in a remarkably sensitive poem cycle, *The Letters of the Fallen* (1935). In this work, he promised the joy of Easter to a suffering people, a nation longing for confirmation of their faith in the words of Christ that appear on the gate of the Langemarck Memorial Cemetery in Flanders: "I have called you. You are mine." Once again the author developed a counterpoint between objective truth and transcendence, in which realistic letters from fallen soldiers are juxtaposed to fantastic revelations spoken by the chorus. Some of the letters conveyed messages to mothers from their sons who were about to die, final words that cause them indescribable pain:

> My dear mother, you must love
> this poor sand that drank our blood.
> Oh what I wouldn't give, just to hold your
> hand again, to caress it gently just one more time.

> Meine liebe Mutter, diesen armen Sand
> musst du lieben, der mein Leben schlürfte.
> Doch was gäbe ich, wenn ich deine Hand
> einmal noch, nur einmal streicheln dürfte.

Not a watery grave, but instead the beauty of Heaven awaited the fallen, for they like Christ would rise up into eternal life. God awaits them there as they enter the heavenly gates:

> And He arises from his throne in sovereign majesty,
> to look into the face of each and every one,
> while fantastic purple banners wave
> solemnly from the heavenly balconies.

> Und er hebt sich mächtig auf und steigt vom Throne,
> einem jeden in das Angesicht zu sehn,
> während feierlich vom himmlischen Balkone
> ungeheure Purpurbanner wehen.

The Heavenly Realm itself is deeply moved by their heroic nobility, rewarded now with the ultimate fulfillment. There were no limits to Möller's ecstasy when describing this, the signal that mystic reverence once reserved for religious ritual had now been transferred to the state:

> All the bells began to sing their somber song.
> the moon and stars themselves stand still

---

[18] Eberhard Wolfgang Möller, *Berufung der Zeit. Kantaten und Chöre* (Berlin: Theaterverlag A. Langen/G. Müller, 1935), pp. 43–59.

and the heavens, which soar high above them,
sob deeply so overwhelmed were they.

Alle Glocken fangen dunkel an zu singen.
Mond und Sterne selbst verhalten ihren Lauf
und die Himmel, welche sich darüber schwingen,
schluchzen tief und überwältigt auf.

Under what other conditions would foot soldiers be reciting the hymns
of Hölderlin, as the flapping wings of angels could be heard overhead?

The final lines of the chorus offer once more the sweet balm of eternal
life for the young heroes, chanting motifs so often repeated in National
Socialist ritual over the coming years:

> Rest you youths at Langemarck
> and wait for the coming of spring,
> the shifting soil will burst open your caskets
> and the warm wind your grave.
>
> As soon as the clouds form in the east
> and the fields turn green once more
> you will see Germany again
> and the forests for which you died.
>
> Into the gardens, for which you departed,
> you will flower in your ranks
> and summer will sing its song
> of your glory and our gratitude.
>
> Ruhet, ihr Knaben vor Langemarck
> und wartet den Frühling ab,
> die treibende Erde sprengt euern Sarg
> und der warme Wind euer Grab.
>
> Wenn nur die Wolken nach Osten stehn
> und der Acker sich wieder benarbt,
> werdet ihr Deutschland wiedersehn
> und die Wälder, für die ihr starbt.
>
> In den Gärten, für die ihr gingt,
> blüht ihr dann im Gerank
> und der Sommer darüber singt
> euern Ruhm und unsern Dank.[19]

Möller was lionized in the press for these gushing works of mystical effusion which in effect represented National Socialist ideology in
poetic form. Goebbels, in awarding *The Call of Destiny* the National

[19] Ibid., pp. 61–74.

Book Prize in 1935, declared that Möller's poems "transmit an unexpectedly grand richness of visionary images with wonderful clarity of language, admirably coming to grips poetically with the experience of our stirring times."[20] This view was echoed by the National Socialist critics, who praised Möller enthusiastically. Ferdinand Junghans, writing in *Der Angriff*, observed that Möller was a singularly outstanding talent, one who linked a wholehearted revolutionary zeal with a disciplined sense of aesthetic form. The noted critic, Eberhard Meckel echoing this view in the *Deutsche Allgemeine Zeitung*, found the poems to be unforgettable in the way they articulated the feelings of an entire generation.[21] It was also a great source of pride for Reich Youth Leader Baldur von Schirach that the leading poet of the young generation was honored in this way. Schirach was a personal friend of Möller and had earlier named him to an honorary position on his personal staff with the Hitler Youth rank of Oberbannführer. His congratulatory telegram to Möller, which received wide publicity, exclaimed, "Young Germany is proud of you. The recognition of your accomplishments confirms for us all that we are marching down the right road."[22]

Möller was extremely active as a playwright in the Third Reich, a regime that offered him considerable opportunity to develop his ideological and cultural agenda. His works deal almost exclusively with the dominant themes of the National Socialist movement, with heroes and antiheroes, with noble races contending with the ignoble. The world was a battleground on which there was a clear delineation between good and evil. On one hand were the enduring values of the past, a world that featured idealized knightly virtues, where peasant men and women tended the soil in a grand union with nature. Comradeship, order, hierarchy, and loyalty to race and nation offered a political framework in which the human spirit could flower beautifully. Juxtaposed to these shining virtues was the materialist spirit of the times in which wretched capitalist greed, treachery, and guile controlled human behavior. For Möller, the Jews were the incarnation of the modern urban spirit, bearers of a parasitical, destructive cancer working from within the body politic, intent on destroying the healthy Germanic Volk.

---

[20] Sammlung Personen, 7008 Eberhard Wolfgang Möller, BHSA.

[21] *Der Angriff*, May 2, 1935 and *Deutsche Allgemeine Zeitung*, May 8, 1935.

[22] Schirach to Goebbels, May 4, 1935, Sammlung Personen, 7008 Eberhard Wolfgang Möller, BHSA. Schirach's telegram to Möller is found in the *Berliner Tageblatt*, May 2, 1935.

Panama Scandal, staged by the gifted director Heinz Hilpert at the Deutsches Theater in Berlin in 1935, was a vitriolic attack against the corruption of Ferdinand de Lesseps, played by Theodor Loos, whose talents as a swindler and blackmailer epitomized for Möller the French Third Republic. His excesses in the Panama Canal scheme cost the lives of thousands of innocent laborers to malaria while at the same time robbed the savings of 800,000 French shareholders in the venture. Money and materialism had replaced honor in French values. Capitalism had destroyed the moral foundation of a great people, who had long since veered away from the heroic spirit of Charlemagne and Napoleon.[23]

Möller's play, *Rothschild Victorious at Waterloo*, enabled him to launch an all-out assault on the marriage of Jewry and capitalism. No Bolshevik writer ever demonstrated a hatred of capitalism that went deeper than that demonstrated by Möller in this play. Writing in the introduction to his work, he observed scornfully that Jewry represented

> a secret power, swimming in money, a secret third power which made numbers and stock market objects out of people, who sucked profits from living beings like parasites and made money from their blood. That is the meaning of this anecdote about capitalism. It is the anecdote of an entire century, in which money became God, materialism the ideal.[24]

Möller was so certain of Jewish perfidy, so assured that Jewry was at the heart of capitalism, that he went so far as to claim that if the actual event concerning Rothschild's "victory at Waterloo" never occurred, the story would have had to have been invented just the same, so accurately did it reflect the depraved Jewish spirit.

According to this myth, widespread in the nineteenth century, Nathan Rothschild made an illicit fortune in 1815, thus establishing the foundation for the most powerful investment bank in the world, by spreading the false rumor on the floor of the London Stock Exchange that Napoleon had been victorious at Waterloo. Having driven English stock prices down to rock bottom, Rothschild moved in like a shark with massive buy orders. The historian Niall Ferguson has proved beyond a doubt that this

[23] Michael Dillmann, *Heinz Hilpert. Leben und Werk* (Berlin: Akademie der Künste, Edition Hentrich, 1990), p. 436. *Panamaskandal* opened in Berlin on September 19, 1935, and together with the performances in Düsseldorf, was staged thirty-five times. The play had premiered at the height of the financial crisis in Frankfurt in 1930, where it ran for only seven performances. Renate Mouchard, *Der Dramatiker und Ideologe Eberhard Wolfgang Möller*, M.A. Universität Köln, 1967, p. 104.

[24] Eberhard Wolfgang Möller, *Rothschild Siegt bei Waterloo* (Berlin: Theaterverlag Langen-Müller, 1934), pp. 5–8.

anti-Semitic tale was a myth, but he also demonstrated that the House of Rothschild was indeed the central banker for the Allied coalition that was victorious against Napoleon. The Rothschilds had made massive profits in this period, making the market for international bonds, trading in international exchange markets, and acting as the conduit for funds in support not only of the duke of Wellington but for the kingdom of Prussia as well. Further, it is true that the Rothschilds made forays in disguise from their London offices to the Continent in pursuit of profits. The House of Rothschild did learn of Napoleon's defeat fully twenty-four hours before news of it arrived in London through official channels. According to the myth, however, as the defining battle of the Napoleonic era approached, Nathan Rothschild crossed the Channel, made his way to the Waterloo battlefield, conferred with Wellington, concocted his plot, and rushed back to London with the false news. In actual fact, the House of Rothschild lost money during the period 1814–15 – when Napoleon escaped from Elba and called his Grand Army to the colors for one last stand – so unstable had international markets become.

The Rothschild family had come a long way from their days in the squalid Judengasse in Frankfurt. Through their financial genius, they had established leading components of their firm in London, Paris, Frankfurt, and Vienna, thereby establishing the foundation and practices for modern international investment banking. They lived entirely like princes. They were awarded titles, lived in sumptuous palaces and country houses, sported tweeds and even went hunting. Yet there was one major difference. They worked hard for a living! It was against this background that the malicious Waterloo myth, based on envy, fear, and fertile racist imagination, was concocted.[25]

Möller took a great delight in writing *Rothschild Victorious at Waterloo*. He presented the figure of Nathan Rothschild as at once cowardly and cunning. He knew loyalty to no single country but instead focused his attention entirely on an unhealthy lust for profits. With opportunities to make money by operating from sophisticated financial bases in four countries, who after all needed a Fatherland? Passing through the French lines, he stated that his nationality was "neutral" and was proud that Rothschild wire-pullers were placed in all strategic locations throughout Europe. He reminded his agent, O'Pinnel, that he had informers on both sides in the war and boasted that "my money is everywhere, the most amiable great

---

[25] The author is indebted to Professor Niall Ferguson for his superb study titled *The House of Rothschild* (New York: Penguin, 1998), vol. 1, pp. 1–31, 83–110.

power in the world." He let others do his fighting. Why should any Jew have to suffer when the Goyim were so intent on doing their bidding? Stooped and flatfooted, it stood to reason that Nathan was a coward as well, getting only as close as necessary to the actual fighting and cravenly seeking cover behind a hill when he approached a battle zone. Once his conspiracy was carried out, the rumor of the Allied defeat at the hands of Napoleon spread like wildfire through the exchanges, and a "Black Friday" panic ensued. Rubbing his plump hands together, he gloated, "The London Stock Exchange is our Fatherland. We rise and fall with the markets." Möller's satirical vignettes were scathing in their contempt, because Nathan Rothschild fancied himself a field marshal directing a battle from his comfortable position atop a hill of gold. When his massive buy orders were carried out, it was the same as if he had "attacked on a broad front." He was gallant as he "bravely held the line" against his enemies. Why, after all, would a Rothschild die for England when it made so much more sense to "buy for England"?

Möller had a field day appearing at performances of his play, sitting in the high-perched loges, drinking champagne and schmoozing with the Nazi apparatchiki like he was born to intellectual royalty. Such a tale, he submitted, summarized Jewry, observing that it was the kind of story even the gods banqueting in Valhalla were wont to recount among themselves – half seriously and half in jest – reflecting as it did the meanspiritedness and shameful conduct of mortals. The Nathan Rothschild that emerged in the play was a coward, even if terribly clever, in his insatiable pursuit of money. He was very conscious of the new power and prestige of his family and firm. His Waterloo triumph was profitable indeed, but in the end, he was left entirely alone with his millions, an isolated, melancholy moral outcast on the unforgiving stage of history. He was less to be held in contempt than to be pitied.[26]

Rothschild Victorious at Waterloo enjoyed a long run after its premiere in Weimar at the prestigious National Theater, where it was directed by Hans Severus Ziegler. The *Völkischer Beobachter*, the Nazi Party organ, praised the work highly, submitting that "it represented the National Socialist program in artistic form."[27] It was a major feature of the Reich Theater Festival Week in Munich in 1936 as well, where a performance

---

[26] Karl-Heinz Schoeps, *Literature and Film in the Third Reich* (Rochester: Camden House, 2004) pp. 142–4.

[27] See "Junge nationalsozialistische Kunst: Der Dichter Eberhard Wolfgang Möller," *Völkischer Beobachter*, October 7, 1934.

was attended by both Hitler and Goebbels.[28] Herbert Frenzel, a leading member of the editorial staff of Goebbels's Berlin organ, *Der Angriff*, compared Möller's talents as a satirist to Aristophanes and Jonathan Swift. He found the play to be a brilliant interpretation of the Jewish mind, quite different from Shakespeare's tragic figure of Shylock. Möller's *Rothschild*, he submitted, was less an emotional propagandistic assault on Jewry than an illumination of the disturbing and utterly isolated situation in which Nathan found himself. In a pungent style reminiscent of the period of struggle, Frenzel judged this isolation to be wholly justified, indeed "a necessary and entirely deserved isolation due to the parasitical Jewish world view, now given a sentence of damnation by the higher principle of justice in the world. Rothschild is a prototype, a representative of the spirit which directs him, mirroring capitalism for the sake of capitalism."[29]

With the production of Möller's *The Frankenburg Dice Game*, which was staged in the Dietrich Eckart Theater at the Berlin Olympic Games in August 1936, Möller reached the height of his success as a playwright in the Third Reich. The work was significant on many fronts, most notably because in barely camouflaged form, it showcased the German claim to pursue the *Anschluss* with Austria and offered justification for the later conquest and colonization of Eastern and Southeastern Europe. Produced in the new outdoor theater in the Olympic complex, the author was clearly embracing theatrical and religious forms in wide use in late medieval Europe. What had earlier served the Catholic Church – the use of choral ensembles and liturgical, mysterious, and supernatural themes – now took on a wholly new form. It had the further effect of significantly advancing Hitler Youth liturgical forms. Married to National Socialist ideology, designed to illuminate the alleged union of justice and morality with the sovereign state, and played outdoors at night under the stars, *The Frankenburg Dice Game* represented the *Thingspiel* program in its most sophisticated form.[30]

---

[28] Oberregierungsrat Leopold Gutterer, Propaganda Ministry, "Exposé über die wichtigsten Veranstaltungen während der Reichstheaterfestwoche in München," Privatarchiv Möller, Bietigheim. Möller was explicit in his instructions submitted to theater directors staging his productions. See "E. W. Möller to Direktor Otto Falckenberg of the Kammerspiele in Munich," May 8, 1936, ibid. Compare George Mosse, "Nazi Polemical Theater: The *Kampfbühne*," *Masses and Man*, pp. 219–20.

[29] Herbert A. Frenzel, *Eberhard Wolfgang Möller*, Reihe Künder und Kämpfer (München: Deutscher Volksverlag, 1938), pp. 12–13.

[30] Möller to Michael Dultz, Erlangen, March 11, April 6, May 14, and October 15, 1965, Privatarchiv Möller, Bietigheim.

The National Socialist *Thingspiel* as a theatrical form for German national drama was conceived by Reich Theater Dramaturgist Rainer Schlösser, Baldur von Schirach, and Möller early in 1934 at a private meeting in Schlösser's villa in Berlin. Its curious name stems from the days of the Germanic tribes, when clan members gathered in sacred assembly ("Ding") to make a judgment on an issue of great importance. In the Third Reich, great importance was placed on the *Thingspiel* as strictly outdoor theater, where *völkisch* affirmations, deliberations, and judgments could be made in a natural setting. Goebbels, for the time being, supported the concept of the *Thingspiel*, reassured when Party intellectuals such as Möller were involved. The Minister was partial to Möller, one of the court favorites whom he had summoned early on to work in the Theater Section of the Propaganda Ministry. Not only was Möller totally committed to National Socialist ideology, he was a fellow intellectual whom Goebbels judged to have "a remarkable genius for language." When they learned of the forerunners who served as models for *The Frankenburg Dice Game* – Möller had credited Euripides's *Orestes*, *Die Bürger von Calais* by Georg Kaiser, and Stravinsky's *Oedipus Rex* as influences on him – even his enemies knew they were dealing with a playwright of real format. Goebbels's trust would not be misplaced, and he noted in his diary that

> Off to the Dietrich Eckart Theater this evening: *The Frankenburg Dice Game*. Except for a couple of choruses it was monumental. Language exudes passion, clarity, and wit. Grand images. I am terribly impressed by it.[31]

What Goebbels witnessed on the Olympic stage under the stars that August night was a blend of classical Greek form and political mystery play, tailored to Nazi racist principles and a zeal for expansion to the East. This was not at all by chance, because the minister himself months before had requested that Möller present several possible themes to him worthy of featuring at the Olympic Games, and he had chosen this one. The production was directed by the noted actor Mathias Wiemann and featured moving original choral music composed by Rudolf Schulz-Dornburg. Seldom have right and wrong been so graphically staged in a work of political theater, in this case featuring a divine judgment of a horrible crime against Protestant Austrian peasants. In the writing of

---

[31] Entry for August 3, 1936, *Die Tagebücher von Joseph Goebbels*, ed. Elke Fröhlich, vol. 2, p. 600.

this play, Möller was influenced greatly by his own family background, at once Protestant, agricultural, Thuringian, and Lutheran. A trial was held in which the highest authorities in the Austrian Catholic Counter-Reformation during the Thirty Years War – the Habsburg emperor Ferdinand II, and Duke Maximilian of Bavaria, the imperial representative in Upper Austria, Adam von Herbersdorf, as well as the Jesuit papal functionaries Wilhelm Lamoraini and Carlos Caraffa III, drunk with incense – are finally brought before the court of world justice. Even today on the Hammersfeld in Upper Austria a memorial reminds witnesses of the horrors that took place there in 1625. On that field, thousands of deceived Austrian peasants had gathered, having responded to a promise of amnesty for their alleged misdeeds. They were an oppressed class that, in an aborted effort to better their miserable economic conditions and servile status, had taken up the revolutionary banner against their feudal overlords in a totally misguided, if understandable, misinterpretation of Luther's Reformation principles. Sixteen of their number lost the throw of the dice and were immediately hanged, their body parts later nailed to church doors in an effort to stamp out the incipient revolutionary spirit in all the provinces of Austria.

With this historical raw material to work with, Möller was in his element. He set about creating a nationalist high mass. In a play that embodied the apogee of the *Thingspiel* movement, he launched a poetic assault on three hundred years of Catholic and Habsburg abuse of Teutonic-blooded Austrian peasants. One by one they become witnesses for the prosecution The farmer Michael Paur intoned the lines that conveyed the heart of Möller's message, saying:

Even if they hang us from the church towers, we will become lanterns, beacons in the night of despair for our grandsons. We will become banners which never are torn to shreds. In some distant day we will inflame passions once more, taking revenge on those who damned us and vindicate the world with our blood.

Tobias Strohmaier answered in words denoting that loyalty was eternal, saying, "In the century that was faithless and disloyal, we had a band that was loyal to the death." Again and again, just as in the great classic past, the chorus chanted lines of truth, proclaiming: "God, you are wonderful, you sacrifice your blood for humanity and die, that we might live."

The peasantry in a thinly veiled affirmation of Hitler's designs on his Austrian homeland, affirmed their cry for freedom, almost two hundred years before the protagonist of Beethoven's *Fidelio* demanded that he, too, must be set free:

> We aren't children and beggars any longer, we are a new people,
> a new army. We are one will and have one demand. In the name of
> God we will finally free ourselves from all corruption, oppression
> and tyranny.

In a final scene, a mysterious representative of divine justice, clothed in black, appeared, forcing the defendants, one by one, to throw the dice themselves to atone for their crimes. First the Emperor Ferdinand was damned for all time for nailing his people to the Cross. Next, Duke Maximilian was humiliated for his crimes, as the smug power-driven Jesuits were sentenced to spend eternity with the Devil. In the finale, foretelling Nazi *Anschluss* propaganda less than two years later, the peasants thank God for their deliverance from murder, injustice, and tyranny. The Volk had been fulfilled and God reigned supreme once more not only in heaven but on earth as well.[32]

Möller himself went to great lengths to reflect on the meaning of his play for the contemporary world. The notes he wrote for the printed programs could have been conceived by Goebbels himself, to wit:

> An event of this consequence cannot be forgotten. The old saying
> that "world history is the world court" is valid today if a people has
> the strength and courage to act as judge and to carry out the sentence
> of eternal justice. For three hundred years the victims of this unnatural
> act of brutality have been crying out for justice. The Third Reich of the
> Germans is powerful enough to hear their plea and to demand that the
> evildoers face a court of law. Even if the dead must arise from their
> graves. Then this play has to be more than just a play. The court of
> today will judge the past and the people will judge their enemies.
> The entire Volk sits as a court. We all will listen, judge, and together
> announce our sentence.[33]

The Frankenburg Dice Game enjoyed a long life in the traditional nationalist passion play repertoire. One garners some sense of the

[32] Eberhard Wolfgang Möller, *Das Frankenburger Würfelspiel* (Berlin: Langen-Müller, 1936). For analyses of the play, see Glen Gadberry, *E. W. Möller and the National Drama of Nazi Germany: A Study of the Thingspiel and of Möller's Das Frankenburger Würfelspiel*, M.A., University of Wisconsin, 1972; Günther Rühle, *Zeit und Theater. Diktatur und Exil, 1933–1945*, vol. 3, pp. 778–93; Schoeps, pp. 153–8.

[33] E. W. Möller, program notes for *Das Frankenburger Würfelspiel*, "under the patronage of Reichsminister für Volksaufklärung Dr. Goebbels und Reichsjugendführer von Schirach," *Das Theater der Jugend*, 1937–8 season, Archiv, Akademie der Künste, Berlin.

importance it had by recalling the Erfurt staging in August 1937, in which
a thousand amateur actors participated in a production mounted on the
steps of the Erfurt Cathedral. There, deep in storied Luther territory, some
seven hundred organizations participated in the planning along with the
Party, the Brown Shirts, Hitler Youth, and the League of German Girls
(BDM), not to mention the Work Front, fraternities, and the historical
costume societies. This clearly was an event for the entire Volk, with an
eye to the annual outdoor performances of Hugo von Hofmannsthal's
Everyman in Salzburg as a successful model of the genre. Hans Joachim
Sobanski wrote a new musical score for the occasion, which featured
"Musikzugführer and Brown Shirt leader Boerner" conducting a spirited
performance by his "Singing Storm, SA Brigade 42."[34]

Nazi bureaucrats who were offended with the seeming religiosity of
The Frankenburg Dice Game and Möller's other works began to become
restive and even resentful of him. At the same time, the author began
boldly to cast judgment on the corruption, stupidity, and arrogance of
many Party members at both the national and local levels, a situation
that troubled him deeply. The cultural vacuousness of so many in the
Nazi leadership corps made him increasingly cynical. As a result, a caustic
irony began to permeate his writing. Möller did not suffer fools gladly,
and he began to make many enemies among Party radicals, a situation that
would come to haunt him. Möller had so alienated Karl Cerff, an official
in the educational wing of the Hitler Youth leadership, that he caused
a scandal at the first Reich Theater Week of the organization staged in
Bochum in the summer of 1937. Cerff, who could counter no opposition,
had met his match in Möller and, to punish him, sent harassment squads
of protesting Hitler Youths to Möller's hotel, where they sang choruses
of songs mocking the poet.[35]

Matters became worse for Möller following the Hamburg premiere of
his play *The Fall of Carthage*, which was the centerpiece of the 1938 Reich
Theater Week of the Hitler Youth. These annual conclaves of youth were
enthusiastically sponsored by both von Schirach and Schlösser. In this play,
Möller once more turned to history to teach a contemporary moral lesson.
Möller's Carthage emerged as a soulless capitalistic state, ruled by greedy
Jews and imperialists, who, having enslaved the indigenous peoples of
much of North Africa, were intent on controlling the entire Mediterranean

[34] *Kulturdienst der NSKG* 6, 45/46, pp. 2–3, Institut für Zeitgeschichte, Munich, MA 679.
[35] Friedrich W. Hymmen, "Zur Entlastung des Schriftstellers E. W. Möller," August 11,
1947, Möller, Denazification Records, Staatsarchiv Ludwigsburg.

basin as well. Devoid of character and any noble qualities – concepts of race and love of the soil were allegedly foreign to them – they were solely concerned with the accumulation of wealth. Gold, not blood, ran through their veins. A bloated capitalist state such as this stood no chance whatsoever pitted against the Roman Republic, where Marcus Portius Cato led a heroic nation of soldiers and farmers.[36]

Möller's negative references to the Weimar Republic were frequent, whereas his attacks on weaknesses in the Third Reich were treated with more subtlety. Herr Professor Lysipp Hüleios, general secretary of the League for Human Rights, was featured as a brazen caricature of Weimar pacifists and left-leaning internationalists. His assault on Baat Baal, a rich, bloated hedonist and libertine, might well have camouflaged an attack on the lifestyle of Hermann Göring and other decadent Nazi leaders. The author's language was devastating, reflecting the hatred and intolerance of the era. One of the characters assailed those individuals and institutions in the Third Reich whom Möller felt had betrayed the National Socialist revolution, lamenting in a devastating outburst:

> The timid ones and the bootlickers, the paper shufflers and
> bureaucrats, the secretaries too and the chancelleries of high
> treason, the parliamentary deputies, the ministers, who are
> none at all and instead filled their pockets, then the editors,
> the newspaper scribblers, the writers of fraud, the big timers
> and the rich Jewish horse traders, the market makers, apostles of
> capitalism, the entire army of scoundrels.[37]

Fighting nobly against weakness and avarice, some Carthaginians demonstrated valor. The Roman field commander, Scipio, regarded Hasdrubal as a hero and a brave adversary in battle, a leader who understood that a proper death guaranteed immortality. What could demonstrate that more graphically than Hasdrubal's dying words, that "death must be sweeter than love." The hero's mother, recalling the brave warriors of Sparta, became a handmaiden to immortality, urging her son to enter the "Reich of the Dead" in one heroic last stand:

> What a thousand years could not destroy will not pass away
> in a thousand years; and the ocean will sing restlessly, the winds
> will sing, and all the hills of graves will sing of your fall,
> my son, my hero.[38]

---

[36] Eberhard Wolfgang Möller, *Der Untergang Karthagos* (Berlin: Theaterverlag Langen-Müller, 1938).

[37] Ibid., pp. 105–6.   [38] Ibid., p. 137.

There is no question that by highlighting the sacrifice motif, Möller was appealing to the Nazi leadership corps to return once more to the spirit of the period of struggle on the route to power. True historical greatness, he affirmed, always demanded a blood sacrifice of the best of the racial community.

Möller *Fall of Carthage* had offended countless Party members and representatives of Party organizations, who felt that they had been pilloried personally. Several rather nasty incidents ensued in some theaters, where loud barking in the Party kennels was heard. Gauleiter Robert Wagner of Baden ostentatiously walked out of a performance of the play in Karlsruhe, a protest that Goebbels felt to be unjustified.[39] Schirach himself, however, had set the tone for this development in the introductory remarks he delivered to the Hitler Youth on the evening of the premiere of *The Fall of Carthage* in which he attacked the opportunism of many writers in the Third Reich, calling them "market writers interested only in money, who have made clichés of the great appeals of the movement and who have mixed an unpalatable gruel with their drivel." These writers were admonished to follow Möller's example, to understand that "the theater in Germany today is a great moral teacher." It was the duty of writers to strengthen the youth of Germany in their devotion to the nation.[40] Herbert Frenzel of *Der Angriff* was unforgiving as well, and far from limiting his criticism only to writers headlined his review of the Hamburg premiere with the admonition, "A Drama That Has to Do with All of Us."[41] Guilty Party members were quite justified in perceiving that Möller had specifically targeted them in his revolutionary political drama.

The Fall of Carthage occasioned a heated controversy within the Nazi Party, and the echo could be heard in Paris and as far away as the Soviet Union. Liberal writers and other émigrés, gathered abroad in their cafés and watering holes of despair, relished the difficulties that "SA Man Möller" had caused the Party, and joyfully drew variations on the themes Möller had showcased. One of the most interesting commentaries appeared in *The Word*, published in Moscow and edited by none other than Bertolt Brecht, Lion Feuchtwanger, and Willi Bredel. Maria Leitner, writing from Paris, was astounded with the play, writing that even the

[39] Goebbels, diary entry, November 3, 1938, *Die Tagebücher von Joseph Goebbels. Sämtliche Fragmente*, ed. Elke Fröhlich, vol. 3, p. 528.
[40] Jürgen Petersen, *Berliner Tageblatt*, October 24, 1938. For other reviews, see Günther Stöve, *Völkischer Beobachter*, October 25, 1938; Max von Brück, *Frankfurter Zeitung*, February 4, 1939.
[41] *Der Angriff*, October 25, 1938.

youngest little Hitler Youth was "bug-eyed" to witness the "deceptive liar" Möller grappling with themes of corruption that had clearly gotten away from him. Unwittingly or not, the author was not focusing on Romans and Carthaginians at all. Instead, he was holding up the "spiritually rotten and morally bankrupt leaders of the Third Reich for ridicule." To cite but one example, she opined that anyone could see that the rich, fat and decadent Carthaginian businessman Baat Baal was a stand in for Hermann Göring. Hitler's Third Reich, Leitner submitted, would be destroyed from within just as had Carthage.[42] The message of the play was clear enough. The Third Reich was doomed to destruction if it stayed on its present path.

Möller's troubles began in earnest with the publication of *Der Führer*, which von Schirach had commissioned him to write in 1938. What began as something modest – the Reich Youth Leader's desire to present each Hitler Youth with a biography of Hitler as a Christmas gift – occasioned a barrage of criticism from Alfred Rosenberg. Rosenberg was a pompous troublemaker and busybody who took his role as Hitler's designated gatekeeper and ideological high priest very seriously. Möller had offended him early on and made no secret whatsoever – both openly and in private – of the fact that he considered him to be a fool and pseudo-intellectual. On the other hand, Rosenberg referred to Möller as a cultural Bolshevik, a front man for the Catholic Action, a spiritual brother of Otto Dix, Georg Grosz, and Bertolt Brecht and the entire gaggle of Weimar communist intellectuals whose day had past once and for all. Rosenberg, in league with such second-rate minds on his staff as the "literature pope" Helmuth Langenbucher, counterattacked forcefully and not without effect. Their bitterness was all the more acidic because Möller had not submitted the book before publication to the small minds on the Margareten Strasse to receive the requisite stamp of approval of their Party office.

Der Führer had hardly seen the light of day when Rosenberg dispatched a thirty-page memo of complaints to Hitler. In this lengthy and turgid missive, Rosenberg tore into Möller ferociously, calling his work a totally unacceptable book, unfaithful to the greatness of the Führer and of the movement. It would not appeal to its youthful audience, being a showy,

---

[42] Maria Leitner, "SA Mann Möller schildert Untergang," *Das Wort. Literarische Monatsschrift* III (1939), pp. 142–3. There is evidence to suggest that Maria Leitner, a Jewish journalist in Weimar Berlin then living as an émigré in Paris, wrote this piece while making one of her bold undercover returns to Germany. The clarity and presentation of her outstanding report certainly point to this possibility.

self-indulgent exercise by its author in a shallow attempt to parade his intellect before the world. It would go over the head of 90 percent of them. Nor was it written in the spirit of National Socialism at all; instead, its very language exuded the "Christian stench of Franciscan monkery." In describing the defining moment of the movement – the abortive march to the Feldherrnhalle in Munich in November 1923 – Möller had not only employed the vision of Mary, Mother of God, looking down sadly from her perch at the Wittelsbach Palace overlooking the bloodied asphalt of the Odeon Square, but even worse, the poet had "Old Testament cherubs" wringing their hands over the Immortals. This tastelessness, he submitted, was nothing more than "overheated kitsch." Rosenberg suggested to Hitler that he order the book to be completely rewritten and to be checked for accuracy in every detail. He simultaneously informed the Führer Adjutancy that he had requested that Reichsleiter Max Amann, director of the Party Central Publishing House (Franz Eher), not to publish more copies of the work until a decision was forthcoming from the Führer.[43]

The response from the Führer Headquarters was not at all what its author expected, lending credence to Möller's contention that his enemies within the SS were always more dangerous to him than those made because of Rosenberg's vendetta against him.[44] Reichsleiter Philipp Bouhler, SS Obergruppenführer and chief of the Führer Chancellery, responded to Rosenberg, noting that the difficulties could have been avoided had the manuscript been submitted for approval before publication to his office, which the deputy Führer, Rudolf Hess, had designated to be responsible for all works dealing with the history of National Socialism. Both the publisher and Möller had already agreed to rework the book with the authorities in the Party Publications Commission to correct the necessary errors of fact and judgment. But he went on to point out that "the charges, so far as they are justified, are not so grave that they should have occasioned such a sharp tone of criticism contained in the memo. I am gratified that the memo has been withdrawn, which I surmise, must have originated among people in your own Publications Office, who in my opinion betray their prejudice against Möller, which in no way is justified

---

43 Rosenberg to die Adjutantur des Führers, "Der Weihnachtsbuch der deutschen Jugend unter dem Titel 'Der Führer' geschrieben von Eberhard Wolfgang Möller," December 15, 1938, Joseph Wulf, *Literatur und Dichtung im Dritten Reich* (Gütersloh: Sigbert Mohn, 1963), pp. 206–11.
44 Heinz Schwitzke to Alice Möller, February 6, 1974, Privatarchiv Möller, Bietigheim. Schwitzke pointed to the SS as Möller's most dangerous enemy: "At least," he wrote, "that is what he told me at the time."

considering the character of the writer."[45] Rosenberg was quite offended by Bouhler's letter and let him know in no uncertain terms that he found the charge of prejudice in his *Amt Schriftumspflege* totally unacceptable.

Rosenberg was determined not to let the matter drop, and he continued to stir up animosity toward the poet at the highest levels of the SA command. SA chief of staff Viktor Lutze wrote to Rosenberg, demanding that the book be withdrawn.[46] Lutze complained that von Schirach was also furious with the harsh treatment Möller meted out to the Brown Shirts concerning the events leading up to the Night of Long Knives in June 1934, charging that Möller's sweeping judgment put the SA in the same category as the Bolsheviks. Möller had defamed the entire SA in such an unspeakable manner, he claimed, that words could not properly convey the stench.[47] Schirach gingerly answered Ernst Röhm's successor, promising that he would have the opportunity to make changes in the edited copy of the next edition of *Der Führer*. Möller meant no harm, he claimed, and had worked from the sources carefully. He had done nothing more than to quote the very words Goebbels used to explain to the nation about Ernst Röhm's conspiracy.[48]

As the months dragged on, the affair began to take on a life of its own. To protect his flanks, Bouhler turned to Rudolf Hess to ask his opinion of the matter. Hess in turn made it clear that he thought Hitler should make the decision. In a vignette reminiscent of the comic opera, Max Amann insisted that he would not submit an edited copy of Möller's book to Bouhler's Party Publications Commission if the "little sausages" in Rosenberg's literature bureaucracy were to be involved. And there the matter rested. Over half a million copies of *Der Führer* were already in circulation, and there was considerable demand for another printing. At a time when Germany was occupying Czechoslovakia and Hitler was preparing for war, four of the Third Reich's Reichsleiters – the highest ranking Nazis – refused to address the issue further. The affair may have been forgotten, but there was to be no second edition of *Der Führer*.

---

[45] Philipp Bouhler, Chef, Kanzlei des Führers to Rosenberg, January 18, 1939, copies to Stellvertreter des Führers, Reichsjugendführer, and Zentralparteiverlag, Berlin, Akten der Parteikanzlei der NSDAP, Institut für Zeitgeschichte, Munich.

[46] Stabschef SA Lutzte to Rosenberg, Tgb. Nr. 257/39. VIII/83, January 10, 1939, Records of the Reichsministerium für den besetzten Ostgebiete, T-454, Roll 75, 000610, NA.

[47] Stabchef Lutze to von Schirach, January 12, 1939, BA NS 11/23a, cited in Gerd Simon, Hitlers Hofdichter, http://homepages.uni-tuebingen.de/gerd/ChrMoeller.pdf. Bormann let it be known that during the war changes in publication policies were neither to be discussed nor proposed. Bormann to Bouhler, November 1, 1939, ibid.

[48] Schirach to Lutze, January 13, 1939, BA NS 11/23a, ibid.

Möller had stirred up a hornet's nest with his provocative manner, and he began to pay the price for his arrogance. He made this clear in a letter to the Paul Rose, director of the Rose Theater in gritty Friedrichshain, Horst Wessel's old Berlin neighborhood of Berlin:

> I want to thank you and your wife for your greetings and good wishes. It was very gratifying right now, at a time when I am sick to death of the hostility, suspicions and curses aimed at me, a mixed brew of envy, misunderstanding and ignorance, and I was in real need of some encouragement from good friends.[49]

Möller had just begun to feel the pain from the unrelenting attacks that lesser minds among his enemies had in store for him. An indication of the depth of hatred toward Möller can be divined from a remark Rosenberg made about him to a group of ranking Party officials at a luncheon in connection with one of his many speaking tours during the war. Referring to *Der Führer*, he denounced the book saying that "this botched up work was written with no respect. Möller can't write about the Führer because he has no spiritual link to him. Möller isn't a National Socialist at all, that's the heart of the matter."[50]

Nevertheless, Möller persevered in what he considered to be his mission – to interpret National Socialism for the ages. He made this clear in a Leipzig address to a Hitler Youth memorial conclave for his favorite author in the Germanic Pantheon, the late Paul Ernst. Writers were called on, he observed, to serve in a very special way. They were assigned the most important role in the service of Hitler, because Providence had placed on their shoulders the obligation to define the "spiritual space" of the German people. As a result, it was the duty of writers to cast the national mission in an "ennobling aesthetic form," thus opening the way to "inner freedom and spiritual peace." This was the true meaning, he submitted, of the poetic truth taught by August von Platen when he wrote that "the lamps of heaven will go out when the last poet dies."[51] It takes little

---

[49] Möller to Direktor Paul Rose, Rose Theater, Berlin, January 12, 1939, Eberhard Wolfgang Möller File, DLAM.

[50] Friedrich W. Hymmen, "Zur Entlastung des Schriftstellers E. W. Möller," August 11, 1947, Eberhard Wolfgang Möller File, Spruchkammer der Interniertenlager, Verfahrensakten des Lagers 76, Hohenasberg 1946–1953, EL 903/4, 205, J/76/1438, Staatsarchiv Ludwigsburg, hereinafter cited as Möller, Denazification Records, Staatsarchiv Ludwigsburg.

[51] Möller, "Darum sind Dichter im Volk!," "Rede bei der Paul Ernst Feierstunde der HJ am 11. Mai 1939 während der Reichstagung der Paul Ernst Gesellschaft in Leipzig," *Die Neue Literatur*, July 1939, pp. 329–39.

imagination to understand that Möller's Olympian ideas were far removed from the Reich's mission as it was conceived by Hitler and Himmler as they prepared to move into action with the coming of the war in 1939.

Ironically, it was the war that offered Möller the proper structure to develop completely his conceptualization of the mission of the poet, because it was only through war that the optimal fusion of power and intellect could be fulfilled. In a definitive essay written in 1941, he contended that the Third Reich had offered the nation the singular opportunity to achieve moral greatness through Germanic tragedy. With the coming of World War II, the way was open for the creative genius of the nation to transcend the material and to be ennobled in what he termed "tragic world feeling." What had been denied to Schiller could now be fulfilled in German drama, that is, to rise to the heights of tragedy that only myth can reveal. In a theoretical construct clearly influenced by Hegel's concept of dialectical idealism, the author posited that

> A people can only live if it is a nation. It is a nation when it possesses culture. It has culture when it consciously expresses itself, its nature and its duty as a people. It discovers this consciousness in its national literature. Tragedy is the consummate literary form. Tragic form is realized when the writer fulfills the will to form which is embedded unconsciously in the soul of the people. The heart of tragedy is the *völkisch* myth, and if there is no living myth in the Volk then it is not possible to have tragedy. Commensurately, tragedy is impossible if the poet and his era do not possess tragic world feeling. It follows that the premise for tragedy is the tragic experience of the world.[52]

What exactly was the nature of this tragic life experience, and how could it be found? It could only be discovered in war, he submitted, observing that war was at once the source and fulfillment of all life. War was the essence of Germany's "tragic world feeling," the true meaning for its existence. Fate had thus endowed Greater Germany with an epic mission of destiny at precisely that point in her history.

Freed from the shackles in which the Nazi bureaucracy attempted to tether him, Möller now felt himself liberated, called once again to commune with heroes. In his poem, "The Duty of the Poet," written during the Battle of France, he rhapsodized that myth had been reborn, now

---

[52] Eberhard Wolfgang Möller, "Die Deutsche Tragödie," notes appended to his play, *Das Opfer* (Berlin: Theaterverlag Langen-Möller, 1941).

that the warrior gods had returned as teachers of men. Poets too were delivered from their blindness and were empowered to approach that place:

> in whose halls the heroes are gathered which after victory in battle resound with festive music and the peoples' celebration.

> And the poet is enthralled as in days of yore sitting among the scarred warriors at high table as the long-awaited arises. Reverence however and devotion

> Go before him, the destroyers of ignorance, and in sacred speech he conjures up the great secrets, that the gods have confided in him and uttering prophecies for the future,

> That he once more divines as poets did from the beginning of time, the better to entwine the noble immortal dead and the brows of the living with the golden wreaths of glory.

> Wo im Saale die Helden stehen und Festmusik nach gewonnener Schlacht tönt zur frohen völkischen Feier.

> Und der Dichter begeistert wie im einstiger Zeit unter den Narbenbedeckten sitzend am hohen Tisch aufsteht, der lang Erwartete, Ehrfurcht aber und Andacht

> Gehn vor ihm her, die Niederzwinger des Unverstands, und mit heiliger Rede hebt er Geheimes an, das ihm die Gottheit vertraut und der Zukunft raunende Boten,

> Dass er des Amtes wieder walte von Anbeginn, zu umwinden der edlen Toten Unsterbliches und auch der Lebenden Stirn mit des Ruhmes goldenen Kränzen.[53]

Möller was soon enough swept out of the billowy clouds of his Nordic fantasies when he was called on as a consultant and scriptwriter for the notorious anti-Semitic blockbuster film, *Jud Süss*.[54] Here the opportunity

---

[53] Eberhard Wolfgang Möller, *Die Maske des Krieges* (Berlin: Verlag Die Heimbücherei, 1941), pp. 7–8.

[54] In the summer of 1939, Möller had signed a contract with Terra Filmkunst Production to deliver a manuscript for *Jud Süss* based on a script written by Ludwig Metzler and

presented itself for him to gain an entrée into the lucrative world of film writing, but there were few decisions that he would later regret as much as this in later years. This film became the iconic Nazi anti-Jewish cinema production, beloved by both Goebbels and Himmler and enthusiastically viewed by more than twenty million people during World War II. Considering the heated controversy about this film – even Lion Feuchtwanger protested from his plush California villa, certain that his best-selling novel *Jud Süss* (1922) had been plagiarized – it is important that its true authorship be traced. As so often in history, following the money trail can be instructive. The original script was written by an obscure film writer, Ludwig Metzler, and Möller was paid a paltry RM 5,000 to improve the script. Goebbels was not pleased with the outcome and turned instead to the flashy young director Veit Harlan, who entirely rewrote the script, receiving RM 25,000 for his efforts. Harlan was upset that Möller's name was included in the byline, because he insisted on writing the scenarios for films that he directed. Known for his arrogance and vanity, Harlan protested, complaining to Goebbels: "Is it really necessary to adorn the byline with the names of extraneous writers?"[55] Goebbels, however, did not back down, and continued to feature Möller's name to keep peace in his literary stables.[56]

Jud Süss drove home the theme of Jewish perfidy in a remarkably cruel manner. Released in 1940, Harlan went over the top in his production, exaggerating alleged Jewish stereotypes of stealth, cunning, greed, lust,

---

delivered the manuscript soon thereafter, on August 31, 1939. See "Normalvertrag für das Film-Drehbuch," Terra Filmkunst G.M.B.H., Babelsberg, July 21, 1939, Privatarchiv Möller, Bietigheim.

[55] Alice Möller, addendum to document, Möller to "Dr. Flügel," Berlin, July 20, 1964, Privatarchiv Möller, Bietigheim.

[56] Goebbels wrote in his diary entry for December 15, 1939, "Studied the manuscript for the Jud Süss film. It is much better now. It was beautifully transformed by Harlan. This will become the anti-Semitic film." *Die Tagebücher von Joseph Goebbels*, vol. 3, p. 666. No less a figure than Werner Krauss, one of the stars of the film, attested that he had no idea whatsoever that Möller was involved in the project. The title page from the *Jud Süss* scenario from which he worked – and still in his possession – stated simply, "Jud Süss, ein historischer Film, Regie: Veit Harlan" (Werner Krauss, Scharfling am Mondsee, to Ministerium für politische Befreiung Württemberg-Baden, Abteilung Interniertenlager, z.H. des Herrn Obersten Klägers, August 1948, Möller, Denazification Records, Staatsarchiv Ludwigsburg). According to the denazification court judgment, Möller's work on the *Jud Süss* manuscript was "insignificant, only a critical editing of the film's dialogue, which was true to the historical facts" (see "Spruch," Spruchkammer d. Int. Lager, May 12, 1948, J/76/1438, Möller, Denazification Records, Staatsarchiv Ludwigsburg).

exploitation, and cowardice.[57] In this film, the motif of miscegenation –
Rassenschande – was married to Jewish putrefaction. Ferdinand Marian,
who played Joseph Süss-Oppenheimer, not only insinuated himself into
the court of Duke Karl Alexander of Württemberg, making him depen-
dent on Jewish money and bankrupting the state but also violates the
gorgeous Kristina Söderbaum, an innocent child of the Volk. The maiden
drowns herself in a desperate attempt to regain her honor, the people of
Württemberg rise up, and Süss is hanged in an iron cage on the market
square of Stuttgart. The message was clear: German and European Jewry
must pay the price for centuries of criminal abuse.[58]

Möller may not have been responsible for writing the complete script
for *Jud Süss*, but he put his authority as an artist on the line in the publicity
attendant upon its release in the film theaters. Playing on the prestige he
enjoyed as a major interpreter of Jewry's place in European life, he was
widely quoted in propaganda releases when he said that

> We let history speak. And it does not show that the Jews
> "are just like all other human beings," no, it makes clear
> that the Jews are entirely different from us and their behavior
> is not at all governed by our innate moral principles. We
> did not want to present a terrible demon, but rather to reveal
> the great chasm between Jewish and Aryan behavior. That is
> the reason we had to transcend chronology and show Jüss's
> roots in the ghetto as a haggling street trader who snuck into
> the country illegally in the dark of night, and gradually
> becomes more audacious and powerful and is able to conceal
> his background by means of his speech, gestures, and clothing.[59]

There is no clearer proof than this that Möller's contempt for Jewry was
as much a part of his nature as that of the SS radicals, who later would
go to such lengths to silence and punish him.

---

[57] For the definitive analysis of the historic Joseph Süss Oppenheimer, see Barbara Gerber,
Jud Süss. Aufstieg und Fall im frühen 18. Jahrhundert (Hamburg: Hans Christians Verlag,
1990).

[58] See David Welch, *Propaganda and German Cinema 1933–1945* (Oxford University Press,
1983), pp. 284–92; Linda Schulte-Sasse, *Entertaining the Third Reich* (Durham: Duke
University Press, 1996), pp. 47–91; Schoeps, pp. 213–15.

[59] "Jud Süss unmaskiert im Film. Eberhard Wolfgang Möller zu seinem ersten Film-
drehbuch," September 1939, Möller file, DLAM. See also Elisabeth Frenzel, *Judengestaltung auf der deutschen Bühne. Ein notwendiger Querschnitt durch 700 Jahre Rollengeschichte* (München: Deutscher Volksverlag, 1940). Möller was credited with his
work on the scenario in the major film reviews. See Karl Korn's review in *Das Reich*,
October 6, 1940, which asserted that the film proved that the "chosen people" were at
last receiving just punishment for their "Talmudic nihilism."

With the onset of the war, Möller volunteered for service as a Waffen SS war reporter. Trained in the war correspondents unit of the elite Leibstandarte SS in Berlin, he was to take part in the campaigns of France (1940), Russia (1941–3), Yugoslavia (1943), Italy (1944), on the invasion front in France (1944), and the retreat into Germany (1945). The title of his book on the campaign in France – *The Mask of War* – reveals an aesthetic grounding on the model of Heinrich von Kleist's *Prince Friedrich of Homburg*. Approaching the war as a transcendent and ennobling experience, such a work could only have been produced in the days of German Blitzkrieg victories early in the war. It is certain that no veteran of the killing fields at Verdun or the Somme could have written the work that emotes a romantic reverence for war. It was not by chance that the initial chapter, titled "The Ninth Symphony," reached for the stars, with the Battle of France presented as the moral equivalent to Beethoven's monumental choral work. For Möller, to participate in this magnificent campaign was a gift of God granted to few people. Its grandeur and beauty were almost indescribable, offering the participant a flight to the great moral heights where will and freedom were enshrined, while offering transcendence from the material in the renunciation of the self, the ephemeral, and the impure. His self-described obligation as an artist was to transfigure war from an experience of horror to one of ecstasy. Thus it was that the victory over France offered Möller the opportunity to express his aesthetic fantasies in a way that would have been unthinkable during the Battle of Russia.

From time to time historical reality crept grudgingly into the composition, nowhere more dramatically than when he described the "unspeakable decadence" of France. The hatefulness of French behavior following the Great War – not only at the vindictive Versailles Peace Conference but continuously thereafter – was now being avenged. Arrogant and supercilious beyond belief, they behaved as if they were still the center of the universe and the Sun King, Louis XIV, ruled the world. But the truth was something entirely different, Möller asserted. The overwhelming power and technical superiority displayed by the Germans had enabled them to tear off the mask that camouflaged the decomposition of the French nation. The death mask revealed France for what it really was, a nation of self-deceivers molded by the tragedy of the revolution of 1789. Everything that was noble and good had been destroyed, opening the way for republicanism, liberalism, materialism, and corruption, fit only for Jewish wine and cattle merchants and greedy politicians. Even before the war, the French did not know what they were living for, propped up as

they were by American millionaires and their infrastructure being supported by German reparations. Worse still, coming face-to-face with their
intrepid adversaries, they did not know what they were fighting for either,
much less whether or not they ready to die for such a miserable republic.
A bloodless people, they were now paying the price for their sloth and
craven pursuit of comfort. Henceforth, their much ballyhooed Maginot
Line and its fortifications would be useful solely for the production of
mushrooms and snails for the French table.

Great Britain ran a close second in this litany of shame, where brutal
evidence of centuries of German envy and feelings of inferiority cascaded
from Möller's acid pen. Falsehood and craven deception were at the heart
of the English character, he claimed. Hypocrisy was the byword for this
nation of sea pirates and imperialist exploiters. What a contrast to German
intellectual and technical superiority, so grandly on display in the somber
majesty of Wehrmacht and Waffen SS officers and men, whose devastating
pincer thrusts and astounding breakthrough to the coast enabled German
forces to surround and annihilate their enemies in one of the greatest military victories in world history. For Möller, the embarkation at Dunkirk
of what remained of the broken English armies signaled that the German
forces, motivated by a revolutionary ideology and inspired by the Führer's
messianic genius, were rewriting history in the key of justice and heroism.
In this vein, he cruelly observed: "It is simply hard to believe, how in one
stroke centuries of English arrogance has finally been shattered."[60] Further, he described the signing of the armistice in the forest of Compiègne –
which in fact signaled the apex of Hitler's power – in the baroque colors
of a Te Deum mass. Such a victory could only have been the result of the
Germans' "total selflessness, that grand and rare flower which can only
grow in the soil of a truly noble people focused on the greater good of
all." In this way, Möller claimed, those who rendered the ultimate sacrifice were transfigured, and the laurel crown of victory guaranteed the
immortality of the entire racial community.[61]

Despite this effort at transcendence, the reality of the biting sting of
death did not escape our protagonist. Deep down, he was a sensitive man
attuned closely to nature and was quick to perceive an abiding meaning
in seemingly ephemeral events. He knew that he shared this particular
gift with both artists and photographers. This was the very human side
of Möller, which would later nearly cost him his life at the hands of

---

[60] Möller, *Die Maske des Krieges*, p. 118.   [61] Ibid., pp. 130–4.

6. Eberhard Wolfgang Möller in His Waffen SS Uniform, Circa 1943. Author's
Private Collection.

the SD when he refused to toe the line on the myth of heroic death. He was deeply shaken by the loss of Lieutenant Otto Keppler, the only son of his best friend, the State Actor Ernst Keppler, who was killed in an assault over the Aisne-Oise Canal. This led him to write an intensely spiritual poem in his memory, which he titled "June 5, 1940":

> Blessed, blessed, blessed swept away
> already dead, even as he jumped,
> already deeply moved from the realization
> of his inescapable imminent destruction,
> he darted out in front like a fire,
> that shoots out from the withered bank,
> suddenly fanned and immense
> in what took just a heartbeat,
>
> the focus of thousands of eyes
> like a star, that descends with a ring,
> from millions of unredeemed years
> redeemed in that one moment,
>
> gigantic and taking everything with it,
> that stood in the way of mortality,
> glittering in a thousand prisms in his leap:
> he waves with his upheld hand,
>
> he stands on the high bank,
> star and flag, fire and signal,
> collapses and with his violent plunge opens the way for
> a flood of victory across the canal.
>
> Selig, selig, selig hingerissen,
> schon gestorben, während er noch sprang,
> ganz durchdrungen schon von jenem Wissen
> um den unentrinnbar nahen Untergang,
>
> war er vor den andern wie ein Feuer,
> das emporleckt am verwelkten Hang,
> plötzlich angefacht und ungeheuer
> für den Pulsschlag eines Herzens lang,
>
> für den Blick von tausend Augenpaaren
> wie ein Stern, der sausend niederstösst,
> aus Millionen unerlösten Jahren
> in den einen Augenblick erlöst,
>
> riesengross und alles niederreissend,
> was an Sterblichem entgegenstand,
> tausendfältig im Zerspringen gleissend:
> also winkt er noch mit hoher Hand,

also steht er noch auf hohem Walle,
Stern und Fahne, Feuer und Signal,
stürzt und liegt und reisst mit seinem Falle
eine Flut des Sieges über den Kanal.[62]

Möller later returned to this sad motif in a bittersweet soliloquy in which he pondered the fate of Keppler once more in very tender words. Nature in all her splendor had reclaimed the embankment where he perished, hallowed ground that lay in the valley of the "Chemins des Dames," the scene of bitter fighting in World War I. Now a sweet summer wind gently blew over the canal, sweeping away all traces of what had transpired there. Möller lamented the fact that only a solemn memory of the hero's noble sacrifice remained in that "valley of love, a garden of peace filled now with sweet wild flora and fauna, awaiting the secret of his soul." Even God was overcome in the face of such "flowering reconciliation," he submitted.[63] Considering the tone of this poetry of death, it is hardly surprising to learn that the chief censor in the Propaganda Ministry, Werner Stephan, criticized *The Mask of War* as did the highest SS officers, finding it to be "Francophile, unsoldierly, and not true to National Socialist principles."[64]

With the German defeat in the Battle of Britain later in 1940 and as corruption and weaknesses in the National Socialist leadership became more glaring, Möller's attitudes gradually changed. His writing revealed more negativism and pessimism than the official line permitted, and he realized that his prestige was declining. More and more he saw the war from the perspective of his own aesthetic vision, less and less from the point of view of ideology. Real trouble lay ahead for him following the publication of his poem, "The Corpse" in the Hitler Youth publication *Will and Power*, which occasioned a vicious campaign of character assault by influential SS officers and their allies. In this poem, a corpse muses on its condition, observing that

I have soil over my lips.
A big stone is in my mouth.
A gentle mole is moving in my ribs
and is my friend. I am no longer alone.
I lie still and cannot move
and do not know, if I am even myself.

---

[62] "5. Juni 1940," ibid., pp. 95–6.   [63] "Beschreibung," ibid., pp. 155–6.
[64] "Kurzer Abriss der Lebensdaten Eberhard Wolfgang Möllers zur Information," Privatarchiv Möller, Bietigheim.

But I am not thirsty, the rain soaks me
and many roots are growing through me.

I am not alive; but there is life in my limbs
and a colony of beetles scurrying over them.
Then it seems that I am breathing again
awakened by their nightly bustle,

and am attentive to the growing roots,
to see if a bud will open,
and listened quietly to the song of the stars
high over me, and lie still once more.

Ich habe Erde über meinen Lippen.
In meinem Munde ist ein grosser Stein.
Der sanfte Maulwurf geht in meinen Rippen
und ist mein Freund. Ich bin nicht mehr allein.

Ich liege still und kann mich nicht bewegen
und weiss nicht, ob ich noch ich selber bin.
Allein ich dürste nicht, mich tränkt der Regen,
und viele Wurzeln wachsen durch mich hin.

Ich lebe nicht; es lebt um meine Glieder
und der Schwarm der Käfer nur, der sie bedeckt.
Dann ist es wohl, als atmete ich wieder
von ihrem nächtlichen Gewühl geweckt,

und lauschte mit den Wurzeln in die Ferne,
ob eine Blüte sich erschliessen will,
und hörte leise den Gesang der Sterne
hoch über mir, und liege wieder still.[65]

Möller considered his poem to be nothing more than the tender impressions of a corpse, reflecting on how its body had returned to nature. His detractors, on the other hand, saw it as a blasphemous violation of the heroic death myth.[66]

Hans W. Hagen, a fiery junior SS officer posted to the Propaganda Ministry who was engaged as an ardent cultural critic, attacked Möller in a sensational article in the SS sponsored journal, *Die Weltliteratur*, bearing the headline, "Aesthetic Desecration of the Dead." The German Reich and its Nordic ethos were founded on the deeds and sacrificial blood of its fallen, he argued, charging that the poet had violated their sacred memory. The dead may have left the fighting ranks of their comrades but would live

[65] Möller, "Der Tote," *Das Brüderliche Jahr. Gedichte* (Wien: Wiener Verlagsgesellschaft, 1941), p. 59.
[66] Möller to Renate Mouchard, March 17, 1967, Privatarchiv Möller, Bietigheim.

ennobled in Valhalla for eternity, he affirmed. Hagen accused Möller of being inspired by Christianity, the Enlightenment, and fin de siècle literary aestheticism. As a result, he had committed a crime against every hero's mother and widow. The writer, Gottfried Benn, he claimed, wrote on the identical subject with much more force and grace, and he had long ago been uprooted from the national cultural scene. Otto Dix had done the same thing in his paintings, and he too had been expelled. Now Möller had appeared, Hagen complained, and tried "to make something aesthetic out of this gooey mess," continuing a decadent cultural motif that can be traced to Rilke. Our soldiers deserve better than this, he asserted. One should glorify the greatness of the fallen, he concluded, "not feel entitled to rhapsodize about all manner of things and certainly not to whistle carelessly in memorial gardens."[67]

Hagen's article had the severest consequences for Möller, and many of his enemies took the opportunity to wage a secret campaign against him. Those who nursed grudges against Möller swiftly took their revenge, not the least of whom was the SS propagandist and poet Kurt Eggers. Eggers had felt terribly diminished when Möller not only turned down one of the manuscripts he had submitted to the Propaganda Ministry in the mid-1930s but had added insult to injury by calling Eggers a purveyor of "nationalist kitsch that showed itself in constant chest-thumping and imitative expressionist flatulence."[68] Eggers was a close friend of Hans Hagen, and together they conspired to incite high-ranking officers of the Reich Central Security Office to take action. Himmler was informed, but the Reichsführer, embarrassed by Möller's breach of ideological discipline, wished for the matter to be handled quietly. He ordered that the offender be sent into military action on the Eastern front (*Frontbewährung*), a disciplinary sentence that often meant certain death. Himmler forbade all further public or private references to the affair, which meant of course that the poet could not defend himself.[69] The anti-Möller clique also approached Reich press chief, Gruppenführer Otto Dietrich, demanding that his services as a war reporter be terminated. Friedrich Wilhelm Hymmen, chief editor of the Hitler Youth organ *Will and Power*, observed that "his reputation was destroyed. Not a single person in public life protected

---

[67] *Die Weltliteratur* 16 (July 1941), p. 191.
[68] Möller reported at length on these events in letters to Michael Dultz (Erlangen) dated October 15, 1964, and March 11, April 6, and May 14, 1965, Privatarchiv Möller. Bietigheim.
[69] Tb Radke, BA ZM 232 A 4 S. 31f, and 97, cited in Gerd Simon, Hitlers Hofdichter, http://homepages.uni-tuebinben.de/gerd/ChrMoeller.pdf.

Möller after this attack. He was branded an enemy and was forced to withdraw from the public arena."[70]

Henceforth, writers and officials in the Nazi cultural-political bureaucracy distanced themselves from Möller and his work. Herbert Frenzel of the Propaganda Ministry, the author of a major essay lauding the poet that had been published in 1938, later observed that Möller was the leading example of a member of the Party who had essentially been banned for his artistic views and writings.[71] Further, Möller was placed under SD surveillance, forfeiting the privileges and freedom of movement he had enjoyed as a war reporter. Even his old friend and patron Baldur von Schirach had forsaken him.

It is certain that as early as 1942, Möller had no standing as a representative Third Reich author. Yet even when fate had turned against him, he still clung to the misguided belief that, despite everything, he remained an exponent of what he considered to be true National Socialism. In effect, he had learned nothing from his experiences in the Third Reich. He still contended that the Germans represented a race of superior intellect and morality, and it was their duty to spread the greatness of their culture in the Eastern territories. He returned to these themes in his final play, *The Sacrifice*, which he managed to have staged at the Landestheater Hermannstadt in Rumania late in 1941.[72] In this work, the Slavic race looms dangerously not only as culture-destroying vandals but as a sexual threat to the integrity of the Nordic peoples. Even when fate had turned against him, Möller continued to try, albeit without success, to have this play performed in Berlin and Vienna.

Cost him what it may – and the danger to him was indeed great – Möller wore the contempt for him of the SS and Rosenberg cliques as a badge of honor. He considered them to be vulgarians and continued to publish poetry in the style condemned by the hard-core Nazis. He had nothing whatsoever in common with radicals such as Kurt Eggers, whose level of sensitivity would never have permitted them to write of a dying soldier as Möller did:

> He lay in a little wagon,
> I saw his mouth;

[70] Friedrich W. Hymmen, "Zur Entlastung des Schriftstellers E. W. Möller," Möller, Denazification Records, Staatsarchiv Ludwigsburg.

[71] Herbert A. Frenzel, June 1, 1947, Möller, Denazification Records, Staatsarchiv Ludwigsburg.

[72] Eberhard Wolfgang Möller, *Das Opfer* (Berlin: Theaterverlag Langen-Müller, 1941). *Bühnenblätter des Landestheaters der Deutschen Volksgruppe in Rumänien*, Spielzeit 1941/42, Heft 6.

he trembled gently without crying out
like a woman giving birth.

His body was torn and bloody,
it was death that he was bearing,
and beads of sweat
rolled off his mangled hair.

His eyes quietly circled,
as if they were ashamed that he suffered so.
Then a comrade cried over him,
and the whole world cried with him.

Er lag in einem kleinen Wagen,
ich habe seinen Mund gesehen,
er bebte leise ohne Klagen
wie eine Frau in Kindeswehen.

Sein Leib war blutig aufgeschnitten,
es war der Tod, den er gebar,
und eine Spur von Schweiss war mitten
im vollen aufgewühlten Haar.

Die Augen gingen still im Kreise,
als schämten sie sich, dass er litt.
Da weinte einer um ihn leise
and alle Dingen weinten mit.[73]

Nor would the dead disappear but would quietly return to those they loved from their graves. He had one of them reflect on the beauty of his return, when on cold winter nights by the light of the full moon, "I will wreathe a crown of death from the snow and twigs. I will look into their houses, where it is warm and light, and will call to the dogs, but they cannot see me."

Then I will knock with jangling bones
On the wooden doors and window glass.
Then I will be with you; because you are not to think
that I am silent because I have forgotten you.

Dann klopfe ich mit klirrenden Gelenken
ans Holz der Türen und ans Fensterglas.
Dann bin ich bei euch; denn ihr sollt nicht denken
Dass ich still bin, weil ich euch vergass.[74]

Möller began the darkest period of his life and was attached as a war reporter to the 5th Waffen SS Division "Viking" on the Russian front. It

---

[73] Eberhard Wolfgang Möller, "Der Sterbende," *Das Brüderliche Jahr. Gedichte* (Wien/Leipzig: Wiener Verlagsgesellschaft, 1941), p. 48.
[74] "Vermächtnis," ibid., p. 57.

was something of a miracle that he lived, and his survival was due in part to the intervention of the commander of the SS war correspondents regiment, Standartenführer Gunter d'Alquen. A journalist who himself had often come under fire for his policies as editor of the *Schwarze Korps*, the official organ of the SS, where he had the reputation as an enfant terrible, d'Alquen succeeded in fighting off the attack wolves. He intervened on several occasions to protect Möller from the severest disciplinary measures, the result of brutal assaults on him from the highest levels of the Reich Central Security Office and the Hitler Youth.[75]

Möller may not have been killed in Russia, but his spirit certainly was. He was heartbroken to learn that his brother, Johann Michael, had been killed in action on the eastern front, a loss that added immeasurably to his morbid spirit. He kept a diary on his experiences there, a work that would not be published until shortly before his death in 1971. It would be brought out by the Munin Verlag, an Osnabrück firm run by and for the postwar SS establishment. Möller's reveries jotted down in the black of night in the frozen east reveal a deeply disillusioned and spiritually broken man:

> Easter 1942. After my defamation as a cultural Bolshevik,
> I am ordered to prove my mettle at the front. Not even my
> war reports are to be used from now on at home. Just about
> done for and placed under surveillance by functionaries
> whose job it is to see that I am finished off, I am experiencing
> the end of all my illusions. Each individual is destroyed in
> this war in a different way. My depression gets worse from
> day to day.[76]

Other diary entries take the Party and its leaders to task for cowardice and corruption. Möller was totally disillusioned with National Socialist ideology, most notably the destructive myth of death. He lamented: "I cry out against this whole noisy era and its miserable bloated lies which make a theater out of suffering and a circus show out of death. They have made men into dogs."[77] Our men at the front don't believe in the heroic myths any longer, which in fact should be described as "heroic sarcasm." Nor did they have faith in the goodness of God, the honesty

---

[75] Gunther d'Alquen, Regimentskommandeur der Standarte "Kurt Eggers," Vatten-Caithness, POW Camp 165, Scotland, October 24, 1947. Möller, Denazification Records, Staatsarchiv, Ludwigsburg.

[76] Eberhard Wolfgang Möller, *Russisches Tagebuch* (Osnabrück: Munin Verlag, 1971), p. 30.

[77] Ibid., p. 29.

of the homeland, or even in the competence of their leaders. They only believed in themselves. Möller observed tellingly that more than ever he held firmly to Hölderlin's affirmation that anything of enduring meaning must be prudent and level-headed. In the Third Reich, on the other hand, inferior men of the worst character had risen to the top, and the war had only made the situation worse. Their corruption wore more heavily on the human spirit than the massive blood sacrifice that they had caused. On hearing the lamentations of an SS officer about the executions that he was ordered to carry out, Möller noted, "We are not competing with the best men in world history as to how high we can climb, but rather to what depths we can fall."[78] It is evident that Möller was more concerned about what effect the murder squad executions would have on the German spirit than any remorse for the fate of the Jews. On the other hand, he admitted that he did not have the words to describe the gallantry, endurance, and accomplishments of the German soldiers on the eastern front, notwithstanding the dishonesty and dissimulation that characterized Nazi propaganda about them emanating from Berlin.

By a miraculous turn of fate, Möller did not die in the Soviet Union after all, and during the winter of 1943 he was able to leave the Russian front for good. Strangely, however, the memory of certain images of his experiences there would remain with him forever. He observed:

> As I take leave of this country, it is hard for me to give
> it its due. The steppes with their undulating hills, towering
> billowy clouds, and unceasing wind cast an irresistible
> magic spell on everyone; once one has experienced this,
> it will never let you go. I think that I will dream of it as
> long as I live and hear in my dreams the call of the owls
> and on winter nights the bursts of wind which resounded
> like cannon shells.[79]

While on leave at home in Berlin in the summer of 1943, Möller was more outspoken than he had ever been had in the past. At private social engagements in the capital, he expressed himself in a way that – had it been reported to the Gestapo – would have sent him packing off to a concentration camp. He attacked the rottenness and brutality of Nazi leaders – especially Rosenberg, Goebbels, and Himmler, and even his old friends von Schirach and Schlösser – his SD handlers, and the anti-Christian policies of the regime as well as the liquidation of the Jews. Some of Möller's outbursts on these occasions were notable. One of his friends quoted him

---

[78] Ibid., p. 22.   [79] Ibid., p. 131.

as saying that "if I have to choose between Christianity and National Socialism, then I will choose Christianity." Further, "the only people who still believe in the Party are those who personally have something to gain. National Socialism has no ideological viewpoint whatsoever."[80] Although he returned to the front as a war reporter in Italy and France, his submissions were written halfheartedly. As a result, his filings were only sporadically published.

With the defeat of the Third Reich becoming ever more a certainty, it was obvious that Möller's dream of witnessing the rebirth of German tragedy and his vision for a grand union of intellect and power under Adolf Hitler was but a chimera. His career, which had begun in the chaos of Weimar Germany, ended as tragically as it had begun. Ironically, he would outlive his enemies among the ranks of Nazi radicals, who in September 1944 arranged for what was to have been his "heroic death" on the invasion front in France. He was commanded to enter the front lines in Normandy with the 12th SS Panzer Division "Hitler Jugend," to take part in their last stand, to gain immortality as the "poet of the German youth" and with his heroic death there to become an immortal symbol of loyalty unto death. In short, he was to relive the myth of Langemarck, the brutal sacrifice of German youth in the front generation of 1914. Möller would relate after the war that the front broke down so swiftly that the cynical plan for his mythical heroic death could not be carried out as planned. His enemies went so far as to publish a notice that he had been killed in action, and his personal effects were returned to his wife, Eva Möller, in Berlin.[81] Although the author's war reports had long ceased to be published, Möller was promoted to the rank of SS Obersturmführer in January 1945, a puzzling development considering his stormy relations with the Nazi establishment yet a sign that despite the machinations of the now totally impotent Rosenberg, he was still very much persona grata with many people who mattered.[82]

Möller took part in the retreat on the western front by way of Soissons, Brussels, and Arnhem, all the way to the Rhine River. When Germany surrendered in 1945, he was in the Ruhr Valley. Totally resigned to an abysmal future, he repaired to his country home in Thuringia where he was soon taken prisoner by the Americans and was incarcerated in

---

[80] Friedrich Wilhelm Hymmen, "Zur Entlastung des Schriftstellers E. W. Möller," Möller, Denazification Records, Staatsarchiv Ludwigsburg.

[81] Bernard Payr, *Kurzinformationen für die Hauptämter und Ämter*, September 1944, Nr. 4, BA NS 15/72, cited in Gerd Simon, "Hitlers Hofdichter."

[82] SS, NSDAP, *Personalveränderungsblatt*, promotions as of January 30, 1945.

Hohenasperg, the fortress prison near Ludwigsburg, where none other than Joseph Süss-Oppenheimer ("Jud Süss") had himself been imprisoned before his execution in 1737. Over the coming years, he was tried three times in the denazification courts, and his judicial ordeal did not come to a conclusion until the summer of 1950. He was set free with no penalty whatsoever.

Möller remarried and spent the rest of his life in obscurity in Bietigheim, a village north of Stuttgart.[83] Although he continued to write profusely – he was able to publish two novels after the war, *The Lover of Mr. Beaujou* and *Chicago* – nevertheless his means were modest indeed.[84] Nazi ghosts have a long life, however, and as late as the summer of 1970, Möller was reading from his works at the Lippoldberg Writers Meeting, where the heirs of Hans Grimm (*Volk ohne Raum*) carried on the decades-old tradition of al fresco readings by right-wing writers in the yard of a medieval cloister situated high above the Weser River.[85] Möller died of a heart attack on New Years Day 1972. Buried in Bietigheim, the strains of Wagner's grief motif from *Parzifal* accompanied his casket to its final resting place, where a group of young adherents placed a laurel wreath over it in his honor.[86]

---

[83] For an authoritative account of the last decades of Möller's life and his postwar writings, see Stefan Busch, *Und gestern, da hörte uns Deutschland. NS-Autoren in der Bundesrepublik*. Studien zur Literatur-und Kulturgeschichte, no. 13 (Mainz: Königshausen & Neumann, 1998), pp. 173–208.

[84] "Kurzer Abriss der Lebensdaten Eberhard Wolfgang Möllers zur Information," Privatarchiv Möller, Bietigheim.

[85] Eberhard Wolfgang Möller File, Institut für Zeitgeschichte, Munich.

[86] *Deutsche Wochenzeitung*, January 7, 1972.

7

The Testament of Zarathustra: Kurt Eggers and the SS Ideal

When Hitler Youth Leader Baldur von Schirach observed that "Goethe's *Faust*, the Ninth Symphony and the will of Adolf Hitler are eternal youth and know neither time nor change," he was portraying a radical world-view whose simplicity belied the profound consequences his words would ultimately have.[1] Every historical movement of importance has its bards and troubadours, the more so with fascism, the political identity of which was consonant with poetic imagery. Without question, Kurt Eggers was the leading muse of the SS, a man whose character embraced at once a volatile temperament, a predilection for romanticism, fanatical racism and nationalism, belligerence, and heroic idealism. Although he could be quite creative as a writer, at heart he was a revolutionary and a freebooter.

Robbed of his youth by the miserable political and economic conditions of the early Weimar Republic, Eggers found himself cast in the role of a Free Corps fighter at a tender age. Ever after, action and political deeds were what counted for him, not words alone. Eggers's vision of the Nordic ideal became a source of energy and life for him, which he celebrated in exaggerated imagery associated with heroic death. Having become widely known for his dramas, novels, poetry, and radio plays, he drew the respect and attention of both Hitler and Himmler. As a result, he was appointed to serve in several SS offices in Berlin dealing with cultural and ideological propaganda.[2] But he longed for battle, and he was later attached to the Fifth SS Panzer Division "Viking" as a tank commander. Eggers would

---

[1] Baldur von Schirach, *Die Hitlerjugend. Idee und Gestalt* (Berlin: Zeitgeschichte, 1934), pp 18–19.
[2] See Kurt Eggers, born November 10, 1905, Berlin-Schöneberg, "Mein Lebenslauf," submitted to his SS superiors on September 1, 1936, personnel file, BAB. Much of this chapter has been corroborated by the evidence to be found in Eggers's NSDAP and SS records, BAB.

7. Kurt Eggers, Circa 1935. Courtesy of Berlin Document Center.

be killed in action on the Eastern front in August 1943, and he became a model of the National Socialist blood cult. Soon thereafter Himmler named the SS war reporters unit – the SS Standarte "Kurt Eggers" – in his honor.

His death thereby served as a testament to the haunting leitmotif of the SS anthem so beloved in circles of the Black Corps, which viewed a brave warrior's death as ennobling. It became the mantra for Eggers, and he was true to its distorted concept of the eternal life to be found in a hero's death:

> When all become disloyal
> then we will remain steadfast,
> so that there will always be a squad
> remaining for us in the world.
> Companions of our youth,
> those images of a better time,
> which have consecrated us for
> manly virtue and love death.

> Wenn alle untreu werden,
> so bleiben wir doch treu,
> dass immer noch auf Erden
> für uns ein Fähnlein sei.
> Gefährten unsrer Jugend,
> ihr Bilder bessrer Zeit
> Die uns zu Männertugend
> und Liebestod geweiht.[3]

Kurt Eggers lived an adventurous life characterized by an endless search for risk and danger. By his own admission, he was a desperado, ever perched dangerously on the edge of the abyss. He did not fear death and went so far as to publish his memoirs at the age of thirty-four, titled *Dancing to My Own Drummer* (*Der Tanz aus der Reihe*) before facing almost certain death on the Russian front.[4] In this autobiography, Eggers addressed the tensions of his era while mocking what he referred to as the "the works of Jewish psychologists who spoke so knowingly of their problems, clinging to the strange notion that somehow their generation was in the grips of a 'father-son complex'." The goal of these effete intellectuals, he submitted, was to dismiss the revolutionary young as hotheaded adventurers who would settle down soon enough as they matured. In reality,

---

[3] See Hitlerjugend Schulung, Reichsjugendführerschule, NSDAP, Hauptarchiv, Roll 342, Folder 342.
[4] Kurt Eggers, *Der Tanz aus der Reihe* (Dortmund: Volkschaft Verlag, 1939).

he submitted, the Great War had fundamentally restructured traditional German values. The young had joined their fathers in molding a new generation of warriors, fighters who amid all the chaos of those days, refused to return to the false norms of the prewar era. "We were determined to live dangerously," he submitted. "Nietzsche had become our great teacher and for us he was an educator, not a prophet." Eggers declared that "We did not want to howl with the wolves but to remain exactly what we were by nature and to steer our own course. We wanted to be soldiers in our daily lives, fearless and spontaneous men. This was the whole problem of my generation."[5] It is not an exaggeration to observe that the seeds of future evil had been planted in Kurt even in his earliest boyhood, as his own remembrances clearly reveal.

Kurt Eggers was born in 1905 in Berlin-Schöneberg into a very well-to-do family. His father, Wilhelm Eggers, held an influential position in the Dresdner Bank. Wilhelm came from a long line of teachers and ministers and had several relatives who were successful in business and large farming operations. Kurt spent the early years of his boyhood close to the land in the family house at Schöneiche near Friedrichshagen, not far from Berlin, where an English governess doted on him and his sister. It pained the lad that some of the farm boys referred to him as a child of the upper classes, but his physical strength, bravery in schoolyard scuffles, and general impishness soon earned him the respect of the country folk.[6] The sensitivity that he later demonstrated for the economic difficulties of farmers and their families are traceable to those early years, where young Kurt took a delight in the simple beauty of nature.

Even as a boy, Eggers had a romantic zeal for everything military. He played with his lead soldiers by the hour, reenacting the German victory over France at Sedan in 1870, and even thought of himself as a young soldier. He was embarrassed by his infatuation with an affectionate young girl, and like so many front soldiers and Free Corps men who faced disappointment when returning home on leave, quickly went back to the security of his wolf pack, declaring, "After a mistaken flight into a hostile world, I returned home with my friends."[7] On the day that Germany declared war in August 1914, Kurt's father took him to the city to witness the historic occasion. He was thrilled to get a glimpse of Kaiser Wilhelm II and Chancellor Bethmann-Holweg and to witness the Christian military ritual held at the Bismarck monument in front of the Reichstag.

---

5 Ibid., pp. 514–15.   6 Ibid., pp.
7 Ibid., p. 60.

Like many boys too young to go to the front, Kurt felt useless and longed
to see action himself. In his youthful zeal, he carried a hunting rifle, had
a military coat tailored to fit him, topped with a soldier's hat and the
shoulder epaulets of the storied 112th Infantry Division. At the tender
age of nine, he declared himself to be the "captain of the entire corps
of military youth between Kleinschönebeck and Rahnsdorf." During one
attack staged in the local forest, where the boys had dug trenches on the
western front model, he managed to set fire to the local forest when his
unit sallied forth against the enemy. For this infraction, there was hell to
pay from the local authorities.

Eggers was considerably influenced by his German teacher, the author
Bruno Wille, who taught his young charge to be strong, come what may.
He never forgot what he learned from Herr Wille on a class outing to the
Müggelberge, an incident that turned out to be a defining moment in the
development of his radical character. There, among the traces of prehis-
toric German tribes, the teacher made the point that men could lead good
lives without the church and without Jesus Christ as their savior. Wille
taught Eggers to write in a totally spontaneous and unself-conscious way,
and he proceeded to do this at once, never in his life wavering from
this premise. Wille was so impressed with an essay Eggers submitted
on a heroic theme that he sent it up to the headmaster, who lauded it
highly.[8]

Eggers's descriptions of his life as a boy during the Great War paralleled
the conclusions drawn by several authorities on the influence the war had
on the children of that era.[9] The pangs of hunger, melancholy, and the
frustration of being too young to go to war hung over him. He felt deeply
the disappointment that Germany had not brought hostilities to an end
with a quick victory in the summer of 1914, and questions about the
nation's military leadership haunted him. A front soldier who returned to
Schöneiche at the end of September 1914 could not keep the tears from
running down his cheeks when describing his contempt for the German
commanders. With victory in their hands, he said, the leaders lost heart
and pulled the stormers back, following the orders from someone far from
the battle line who had lost his sense of purpose and will to victory. "All
of a sudden it was over," he cried, "the attacks, the victory, our trust.
Everything was in vain. Take note of the names Moltke and Hentsch,

[8] Ibid., pp. 81–2
[9] See Peter Loewenberg, "The Psychohistorical Origins of the Nazi Youth Cohort," *American Historical Review* 76 (December 1971), pp. 1457–502.

they have us on their consciences."[10] Kurt Eggers thus learned at an early age the rallying cry of the front soldiers and officers that would later develop into the sinister claim that the German defeat was the result of Jewish traitors and communists who "stabbed the nation in the back." Kurt fantacized that he, too, was a soldier with a passionate love for the Fatherland. When German units took Fort Douaumont at Verdun in February 1916 – final victory seemed so near at that point – he was thrilled to sing "Ich hatt' einen Kameraden" at a school celebration in the freezing school auditorium, where the children were huddled together in their winter coats to keep warm.

Eggers was devastated when in the summer of 1916, just as the Battle of the Somme was beginning, the family had to leave their country idyll and move to Berlin. His father became an officer in the Third Guard Regiment and the family lived in fashionable Wilmersdorf. The city seemed huge and foreign to Kurt and exacerbated the rebellious behavior he evidenced after his father refused to allow him to enroll at the prestigious naval cadet academy at Plön in Schleswig-Holstein. Instead, he attended the Bismarck Gymnasium where the sons of Gustav Stresemann, Wolfgang and Joachim, were among his classmates. Kurt constantly challenged the school authorities, showing little respect for his upper bourgeois surroundings, and performing poorly in his studies. All the more did he delight in the company of his fellow hooligans, boys who set records in the annals of student escapades in the capital. One of their favorite activities was to climb the roofs of apartment houses, where Eggers and his friends scampered like cats from roof to roof in extraordinary feats of daring over an extensive area of the West End, frightening the housewives in their kitchens with their dangerous antics. The entire city soon became the boys' playground, and they even engaged in shoplifting at the famous department stores on the Kurfürstendamm.

At the age of twelve, Eggers became a cadet in the new naval academy in Berlin, founded under the sponsorship of Kaiser Wilhelm II. Organized from scratch by a former naval officer, Kommandant Schmitt, the military school took the name "Deutscher Schulschiff-Schülerverein" (DSSV) and operated on the Wannsee, plying the waters of the Havel River around Berlin. At last, the restless youth had found his spiritual home. Sporting his new naval uniform, lustily singing nationalist songs such as "Stolz weht die Flagge Schwarz-Weiss-Rot," adapting to the rigor of military discipline, and responding to all manner of challenges to his physical

[10] Eggers, *Tanz*, pp. 90–1.

stamina, Kurt was as content as an osprey diving for a prize fish. Musing on his first days at school, he wrote: "I was so happy, that I did not dare fall asleep, simply for fear that I might have been dreaming."[11]

Every child needs a role model, and young Eggers found his in the commandant of the academy, a man who inspired so many of Eggers's fellow cadets, all of whom were trying desperately to find their place in a world that was rapidly disintegrating. Every inch the naval officer in style and bearing, the commandant greeted his cadets at inspection by barking the word "Hiddek"– "Hauptsache ist dass die Engländer Kloppe Kriegen/The main thing is that the English get a thrashing!" – an amusing yet revealing testament to the hatred and envy German naval officers felt for their much more successful counterparts in His Majesty's Royal Navy.

Commandant Schmitt was contaminated with the anti-Semitism and paranoia so common to his generation. All cadets had the anti-Semitic publication *Hammer* on their reading lists, which included selections from Theodor Fritsch's notorious *Anti-Semitic Catechism*. These authors exacerbated the mistrust of Jewry in Eggers's mind, ideas already taught him by his father who was a strong supporter of the Nationalist Party. Schmitt firmly believed in a Jewish world conspiracy, and when the Austrian Minister President Count Karl von Stürgkh was murdered by "the Jewish Marxist leader Friedrich Adler" in October 1916, he had this to say:

> Believe me, the Jews are trying with all their power to gain control over the world, which they have been dreaming of since Moses started this mischief in the Sinai Desert. Their hope is that the world war will bring them to this goal. I am afraid that the murder of Stürgkh is simply the beginning of what will become the mass murder of all those who try to get in their way.[12]

The year 1917 brought with it serious misgivings for the young fanaticized patriots. Hunger was everywhere and took a terrible toll on Kurt, whom the commander sent to a farm in Pomerania to regain his health. Despite the Russian Revolution and German victories on the eastern front, the war had obviously taken a serious turn against the Central Powers when the United States entered the hostilities. Depression and fear gripped the home front, and traitors seemed to be everywhere. Not only were the communists spreading rebellion, the Majority Socialist SPD was showing signs of serious doubt in the national effort. The mood in Berlin was ominous, and the cadets learned firsthand the meaning of class hatred and

---

[11] Ibid., pp. 130–7.   [12] Eggers, *Tanz*, p. 140.

political division. Appearing in the streets in their sailor uniforms, they were mocked and spat on. There were no gifts in the Eggers home for the holidays in 1917, no Christmas tree, just the pall of hunger. Kurt's mother was seriously ill due to stress, malnutrition, and worry about the sad state of her family. Eggers became terribly melancholy and, remembering those days in later years, observed: "I closed my eyes and dreamt of the future, when I would be able to celebrate Christmas with my fellow sailors in some unknown distant place. I knew then that my home was now the school ship."[13]

On New Years Day, 1918, the commandant addressed the cadets, stressing the seriousness of the political and military situation, pointing to the crisis on both the home and fighting fronts. Mass strikes were under way, criticism of the Kaiser and the military elite became louder, and left-wing insurgents prepared for a revolution. Under these conditions, believing that traitorous enemies of the Reich wanted the total destruction of Germany, Commandant Schmitt called for a dictatorship under Field Marshal Erich Ludendorff "to flush the destructive poison out of the German body politic once and for all." Then, in the spirit of what would become Free Corps and National Socialist radicalism, he sounded the ultimate call to valor: "If we must die, then we want to take our enemies with us to the grave. Use the time that you still have to prepare for the final decision."[14] Misguided, the entire corps of cadets prepared to sacrifice their lives for the sake of the old, rotten order and volunteered to join their counterparts from the elite Prussian cadet schools at Berlin-Lichterfelde and Potsdam.

The situation went from bad to worse during the course of the year, as the last great offensive on the western front ground to a halt. The pall of death lay over the capital. It was during these critical months that Eggers suddenly came to understand that he had skipped a stage in life and had already become a man. He and his fellow naval cadets had become a bonded community of men, alienated from their families. It was a bitter pill for them to swallow when they were not deployed to defend the Imperial Castle as the old regime went down to defeat in November 1918, as communist revolutionaries joined their comrades at the front in fomenting insurrection. In the chaos that ensued following the Kaiser's abdication and flight to the Netherlands, the commandant refused to offer his cadets as a nihilistic blood sacrifice. Ordering them to

[13] Ibid., pp. 189–91.   [14] Ibid., p. 190.

be prepared for action, he observed, "Take note of these traitors. They are all Free Masons, Jews, and Papists."[15]

The sadness Kurt felt when his naval cadet school was disbanded on November 10, 1918, was indescribable. He would never forget Schmitt's final words:

> My young comrades, you will only later realize what it means
> to lower our flag for the last time. You now have the duty
> to raise our desecrated German war flag in all its glory some day.
> Never forget your duty![16]

Eggers was shattered and inconsolable: "I suffered the deeply felt pain of a young heart awakened from a delirious nightmare and understood then that the only real thing in life is iron and the sword." Returning to the Bismarck Gymnasium, ironically he was elected class representative to the "Student Soviet Council," where he promptly picked fights with Jewish students and was severely disciplined by the headmaster. He wandered aimlessly through the Grunewald and his other familiar haunts in Berlin and was surprised how often tears poured down his cheeks. He would later reflect on the carefree days of his boyhood in the country, when life seemed but a dream in a land of sunshine, fresh grass and trees, birds and butterflies, where animals and men were brothers and the moon and sun were his companions. But the dance of youth he had enjoyed had been but a delusion. Now he understood that conflict governed the world order and that henceforth hatred and alienation were to be his companions on the tortured journey of life.[17]

Years later Eggers reflected on what he considered to be the redemptive suffering of those days of shattered illusions in his work, *The Home of the Strong*. In a chapter titled "On Childhood and Longing," he observed that "Even in boyhood the weak are separated from the strong in their longing for danger and testing. But those called to the home of the strong actually merge with the eternal grand idea."[18]

Sadly, however, the contempt he would later show for the Jews as an SS officer was also born in the trauma of 1918–19. More and more he came to blame them for Germany's woes, and he was merciless in his mockery and castigation of Eastern Jews. The Jews were the alleged

---

[15] Ibid., p. 223.   [16] Ibid., pp. 226–7.

[17] The poem "Kinderland – Vaterland" offers eloquent testimony to the sadness fate cast on the war generation. See Kurt Eggers, *Schicksalsbrüder. Gedichte und Gesänge* (Stuttgart-Berlin: Deutsche Verlagsanstalt, 1935), pp. 9–11.

[18] *Heimat der Starken* (Dortmund: Volkschaftsverlag, 1938), p. 28.

wire-pullers of finance, media, and modernist culture. Whereas German veterans either could not get jobs or were simply psychologically unable to make the radical transition to employment on the home front, the Jews prospered because the instability and chaos of the Weimar Republic was their natural milieu. One could see them scurrying about like rats in the foyers and back alleys of East Berlin, he charged, selling their black-market jewelry, or on the posh West side, lounging about in fashionable Kurfürstendamm cafés as if they had lived there for generations. To make it worse, he complained, Jews were streaming in by the thousands each day from Poland. "These jackals," he deplored "were hurrying about in their filthy, frazzled caftans, sporting greasy felt hats, making their deals, stroking their frizzled beards, mumbling Yiddish and gesticulating." They had succeeded in turning the neighborhood around the Silesian Railroad Station into a ghetto.[19] When Karl Liebknecht and Rosa Luxemburg were brutally murdered in January 1919, Kurt joined the celebrations in the streets and the singing of the ghoulish song, "A Corpse Is Swimming in the Landwehr Canal." Regrettably, Eggers had learned his anti-Semitic lessons quite well, and they would later form the basis of his ideology.

Kurt soon contributed to the propaganda efforts of right-wing organizations. He joined the Deutscher Schutz und Trutzbund, whose commander engaged him as his personal aide-de-camp because of his loyalty and bravery. Eggers was now leading a double life, that of a troublemaker by day at school and an activist by night. He painted swastikas on the doors of synagogues, on the homes of wealthy Jews, and on public buildings. Gratified to be back in uniform, he sported the colors of the Schutzbund, a dark blue, small sunflower on a silver patch and a silver swastika. Kurt was home again among his comrades, and he delighted in singing the freebooter's song, whose first line celebrated the "swastika on steel helmet, black, white, red ribbon." He first saw action when his unit participated in the abortive Kapp Putsch in March 1920, joining in the hue and cry that Jewish communists were responsible for its failure.[20] Kurt was more committed to the German cause than ever, observing that he had become a "citizen of a secret Reich that lived only in the hearts of the free, men who hoped with all their heart that the day would come in which the

---

[19] Eggers, *Tanz aus der Reihe*, pp. 232–3. On these anti-Semitic motifs, see Steven E. Aschheim, *Brothers and Strangers: The East European Jew in German and German Jewish Consciousness, 1800–1923* (Madison: University of Wisconsin Press, 1982).
[20] Eggers, *Tanz aus der Reihe*, pp. 287–327.

inner Reich once more would become the Fatherland, the home of all Germans."[21]

Kurt Eggers was a considerably more complex personality than one might believe. He was intellectually gifted and set his mind to serious study in the gymnasium, especially Latin and Greek. He was confirmed into the Brandenburg Protestant Church in his home congregation, the Auenkirche parish in Berlin-Wilmersdorf in March 1921. How a belief in the tender mercy of Jesus Christ could be integrated into his nationalist obsession can only be explained by consideration of his age upon entering the church. He was only fifteen years old at the time and still clung to many of the traditional biases of the imperial social elite, including the established church and respect for the monarchy.

Eggers marched in uniform with his Trutz und Schutzbund comrades across Berlin to Potsdam to take part in the monarchist rally following the death of the Empress, Auguste Viktoria in April 1921. His company took up guard duty near the Neues Palais, where both Field Marshals Erich Ludendorff and Paul von Hindenburg took their salute in a march by. Eggers's romanticism could get the better of him as evidenced by a humorous event that took place a few days later while his company was guarding the entrance to the Kaiser Wilhelm Memorial Church. Eggers, now dressed in his naval cadet uniform, rushed to open the door of the crown princess's carriage upon its arrival. Bowing in deep respect, he cavalierly accompanied the princess into the church past the uniformed dignitaries of the past. Like a little boy happily reporting that he had won his mother's approval for a good deed, he commented later that the crown princess had asked him his name. Such were the youthful experiences of a future SS officer and self-appointed spokesman for the testament of Zarathustra![22]

In fact, Eggers was about to address infinitely more serious matters. In 1921, renewed trouble broke out with Poland in Upper Silesia, where a plebiscite was to decide the future of the province. Following the German victory at the polls in March, Polish Free Corps units under the command of Wojciech Korfanty rose up in an effort to conquer all of Upper Silesia. To make matters worse, in the view of German nationalists, the French had gone far beyond the role mandated to them by the League of Nations to function as overseers of the plebiscite, going so far as to supply their Polish ally with deliveries of weapons and intelligence information. German volunteer Free Corps units were quickly formed, and once more

---

[21] Ibid., p. 327.   [22] Ibid., pp. 339-55.

Eggers hurried into action. Knowing that it was impossible to get his parents' permission to head eastward immediately, Kurt sought the blessing of his old naval commandant who sent him off to war with the words: "I am proud to have played a part in your military training, and I know that you will be brave. I hope that you make it back home. But if you don't, at least you know that you had the privilege of dying a free man."[23]

With time so short before heading to the front, Eggers was not able to request leave from the director of the Bismarck Gymnasium. Instead, he simply dropped a note off at the school, which conveyed the following brief, yet telling, message:

> Dear Honorable Herr Director! I want to inform you that I will have to be absent for some time from the Gymnasium, because I am going to join my comrades with the Free Corps and am now on the way to Upper Silesia. Kurt Eggers[24]

Eggers's reminiscences of his Free Corps experience reflect its defining role in both the development of his character and in the clarification of his radicalism. He exuded a boyish delight in the adventure and was completely in harmony with the freebooter spirit of the paramilitary groups whose ethos and behavior had much in common with marauding wolf packs. He shared the reckless abandon that gripped the rebellious Free Corps men, who were eager to put their frustrations behind them and to swing into action. They were certain that they had to fight a war on two fronts – against the Poles on one hand and what they considered to be the traitorous German government on the other. The clandestine nature of their bold enterprise acted as a tonic for them as well. Eggers was deployed in a light machine gun unit attached to the Schwarze Schar, commanded by First Lieutenant Karl Bergerhoff, whose emblem was the death's-head skull and crossbones.[25] Their weapons consisted of World War I equipment secreted by right-wing groups in a barn along the Neisse River. It was a source of great pride for the members of the Schwarze Schar to march out singing their favorite songs while the yellow-white flag of Silesia – made for them by the local inhabitants – waved briskly in the wind before them. In the event, they were to be deployed in the legendary storming of the heights of the Annaberg, perched above the Oder River, an

[23] Ibid., p. 358.   [24] Ibid., p. 360.

[25] See book by Lt. Karl Bergerhoff, *Die Schwarze Schar in O/S. Ein historischer Abschnitt aus Oberschlesiens Schreckenstagen* (Gleiwitz: Selbst-Verlag "Schwarze Schar," 1932), which details the campaign waged by the unit. Remarkably, an approving letter from General von Seeckt was included as a dedication to the book.

engagement that assumed the aura of a Station of the Cross for German nationalists.

The Annaberg engagement featured names that were to become legendary in Free Corps annals. While units of the Storm Battalion Heinz, the Free Corps Oberland, and Heydebreck's Werewolves actually stormed the Annaberg, it was Lieutenant Bergerhoff's Schwarze Schar that took Wynona Hill and a nearby town, thus securing the right wing in the attack.[26] The fighting was bitter, and Eggers noted that no prisoners were taken, a rather telling description for murder. The victory was profoundly moving to many veterans of the Great War, men who had known only sadness since their humiliating defeat in 1918. General von Hülsen remarked on the delight German units took in once more raising their war flags "on conquered territory." He reported how a veteran of the Annaberg engagement, gazing at the German battle flag waving from the tower of Annaberg Cloister, sighed and said that "he could die in peace" now that the German battle flag had been raised from the filth of Versailles to the place of honor it always had deserved.[27]

Young Eggers shared in this triumph, although he admitted that his own baptism of fire was not entirely heroic. Suffering a punctured eardrum and a wound in his left foot, he had felt tears rolling down his cheeks at the moment of crisis.[28] But the real agony set in when, at the very moment of victory, the Free Corps felt that they were betrayed by their own government. On May 24, 1921, Reich President Friedrich Ebert and Chancellor Joseph Wirth issued an order closing the border to Upper Silesia, and deployed a thousand troops to secure it. They were commanded to block any movement by armed Free Corps units heading east and to disarm those returning home. Disobedience to the order would bring perpetrators a fine of 100,000 marks and possible imprisonment.[29] The men of the Free Corps were hoping to conquer and occupy the entire province of Upper Silesia in another spectacular feat of arms and were furious that

[26] Kompanieführer der 1.III. Sturmfahne Freikorps Oberland, Captain Viktor Scheffel, paid Eggers's unit a tribute for breaking through on the right wing and thus guaranteeing victory. See V. Scheffel, "Annaberg," in Ernst von Salomon, *Das Buch vom deutschen Freikorpskämpfer* (Berlin: Wilhelm Limpert Verlag, 1938), pp. 270–9. Compare Robert G. L. Waite. *Vanguard of Nazism. The Free Corps Movement in Postwar Germany 1918–1923* (Cambridge, MA: Harvard University Press, 1952), pp. 227–32.

[27] Generalleutnant von Hülsen, "Freikorps im Osten," in Han Roden, *Deutsche Soldaten* (Leipzig: Breitkopf & Härtel, 1935), p. 115.

[28] Eggers, *Tanz aus der Reihe*, p. 383.

[29] For a copy of the Reich government's order, which appeared in poster form throughout the country, see von Salomon, p. 301. Compare Waite, pp. 231–2.

they were being forced to return home. Was this to be the thanks of the Fatherland, they queried, for their efforts to secure dignity for the nation and a peaceful life for German citizens in the East?

The Schwarze Schar released a statement to the press in honor of their fallen, appending a bitter statement that: "Far from the homes of their parents, these men gave the best they had in the battle against the Polish rabble. Their patriotic spirit, valor, and readiness for self-sacrifice assures them a place in our hearts forever."[30] Eggers's radical spirit was only hardened by this experience, and it is fair to say they he remained a freebooter until the end of his days. He later bemoaned the fate of his beleaguered compatriots: "Hopeless and not knowing where to turn, we headed home and were lost in a Germany that did not know us. We could only shrug our shoulders and secretly shed tears for Germany."[31]

Years later, in 1937, Eggers would publish a novel, *Rebels' Mountain*, that drew on his experiences in Upper Silesia.[32] Part memoir, part novel, the work features as protagonist the student Konrad Ertel, a member of the Schwarze Schar. Like Eggers, he received his baptism of fire in the storm on Annaberg. Ertel was presented as a bridge from the past to the future Reich, representing the many idealistic students who joined the hardened and experienced veterans of World War I in the Free Corps. His death was redemptive, and the commander of the Schwarze Schar lowers the unit's battle-torn flag in his honor, saying, "I served at both Langemarck and Verdun. These were the most important battles of the Great War. But Annaberg will become the symbol of German youth, who will lead us into a new world, to that summit we call freedom." Before their great victory, the Free Corps were known as rebels, he claimed. But ever after they would be regarded as the real founders of the great new Reich to come, the Third Reich, the "Empire of the Free."[33]

Upon his return to Berlin, where he enrolled once more in the Bismarck Gymnasium, Eggers was a lost soul. The vulgarity of materialist capitalism, the perceived Jewish influence in the government and media, and the suffering of the people all distressed him terribly. The only bright point

---

[30] Bergerhoff, pp. 55–7.
[31] "Wir hatten keine Zeit," in *Schicksalsbrüder*, pp. 26–9.
[32] Kurt Eggers, *Der Berg der Rebellen* (Leipzig/Berlin: Schwarzhäupter Verlag, 1937).
[33] Friedhelm Kaiser praised the work highly in a 1937 review published in Dortmund. He noted that it was difficult to judge the work's literary merits, "because Eggers has succeeded in not simply writing a factual history of Annaberg, but rather viewing it as a symbol of eternal Germanness". See Friedhelm Kaiser, "Kurt Eggers/Der Berg der Rebellen." Des Dichters und Mitkämpfers Buch von Annaberg, Kurt Eggers Collection, Institut für Zeitgeschichte, Munich.

in his life surfaced when Minister of Economics Matthias Erzberger was murdered by Free Corps officers while vacationing in the Black Forest in the summer of 1921, followed by the assassination of Foreign Minister Walther Rathenau en route to his office in June 1922. Eggers was so much in harmony with violence that he made it known that as far as he was concerned, the entire pack of "Weimar traitors" should meet the same fate. He could not keep a job, was expelled from school for bad behavior, and served short stints in jail for assaulting political enemies on the streets of Berlin. Thereupon, he matriculated in the Agricultural University in the capital to prepare for a career on the land. He joined a fraternity and took a great interest in fighting the traditional regulated fencing bouts (*Mensur*) which he felt to be a test of physical skill, personal courage, and character. He wore his facial scars from the duels as a badge of honor.

Eggers took his agricultural internship at the Rittergut Vogelsang in Mecklenburg, where he learned at firsthand the economic difficulties that farmers encountered in the Weimar Republic. Despite its hardships, life on the land was supremely happy for him, because there he found himself at one with nature. He was certain that this was not the craven romanticism of a city dweller, nor was it Tolstoyan escapism. Instead, he observed, "a real farmer has to love his fields, as if they were blood of his blood."[34] Only the farmer who plows the soil realizes that he has a blood relationship with the earth, which he passes on to his son, from generation to generation. Although he may own the farm, he is nevertheless subject to the immutable laws of nature. There is a rhythm in nature, in the organic recurrence of the seasons, while the simplest things – the singing of the birds, the hum of the bees, and the behavior of animals – all have a lesson to tell. To live in the country – as opposed to the city – was to experience the reality of life itself. Eggers lent an historical dimension to his love of the land and on Sundays went with other farmers into the forest to discover graves of Huns, to recite the werewolf poetry of Hermann Löns, and to stage readings of some of his own poetic creations.

Eggers argued that agricultural reform was the order of the day, because far too many people on the farms were simply rural proletarians, wage earners with no organic union with the land.[35] Such radical sentiments about the agricultural crisis were anathema to the owners of Vogelsang

---

[34] Eggers, *Tanz aus der Reihe*, pp. 413–16.

[35] Talk of agricultural reform was anathema to the estate owners who were sensitive to challenges to their authority. See Shelley Baranowski, *The Sanctity of Rural Life. Nobility, Protestantism & Nazism in Weimar Prussia* (New York: Oxford University Press, 1995), pp. 68–70. For an authoritative analysis of the desperate crisis in agriculture during the Weimar Republic, see Baranowski, pp. 118–26.

Castle who became uneasy observing how much time their restless intern was spending with the farmhands and stable boys. His pronouncements at social events and over dinner in the castle were poorly received by the owners, who considered him a threat to their privileged order. His days in the country were cut short when, following an especially nasty exchange with the incensed Junker, Eggers departed the estate in a fit of rage. Shortly thereafter, he did another stint on an estate at Giesendorf, southeast of Berlin.

Years later, Eggers tended to exaggerate his rural heritage, the better to fit the Nazi antiurban model. In fact, this was just one more component of his myth making. He tended to overlook the fact that he was born in prosperous Berlin-Schöneberg and totally ignored the wealthy businessmen in his family, preferring to point to the teachers, preachers, and farmers in his family tree. Eggers was joined in this distortion by Eberhard Wolfgang Möller, who exaggerated his rural roots in Thuringia, the home of the Reformation, while in truth he was very much a product of the urban milieu of Berlin that he denigrated.

Once more the young rebel searched in vain for his proper life's calling. Fortunate enough to succeed where so many before him had failed, he was inducted into the Reichswehr as a gunner in the Third Prussian Field Artillery Regiment, posted at Frankfurt on the Oder.[36] He was certain that Poland was about to strike westward, and he longed to see military action once more. This was not to be. He was also disappointed in the government's passive resistance campaign against the French occupation of the Ruhr. It galled him when in March 1923, French troops occupied the Krupp Works in Essen, killing thirteen German workers and wounding forty-one others. There was no chance that the army would be deployed against the French, however, and Eggers became ever more restless, a situation compounded when Albert Leo Schlageter was executed as punishment for sabotage by the French in the Golzheimer Heath outside Düsseldorf in May 1923. Eggers felt that this case of unredeemed martyrdom was reprehensible. When in 1924 his regiment was assigned to Berlin to guard the highest officials of the Weimar government, it was more than he could stand. Despite having enlisted in the Reichswehr for twelve years, Eggers's superiors understood his predicament and granted him an honorable medical discharge.

After a brief period at Göttingen University where he heard lectures and became convinced that history was not being taught the way it should

---

[36] Eggers enlisted in the Reichswehr in the fall of 1923. See Eggers, *Tanz aus der Reihe*, pp. 459.

be, Eggers returned to Berlin. With nothing to lose, he appealed to the director of the Bismarck Gymnasium to readmit him, jokingly observing that "After the last amnesty we old Free Corps veterans are citizens with unblemished records." The director would have none of it, observing caustically that "You always danced to your own drummer, Herr Eggers. Do you really believe that I would be so idiotic as to readmit you as a senior student, so that you could put our school on its ear with your bad influence?[37] Fortunately for Eggers, an understanding former army lieutenant, the director of the Kaiser Friedrich Gymnasium on the Savigny Platz, admitted him to the school where, it turned out, more than 90 percent of the students in his class were Jewish. Because advanced study now meant so much to him, he bore down on his reading of Greek, Roman, and German literature, as well as Hebrew, in preparation for the study of archeology at university. Within less than a year, he had passed his final examinations with high marks.

To the dismay of his family, at the age of twenty Eggers began a rigorous curriculum at the Humboldt University of Berlin, which included study of philosophy, Sanskrit, classical and Biblical archeology, Aramaic, and Hebrew.[38] Even though his father had considerable means, he felt it necessary to earn money for college and took a job as a waiter in a café on the Müller Strasse in Berlin. An ambitious owner wished to make an impression in this smoky milieu by hiring college students and dressing them for work in rather rumpled tuxedos. It would be difficult to conceive of a more solidly communist neighborhood than Berlin-Wedding, where the communist leader Ernst Thälmann often held forth, and the vision of Kurt Eggers waiting on proletarian tables there is absolutely Chaplinesque. He was able to survive this setting for only a few weeks, before taking another job that also brought him into close proximity to working people, this time as a red cap carrying baggage at the Stettiner Railroad Station.[39]

Eggers continued his study of theology and related fields at Rostock University. There he joined the Corps Vandalia, at that time a right-wing, elitist fraternity under the umbrella of the corporate Kösener S.C. organization. The Vandalians had associated themselves with the *Hochschulring Deutscher Art*, an intellectual hotbed for racist and National Socialist ideology, and some noteworthy brothers cast their lot with Adolf Hitler.

---

[37] Ibid., pp. 505–6.
[38] See Kurt Eggers, "Mein Lebenslauf," September 1, 1936, Kurt Eggers File, BAB.
[39] Eggers, *Tanz aus der Reihe*, pp. 523–4.

Eggers went to work on his major research paper in archeology as well, choosing Byzantine basilica architecture as his field of concentration, a remarkable course of study for a future SS propagandist. His red facial scars from recent duels did not serve to endear him either to the theology faculty or his fellow students.

The project Eggers chose for his theological concentration dealt with Jesuit influences in the powerful "Catholic Action" organization, an activist endeavor of the Mother Church begun by Pope Pius IX with the goal of influencing political, moral, and family relations in the modern state. Focusing on the significant writings of Erich Przywara, S.J., Eggers's research took him to the excellent collections of the Prussian Secret State Archive housed in Berlin-Dahlem. There he ferreted out evidence that convinced him that he was on the trail of a Catholic conspiracy. His theory centered on the activities of Ludwig Windhorst, leader of the Catholic Center Party who, he was certain, forced a misunderstood Otto von Bismarck into the notorious *Kulturkampf*, the assault on the Catholic Church in the newly united Germany in the 1870s. Eggers was actually in the initial stages of what for him would become a lifelong attack on the Roman Catholic Church, which he pursued with a venomous obsession not unlike that of the Nazi court philosopher, Alfred Rosenberg.[40]

The Vandalia Corps had an active social life, and Eggers was cast into situations that defy belief. One such encounter took place at the locale favored by Vandalia's brother house in Berlin, the famed Normannia Corps. There he imbibed several beers with none other than Horst Wessel, the yet uncrowned martyr and commander of the SA Storm 5 in Berlin-Friedrichshain, whose death Goebbels would transfigure into a political apotheosis. Wessel, known for his outbursts, looked at Eggers and drew his attention to two Normannia brothers across the table, saying: "There's a couple of strange opposites! The one is Friedrich Hielscher, standing on his head today trying to perceive of a Reich that will tower over even our own Third Reich. The other is Hanns Heinz Ewers, whom you surely know from his weird novels!" Later the group was joined by "Hugi," who turned out to be the son of Alfred Hugenberg, the media magnate and leader of the German Nationalist Party. Late into the night, the band of future party leaders debated the desperate condition

---

[40] Ibid., pp. 536–47. According to Eggers, Bismarck was forced to become a "heretic," a designation he delighted in taking for himself and for every "freedom-loving German" since the days of the Reformation.

of their Fatherland.[41] Little did Eggers presage the significance of that evening.

As Eggers prepared for his state examination, he became engrossed in the period of the German Reformation, less for his interest in Luther's dramatic campaign for spiritual renewal than for his fascination with the volatile political milieu of the early sixteenth century. Eggers was drawn especially to the evangelical revolutionary, Ulrich von Hutten, and throughout his life, he would return for personal inspiration to the life and legends of this zealous knight. He also admired the left-wing radicalism of Thomas Müntzer, and attacked the cold intellectuality of the ivory tower humanists of the Reformation era. As for modern theologians, he was convinced that they were more interested in engaging in intellectual word games than in bringing social justice to the world. Eggers heard the distinguished theologian Paul Tillich speak at Rostock and was appalled with what he perceived to be misguided modernist theories bridging theology and philosophy, religion and culture, Lutheranism and socialism. He referred to Tillich as "the founder of religious communism," whose teachings provided a gathering point for "Jews, republicans, pacifists, communists and the other supporters of the weakness of the spirit of Geneva." He noted with contempt that true Christians were rare in seminaries and academic departments of religion. Eggers wanted something radically different than they professed. As he expressed it: "I did not want to return to Christ, but instead to continue what Luther had started. I wanted to be a Protestant and, the way I saw it, the church should be the springboard for spiritual action, without which the struggle for freedom would be impossible. Only Nietzsche and von Hutten could lead me to freedom."[42]

What a scene it must have been in the Rostock University Church when Eggers, wearing the traditional black gown and white collar favored by the evangelical clergy, delivered his first sermon. The congregation that day was a colorful mixture of people and included fraternity men in full regalia, former girlfriends, assorted longshoremen from the port with whom he had tipped many a glass, fellow students, and in the front two rows, the assembled fighting corps students, dressed in assorted tuxedos, cutaways, and seedy blue suits. After the singing of the hymn "Wake up, wake up, you German land!," the stirring call to action inspired by the Reformation, Eggers launched into an atypical Protestant sermon. The word "Jesus" never crossed his lips. Instead, he drew variations on the themes of freedom and responsibility, sacrifice and struggle. Clearly, this was an

---

[41] Ibid., pp. 548–9.   [42] Ibid., p. 553.

exhortation on the willingness of Germans to sacrifice for their nation, ideas cherished by his fraternity brothers but rejected by the theology students in attendance, who did not see a future Christian minister in Eggers but instead a hopeless outsider.[43]

It is puzzling why a nationalist desperado like Eggers would even endeavor to become a minister. Here was a man who at his ordination in 1930 was twenty-five years old and fit the profile of a National Socialist activist. Eggers himself saw the situation quite differently. In his own words, he had entered the service of the church to minister to the strong, not to console the weak. Furthermore, he considered himself to be an educator, not a prophet, a herald of a new era of freedom, like his mentors Friedrich Nietzsche and Ulrich von Hutten. He was first of all a writer and only secondarily an activist. This explains why he did not join the Party or the SS until 1935, when he realized that the time had come to live the life he had extoled in his literary creations.[44] Evidence that he was a misfit as a clergyman was not long in coming.

Having completed his examinations for the theological degree with honors, Eggers was assigned to the position of assistant minister in a backwoods community in Mecklenburg. There, by his own account, he began what he hoped would be a new German Reformation, "free of dogma and the Bible."[45] He had a deep affection for simple peasants and farmers, knowing from personal experience how they suffered economically and psychologically in an unfavorable economic environment. He saw how week after week, more deeply indebted farmers suffered the tragic fate of having their property foreclosed. As a result, Eggers's sermons were more political speeches than Christian homilies, and often the Bible was not even opened. Instead, he spoke the language of the peasantry movingly, calling on them to break their chains and demand major improvements in their lot. He joined in the effort to sabotage public auctions of farms and estates. He scorned the farm policies of both the Stresemann and Brüning administrations, berated "traitors" to the national cause, and attacked both communism and capitalism.

[43] Ibid., pp. 556–65.

[44] Further, in a period of severe unemployment, Eggers needed time and financial support to begin his writings on Ulrich von Hutten. See SS Oberführer Fuchs, i.v. Der Chef des Rasse- und Siedlungshauptamt SS, Stabskanzlei, March 10, 1938, "Dienstleistungszeugnis for SS-Untersturmführer Kurt Eggers," SS-Nr. 273 203, NSDAP Mitgliedsnummer 3 953 817, Kurt Eggers File, BAB.

[45] Eggers, *Tanz*, p. 573. Eggers was assigned to the village of Kratzeburg in Mecklenburg, a parish which included the rural communities of Dalmsdorf, Granzin, and Krienke.

The Lutheran church in Prussia was a bulwark of conservatism and for centuries had buttressed the union of church and state. The Junkers viewed it as a necessary firmament in the edifice of inherited privilege that they had traditionally enjoyed, serving both as a moral teacher and learned vehicle of conservative Scriptural authority.[46] Eggers's political agenda offended the rural establishment greatly, and there were serious rumblings of discontent in the provinces. As he became more and more outspoken, his radicalism and unsettling presence drew the attention of superiors in the church. There was gossip in his own parish to the effect that Eggers had been sent by the Devil to test the faith of the congregation. One Sunday morning he went so far as to dispense with the liturgy entirely. Instead, he delivered a political speech, urging the poor farmers to offer armed resistance to their oppressors under the black banner of the *Bundschuh*, just like their forefathers had four hundred years before. The peasants roared their approval and sang the national anthem lustily. Soon Eggers, who referred to himself as Mecklenburg's first Bauernführer, led acts of resistance against court-appointed representatives who appeared in the country to evict peasants from their farms.[47] His poem, "Song of the Struggling Peasants," was nothing less than an incitement to violence, calling for resistance unto death. The red and blue flames of burning farms, he proclaimed, would announce to the world the dawning of Germany's rebirth.[48]

By declaring himself the leader of a twentieth-century Peasants Revolt, Eggers had clearly crossed the Rubicon. The Church authorities were moved to action, citing the authority of Luther, who had opposed the Peasants Revolt vigorously, even urging the princes to slay the rebels in his famous tract, "Against the Murderous and Thieving Hordes of Peasants" (1525). Eggers threw fat on the fire when, in a café frequented by the bourgeoisie, he demanded the overthrow of the Berlin regime for their handling of the funeral of Horst Wessel. Nor did the uninhibited pastor shy away from love affairs. At length, church administrators from Berlin called Eggers to account, warning him to mend his ways. Nevertheless, he allowed his name to be placed on the combined conservative party electoral list for the Mecklenburg state elections. Called before the High Consistory late in 1930, he was summarily dismissed from his post and given a replacement appointment in a Berlin church.

---

[46] Baranowski, pp. 83–102, 128–44.   [47] Ibid., pp. 586–90.

[48] "Lied der kämpfenden Bauern," *Deutsche Gedichte* (München: Chr. Kaiser, 1934), p. 34. Eggers went so far as to call on the Virgin Mary for help in the poem, "Ave Maria": "Was weisst du von dem Kinde, Weisst du von seiner Not: Heut jauchzen ihm die Winde – Und morgen ist es tot" (ibid., p. 35).

Eggers witnessed firsthand the growth of poverty, hunger, and desperation as the economic and social crisis worsened. "Germany," he submitted,
"was at death's door."[49] Within a matter of months, Eggers had resigned,
convinced that the church leaders were entirely under Jewish-Marxist
influence. As he would later attest, he had resigned because he was "sick-
ened by the deception of the organized church and the untruthfulness of
Christianity."[50] The ministry of the young radical had lasted but eighteen
months.

With his career in the church ended, Eggers was determined to become
a writer for the nationalist cause. He pointedly refused to accept the assistance of family members who offered to use their influence to place him
in a job with a Berlin firm. Having willfully joined the millions of hopeless unemployed in the capital, Eggers tried in vain to find a publisher for
his recently completed novel, *Hutten*. Just like Joseph Goebbels, another
frustrated novelist of that era, he would blame Jewish publishing firms
such as Ullstein and Mosse for his own failures. When trying to find an
outlet for his Free Corps radio drama *Annaberg*, Eggers was shown the
door by a supercilious radio executive. His personal disappointments were
exacerbated when he was approached by his former comrade in the border wars, the former Free Corps Oberland officer Josef "Beppo" Römer,
to join him in a radical workers organization attached to the communist
front. He was deeply saddened that Römer had gone over to the Marxists,
remarking on this odd twist of fate during the worsening German crisis.[51]
He was now without proper food or clothing. The last straw came when
the courts confiscated everything Eggers owned in his pathetic little rented
room in Berlin. In an act of desperation, he headed to East Prussia in 1932,
claiming that he would be among the first to see action when fighting with
the Poles broke out once more. In fact, he was seeking food and shelter
on one of the many estates that for years had served as way stations for
so many former Free Corps men.

The works of Kurt Eggers written during the transition from the Weimar
era to the Third Reich were characterized more by revolutionary passion
than intellectual depth. Unlike many authors on the nationalist right,
Eggers never darkened an archive, indulging rather in what was often a
childlike adoration of his cultural heroes. As a result, he focused on the

---

[49] Eggers, *Tanz aus der Reihe*, p. 597.   [50] Kurt Eggers File, BAB.
[51] Josef Römer also wrote for the communist newspaper, *Aufbruch*. As early as 1934 he
    became involved in plots to assassinate Hitler, was sent to Dachau, and was executed in
    1944.

career of the most hopelessly romantic nobleman of the Reformation era, the vehemently antipapal humanist, Ulrich von Hutten. Crowned poet laureate in 1517 by the Holy Roman Emperor, Maximilian I, Hutten did not possess the brilliance and political astuteness of his contemporary, Erasmus. Instead, it was his revolutionary spirit that Eggers wished to emulate, as well as his strength in adversity and determination to play a role in returning Germany to the glory it had once known.

As Eggers himself noted: "As long as I can remember, I have felt a certain prophetic calling, a feeling that I must stir things up, cry out and awaken the unaware, and keep the flame alive. There was no question that Hutten would be the subject of my first play."[52] He was attracted to Hutten because of his legendary struggle for German freedom and unity. Freedom from Rome, freedom from foreign influence, freedom from the concept of sin, and freedom from all unnatural controls. Eggers dreamt of the day when the young knights of the Third Reich would ride forth into the light of morning, side by side with Ulrich von Hutten, to restore the greatness of the German empire.[53]

By focusing on von Hutten, Eggers was drawing variations on a major theme in Nazi education of the young. For example, on view at the Ordensburg Vogelsang – the elite school for future National Socialist Party leaders – was a work by Georg Sluyterman von Langeweyde, which featured Ulrich von Hutten and a Junker of the Third Reich traversing the landscape of the Eifel on horseback, with the castle of the Ordensburg towering over them.[54] As Eggers wrote in *Germany Aflame. A Hutten Ballad*: "Wake up, Germans! The dawn will soon be breaking when the flame of freedom will shine down from the mountains and illuminate the valleys, giving us hope once more!"

Eggers also employed the figure of Hutten as a trope in the racial question. By focusing on race as a major factor in German renewal, he struck a sinister chord by claiming that the time was coming when Germans once more must answer the call of their blood. Eggers was after all on the syllabus of every student enrolled in a Party school, and the young Nazi guard was not long in taking up this motif as well. One can ascertain the importance of the education of the young by Eggers and other propagandists by citing but one example. At an Ordensburg function held in

---

[52] "Junges Schrifttum," *Das Deutsche Wort*, 10.

[53] Kurt Eggers, *Feuer über Deutschland. Eine Huttenballade* (Oldenburg/Berlin: Gerhard Stalling, 1939), pp. 18–19. See also Kurt Eggers, *Hutten: Roman eines Deutschen* (Berlin: Propyläen, 1934).

[54] See H.-Dieter Arntz, *Ordensburg Vogelsang 1934–1945. Erziehung zur politischen Führung im Dritten Reich* (Euskirchen: Kümpel, Volksblattdrückerei, 1986), p. 108.

the Rudolf Oetker Hall in Bielefeld in June 1939, attended by some two hundred young National Socialist "knights," the speaker pointed to the importance of Ulrich von Hutten as their historic exemplar. Hutten, it was claimed, had been a revolutionary who in his own day set an example for them by stressing that the Germanic race was engaged in a battle for blood and soil, freedom and honor. It was the obligation of the young Party stalwarts to join the vanguard in this struggle of world-historic importance.

By focusing on the theme of racism, Eggers was recklessly distorting his hero's views by superimposing on him a National Socialist racist exclusivity. Eggers's interpretation of Hutten became a component in the pedagogical canon of the SS, with the result that he took on considerably more importance in National Socialist propaganda than he actually enjoyed in history.[55] According to this interpretation, for over two thousand years Germans had fought to free themselves from foreign influence. Whenever their desperate situation seemed as if it could get no worse, providentially a "Nordic bearer of light would spring forth to protest in the name of the German blood." Whereas in A.D. 9, it was Arminius who rose up against the Roman legions, later it was to be Widukind and Walther von der Vogelweide who stood up for Germany. In this curious historical falsification, Luther was deemed to have been a weak individual, merely a transitory historical figure. Rather Hutten alone was the genuine revolutionary, serving as a significant link to the Third Reich. "True revolutionaries," Eggers opined, "influence the course of history for a millennium."[56]

Eggers simply went over the top when he claimed that the spirit of Hutten had called him to be a modern apostle for freedom. As he wrote: "I cannot rest. You have become my fate. You were a revelation for me. I must follow your will: to carry the flag and to summon others to the attack. You live in me! Through you I have learned to hate and carry my head high. I laugh at danger and will never surrender."[57] This zealous spirit was reflected in the plays and choruses that Eggers wrote soon after Hitler's assumption of power, works that appear crude today but that in their era reflected a nearly religious statement.[58] Young boys, the Reich's future political soldiers, loudly chanted such lines as these:

"We will grow into an elite race of the unspoiled brave."
"We know the meaning of the freedom our blood gives us."

[55] *Hutten* was also widely featured on German radio in the 1933 and 1934.
[56] "Lasst Hutten nicht verderben!" in *Ich habs gewagt! Hutten ruft Deutschland*, ed. Kurt Eggers (Berlin/Lichterfelde: Widukind & Boss, 1939), pp. 5–8, 17
[57] Eggers, "An Hutten," in *Der deutsche Dämon* (Leipzig/Berlin: Schwarzhäupter, 1937).
[58] See Kurt Eggers, *Sturmsignale. Revolutionäre Sprechchöre* (Leipzig: Ferd. Peter, 1934).

"Come to us, all you who have not died, Nordic blood flows through your veins, and together we will fight and win the day."[59]

Hutten's model inspired Eggers to compose the chorus, "Flyers," focusing on the motif of freedom. Appealing to the spirit of adventure of the young generation who were thrilled with the new world that flying presented them, he rhapsodized:

> Heaven and earth lie at our feet, they are far behind us now, and the stars greet us flyers.
> We fly and hover between life and death, between happiness and pain, transcending space and time.
> Far beneath us people wave and sink back into their tedium.
> But we are liberated.
> We fly toward the light, past the night.
> We are free in the clouds.[60]

Eggers's radical views soon drew him to the attention of the power brokers in Berlin. As a result, after Hitler was named chancellor, he was appointed director of broadcasting for Reich Sender Leipzig, which offered him ample opportunity to present his plays, poetry, and songs to the German public. He was also included in the circle of writers around Goebbels, a position he used to ingratiate himself with influential members of the Party and the SS. A year after joining the SS, Eggers was named to the Race and Settlement Central Office, where he headed the department responsible for indoctrination and ritual.[61] Although he moved in and out of various influential cultural positions, Eggers remained first and foremost an independent writer and propagandist.

As might be expected, Eggers became part of the short-lived *Thingspiel* movement, begun with such passion, but that had little chance of winning an enduring place in the theater of the Third Reich.[62] His works in this genre included *Job the German*; *Annaberg*, which played in theaters throughout the Reich; and *The Great Journey*, which premiered in the *Thing* theater in Halle. They all reflected the same pathos and sacramental

[59] "Das Sonnenkreuz der Freiheit," "Junge Kolonne" and "Kriegsruf," ibid., pp. 4–13.
[60] "Flieger," ibid., pp. 21–4.
[61] Rasse-und-Siedlungs Hauptamt, III. Schulungs und Feiergestaltung. See "Mein Lebenslauf," Kurt Eggers File, BAB.
[62] See George Mosse, *The Nationalization of the Masses* (Frankfurt/Berlin: Ullstein, 1975), pp. 140–1. Compare, Klaus Vondung, *Magie und Manipulation* (Göttingen: Vandenhoeck & Ruprecht, 1971), p. 184. See also Uwe-Karsten Ketelsen, *Von Heroischen Sein und Völkischen Tod. Zur Dramatik des Dritten Reiches* (Bonn: Bouvier, 1970), pp. 299–301.

fervor to be found in Richard Euringer's bombastic *German Passion 1933* or Hanns Johst's *Schlageter*, two other representative yet time-bound plays of that period. Clearly, the author's goal was to cast suffering Germany in the role of the world's savior, the identical concept one could see on the wall of Hitler's birthplace in Braunau, where an artist had inscribed in bold letters, "Let the World be Healed Through the German Spirit."

Job the German was written in a style reminiscent of the ancient mystery theater, in which Job symbolized Germany and was subjected to every conceivable mode of suffering. The Archangel Michael acted as the guardian of Germany, as God's testing of Job assumed many painful turns. Choirs of angels as well as "bearers of death" enter the lists, yet Job endures throughout the brutal siege. Finally, God rewards Job, saying, "Go back to the earth and your longings will be fulfilled! I give to you the splendors of the world, your possessions, and your sons. I will reveal myself to the world from this time forward through your people. Go from me in peace, German! My spirit will be with you until the end of time. You came enslaved but leave as the master, you German. Take over your Reich as king!" The chorus answered joyfully: "He will rule over the whole world, clothed in godly royal garb. The German is free! Free forever."[63]

As early as 1933, Eggers began what he considered to be his testament for the German people, which he arrogantly referred to as a "catechism for a total German ethic." In fact, it became but the first component of what would eventually become a trilogy on the motif of heroic freedom. It commenced with the publication of *On Courageous Living and Brave Death*, which appeared in the triumphalist *Writings for the Nation* series edited by the prominent author of military works, Werner Beumelburg. *The Birth of the Millennium* was the next title, which clearly was written as propaganda for the Third Reich, yet which in its sweeping universalist scope offered a Nazi antidote to Oswald Spengler and Arnold Toynbee. *The Home of the Powerful*, which completed the trilogy, presented epigonal

---

[63] Kurt Eggers, *Das Spiel von Job dem Deutschen. Ein Mysterium*, Wilhelm Karl Gerst, ed., *Aufbruch zur Volksgemeinschaft. Eine Sammlung deutscher Volksschauspiele* (Berlin: Volksschaft-Verlag, 1933). Although the play premiered before five thousand people in the Messehalle in Cologne and featured Eugen Klöpfer as Job, the critics were less than supportive of it. Otto Brües noted that Eggers simplified ideas to the point that they appeared banal. In his effort to reach everyone, he underestimated the intelligence of his audience. Just like the mystery plays presented in the Weimar era by Max Reinhardt, Eggers's *Job* was so weighed down by its priestly trappings that the artistic mission of the production was lost. However, Brües praised Werner Egk's musical score highly. See Otto Brües, *Job, der Deutsche*, Uraufführung in Köln, in *Von Fest und Feuer*, Kurt Eggers File, DLAM.

Nietzschean variations on Nordic racist themes. Focusing on the Germanic warrior Valhalla, the eternal home of the brave, it sounded the death knell to the Christian concept of Heaven. Eggers was certain that his work surpassed Nietzsche by positing that the future thousand years would belong to Nordic supermen, blond warriors of the Teutonic race.

With the coming of the war, Eggers attached a coda to his heroic trilogy, a militant catechism consisting of poems and essays on the subject of fulfillment. The opportunity to die a "brave death" in the service of the "German millennium" and to find an eternal life among the brave knights in Valhalla, the "home of the strong," had finally been realized. For Eggers, the time had come to put his pen aside and to bathe in the waters of eternity. The result was *On the Freedom of the Warrior* and *The Martial Revolution*, books that purportedly represented the German warrior's path to fulfillment but that in fact were characterized by a macabre funereal euphoria. Begun during the years of Blitzkrieg victories, Eggers's works reached a crescendo of emotion when the initial successes on the Russian front gave way to defeat and death on an unimagined scale.

On Courageous Living and Brave Death, published in 1935, preached a philosophy based on the Germanic "will to life." Above all, Eggers signaled a break with Christianity in this work, which affirmed man as master of his own fate, devoid of original sin, need for a savior, a resurrection or a heavenly afterlife.[64] The German racial community, united in blood in a way not witnessed since the era of its tribal origins, stood ready to perform glorious deeds of valor that would be celebrated in legend, myth, and song. The racial community was the bearer of will and law. Above all, the community of the Volk stood against the concept of mass man, the source of evil, liberal decadence, and pedestrian mediocrity. The elite brotherhood of warriors, loyal to the death and attuned to the will of the Führer, must remain on guard to liquidate this social disease wherever it appeared.

Immanent in the Volk was its spiritual essence, which Eggers referred to as "the Order," a racial holy temple, at once bearer of the Idea and witness to its eternal nature. The Order was the incarnation of the will of the Volk, supplanting the role Robespierre assigned to the general will, Hegel to the idea of freedom, Darwin to natural selection, or Marx to the

---

[64] Readers may wish to place Eggers's absolutely clear stand against Christianity within the context of Richard Steigmann-Gall's *The Holy Reich. Nazi Conceptions of Christianity, 1919–1945* (New York: Cambridge University Press, 2003), pp. 252–67.

dialectic. The warrior stood foursquare in the service of the Order, honor bound to be courageous, to act nobly, and to employ violence only in the service of a higher ideal. The fighter must die proudly, robbing death of its sting, certain that the shedding of his blood would further the fulfillment of the law of the nation. Reason, Enlightenment concepts, and all traces of Christian thought were eradicated. As for himself, Eggers announced, "I hope to die bravely doing my duty and know that a blessed death comes only to those who die in fulfillment of the law. I hope to die in a way that my death is a worthy culmination of a strong life."[65] Eggers appended "The Song of Comrades" as poetic affirmation of this motif, attesting that death was part of the great chain of life. He concluded the poem with a joyful celebration of his assured warrior's sacrifice: "Let the drums roll! The world is grand! I too will die a soldier's death."[66]

The Birth of the Millennium provided an historical basis for Kurt Eggers's worldview, but its pretentious conceptual framework, claiming to represent an all-embracing historical scheme, was actually narrow in its vision. The author divided the history of the West into two periods, symbolized by dream and reality, darkness and light, good and evil, putrefaction and strength, thereby offering an explanation for German suffering over the previous thousand years. The past was an era in which Germans did not see themselves as Germans but often as servants of retrograde Christendom. He assailed Rome as the parasitical seat of nihilistic collectivism, shackling the great northland to the power and whims of an alien Mediterranean people. Instead of building their own empire, Germans were satisfied to waste their energy on Crusades, the only purpose of which was to strengthen the imperialist program of the papacy. Christian humility and weakness characterized the era, which was often given over to the abnegation of man's natural instincts. The peasantry subjected itself to the nobility, the only goal of which was self-aggrandizement. Jewry ran rampant with its own cultural and spiritual program, which camouflaged the imperialist goals of the Hebrew people. During the entire historical process, Nordic blood was weakened and polluted. Learning replaced strength, and an exaggerated and overly subtle intellectuality blinded the Volk to the truth. Cosmopolitanism overshadowed any sense of Germanic racial substance.

[65] Kurt Eggers, *Vom mutigen Leben und tapferen Sterben* (Oldenburg i.O: Gerhard Stalling: 1935), pp. 94–5.
[66] *Schicksalsbrüder*, pp. 42–43.

These trends were taken to their extreme during the Great War. The conflict between the values of the warrior class and the bourgeoisie came to a head and ultimately determined the outcome of the war, as the heroism of the German soldiers gave way to the weakness and lack of will at the top. The enemies of Nordic man – the organized Church, Jewry, and Bolshevism – combined to destroy the Reich. Yet out of the darkness the Promethean Antichrist exploded like a starburst, flooding the cosmos with the light of freedom and signaling the birth of a new era.

Eggers's poem, "The Road to Freedom," formed the centerpiece of his most representative work, *The Birth of the Millennium*. Nordic man awakened to divine the testament of Zarathustra, greeting the dawn of the new century. Freedom, after one final glance into the bright light of the omniscient sun, with a bold heart clutched its sword and leapt through cosmic space down to the lowlands, where it would either emerge victorious in battle, bathed in the bright light of the sun, or go down to defeat and be forced to retreat into the shadows of night's eternal darkness. Through valiant effort, freedom was fated to win the final victory.[67]

With the onset of the new era, which the author referred to as the "millennium of heroic realism," the Church, the Jews, and Bolshevism would all be overcome. The strong would rule according to the law of nature, as the total state became the vehicle for Nordic man to fulfill the revolution. The Soviet star, the gold of Jewry, and the hypocrisy of Christianity would all fade into history. Political parties, bourgeois property and comforts, and all manner of decadence would disappear as individual wills were merged into the larger community of the Germanic race. The new millennium would not be a paradise, but rather a Spartan, soldierly state, ever on alert against enemies determined on its destruction. Rule by a Nordic elite protecting the nation from all corrosive foreign concepts would guarantee eternal justice. Led by courageous knights of the blood, who knew no fear, a golden age was fated to last a thousand years. Myth, reality, and a purified race would form a great union, inspiring a loyalty so intense that young warrior-knights would consider it a sacred privilege to die for

---

[67] Kurt Eggers, *Die Geburt des Jahrtausends* (Leipzig: Schwarzhäupter, 1936), pp. 147–48. This work was well received in SS circles. See letters from the Deutsches Ahnenerbe, Kommission für Schriftum, S/B, to Dr. Wilhelm Kinkelin, SS Standartenführer, Stabsamt des Reichsbauernführers, July 18, 1936, and to Dr. von Hase, Verlag Koehler und Amelang, Leipzig, July 22, 1936, which praise the work highly and recommend its acceptance in the appropriate Ahnenerbe book series. Eggers was compared to Nietzsche and lauded for his "clarity" and "fierceness of language" (see Kurt Eggers File, BAB).

it. "The storm winds are raging," he asserted. "The time has come to die."[68]

The Home of the Strong completed Kurt Eggers's catechism for Nordic renewal. In this work, the author returned to the world of tribal mythology, describing the future Reich in extremely romantic terms. At a time in the distant past when neither Christians nor Jews ruled the world, when the wind rustled through the leaves of ancient trees towering high over the groves of fallen heroes, Germanic ancestors heard the call of Odin the Strong. They soar like eagles in the gorgeous sky, embracing the eternal rainbow that only the brave may admire. He hearkened back to the days of the Garden, when Asgard, the source of eternal creativity, stood guard over the treasure hoard of Freedom in the castle of Asen, the center of the cosmos from which the spirit of Odin flowed into the blood of heroes below. The realm of Asen knew neither darkness nor dawn and was free from the shackles of time and space. From here Odin ruled over Valhalla, a majestic Hall of Heroes, the roof of which was decorated with swords and shields with gold that sparkled in the candlelight by night. Here the heroes lived only among themselves, gods among their fellow gods. Asgard's glorious rule of the world came to an end, and Valhalla fell into darkness when the knights lost sight of their ideals, having ignored the eternal law that was the source of their strength. The stage was set for Jewish arrogance and Christian hypocrisy. Eggers charged that "the Asen betrayed themselves by their unworthy blood mixing and sank from the heights of pure wisdom into the valleys of carnal decadence. Destruction always results from blood mixing!"[69] The result of this tragedy had deleterious effects for centuries and centuries thereafter.

Only in the modern age did the forces of good awaken once more, he observed, commencing a rebirth of timeless virtue. Rebellious Nordic man, realizing the truth, reestablished "the home of the strong" once more. This victory could only have been realized in Germany, the northern heartland. Their fallen heroes were said to be brothers of the gods and trace their lineage directly to them. Realizing from whence they came, they have returned home to Valhalla. They sit at table with the Asen, drinking from the same cup. They are the bravest of the brave, the fire of fire, and the light of light. Knowing what a solemn responsibility fate had cast upon them, they "listen to the harmony of the spheres and are filled

---

[68] Eggers, *Die Geburt des Jahrtausends*, p. 7.

[69] Kurt Eggers, *Die Heimat der Starken* (Dortmund/Berlin: Volkschaft Verlag, 1938), pp. 13–20.

with the melodic rhythm of creation."[70] Victorious against their enemies
and prepared to build the cathedral of eternity, they ride the cosmic wave
of freedom toward the great dawning in joyous exaltation.[71]

The Propaganda Ministry showcased the writings of Eggers in its annual
"Week of the German Book" in 1938, at which time he received laudatory
coverage nationwide. Hans W. Hagen, the SS literary propagandist, wrote
the featured article, in which he praised the author for the success of his
trilogy in contributing to the mobilization of Germany for the great deeds
to come. The onset of the Third Reich signaled not only a political revolution, Hagen submitted, but also a revolution of the spirit. Field Marshal
Ludendorff had shown the way, he wrote, by admonishing the German
people to strengthen the nation by steeling their souls. Now writers like
Kurt Eggers were carrying out a poetic mission to lead the way to inner
freedom and strength, offering enlightenment to guide the Nordic people,
not simply for decades but for centuries to come. His teaching was said
to offer a commendable embodiment of Nietzsche's prophecy that upon
the death of the gods, supermen would arise to take their place. It was
Eggers's great gift, he noted, to be the educator of supermen in the Reich's
fateful hour.[72]

Eggers managed to balance his career as a writer with various influential
positions in the SS cultural apparatus in Berlin. He was adept at cultivating
the highest-ranking Party functionaries, who found his enthusiasm for the
Nazi mission very stimulating. The key to Eggers's success in these various
roles was that he disarmed his contemporaries, who seldom saw him as
a rival but rather as a propagandist with great flair. They overlooked
his personal weaknesses, reputation as a bully, and exploitation of other
people. His first marriage in 1931 to Gerda Boldt of Magdeburg, the
sweetheart from his student days in Rostock, was a disaster because of
his philandering. It lasted only eighteen months and ended in divorce in
February 1933.[73]

There is evidence that Eggers misused his position in the SS, allegedly
going so far as to impersonate the Reichsführer SS Himmler on the
telephone while investigating a supposed case of espionage following
the banning of the periodical *The Inner Reich*. Eggers, who could be a

[70] Ibid., pp. 27–9.   [71] "Schicksalsbrüder," in ibid., pp. 206–7.
[72] For one example of many demonstrating the increasing prestige of Eggers as a writer and
propagandist, see Hans W. Hagen, "Der Dichter Eggers," and Friedhelm Kaiser, "Um die
Freiheit der deutschen Seele. Zu den weltanschauisch-kämpferischen Büchern von Kurt
Eggers," in *Westphälische Landeszeitung*, November 6, 1938.
[73] Judgment of the Preussische Landgericht III, Berlin-Charlottenburg, Case number
8.R.4238.32., February 17, 1933.

mischievous busybody, had originally fomented the crisis, when he wrote an unsigned article for *Das Schwarze Korps* in 1936, attacking the journal for publishing what he considered to be an unpatriotic article on Frederick the Great. He was successful in his original intent to close down *The Inner Reich*, which he deemed to be subversive. But Eggers overreached himself by becoming involved in Gestapo affairs in his search for internal enemies among the publication's often independent writers. Although his case was reported to several highly placed SS officers and led to an internal investigation of his indiscretions, Eggers was given the benefit of the doubt and the matter was dropped.

Yet another affair involved a dispute with Edgar Maria Moog, his predecessor as district leader of the South Westphalian office of the Reich Literature Chamber, which led to the convening of an SS Court of Honor. The matter was deemed important enough by Gruppenführer Schmitt, head of the SS Personnel Chancellery, to refer the matter to the offices of Reinhard Heydrich, who headed the SS Central Office, for his opinion. According to the judgment of the court, both men were deemed guilty of dishonorable conduct. It turned out that both Eggers and his adversary had improperly contacted Obergruppenführer August Heissmeyer to intervene on their behalf to influence the outcome of their case before the court.[74]

None of these entanglements had any noticeable effect on Eggers's career in the SS. His fellow officers in the SS Race and Settlement Central Office attested that he "was very highly regarded for his exemplary ideological firmness and also was a much loved comrade because of his fine human qualities."[75] With the onset of the war, Eggers somehow balanced his SS staff positions with service at the front, took a doctorate, and at the same time continued his extensive publishing activities.[76] He skillfully exploited his influence as a writer, even insinuating himself

---

[74] "Aktennotiz für die Pers. Akte E 248 des SS-Ostuf. Kurt Eggers. Der Vorgang, Ehrenhandel des SS-Ostuf. Ferdinand Thürmer gegen SS Ostuf. Eggers, befindet sich in der Pers. Akte M 1595 Edgar Moog." Eggers, Dortmund, February 11, 1939, to Personalkanzlei der Reichsführung SS, requesting "übersendung der Ehrenordnung betr. Ehrenangelegentheit zwischen SS-Führern." Der Chef der SS-Personalkanzlei Schmitt to Chef des SD-Hauptamtes, Heydrich, Abteilung Versorgung und Gericht, Kurt Eggers File, BAB.

[75] From his position as an officer in the Race and Settlement Central Office, he moved to a staff position with the SS Central Office, followed by an assignment with the Einwanderer Zentralstelle. Kurt Eggers, Dienstleistungszeugnis, Kurt Eggers File, BAB.

[76] See Egger's letter to the Rasse und Siedlungshauptamt, November 12, 1941, requesting his proof of Aryan background, because he needed the document in connection with his final doctoral examination. Eggers File, BDC. The title of Eggers's doctoral dissertation, which was a mere forty pages long, was "Neue Lösung des ersten ballistischen Hauptproblems. Eine Methode von grosser Einfachheit und Genauigkeit zur Berechung e. Geschossflugbahn und ihrer meteorol. bedingten Abänderungen." Berlin: J. Springer, 1939). The degree

into the closed circle around Hitler. The nimble SS propagandist Gunter d'Alquen used his influence with Himmler to place Eggers on the staff of the Party Chancellery, headed by Martin Bormann. Bormann, in turn, went so far as to recommend that Eggers's book, *The Home of the Strong* and d'Alquen's *This Is Victory* be distributed as Christmas gifts to members of the Wehrmacht, Waffen SS, and NSDAP in 1940.[77] Bormann also emerged as a protector of Eggers in the internecine cultural warfare pursued by Nazi ideological purists. When Hans W. Hagen – he was an SS officer on the staff of the Party Chancellery office approving the publication of literary works – attacked Eggers behind his back in 1942, Bormann had him summarily fired.[78]

As the war on the eastern front began to slow before Moscow in the early winter of 1941, Hitler himself read Eggers's vehement book *The Bonfire (Der Scheiterhaufen)*, an anthology of historical German anti-Christian thought, and commented on it very favorably.[79] According to Bormann, he went so far as to read passages aloud to his staff on several occasions and requested that the book be given to every member of his headquarters staff.[80] Hitler might well have sensed that he had found a

---

was awarded by the University of Rostock on August 23, 1939. See *Jahresverzeichnis der deutschen Hochschulschriften 1939*: 55, p. 609.

[77] See M. Bormann, NSDAP, Der Stellvertreter des Führers, Rundschreiben, December 7, 1940 to Reichsleiter, Gauleiter and Verbändeführer, "Buchgeschenke an Soldaten usw. zu Weihnachten," 41930, BA: NS18, *Akten der Parteikanzlei der NSDAP* (Munich: Saur, 1992). On Eggers's growing influence, see Obersturmführer (D. O., illegible), den Haag, February 22, 1941, to Untersturmführer Boehm, Ahnenerbe, Berlin-Dahlem: "Seine Beziehungen zu Bormann und damit indirekt zum Führer selbst können uns von grösster Bedeutung werden, da dort sehr konstruktive Pläne in kultureller Hinsicht vorbereitet werden. Eggers will auch die ersten 3 Nummern der neuen Weltliteratur an den Führer zur Beurteilung übergeben." Ibid. Eggers is also listed as a member of the Führungsstab (Organisationsleiter) of the SS Einwanderer Zentralstelle in *The Holdings of the Berlin Document Center, A Guide to the Collections*, p. 36.

[78] Bormann, Der Leiter der Partei Kanzlei, Führerhauptquartier, February 18, 1942, to Reichsleiter Philipp Bouhler, Leiter der Parteiamtlichen Prüfungskommission, announcing that he had had Hagen fired from his position. Hagen was later vindicated because he spoke at Egger's funeral ceremony staged in Berlin the next year (Hans W. Hagen File, BAB).

[79] Adolf Hitler, *Monologe im Führerhauptquartier. Die Aufzeichnungen Heinrich Heims*, ed. Werner Jochmann (Hamburg: Albrecht Knaus, 1980), pp. 96–8. Even the prickly Alfred Rosenberg noted in his diary in February 1940 that he had just read Eggers's *Tanz aus der Reihe*, observing that it was a decent effort but "really failed to come to grips with the great epic of our period of struggle." See *Das politische Tagebuch Alfred Rosenbergs 1934/35 und 1939/40*, ed. Hans-Günther Seraphim (München: Deutscher Taschenbuch Verlag, 1964), pp. 121–2.

[80] See Walter Tiessler, Propaganda Ministry, "Vorlage für Reichsleiter Bormann," December 8, 1941, *Akten der Parteikanzlei der NSDAP*, BA NS 18/33.

radical soulmate in Kurt Eggers, whose contempt for Christianity paralleled his own. Eggers's introductory poem to the work certainly spoke Hitler's language:

> You, my brothers,
> Take the torch
> And lighten the darkness!
> Set fire to the rotten world of lies
> And light the flame of zeal!
> Drive out with light and fire,
> The spooks,
> The sorcerers and conjurers
> The bewitched in the darkness
> Startle the souls
> Of the doubting.
> Set fire to the old rafters
> Where bats are hanging!
> The bright light of truth
> Announces the birth of freedom.
> You, my brothers,
> Attack.[81]

Both Hitler and Bormann ultimately wished to eliminate Christianity from German soil, and the propagation of writings by Kurt Eggers could be useful in this effort. Accordingly, with the hopes of gradually winning public support for this policy, Bormann recommended to the Propaganda Ministry that sixty thousand copies of *Der Scheiterhaufen* be printed and distributed immediately. Bormann was irritated when Goebbels personally rejected this plan, arguing that the time was not right for mass distribution of this kind of fiery anti-Christian propaganda. At the height of the war, it would unnecessarily upset many people of faith and would be counterproductive. In the event, Bormann had his way, and subsequent editions were published in both 1942 and 1943.[82]

---

[81] See Kurt Eggers, *Der Scheiterhaufen. Worte Grosse Ketzer* (Dortmund: Volkschaft Verlag, 1941). This particular poem, called "Ein Feuerspruch," was written on Heroes Memorial Day for added theatrical effect (ibid., pp. 5–7). It is clear that Eggers – just like Hitler and Bormann – hoped to see the church eradicated. He said as much at the conclusion of his passionate work, *Rom gegen Reich* (Stuttgart: Truckenmüller, 1935, p. 61) when he observed that "Germany is fighting for a Northland free of Roman influence."

[82] See Walter Tiessler, Propaganda Ministry, "Vorlage für Reichsleiter Bormann," December 8, 1941, *Akten der Parteikanzlei der NSDAP*, BA NS 18/33. Bormann personally scribbled several notes on Tiessler's memorandum, confirming Hitler's enthusiasm for Eggers's ideas and reflecting his impatience with the Propaganda Ministry. Compare Steigmann-Gall, pp. 249–51.

Feeling his new power, like so many among the Third Reich's parvenus, Eggers could be quite arrogant. Early in 1942, he went so far as to complain to Hans Hinkel – an Old Fighter, holder of the Blood Order, and a ranking official in the Propaganda Ministry – that a war song he had composed at the request of various Waffen SS leaders had not yet been played on the radio and that Hinkel should set about addressing the problem.[83] Eggers was also terribly proud of himself for fathering four sons with his second wife, Traute Kaiser, the daughter of a Berlin pastor. In September 1941, he reported the birth of his fourth son Jens to the proper SS authorities with great joy.[84] To add to his euphoria, more than a million copies of his works were in circulation at the onset of the war. He was gratified with the success he had enjoyed, boasting that although he had many enemies, he had played a role in "mobilizing the German soul."

A born fighter, Eggers was now in his milieu. Myth and reality were at last to merge in his life. Living his own myth, Eggers was assured that his almost certain death at the front would secure a place for him among the warrior gods in Valhalla. As he wrote at the time: "The hour has come when we can show that our love for Germany is worth the supreme sacrifice."[85] When the war broke out, he headed immediately for the front, serving on the staff of an Army Panzer company in Poland. Now he himself would face life's supreme test at a time when words must give way to deeds. "Our heaven," he observed, "is the great war on earth."[86] "We are not afraid of the great valley of death because it opens the gate to fulfillment." "Now we have become a gray front again! Now the old, wild songs which inspired our fathers on their path to death ring out in our hearts again."[87]

With the onset of the war, Eggers's emphasis on the Nordic race became more intense. The bizarre blood-based romanticism that ran through

---

[83] Eggers to Staatsrat Hans Hinkel, April 20, 1942, with the music to the song composed by one Küssel. Kurt Eggers File, BAB. For an example of Eggers's activity as a songwriter, see "Heute müssen wir marschieren," *Liederbuch der SS*, in Denkler and Prümm, *Das deutsche Literatur im Dritten Reich*, p. 271.

[84] SS Obersturmführer Kurt Eggers to the SS-Personalamt, Prinz Albrecht Strasse 9, Berlin, September 23, 1941, Kurt Eggers File, BAB.

[85] Kurt Eggers, *Vom Kampf und Krieg*, 3rd ed. (Erfurt: Verlag Sigrune, 1940). One hundred thousand copies of this work circulated among servicemen of the Wehrmacht and Waffen SS.

[86] Kurt Eggers, "Soldatisches Bekenntnis," February 1940, in *Krieg und Dichtung*, ed. Kurt Ziesel (Wien: Wiener Verlag, 1943), pp. 137–8.

[87] Kurt Eggers, *Kamerad. Gedichte eines Soldaten* (Leipzig: Schwarzhäupter Verlag, 1940), p. 5.

many of his works was cast in graphic relief in an essay titled "The German Soul." He submitted that the Volk, rising out of the gray fog of the Northland, was characterized by total rejection of the weak, whose racial inheritance fated them for destruction. The strong, on the other hand, tested in the fire of battle, were lauded as a race destined to emerge victorious. They embraced the "myth of the German soul," modeled on the epic *Song of Edda*, which merged the dual qualities of naïve purity and martial instincts. Only Nordics could comprehend the splendor of its secret signs that were unfathomable to those not graced with German blood and who alone were singled out for genius. Among the chosen, only a select few were called to give poetic expression to their unique gift. The lyric artists integrated creative melancholy with cosmic naïveté, like the all-knowing fool Parzifal, while perceiving the light of eternal wisdom, accompanied by heavenly chords from on high. The Germans, he noted, are a people of longing not fulfillment, of battle not peace, of hunger not satiety. The time had come, he announced, when darkness would give way to a great dawning as the sun shone forth in all its splendor over the new Reich.[88]

During the winter of 1939–40, Eggers returned from the front and wrote *On the Freedom of the Warrior*, a testament to what he perceived to be the brutal splendor of war as well as a celebration of Germany's victories. Here one finds a barely camouflaged Dionysian ecstasy clearly inspired by Nietzsche and cascading waves of praise for the few who, like Zarathustra, leave the banality of the warm and comfortable valleys to climb the "mountain in midnight," the "home of the free." They move in the realm of the sun and stars, breathing deeply of the crisp air at those rarified heights that unite heaven and earth in ethereal light. They alone guard the fires of freedom on the heights of heroism, whose flames bathe the entire universe in their grand light. They feel pity for the masses far below in the valley, those who will never know heroic commitment, and who will never shine forth in the darkness like torches of sacrificial light, bearing testament to the faith of the Nibelungen: "I know only one thing that is eternal: The epic deeds of heroes!"[89] As the hearts of the weak grow cold with dreams of peace, those of the elite glow like torches in the glory of their calling. They harden their swords in the fire of eternity, preparing for the titanic struggle to come to fulfill the law of the universe.

---

[88] Kurt Eggers, "Die Deutsche Seele," in *Deutsches Bekenntnis*, pp. 9–10.
[89] Kurt Eggers, *Von der Freiheit des Kriegers* (Berlin: Nordland, 1940), pp. 1–18.

One would expect that Eggers's call to battle would be lauded by Himmler, but this was not the case. The Reichsführer sent a letter of complaint to the editors of the Nordland Press that the SS controlled, demanding that henceforth all books should be dispatched to him in manuscript form for his approval before publication "to be certain that they do not contain any dangerous passages." "The Reichsführer SS does not want books to be released behind his back that ultimately bear his imprimatur," the letter continued, noting that the work by Eggers brought about this order.[90] Although Himmler did not comment about what had irritated him, it is obvious that Eggers's treatment was far too metaphorical for his tastes. At this juncture in the war, he obviously expected that the mission of the SS in the eradication of the Jewish world enemy should be stressed.

Obviously Eggers incurred no lasting damage from this incident, because his next major work, *The Warlike Revolution*, published in 1941, reached the 500,000 sales mark within two years, a clear indication that it received widespread Party approval as a propaganda medium.[91] The fiery essay called for total war and would later fit in well with Goebbels's propaganda following the disaster at Stalingrad. No enemy escaped attack in this work, which commenced with an assault on the pensioner mentality of the bourgeoisie. The battle cry of the SS must not be "Peace at any price," he declared, but rather "Howl with the wolves!" The beauty of the war, he argued, was that it made soldiers out of the bourgeoisie in spite of themselves, a class of people who now perceived that the time had come for a great historical transformation. "We are bidding the bourgeoisie goodbye, once and for all," he boasted.[92] It was imperative that this selfish class that had outlived its time meet its world-historic responsibility to support the National Socialist revolution. This fundamental transformation was possible because, as bearers of German blood, they were warriors by nature. They were now being forced to trade their infatuation with reason, enlightenment, and money for the enduring Germanic values of discipline, courage, comradeship, and sacrifice. Only now were they beginning to understand the meaning of the sacred words, "The Führer is Germany," and to realize that Hitler was the incarnation of all soldierly virtue. Eggers warned that "misguided Aryans" who refused to understand their responsibilities in the New Order must be dealt with

---

[90] SS Hauptsturmführer Brandt, Der Reichsführer SS, Persönlicher Stab, February 12, 1940, to Nordland Verlag, Berlin, Kurt Eggers File, BAB.

[91] Kurt Eggers, *Die kriegerische Revolution* (Berlin: Zentralverlag der NSDAP, Franz Eher, 1941), in *Gesamtverzeichnis des deutschsprachigen Schrifttums 1911–1965*, p. 350.

[92] Ibid., pp 5–11.

harshly. As a result, henceforth Rome and the church were no longer to influence the German conscience.

Eggers also elaborated on the configuration of life in the future National Socialist state, contending that as a result of the radical cultural changes, Germany was entering a great period in its history. Youth belonged to the Führer heart and soul, and the best were being educated in the *Napolas*, elite National Socialist schools. Weimar political chicanery had been eradicated, he observed, and henceforth the nation would be governed by Party leaders given proper administrative training in *Ordensburgen*, the Castles of the Order. The *Hohe Schule*, the National Socialist University, would gather the best minds at its campus on the banks of Lake Chiemsee for advanced training in all fields of intellectual attainment. The entire curriculum there would be based on Germanic racial consciousness. Farmers who once had known only poverty would be given generous plots of land whose bounty would feed a healthy and growing population. After winning the final victories on the battlefield, the veterans would return to oversee the building of the Reich for centuries to come.[93]

In mid-1942, Eggers, who was still functioning as a writer attached to the Party Chancellery headed by Bormann, approached his chief with the wish to return to the front. He had become restless, and according to the SS war reporter Fritz Helke, who visited Eggers in his office in Berlin at that time, he seemed like a frustrated lion in captivity. "Did anyone think that I could live for very long in this cage?," he queried?[94] This situation would soon change because Bormann, without the knowledge of Hitler, arranged for what was to have been a limited period of service in battle. In September 1942, Eggers was attached to the SS Panzer Reserve (Section Weimar-Buchenwald) and undertook a short course in armor tactics with this unit. In October of that year, he attended the writers'

---

[93] Ibid., pp. 19–51.

[94] SS Kriegsberichter Fritz Helke, "Begegnungen mit Kurt Eggers. Zum Todestag des Dichters und Soldaten," *Berliner Börsen Zeitung*, August 11, 1944. During this period, Eggers was active in the creation of propaganda for the SS. For an example of his activities, see "Teilnehmer an der Tagung des 'Födererkreises der Germanischen Leithefte' in Magdeburg vom 27.4.–30.4.1942," noting his participation at this planning conference for the central SS book series. The list of participants reads like a "Who's Who" of the SS literary establishment. It included not only Eggers but Gruppenführer Gottlob Berger, Chef des SS Hauptamtes, Gunter d'Alquen, Kommandeur der SS Kriegberichterabteilung, Hans Hagen of the Propaganda Ministry, Brigadeführer Albert (Litzmannstadt/Lodz), Dr. Carstens, Rektor der Universität Posen, Dr. med. Habelmann, surgeon, Robert Koch Krankenhaus, Berlin, and Brigadeführer Heider, Amtschef im Rasse-und Sieglungshauptamt SS. Kurt Eggers File, BAB.

conference in Weimar, which met each year in connection with Goebbels's birthday. A participant reported on Eggers's appearance there, noting that his friends had never seen him happier or more at peace with himself. The reason was easy to divine. He had at last reached his goal to serve on the eastern front in a Waffen SS Panzer division, where the fighting was most dangerous and the military situation extremely threatening. It was as if he were but a boy again, heading out to serve with the Free Corps: "I am going to the 'Viking' Division," he reported. "I'm getting a tank!" Once again a soldier, he was certain that his division would join the vanguard of the Nordic community intent on forming the European New Order.[95]

Later that month, Eggers was dispatched to Terek in the Caucasus, where he was deployed to the 5th SS Panzer Division, an entirely volunteer division composed of Walloon, Dutch, Norwegian, Baltic, Finnish, and German units. His division was attached to Army Group A under Field Marshal von Weichs, which in the massive offensive of 1942 was charged with covering the right shoulder of the assault on Stalingrad, securing the mineral-rich Don and Donetz basins, and conquering the rich oil fields of the Caucasus. Eggers entered the scene just as the tide was about to turn on the Russian front, when the Russians succeeded in surrounding the German Sixth Army in November 1942 and proceeded to squeeze its prize to death in the early winter of 1943. He took part in the bitter fighting during the withdrawal of Army Group A from the Caucasus and the subsequent pullback from Rostov to the Donetz River.[96]

Eggers's comrades in the Fifth Panzer Division were curious upon hearing that the famous writer Kurt Eggers was about to join their ranks in the Panzer corps, and they closely observed his behavior in battle. It did not go unnoticed that the ardent Panzer commander destroyed three Soviet tanks on his first deployment at the front. Commenting to an SS war reporter, members of Eggers's unit lauded his bravery and willingness to spring into action under the most dangerous conditions. Observers have left graphic accounts of his participation in the defensive engagement in the Kalmuck steppes as well. There the invaders were not only heavily outnumbered by Russian T-34 and KW I tanks, they also faced heavy snow, terrible cold,

---

[95] "Dichtertreffen, Herbst 1942," Kurt Eggers File, Bundesarchiv Potsdam.

[96] For accounts of the deployment of the Division "Viking" in these campaigns, see Peter Strassner, *Europäische Freiwillige. Die Geschichte der 5. SS Panzer-Division WIKING* (Osnabrück: Munin Verlag 1968), pp. 124–204. See also Jean Mabire, *Die SS-Panzer-Division "Wiking"* (Preussisch Oldendorf: Verlag K. W. Schütz, 1983) for a general history of the Fifth SS Panzer Division in World War II.

8. Kurt Eggers in His Panzer Corps Uniform, Circa 1939. Author's Private Collection.

and the continuous assault of brave Soviet partisans.[97] Over the coming
months Eggers displayed both outstanding ability as a Panzer commander and gallantry under fire. In one incident, even though Eggers was
severely wounded and his tank destroyed, he held his ground and continued to command his unit. As a result, he earned the Iron Cross, Second
Class, and the Panzer Combat Medal in Silver; he was also praised by his
commanding general, Felix Steiner.[98]

Early in the summer of 1943, Bormann wished to have Eggers recalled
for service in the Party Chancellery, and he dispatched a request to this
effect to the appropriate SS authorities. Although coming from the highest levels of the SS Central Office, bureaucratic red tape determined that
this request would be denied. "Should Eggers be needed by the Party
Chancellery," the answer read, "a request must be made through the normal channels and Eggers would have to be dismissed from the Waffen
SS."[99] Bormann then turned to Himmler who immediately commanded
that Eggers be withdrawn from the front, where his division was engaged
in a defensive campaign along the Don River. He was dispatched to Berlin
to take part in the writers' conference sponsored by the Propaganda Ministry, which in 1943 would be held in the capital instead of Weimar because
of the exigencies of Goebbels's total war offensive.[100] Before Eggers set
out for Germany, he celebrated the summer solstice in the field with his

---

[97] For an excellent account of Eggers's service at the front, see "Vom mutigen Leben und
tapferen Sterben," *Das Schwarze Korps*, November 18, 1943, pp. 6–7.

[98] SS-Sturmbannführer und Abteilungs-Kommandeur, I./SS Panzer Regiment 5, Abt. Gef.
St., March 20, 1943, "Beurteilung des Oberscharführer Kurt Eggers," Kurt Eggers
File, BAB; Gruppenführer Gottlob Berger, SS Hauptamt, June 17, 1943 to Chef des
SS Personalhauptamtes, Gruppenführer von Herff, ibid.; SS Gruppenführer Steiner,
Generalleutnant der Waffen SS und Divisionskommandeur, March 12, 1943, wrote:
"Recommended! Eggers has taken part in some tough battles and has fully stood the
test" (ibid.).

[99] For the request, see Gruppenführer Gottlob Berger, SS Hauptamt, June 17, 1943, to
Chef des SS Personalhauptamtes, Gruppenführer von Herff, Kurt Eggers File, BAB. In
this letter, it was noted that Bormann had acted on Eggers's request for deployment at
the front "without the Führer knowing about it." For the denial of the request, see SS
Personalhauptamt, Berlin, June 22, 1943, to SS Hauptamt, ibid.

[100] Telegraph: Reichsführer SS, Führungshauptamt, Amt V, IIa, to SS-Pz. Gren. Div. "Wiking," June 10, 1943; Telegraph: SS-FHA. Amt V to Gen.Kdo. III (germ.) SS-Pz Korps,
Bayreuth, June 22, 1943 (a request regarding the date Untersturmführer Eggers would
arrive in Berlin); SS Staf., Diebitsch, General Kommando III, (Germ), SS Panzer Korps
II a, June 29, 1943, Bezug: FS. SS-FHA vom 25/6/43 to SS-Führungshauptamt, V: SS
Untersturmführer Eggers wurde am 22/6/43 von Division Wiking nach Berlin in Marsch
gesetzt."

comrades, complete with crackling bonfires in the Viking style.[101] It would be his final trip home.

After spending time with his family and friends, Eggers spoke before a gathering at the University of Berlin and delivered a Sunday afternoon radio address on the Grossdeutsche Rundfunk on the anniversary of the death of Ulrich von Hutten. It was suggested to Eggers that he remain in the capital, accepting Bormann's request that he once more take up his role as a writer and ideological propagandist. Eggers would have none of it, however, feeling that the Viking Division would continue to be a significant component of the German defensive campaign. Yet without question, there was a deeper reason for his feeling compelled to return to his unit, because Eggers was convinced that fate had predetermined that he must die for his beliefs. Two years earlier, on being confronted by his friend, Hans Hagen, as to why a thirty-five-year-old man would deem it prudent to publish his memoirs, an astounded Eggers responded with the words: "Don't you know that I will die a soldier's death in Russia?"[102] Furthermore, he had published a poem titled "To My Sons," making it clear that he must be fulfilled in heroic death. It concluded with the lines: "So go your way to the end and laugh at all danger. Build the Reich that is your fate. Build the Reich! Stay at my side, my sons."[103]

Eggers rejoined the Viking Division in late July 1943, at a point when "Operation Citadel," the massive German offensive at Kursk, commanded by Field Marshal Erich von Manstein, had ground to a halt. The Russians, attacking in great strength, were desperate to break into the Ukraine and began an encirclement of Kharkov. Their ultimate goal was to break through westward to the Dnieper River, thence to encircle and wipe out the entire German southern front. Von Manstein, describing this campaign in his memoirs, *Lost Victories*, commented on the extremely difficult situation he faced at the time, stressing the serious imbalance of forces on that front.[104]

Eggers was killed southwest of Bjelgorod on August 12 as his division took a gamble and counterattacked, deploying its tanks on a broad front in an attempt to take Hill 208, which commanded the northern

---

[101] *Verweht sind die Spuren. Bilddokumentation SS-Panzerregiment 5 "Wiking"* (Coburg: Nation Europa, 1998), 2nd ed., p. 95.

[102] Hans W. Hagen, "Kurt Eggers," *Klütter Blätter* (16), 1965, pp. 62–4.

[103] "Kurt Eggers gefallen," *Die Weltliteratur* 8/9 (August-September 1943).

[104] Field Marshal Erich von Manstein, *Lost Victories* (Chicago: Henry Regnery, 1958), pp. 450–8.

approaches to Kharkov.[105] The *Schwarze Korps* reported that "the tanks, burning as far as the eye could see, seemed to offer a sacrificial fire for you, Kurt Eggers – our comrade. Just a few meters from me, the steel body of your tank took the direct hit of an artillery shell, snuffing out your life, which glowed like a torch in the night – bright and shining, the enemy of all darkness."[106] His obituary in the SS organ was an exercise in elegiac lamentation, claiming that Eggers's life had been characterized by great love and boundless enthusiasm for the German cause, a zeal that inspired countless others to take up the cause and to be ready to die for it. Eggers had embraced the "freedom of the warrior," the Germanic idea of freedom, in which victory shines forth even in death. His fighting spirit, his flag of freedom, would serve to encourage his comrades to give their all for the beloved Reich.[107] Eggers's wife, Traute, published a newspaper notice extolling her husband's "courageous life and brave death for an eternal Germany." He would live on in the lives of his three surviving sons – Jörg, Götz, and Jens – she asserted.[108]

The SS-sponsored periodical, *World Literature*, gave a sinister racial gloss to their hagiographic article, claiming that Kurt Eggers would not want his death to be mourned. Quite the contrary, he willingly gave his life for his race and Volk. For Eggers, there were only victors and vanquished, it concluded, and any other reading of the matter would reflect effeminate bourgeois sentiment. Eggers was certain that only the armed forces of the German Reich stood between the "storm from the west of crass materialism and aimless technology and the bestial physiognomy of the Eastern Jewish-Bolshevik hordes." The essay continued in the spirit of the somber propaganda that Goebbels had orchestrated after the Stalingrad debacle, presenting images that appear bitterly ironic as the ovens of Auschwitz continued to incinerate their victims: "We must be ready to perish in our own flame. Always in the great battles of destiny in which our Volk has been engaged, noble Germanic martyrs have come forth to show us the way. Kurt Eggers has joined the great ranks of the immortals."[109]

Soon after receiving the news of the death of Eggers, Himmler ordered that he be promoted posthumously to the rank of SS Obersturmführer (1st Lieutenant), and he was awarded the Iron Cross, First Class, as

[105] Strassner, pp. 213–15.
[106] *Das Schwarze Korps*, November 18, 1943, p. 7.
[107] "Das war Kurt Eggers," *Das Schwarze Korps*, September 9, 1943.
[108] *Völkischer Beobachter*, September 6, 1943.
[109] "Kurt Eggers gefallen," *Die Weltliteratur* 8/9 (August–September, 1943).

well.[110] On September 26, 1943, the life and death of Kurt Eggers was celebrated in the Kroll Opera House. It was the kind of ceremony that Eggers himself relished, merging National Socialist ideology with classical German culture. Both Beethoven's "Funeral March" and Brahms's "Tragic Overture" were featured in the memorial. Heinrich George, one of the most important actors of the era and a personal friend, recited several of Eggers's poems in his grand stentorian tones. These included "Viking Journey," "How the Strong Go to Their Death," and "We Fought the Good Fight."[111] Lieutenant Hans W. Hagen, a close friend, gave the eulogy.[112] Exactly two days later, English bombers completely destroyed the Kroll Opera House, where ten years before the Reichstag had voted Hitler dictatorial powers.

Through the good offices of Gunter d'Alquen, commander of the SS War Reporters Section, Himmler prevailed on Hitler to order the unit to be renamed SS Standarte "Kurt Eggers."[113] D'Alquen wrote to Himmler, thanking him profusely for the trust he had placed in him, his officers, and men, because the name Kurt Eggers meant so much to them all. In early November 1943, the unit was renamed in a Berlin ceremony attended by his widow, Traute, and his three sons. D'Alquen assumed command of the Standarte, and henceforth all war reports from the field bore his name.[114]

Eggers died before having to witness the shattering of all his dreams and his demise signaled the coming destruction of the Third Reich. It is sad to recount that at the height of his success, he had inspired many

---

[110] September 1943, Der Reichsführer SS, Persönlicher Stab, to SS Personalhauptamt, Berlin. The date of the promotion was backdated to June 21, 1943. Kurt Eggers File, BAB.

[111] September 26, 1943, "Gefallenen-Gedenkfeier der NSDAP für Kurt Eggers in der Berliner Krolloper," *Tondokumente zur Zeitgeschichte 1939–1945* (Bild-und Tonträger-Verzeichnisse. Hsg. Vom Deutschen Rundfunkarchiv), ed. Walter Roller (Frankfurt am Main: Decker & Wilhelm, 1975), pp. 191–2.

[112] Hans W. Hagen, *Klütter Blätter* (16), 1965, pp. 62–4.

[113] November 7, 1943, "Die SS Kriegsberichterabteilung erhält den Titel SS Standarte Kurt Eggers," Gunter d'Alquen, "Bekanntgabe des Führerbefehls vom 31.10.1943," *Tondokumente zur Zeitgeschichte 1939–1945*, p. 199. See also William L. Combs, *The Voice of the SS. A History of the SS Journal "Das Schwarze Korps"* (New York: Peter Lang, 1986), pp. 382–3.

[114] D'Alquen to Himmler, November 8, 1943. D'Alquen reported that Traute Eggers would soon be writing to the Reichsführer, thanking him for his suggestion to Hitler that Kurt be honored in this way. This letter shows the respect that d'Alquen had for Kurt Eggers, who went to great lengths to support Traute Eggers and the family in their grief. Eggers had taken good care of his family in his will. The royalties from his extensive publications made the family more than comfortable, and the Gauleiter of Mecklenburg had arranged for the family to live in an appropriate manner for the duration of the war in the village of Dobbetin.

young people to see their future sacrifice for the nation as redemptive. As a major SS propagandist, he played his role in educating recruits to embrace a radical ideology of death, according to which many SS men came to believe that those whom the gods love are called home at a tender age. Their end was to come in violent acts of divine immolation.

Felix Lützkendorf, also a member of the Fifth SS Panzer Division "Viking" who served at the front with Eggers, composed a poem dedicated to this motif titled "On the High Banks of the Dnieper." Written a matter of months before the death of Eggers, the work offers graphic testimony to the perceived historic dimension of the SS mission in the east, conjuring up images of the Goths and Vikings who had fought, died, and been buried in the same soil centuries before. Lützkendorf offered no hint that his symbolic representation was in fact a chimera, bathing a criminal organization in the rays of heavenly light. Man and nature were joined in the poem, which in reality was a prayer that God would bless the deaths of his SS comrades. He referred to an ancient tree he saw there, "as deeply rooted as God was in this land," its leaves rustling in the winds of the steppes as they had for hundreds of years, standing firmly against the raging storms which threatened it. The somber majesty of the Russian landscape can be perceived in every line:

> High over the banks of the Dnieper
> stands an ancient and lonely tree
> the winds of the steppes blow the leaves
> accompanying its millennial dreams.
>
> It buried the shafts of its roots
> as deeply as God in that land –
> Oh the thunderous showers of the days and nights,
> Oh the storms that it withstood.
>
> Among its roots we dug
> a grave for our dead brothers,
> there where in that sacred grove
> it cast its undulating shadows.
>
> You heard the songs of the Goths,
> you witnessed the Vikings' journey –
> Oh protect these dead blond warriors,
> they are the very same type.
>
> And teach them the wonderment of God,
> that you, his poet, perceive,
> when they listen to the storms,
> which blow across the plains.

Am hohen Ufer des Dnjepr
steht uralt ein einsamer Baum
der Steppenwind rührt seiner Blätter
Jahrtausendverwobenen Traum.

Er grub seiner Wurzeln Schächte
tief wie Gott in das Land–
O Schauer der Tage und Nächte,
O Stürme, die er bestand.

Wir hoben im Wurzelgrunde
den toten Brüdern das Grab,
da wo er in heiliger Runde
warf wogende Schatten herab.

Du hörtest die Lieder der Goten,
Du sahest der Wikinge Fahrt –
O hüte die blonden Toten,
Sie sind nicht anderer Art.

Und lehre sie Gottes Rauschen,
Du, sein Sänger, verstehen,
Wenn sie den Stürmen lauschen,
Die über die Ebene wehn.[115]

In the final reckoning, Eggers and his fellow poets called on heroic imagery in their endeavor to confer enduring meaning to the sacrifice of nearly an entire generation of young men. Today their poems stand as lonely sentinels on the distant horizon, offering evidence for the curious phenomenon that, even as Nazism faced its death throes, writers stood ready to glorify the dying National Socialist regime with the gift of their often seductive and macabre lyric works.

---

[115] Felix Lützenkendorf, "Am Hohen Ufer des Dnjepr," *Die Weltliteratur* 18 (January 1943).

Epilogue

Prose and poetry invariably take on more importance in autocratic regimes than is the case in democratic countries. In Germany, a long tradition had developed in which literary works reflected glory on the crown, most notably in Heinrich von Kleist's memorable *Prinz Friedrich von Homburg*. This work represented the apogee of the Prussian aphorism according to which "the security of the crown rests on poetry."[1] However, when literature is used to buttress a totalitarian system, as it was under Hitler, Stalin, and Mao Tse-tung, where it was subjected to censorship and filtration through the bureaucratic sieve, quality varied considerably. In the Third Reich, however, the results were irregular indeed, stretching from the pedestrian rhymed couplets of Heinrich Anacker to the often brilliant lyric poetry of Eberhard Wolfgang Möller.

Whereas Prussian kings and German emperors often relished the poetic works dedicated to them, Adolf Hitler generally ignored the Nazi writers and their works, with the exception of Kurt Eggers. Although some of them continued in the pretentious belief that the soul of the nation found its expression in their literary works, the worm had turned. Henceforth, writers were expected to reflect on the political, ideological, and racial struggle of the era. Further, Hitler was convinced that literature was an ineffective weapon in the propaganda wars. Rather his heart lay with architecture, music, and art and sculpture, and there is considerable evidence that his enthusiasm for artists in these fields often reached a childlike intensity. Figures close to Hitler remarked that over the many years they knew him, not once did he utter a word about any of the

[1] See Jan Andres, *"Auf Poesie ist die Sicherheit der Throne gegründet": Huldigungsrituale und Gelegenheitslyrik im 19. Jahrhundert* (Frankfurt/Main: Campus, 2005).

leading National Socialist writers.[2] With just a few exceptions, they were simply marginal for him, even though their works became important in the propaganda buttressing the regime. Literary figures were never invited to dine or socialize at functions hosted by the Führer, who delighted in the company of architects and film stars. This was graphically reflected by his entourage while visiting the cultural sights of conquered Paris in 1940. The architects Albert Speer and Hermann Giesler as well as the sculptor Arno Breker, were featured as the cultural paladins flanking him there. There was no literary figure in sight. Hanns Johst, Bruno Brehm, and a gaggle of other writers had to be satisfied with a trip to the battlefields arranged and directed by the Propaganda Ministry.

The poets and writers who remained in Germany during the Third Reich never truly understood that the adulation they showered on Hitler fell on deaf ears, even though they represented what Sander Gilman has referred to as "the guardians of the Holy Grail."[3] In the final analysis, theirs was an unrequited love. The authors paid a high price for this, because not only were many of them marginalized in their own day, but after the destruction of the Third Reich, they were pilloried mercilessly. Critics took their cue from Thomas Mann, who deemed rubbish everything published in Germany between 1933 and 1945. As a result, the works of these authors were considered to be egregiously bad – often by people who had never read any of them – and deemed to be unworthy of any consideration whatsoever. They were widely attacked by historians and literary critics as well. This in turn led to serious imbalance and misrepresentation in the historical interpretation of the period.

For decades after World War II, the literature of the Third Reich era was avoided like the Devil avoids Holy Water. Moral repulsion alone cannot substitute for sober historical analysis, however. The writers under consideration in this study together sold millions of copies of their works, and there is no question that the great liberal intellectual figures who dominated the literary scene during the 1920s were losing influence in the years just preceding Hitler's assumption of power. Indeed the case has been made that a paradigmatic shift had occurred in literature paralleling the political move to the right after the onset of the economic crisis in 1929, when such figures as Ernst Jünger, Hans Grimm, Edwin Erich

---

[2] Karl Corino, ed., *Intellektuelle im Bann des Nationalsozialismus* (Hamburg: Hoffman und Campe, 1980), pp. 245–6.

[3] Sander L. Gilman, *NS-Literaturtheorie* (Frankfurt/Main: Athenäum Verlag, 1971), pp. x–xi.

Dwinger, Josef Magnus Wehner, Franz Schauwecker, Werner Beumelburg, and Erwin Guido Kolbenheyer took center stage at the expense of the intellectual elite.[4] Whether or not they later supported the regime directly, these conservative revolutionaries contributed in no small way to opening the way for Hitler. Through their literary works, they also contributed to the success Goebbels had in persuading the German people that National Socialism was the only alternative to Bolshevism. Without question, the interface between art and politics had profound implications in the Third Reich. Ultimately, whether or not they willed it, these literary figures provided aesthetic accompaniment to criminality. My goal has been to assess why this was done, how it was accomplished, and where possible, to analyze its political and social significance.

It is indisputable that the intellectual depth and literary quality of the works of the new elite were in most cases a cut below those of the waning literary establishment. But the immediate future – as brief as it was and certainly less than a thousand years – lay with the conservative revolutionaries and National Socialists. In truth this work is less about literature than the interplay between literature and politics and the indisputable deleterious effect their writing had on political developments.

All of the major writers in question came to grips with by far the most important and portentous event of the period, World War I, whose profound economic repercussions and traumatic psychological effects would ultimately have monstrous consequences. All of them were obsessed with its memory, and they drank deeply and unremittingly from this source, which became for many of them the alpha and omega of life. Most of them constructed a philosophy of life based on battle and struggle that in turn provided a framework for their reactionary ideology. The tragic war experience formed the basis for their entire political program and raison d'etre. Werner Wirths summarized this program succinctly when he wrote that

> We want to return to the war experience. We want once more
> to find the true meaning of life that we knew out there and
> simply does not exist anymore. We seek it in the future. We are
> going to put the question into the hands of fate and urgently want
> the answer to it.[5]

Ernst Jünger was by far the most eloquent figure in the stable of conservative writers, whose *Storm of Steel* launched a brilliant literary career.

4 Susanne Meinl, *Nationalsozialisten gegen Hitler. Die nationalrevolutionäre Opposition um Friedrich Wilhelm Heinz* (Berlin: Siedler, 2000), pp. 174–5.
5 Werner Wirths, "Das Erlebnis des Krieges," *Die Neue Front*, p. 76, cited in Sontheimer, p. 116.

However, the overintellectualized political ruminations that formed the basis of his subsequent writings during the Weimar Republic were far too rarified to place him in the Nazi camp, even though he was welcome there. Although contributing in no small way to the newly articulated cult of violence, Jünger refused to align himself with the National Socialists. Although he was offered membership in the prestigious Academy of Arts, he declined this honor.

Jünger formed the vortex around which a group of writers referred to as the "Five Apostles of the new nationalism" gathered. These "apostles" shared the values molded by their military and Free Corps experiences, and they longed for a new Germany that would embrace their Spartan ideals. They were united in the belief that National Socialism stood in marked contrast to their idealized vision of a revolutionary political world and had been unable to transform their own myths into political reality. This became dramatically clear when Hitler's mythical world became a political reality and they were expected to fall into line. Jünger was joined by Franz Schauwecker, Friedrich Hielscher, Ernst von Salomon, and Friedrich Wilhelm Heinz, and together they formed a nationalist anti-Hitler opposition cell that would survive to the end of World War II.[6] These five were joined by other enemies of Hitler, a group composed of alienated former Stahlhelm leaders, a number of disaffected army officers, and certain Free Corps figures who felt that their dreams for political change had been betrayed in the Third Reich.

Schauwecker's alienation to the new regime was the most surprising, but he was viewed as an outsider by Goebbels and the Nazis even though the title of his war novel *Aufbruch der Nation* (*The Awakening of the Nation*) had become a Nazi slogan. His memorable observation that "we had to lose the war to win the nation" formed the basis for the National Socialist creed, but Schauwecker never felt drawn to the Party.[7] Friedrich Hielscher, on the other hand, a brilliant and charismatic dreamer, elitist theoretician, and hopeless romantic, left no one in the dark about his anti-Nazi attitudes. His utopian blueprint for a profound Germanic future, formulated in his book titled *Das Reich*, which was published in 1931 was banned early on by the new regime.[8] Hielscher would later lead an active

---

[6] Meinl, p. 212.

[7] Franz Schauwecker, *Aufbruch der Nation* (Berlin: Deutsche Buch-Gemeinschaft, 1929).

[8] Friedrich Hielscher, *Das Reich* (Berlin: Verlag Das Reich, 1931). See also Michael Kater, *Das "Ahnenerbe" der SS 1935–1945. Ein Beitrag zur Kulturpolitik des Dritten Reiches.* Studien zur Zeitgeschichte. Herausgegeben vom Institut für Zeitgeschichte. Stuttgart: Deutsche Verlags-Anstalt, 1974, pp. 30–6.

resistance group against Hitler and because of his contacts with leading SS figures – he on more than one occasion carried papers as a department head of the SS Ahnenerbe cultural office – his followers remained active throughout the war.

The program of the conservative revolutionaries appeared benign when compared with the goals of those who took the experience of wholesale slaughter and bloodshed in the war to a new level. Activists such as Alfred Rosenberg grafted the poisonous *völkisch* and racist agenda to the revolutionary program born in the trenches and joined Hitler's vanguard. For many of them, the blood motif formed the cohesive force for a new politics of violence that became second nature to them and formed the basis for hateful theories of integral racism.[9] According to their mythical views, the loss of life and the gaping wounds of the nation were ennobled by the fallen in the same way that Siegfried had transcended the insidious betrayal of Hagen to take on cosmic significance for the Nibelungen and the tribal Germanic vision.

Hell had no fury to compare with rabid nationalists who felt offended by attacks on their interpretation of the war experience. According to George Mosse, "The Myth of the War Experience was designed to mask war and legitimize it and to displace the reality of war."[10] The publication of Erich Maria Remarque's *All Quiet on the Western Front* in 1929 became a clarion call rallying those determined to protect their image of the Germanic Reich redeemed by the blood of the fallen. Rudolf Binding, Edwin Erich Dwinger, Josef Magnus Wehner, and Hans Zöberlein all wrote their war novels and memoirs in response to this assault on what they deemed to be truly sacred. Eberhard Wolfgang Möller, who was all of nine years old when the Great War broke out, fashioned his entire literary career under the sacred canopy of the war mythology. In turn, the youthful Kurt Eggers who was also a Nazi by nature, clustered among those who developed a new and even more sinister racial mythology based on aggression, violence, and death. This self-proclaimed Zarathustrian prophet presented his ideology in such a strikingly rhapsodic form that its Dionysian otherworldliness even tested the patience of the hopelessly mystical racist Reichsführer SS Heinrich Himmler.

As we have observed, the translation from myth to real political life was paralleled in the literature of the era, where the prosaic events of the

[9] See Sontheimer, pp. 115–16.
[10] Mosse, *Fallen Soldiers*, p. 7. Compare Bessel, p. 270.

day took on belletristic form. Novel after novel celebrated the concepts of comradeship, sacrifice, and heroism. Blood, instinct, and violence were celebrated as positive virtues. Considerations of love, international understanding, and the entire gamut of humanistic values were considered to be *Humanitätsdüselei* (insufferable cosmopolitanism). The comradeship experienced at the front was considered to be as transformative to the human experience as the blood and body of Christ.

In the novels of Binding, Zöberlein, Wehner, and Dwinger, the individual warrior was said to have found himself through surrender to the greater good, to the Germanic whole. With such a philosophy of life, one did not suffer disillusionment, fear, neurosis, or loss of identity. Rather, by this transformation from bourgeois decadence to the front spirit, the soul was renewed, and the conscience became as pure as the driven snow. By understanding the will of Providence for the German nation, the warrior found his identity through a blissful transfiguration. He had become whole in the knowledge that he was a member of an elite corps, reborn and blessed by the healing effects of catharsis. The way was open to transform the values of the fighting front to a new way of life on the home front. The spirit of Verdun and the Somme was transferred to the struggle against Bolshevism in the postwar civil strife, as the officers and men carried the banner of their new faith into the battle in the streets of German cities. Those who shed their blood on the asphalt of Berlin, the Ruhr, and Saxony were but extensions of the heroic fallen in Flanders Fields. The authors discussed here were at the forefront of those who believed that the National Socialists were fighting for a noble cause. The future lay with those who shared their vision of a renewed nation, of a community of the Germanic people based on blood, soil, and Nordic culture.[11] First, Eberhard Wolfgang Möller drew variations on this central motif, in both poetic and dramatic works, but the apogee of his distorted vision was realized in his successful play, *Rothschild Victorious at Waterloo* and the notorious film, *Jud Süss*. It was left to Kurt Eggers to carry the torch of murderous SS racial concepts to their final conclusion. Considering himself a Zarathustrian figure sent from above to spread the truth, his Dionysian fantasies contributed in no small way to the tragedy to follow. Many members of the young generation found all of this intoxicating and joined the conquering Nazi legions, first westward and finally into

---

[11] These concepts were well illustrated in a graph produced in Michael Gollbach's *Die Wiederkehr des Weltkrieges*, pp. 245–6, which forms the basis for much of this synopsis.

the killing fields of the Soviet Union. They had succumbed to what Fritz Stern has called the "temptation of National Socialism" and would pay a dear price for their misplaced trust.[12]

When the arts were joined to political violence, the stakes became high indeed. What began as politicized aestheticism would end in the unspeakable brutality of the Holocaust. Sadly, the route to this tragedy was often camouflaged, because force had been cleverly married to art. Enduring masterworks of German culture often provided ravishingly beautiful accompaniment to acts of criminality. It might seem innocent enough to some when propounded by Paul Alverdes, a representative figure of "inner emigration," who edited the journal *The Inner Reich* in league with Karl Benno von Mechow. He reached heights of eloquence when speaking to Munich University students in July 1934. Wrapping himself in the mantle of Friedrich Hölderlin, Alverdes called the young "to their inner selves, the mansion where the nation's culture resides," exhorting them to turn to the "great works of art and literature which make the transitory eternal." There they would find their home in that which is quietly reassuring and warm, bright and shining.[13] The truth was something entirely different from this, however. The stage was set for disaster when the myth of racial and cultural superiority became a philosophy of life and assumed political form. When Richard Strauss cast the poetry of Hugo von Hofmannsthal to music in his opera, *Ariadne auf Naxos*, the finale of which finds Ariadne transported to the *Totenreich*, the Reich of the dead where "everything is pure" by the beautiful god Bacchus, the will to transcendence through a violent end was said to have been redemptive.[14] During World War II, when exhausted German infantrymen gathered in the Kharkov railway station en route to a new posting, they lit their cigarettes and gathered around a quartet playing Beethoven, tears welling up in their eyes as they longed for family and home. Surely, many of them thought, all the suffering had to be for a reason. And when an SS officer grew claustrophobic in his winter quarters and withdrew to hear a Schubert quartet on his

[12] Fritz Stern, *Dreams and Delusions. National Socialism in the Drama of the German Past* (New York: Random House, 1984), pp. 147–91.

[13] Paul Alverdes, "Rede vom inneren Reich der Deutschen," July 19, 1934, from *Das Innere Reich* 1 (October 1934), pp. 829–43.

[14] See Michael Geyer's lyrical remarks on this motif in his essay, "There Is a Land Where Everything Is Pure: Its name Is Land of Death. Some Observations on Catastrophic Nationalism," in *Sacrifice and National Belonging in Twentieth-Century Germany*, eds. Greg Eghigian and Matthew Paul Berg (College Station: Texas A&M University Press, 2002), pp. 118–47.

portable Gramophone, it seemed to prove that Nazi cultural propaganda was on the mark. Surely, according to this thinking, it was ennobling to die for Germany, the protector of Western civilization and for the Führer, Adolf Hitler. The union of art with politics, the heart of Hitler's mission, proved to be lethal indeed.

As a result of the onset of the Third Reich, Germany's greatest literary figures were forced into exile. Thomas and Heinrich Mann, as well as Bertolt Brecht, led the list of those who felt that they had no choice except emigration. Others, such as Lion Feuchtwanger, Alfred Döblin, Ernst Toller, Franz Werfel, and Stefan Zweig, were Jews, and on racial grounds alone were no longer welcome in the nation that was their true home and whose culture they revered. As a result, the marriage of Jewish intellectual and literary talent with the greatness of classic German culture, a productive union that flowered during the modern period of Jewish assimilation, disappeared, and could never flourish in the same way it once had. Ephraim Lessing's dream for the celebration of interracial and intercultural difference – that Christian, Jew, and Moslem would mutually celebrate the genius inherent in all three religions, the lesson taught in *Nathan the Wise* – turned out to be but a fantasy, an idealistic celebration of tolerance forever destroyed. Instead, an era of base provincialism ensued, which followed the model laid out by the Nazi critic Ludwig Friedrich Barthel, who proclaimed in an essay titled "On the Nature and Value of Political Literature" that

> Political literature is nothing but the love of Germans for everything German expressed in language. A love that opens up the infinite for us, because the Fatherland expresses our identity, our all-embracing religion. One is enriched not only by turning within for strength, but by establishing boundaries to repel everything foreign. Thus our political literature is entirely German, understandable to us and only to us. This after all was what Kleist, Schiller, and Hölderlin meant when they urged the Volk to engage in its rendezvous with fate. This intimate intertwining with Germandom will ultimately result in a literature of eternal distinction.[15]

In a coda that was strangely prophetic, Barthel warned that "Our contemporary literature will no longer be poisoned by a mood of decline, rather it will either be daring and great or it will no longer exist."[16]

---

[15] Barthel, *Vom Eigentum der Seele*, pp. 166–7, 170–1, 177–8.
[16] Barthel, pp. 177–8.

The authors presented in this work played their part in creating the literary accompaniment for what was to have been the "Thousand Year Reich." They themselves proved to be as ephemeral as the National Socialist dream to which they devoted their lives. Although they played a major historical role as writers of political literature, with a wide and ultimately influential readership, they have disappeared from most general histories of German literature and from the reference books on the subject as well.

Bibliography

Archival Sources

Akademie der Künste, Berlin
  Theater Archive, Eberhard Wolfgang Möller
Bayerisches Hauptstaatsarchiv, Munich
  Sammlung Personen
    3989 Rudolf G. Binding
    7008 Eberhard Wolfgang Möller
    4747 Josef Magnus Wehner
    3229 Hans Zöberlein
    4663 Edwin Erich Dwinger
  Polizei Direktion München
    10179 Hans Zöberlein
  Landgericht München I
  Oberlandesgericht München, 1. Strafsenat
Berlin Document Center
  NSDAP Personnel Files, Reichsschriftumskammer
    Werner Beumelburg
    Edwin Erich Dwinger
    Kurt Eggers
    Hans W. Hagen
    Hanns Johst
    Eberhard Wolfgang Möller
    Franz Moraller
    Herybert Menzel
    Otto Paust
    Baldur von Schirach
    Josef Magnus Wehner
    Hans Zöberlein
Bundesarchiv Potsdam
  Sammlung Kurt Eggers
Deutsches Literaturarchiv, Marbach
  Nachlass A. Beuttenmüller

Nachlass Rudolf G. Binding
Nachlass Paul Ernst (Pseud. P.W. Spassmöller)
Nachlass Hans Grimm
Eberhard Wolfgang Möller File
Nachlass Paul Rose
Institut für Zeitgeschichte, Munich
    Akten der Parteikanzlei der NSDAP
    Sammlung Kurt Eggers
    Hans Zöberlein, "Eidesstattliche Erklärung zur Denkschrift Max
    Jüttners für IMT Nürnberg", March 20, 1946, Kornwestheim, ZS 31
National Archives
    Records of the Reichsministerium für den besetzten Ostgebiete, T-454, Roll
    75
    Hitlerjugend Schulung, Reichsjugendführerschule, NSDAP, Hauptarchiv,
    Roll 342
Private Archive: Ellen Dwinger, Wildbad Kreuth
    "Urteil der Spruchkammer Füssen vom 28. Juli 1948 über den Schriftsteller
    Edwin Erich Dwinger"
Private Archive: Alice Möller-Trinkle, Bietigheim-Bissingen
    Eberhard Wolfgang Möller
Staatsarchiv Ludwigsburg
    Denazification Records, Eberhard Wolfgang Möller
    Spruchkammer der Interniertenlager, Ludwigsburg, Kornwestheim,
    Verfahrensakten des Lagers 76, Hohenasperg, EL 903/4
Stadtbibliothek München
  Handschriftensammlung
    Sammlung Josef Magnus Wehner
  Monacensia Literaturarchiv
    Nachlass Klaus Mann
    Nachlass Josef Magnus Wehner

Interviews

Baumann, Hans. Murnau am Staffelsee, April 23, May 1, 1985.
Dwinger, Ellen. Wildbad Kreuth, January 5, 1988.
Frenzel, Elisabeth. Castell/Unterfranken, July 28–9, 2002.
Frenzel, Herbert. Berlin, March 20, 21, 30, 1990
Haegert, Wilhelm. Berlin, June 8, 1992.
Hippler, Fritz. Berchtesgaden, January 18, 1988.
Hymmen, Friedrich Wilhelm. Würzburg, May 4, 1991.
Möller, Eva. Wandsbek bei Hamburg, March 3, April 3, 1991.
Möller-Trinkle, Alice. Bietigheim-Bissingen, January 16, 1988.
Möller, Johann Michael. Bietigheim-Bissingen, January 16, 1988.
Schumann, Gerhard. May 19, 1985; March 10, 1990, Bodman/Bodensee.
Schwitzke, Heinz. Eutin, April 6, 1991.
Wien-Dwinger, Waltraut. Munich, January 6, 1988.

Feature Films

Library of Congress
  Stosstrupp 1917 (Arya Films 1934)
  Um das Menschenrecht (Arya Films 1934)
  Jud Süss (Veit Harlan 1940)

Other Documentary Sources

Der Angriff
Aufbau
Die bayerische Tapferkeitsmedaille
Berliner Börsenzeitung
Berliner Tageblatt
Berliner Tagespiegel
Börsenblatt für den deutschen Buchhandel, Frankfurt
Die Bühne
Deutsche Allgemeine Zeitung
Der deutsche Schriftsteller. Zeitschrift für die Schriftsteller in der
   Reichschriftumskammer
Deutsche Studenten Zeitung
Deutsche Wochenzeitung
Frankfurter Rundschau
Frankfurter Zeitung
Germania
Heute und Morgen. Literarischer Monatschrift
Das Innere Reich
Klütter Blätter
Kürbiskern
Die Literarische Welt
Münchener Neueste Nachrichten
Münchener Post
National Zeitung und Soldatenzeitung
Nationalsozialistische Monatshefte
Die Neue Literatur
Die Neue Rundschau
Neues Deutschland
Osteuropa
Das Reich
Reichsruf
Der SA-Mann
Die Sammlung
Das Schwarze Korps
Saarbrückener Theaterblätter
Süddeutsche Sontags Post
Der Türmer
Völkischer Beobachter

Die Weltliteratur
Westdeutscher Beobachter
Wille und Macht
Das Wort
Zeitschrift für Deutsche Bildung

Reviews and Newspaper Articles

Böse, Georg. "Zwischen den Fronten," *Berliner Tagespiegel*, February 5, 1967.

Dwinger, Edwin Erich. "Deutsche Dichter unserer Zeit," *Völkischer Beobachter*, March 22, 1939.

"Ein Ehrenabend für Zöberlein und Adam," *Völkischer Beobachter*, December 11, 1933.

Ferber, Christian. "Märtyrerkronen ohne Köpfe. Ein deutliches Wort zu einer Literatur, die keine ist." *Die Neue Zeitung*, September 27, 1952.

Grothe, Hans. "Begegnung mit Hans Zöberlein." *Völkischer Beobachter*, February 24, 1938.

Hagen, Hans W. "Der Dichter Eggers." *Westphälische Landeszeitung*, November 6, 1938.

_____. "Kurt Eggers," *Klütter Blätter* (1965) 16.

"Hans Zöberlein vor den Inhabern der bayerischen Tapferkeitsmedaille," *Völkischer Beobachter*, May 7, 1934.

"Hans Zöberlein liest vor Feierstunde des BDM," *Münchener Neueste Nachrichten*, November 18, 1937.

"Hans Zöberlein liest in Italien," *Münchener Neueste Nachrichten*, November 28, 1937.

"Hans Zöberlein liest: Kundgebung zur Buchwoche," *Münchener Neueste Nachrichten*, October 21, 1936.

Helke, Fritz, SS Kriegsberichter. "Begegnungen mit Kurt Eggers. Zum Todestag des Dichters und Soldaten," *Berliner Börsenzeitung*, August 11, 1944.

"Junge nationalsozialistische Kunst: Der Dichter Eberhard Wolfgang Möller," *Völkischer Beobachter*, October 7, 1933.

Kaiser, Friedrich. "Um die Freiheit der deutschen Seele. Zu den weltanschaulich-kämpferischen Büchern von Kurt Eggers," *Westphälische Landeszeitung*, November 6, 1938.

_____. "Kurt Eggers/Der Berg der Rebellen. Des Dichters und Mitkämpfers Buch von Annaberg," Sammlung Kurt Eggers, Institut für Zeitgeschichte.

Köhn-Behrens, Charlotte. "Die Sekunde, da ich Dichter wurde/Der Träger des National-buchpreises 1935 Eberhard Wolfgang Möller erzählt," *Berliner Illustrierte*, May 4, 1935.

"Kurt Eggers gefallen," *Die Weltliteratur* 8/9, August–September, 1943.

Leitner, Maria. "SA Mann Möller schildert Untergang." *Das Wort. Literarische Monatsschrift* 3 (1939), pp. 142–3.

Schönfeld, Herbert. "Eberhard Wolfgang Möllers Dichtung im Deutschunterricht," *Zeitschrift für Deutsche Bildung* 10 (1936), pp. 503–10.

Spitz, Rudolf T., "Edwin Erich Dwinger – gestern und heute," *Hochland Bote*, November 8, 1948.

Ulsamer, Hubert. "Hans Zöberlein: Der Glaube an Deutschland," *Völkischer Beobachter*, December 15, 1933.

"Vom mutigen Leben und tapferen Sterben," *Das Schwarze Korps*, November 18, 1943.

Weyrauch, Wolfgang. "Über Rudolf G. Binding," *Berliner Tageblatt*, November 25, 1934.

"Das Wort und die Nation: Akademierede Rudolf G. Bindings," *Berliner Börsenzeitung*, April 29, 1933.

Zöberlein, Hans. "Adolf Hitler – damals und heute," *Völkischer Beobachter*, August 18, 1934.

―――. "Antwort eines Frontsoldaten auf das Buch Remarques," *Völkischer Beobachter*, August 14, 1929.

―――. "Das Beispiel. Zum 10. Todestag Horst Wessels," *Völkischer Beobachter*, February 23, 1940.

―――. "Hans Zöberlein erzählt. Der Träger des Münchener Dichterpreises über seinen Werdegang," *Völkischer Beobachter*, August 14, 1929.

―――. "Kameraden," *Völkischer Beobachter*, April 14, 1928.

Primary Sources

Alverdes, Paul. *Reinhold oder die Verwandelten*. München: G. Müller, 1931.

―――. *Über Rudolf G. Binding*. Frankfurt: Rütten & Loening, 1925.

Anacker, Heinrich. *Über die Maas, über Schelde und Rhein. Gedichte vom Feldzug im Westen*. München: Franz Eher, 1940.

Arntz, H.-Dieter. *Ordensburg Vogelsang 1934–1945 – Erziehung zur politischen Führung im Dritten Reich*. Uskirchen: Kümpel, Volksblatt-Drückerei, 1986.

Barthel, Ludwig Friedrich, ed. *Das war Binding*. Wien/Berlin/Stuttgart: Paul Neff, 1935.

―――. *Vom Eigentum der Seele*. Jena: Eugen Diederichs, 1941.

Benjamin, Walter. *Gesammelte Schriften*. Vol. 8. Frankfurt: Suhrkamp, 1977.

Bergerhoff, Karl. *Die Schwarze Schar in O/S. Ein historischer Abschnitt aus Ober-Schlesiens Schreckenstagen*. Gleiwitz: Selbst-Verlag "Schwarze Schar," 1932.

Binding, Karl, and Hoche, Alfred. *Die Freigabe der Vernichtung lebensunwerten Lebens. Ihr Mass und Ihre Form*. Leipzig: Felix Meiner, 1920.

Binding, Rudolf G. *Der Opfergang*. Leipzig: Inselverlag, 1912.

―――. *Deutsche Jugend vor den Toten des Krieges*. Dessau: Karl Rausch, 1924.

―――. *Rufe und Reden*. Frankfurt: Rütten & Loening, 1928.

―――. *Unsterblichkeit*. Frankfurt: Rütten & Loening, 1928.

―――. *Gedichten um den Krieg. Ausgewählte und Neue Gedichte*. Frankfurt: Rütten &: Loening, 1930.

―――. *Sechs Bekenntnisse zum neuen Deutschland*. Hamburg: Hanseatische Verlagsanstalt, 1933.

―――. *Wir fordern Reims zur Übergabe auf*. Potsdam: Rütten & Loening, 1934.

―――. *Von der Kraft Deutschen Wortes als Ausdruck der Nation*. Mainz: Werkstadt für Buchdruck, 1936.

―――. *Aus dem Kriege*. Potsdam: Rütten & Loening, 1937.

―――. *Erlebtes Leben*. Frankfurt: Rütten &: Loening, 1937.

_____. *Die Briefe*. Edited by Ludwig Friedrich Barthel. Hamburg: Hans Dulk, 1957.

Bloch, Ernst. *Erbschaft dieser Zeit*. Frankfurt: Suhrkamp, 1962.

Böhme, Herbert. *Rufe in das Reich. Die heldische Dichtung von Langemarck bis zur Gegenwart*. Berlin: Junge Generation Verlag, 1934.

Brändström, Elsa. *Unter Kriegsgefangenen in Russland und Siberien 1914–1920*. Leipzig: Koehler & Ameland, 1931.

Bühnenblätter des Landestheaters der Deutschen Volksgruppe in Rumänien. Spielzeit 1941/42, Heft 6.

Decker, Will. *Kreuze am Wege zur Freiheit*. Leipzig: K. F. Koehler, 1935.

Diewerge, Wolfgang, ed. *Deutsche Soldaten sehen die Sowjetunion. Feldpostbriefe aus dem Osten*. Berlin: Wilhelm Limpert, 1941.

Dwinger, Edwin Erich. *Die Armee Hinter Stacheldraht. Das Sibirische Tagebuch*. Jena: Eugen Diederichs, 1929.

_____. *Zwischen Weiss und Rot. Die Russische Tragödie*. Jena: Eugen Diederichs, 1930.

_____. *Wir rufen Deutschland*. Jena: Eugen Diederichs, 1932.

_____. *Die letzten Reiter*. Jena: Eugen Diederichs, 1935.

_____. *Und Gott schweigt. . ?* Jena: Eugen Diederichs, 1936.

_____. *Ein Erbhof im Allgäu*. München: F. Bruckmann, 1937.

_____. *Spanische Silhouetten. Tagebuch einer Frontreise*. Jena Eugen Diederichs, 1937.

_____. *Auf halbem Wege*. Jena: Eugen Diederichs, 1939.

_____. *Der Tod in Polen. Die volksdeutsche Passion*. Jena: Eugen Diederichs, 1940.

_____. *Panzerführer. Tagebuchblätter vom Frankreichfeldzug*. Jena: Eugen Diederichs, 1941.

_____. *Wiedersehen mit Sowjetrussland. Tagebuch vom Ostfeldzug*. Jena: Eugen Diederichs, 1942.

_____. "Der Bolschewismus als Bedrohung der Weltkultur." In *Dichter und Krieger. Weimarer Reden 1942*. Edited by Rudolf Erckmann. Hamburg: Hanseatische, 1943, 13–22.

_____. "Der russische Mensch." Der Weg zur Überwindung des Bolschewismus." *Wille und Macht* 11 (April-June 1943).

_____. *General Wlassow. Eine Tragödie unserer Zeit*. Frankfurt: Otto Dikreiter, 1951.

_____. *Zwölf Gespräche, 1933–1945*. Essen: Blick & Bild Verlag, 1966.

_____. "Wie ich die Revolution erlebte." *Osteuropa* 9 (July 1967): 606–24.

Dwinger, Norbert. "Zwischen Lanzen und Pershings." In *Väter Unser. Reflexionen von Töchtern und Söhnen*. Edited by Susanne Feigl and Elisabeth Pable. Wien: Staatsdrückerei, 1988, pp. 179–210.

Eggers, Kurt. *Das Spiel von Job dem Deutschen. Ein Mysterium. Aufbruch zur Volksgemeinschaft. Eine Sammlung deutscher Volksschauspiele*. Edited by Wilhelm Karl Gerst. Berlin: Volksschaft Verlag, 1933.

_____. *Der deutsche Dämon*. Leipzig/Berlin: Ferd. Peter, 1934.

_____. *Deutsche Gedichte*. München: Chr. Kaiser, 1934.

————. *Das grosse Wandern. Ein Spiel vom ewigen deutschen Schicksal.* Berlin: Volkschaft Verlag für Buch, Bühne und Film, 1934.

————. *Hutten. Roman eines Deutschen.* Berlin: Propyläen, 1934.

————. *Sturmsignale. Revolutionäre Sprechöre.* Leipzig: Ferd. Peter, 1934.

————. *Schicksalsbrüder. Gedichte und Gesänge.* Stuttgart-Berlin: Deutsche Verlagsanstalt, 1935.

————. *Die Geburt des Jahrtausends.* Leipzig: Schwarzhäupter, 1936.

————. *Vom mutigen Leben und tapferen Sterben.* Oldenburg: G. Stalling, 1935.

————. *Der Berg der Rebellen.* Leipzig/Berlin: Schwarzhäupter, 1937.

————. *Die Heimat der Starken.* Dortmund: Volkschaft Verlag, 1938.

————. *Deutsches Bekenntnis.* Berlin: A. Boss, 1939.

————. *Feuer über Deutschland. Eine Huttenballade.* Oldenburg/Berlin: Gerhard Stalling, 1939.

————. *Der Tanz aus der Reihe.* Dortmund: Volkschaft Verlag, 1939.

————. *Von der Freiheit des Kriegers.* Berlin: Nordland, 1940.

————. *Hutten. Roman eines Deutschen.* Berlin: F. Eher, 1940.

————. *Kamerad. Gedichte eines Soldaten.* Leipzig: Schwarzhäupter, 1940.

————. *Vom Kampf und Sieg.* Erfurt: Verlag Sigrune, 1940.

————. *Das Ketzerbrevier. Zeugnisse des Kampfes um die Freiheit des deutschen Menschen.* Dortmund: Volkschaft Verlag, 1940.

————. *Die kriegerische Revolution.* Berlin: F. Eher, 1941.

————. *Rom gegen Reich. Ein Kapitel deutscher Geschichte um Bismarck.* Berlin: Nordland, 1941.

————. *Ich habs gewagt! Hutten ruft Deutschland. Huttens Gedichte und Rufe* Berlin-Lichterfelde: Widukind, 1943.

————. *Vater aller Dinge. Ein Buch des Krieges.* Berlin: F. Eher, 1943.

————. *Tausend Jahre Kakeldütt. Ein lustiger Roman.* Leipzig: Schwarzhäupter, 1944.

Ehrentafel des reichsdeutschen Adels 1914–1919. Gotha: Justus Pertes, n.d.

Elsner, Richard, ed. *Das Deutsche Drama. Ein Jahrbuch.* Berlin-Pankow: Verlag der Deutschen Nationalbühne, 1929.

Fechter, Paul. *Geschichte der Deutschen Literatur.* Berlin: Th. Knaur Nachf., 1941.

Flex, Walter. *Der Wanderer zwischen beiden Welten.* München: Beck, 1918.

Frenzel, Elisabeth. *Judengestaltung auf der deutschen Bühne. Ein notwendiger Querschnitt durch 700 Jahre Rollengeschichte.* München: Deutscher Volksverlag, 1940.

Frenzel, Herbert A. *Eberhard Wolfgang Möller. Reihe Künder und Kämpfer.* München: Deutscher Volksverlag, 1938.

Frey, V. A., ed. *Mütter und Männer. Ein Buch vom tapferen Herzen.* Stuttgart/ Berlin, Truckenmüller, n.d.

Frisé, Adolf. "Edwin Erich Dwinger." *Die Neue Rundschau* 44 (1933): 840–50.

Gaiser, Gerd. *Reiter am Himmel.* München: Langen/Müller, 1941.

Gerstner, Hermann, and Schworm, Karl, eds. *Deutsche Dichter unserer Zeit.* München: Franz Eher, 1939.

Gilman, Sander L., ed. *NS-Literaturtheorie. Eine Dokumentation.* Schwerpunkte Germanistik Series, no. 2. Frankfurt/Main: Athenäum Verlag, 1971.

Goebbels, Paul Joseph. *Die Tagebücher von Joseph Goebbels. Sämtliche Fragmente*. 4 vols. Edited by Elka Fröhlich. München: K. G. Saur, 1987.

Der Gute Kamerad. Die "Grauen Hefte" der Armee Busch. Schriftenreihe zur Truppenbetreuung: 21.

Hagen, Hans W. *Deutsche Dichtung in der Entscheidung der Gegenwart*. Berlin/Dortmund: Volkschaft Verlag, 1938.

Hartkopf, Angelus. "'Mitläufer Edwin Erich Dwinger,'" *Aufbau* 8 (1948): 807–8.

Hitler, Adolf. *Monologe im Führerhauptquartier 1941–1944*. Die Aufzeichnungen Heinrich Heims, Werner Jochmann, ed. Hamburg: Albrecht Knaus, 1980.

Hülsen, Generalleutnant Walter von. "Freikorps im Osten." *Deutsche Soldaten*. Edited by Hans Roden. Leipzig: Breitkopf & Härtel, 1935.

Kaes, Anton, ed. *Weimarer Republik. Manifeste und Dokumente zur deutschen Literatur 1918–1933*. Stuttgart: Metzler, 1983.

Kampfgedichte der Zeitenwende. Eine Sammlung aus deutscher Dichtung seit Nietzsche, Die Junge Reihe. Kampfgedichte der Zeitenwende, no. 8. München: Langen-Müller, 1935.

Kindermann, Heinz. *Die deutsche Gegenwartsdichtung im Kampf um die deutsche Lebensform*. Wien: Wienerverlagsgesellschaft, 1942.

Koeppen, Anne Marie. *Wir trugen die Fahne*. Leipzig: Hesse & Becker, 1938.

Kulturamt der Reichsjugendführung. *Liederblatt der Hitlerjugend*. Wolfenbüttel/Berlin: Georg Kallmeyer, 1936.

Langenbeck, Curt. "Wiedergeburt des Dramas aus dem Geist der Zeit." *Das Innere Reich* 10/11 (January/February 1940): 923–57.

Langenbucher, Hellmuth. *Volkhafte Dichtung der Zeit*. Berlin: Junker & Dünnhaupt, 1937.

Die Lippoldsberger Dichtertage. Bielefeld: Klosterhaus Verlag Lippoldsberg, 1960.

Mann, Klaus. *Heute und Morgen. Schriften zur Zeit*. Edited by Martin Gregor-Dellin. München: Nymphenburger, 1969.

Mayer, Anton. *Der Göttergleiche*. Potsdam: Rütten & Loening, 1939.

Menzel, Herybert, "Auf eine Frühvollendeten: Dem Freiherrn von Richthofen," *Das Reich*, August 18, 1940.

Meyer, Jochen, ed. *Berlin. Provinz. Literarische Kontroversen um 1930*. Marbach: Deutsche Schillergesellschaft, 1985.

Möller, Eberhard Wolfgang. *Berufung der Zeit. Kantaten und Chöre*. Berlin: Theaterverlag A. Langen/G. Müller, 1935.

———. *Das brüderliche Jahr. Gedichte*. Wien: Wienerverlagsgesellschaft, 1941.

———. *Douaumont oder Die Heimkehr des Soldaten Odysseus*. Berlin: Vertriebsstelle des Verbandes Deutscher Bühnenschriftsteller und Bühnenkomponisten, 1929.

———. *Das Frankenburger Würfelspiel*. Berlin: Theaterverlag A. Langen, G. Müller, 1936.

———. "Junges Schrifttum." *Das Deutsche Wort*, no. 7, 1935.

———. *Die Maske des Krieges*. Berlin: Verlag Die Heimbücherei, 1941.

———. *Das Opfer*. München: Langen/Möller, 1941.

———. *Panamaskandal*. Berlin: Theaterverlag A. Langen, G. Müller, 1936.

———. *Rothschild siegt bei Waterloo*. Berlin: Theaterverlag A. Langen, G. Müller, 1936.

———. *Russisches Tagebuch*. Osnabrück: Munin, 1971.

———. *"Über Douaumont oder Die Heimkehr des Soldaten Odysseus."* Saar-brückener *Theaterblätter*, Halbmonatsschrift des Stadttheaters Saarbrücken, 1930–1.

———. *Der Untergang Karthagos*. Berlin: Theaterverlag A. Langen, G. Müller, 1938.

Mulot, Arno. *Der Soldat in der deutschen Dichtung unserer Zeit*. Stuttgart: J. B. Metzler, 1938.

Nierentz, Hans Jürgen, *Kampfgedichte der Zeitenwende*. München: Langen/Müller, 1936.

Paust, Otto. *Nation in Not*. Berlin: W. Limpert, 1936.

———. *Volk im Feuer*. Berlin: F. Eher, 1938.

———. *Land im Licht*. Berlin: W. Limpert, 1941.

Pongs, Hermann. *Krieg als Volkschicksal im deutschen Schriftum*. Stuttgart: J. B. Metzler, 1934.

Roden, Hans. *Deutsche Soldaten*. Leipzig: Breitkopf & Härtel, 1935.

Rosenberg, Alfred. *Festgabe deutscher Dichter für Adolf Hitler*. Berlin, 1939.

———. *Das politische Tagebuch Alfred Rosenbergs 1934/35 und 1939/40*. Edited by Hans-Günther Seraphim. München: Deutscher Taschenbuch Verlag, 1964.

Roters, Eberhard, ed. *Berlin 1910–1933*. New York:Wellfleet Press, 1982.

Rühle, Günther, ed. *Zeit und Theater*, 3 vols. Berlin: Propyläen, 1972–4. Vol. 3: *Diktatur und Exil*.

Salomon, Ernst von, ed. *Das Buch vom deutschen Freikorpskämpfer*. Berlin: Wilhelm Limpert, 1938.

Schäfer, Wilhelm. *Vom deutsche Rückfall ins Mittelalter*. München: Langen/Müller, 1934.

Scheffel, V. "Annaberg,", in *Das Buch vom deutschen Freikorpskämpfer*. Edited by Ernst von Salomon. Berlin: Wilhelm Limpert, 1938, pp. 270–9.

Schirach, Baldur von. *Die Fahne der Verfolgten*. Berlin: Zeitgeschichte Verlag, 1935.

———. *Die Hitlerjugend. Idee und Gestalt*. Berlin: Zeitgeschichte, 1934.

———. *Das Lied der Getreuen*. Verse ungenannter österreicher Hitler-Jugend aus den Jahren der Verfolgung 1933–1937. Leipzig: Philipp Reclam jun., 1938.

Schönfeld, Herbert. "Eberhard Wolfgang Möllers Dichtung im Deutschunter-richt." *Zeitschrift für Deutsche Bildung* 10 (1936): 503–10.

Schuldt-Britting, Ingeborg. *Sankt Anna Platz 10*. München: Buchendorfer, 1999.

Schumann, Gerhard. *Wir aber sind das Korn*. München: Langen/Müller, 1936.

"Selbstdarstellung deutscher Dichter. Edwin Erich Dwinger." *Die Literarische Welt* 9 (April 28, 1933): 1–2.

Simon, Gerd, ed. "Hitler's Hofdichter." http://homepages.uni-tuebingen. de/gerd/ChrMoeller.pdf.

Tucholsky, Kurt. *Ausgewählte Briefe 1913–1935*. Reinbek: Rowohlt, 1962.

Volksbund Deutsche Kriegsgräberfürsorge e.V. *Den Gefallenen. Ein Buch des Gedenkens und des Trostes*. München/Salzburg: Akademischer Gemein-schaftsverlag, 1952.

Wehner, Josef Magnus. *Der Weiler Gottes*. München: Delphin Verlag, 1921.

———. *Die Hochzeitskuh. Roman einer jungen Liebe*. München: Georg Müller, 1928.

————. *Das Land ohne Schatten. Tagebuch einer griechischen Reise.* München: Georg Müller, 1930.

————. *Sieben vor Verdun.* München: Langen/Müller, 1930.

————. *Langemarck: Ein Vermächtnis.* München: Langen/Müller, 1932.

————. *Das unsterbliche Reich.* München: Langen/Müller, 1933.

————. *Mein Leben.* Berlin: Junker & Dünnhaupt, 1934.

————. *Schlageter.* Berlin: Franz Schneider, 1934.

————. *Hindenburg.* Berlin: Franz Schneider, 1935.

————. *Stadt und Festung Belgerad.* Hamburg: Hanseatische, 1936.

————. *Als wir Rekruten waren.* Hamburg: Hanseatische, 1938.

————. *Bekenntnis zur Zeit.* Köln: Staufen Verlag, 1940.

————. *Erste Liebe. Roman aus der Jugendzeit.* Hamburg: Hanseatische, 1941.

————. *Vom Glanz und Leben deutscher Bühne. Eine Münchener Dramaturgie. Aufsätze und Kritiken 1933–1944.* Hamburg: Hanseatische, 1944.

Ziesel, Kurt, ed. *Krieg und Dichtung.* Wien: Wiener Verlag, 1943

Zöberlein, Hans. *Der Glaube an Deutschland.* München: Franz Eher, 1931.

————. *Der Befehl des Gewissens.* München: Franz Eher, 1936.

————. *Der Druckposten. Eine Frontgeschichte aus des Jahres 1917.* München: Franz Eher, 1939.

————. *Der Schrapnellbaum. Vom Stellungskrieg an der Somme.* München: Franz Eher, 1939.

Secondary Sources

Andres, Jan. *"Auf Poesie ist die Sicherheit der Throne gegründet": Huldigungsrituale und Gelegenheitslyrik im 19. Jahrhundert.* Frankfurt/Main: Campus 2005.

Aschheim, Steven E. *Brothers and Strangers. The East European Jew in German and German-Jewish Consciousness, 1800–1923.* Madison: University of Wisconsin Press, 1982.

Baird, Jay W. *To Die for Germany: Heroes in the Nazi Pantheon.* Bloomington/Indianapolis: Indiana University Press, 1990.

————. *The Mythical World of Nazi War Propaganda, 1939–1945.* Minneapolis: University of Minnesota Press, 1974.

Baranowski, Shelley. *The Sanctity of Rural Life. Nobility, Protestantism & Nazism in Weimar Prussia.* New York: Oxford University Press, 1995.

Barbian, Jan-Pieter. *Literaturpolitik im Dritten Reich. Institutionen, Kompetenzen, Betätigungsfelder.* Munich: Deutscher Taschenbuch, 1995.

Bärsch, Klaus-Ekkehard. *Die politische Religion des Nationalsozialismus.* München: Fink, 2002.

Berg, Jan, ed. *Sozialgeschichte der deutschen Literatur von 1918 bis zur Gegenwart.* Frankfurt: Fischer, 1981.

Bessel, Richard. *Germany after the First World War.* Oxford: Clarendon Press, 1993.

Brenner, Hildegard. *Ende einer bürgerlichen Kunst-Institution. Die politische Formuierung der Preussischen Akademie der Künste ab 1933.* Schriftenreihe der Vierteljahrshefte für Zeitgeschichte. Stuttgart: Deutsche Verlagsanstalt, 1972.

Der Bromberger Blutsonntag. Eine Legende in Polen und Deutschland. Zebra Film: TVP Gdansk/Südwest 3/1996. Buch und Regie, Ute Boennen and Gerald Endres.

Busch, Stefan, *"Und gestern, da hörte uns Deutschland." NS-Autoren in der Bundesrepublik.* Studien zur Literatur-und Kulturgeschichte, no. 13. Mainz: Königshausen & Neumann, 1998.

Carroll, David. *French Literary Fascism: Nationalism, Anti-Semitism, and the Ideology of Culture.* Princeton: Princeton University Press, 1995.

Conquest, Robert. *The Harvest of Sorrow: Soviet Collectivization and the Terror-Famine.* New York: Oxford University Press, 1986.

Corino, Karl, ed. *Intellektuelle im Bann des Nationalsozialismus.* Hamburg: Hoffmann und Campe, 1980.

Courtois, Stéphane and Nicolas Werth, Jean-Louis Panné, Andrzej Paczkowski, Karel Bartosek, Jean-Louis Margolin. *The Black Book of Communism. Crimes, Terror, Repression.* Cambridge, MA: Harvard University Press, 1999.

Cuomo, Glenn R. *National Socialist Cultural Policy.* New York: St. Martin's Press, 1995.

Dallin, Alexander. *German Rule in Russia 1941–1945.* London: Macmillan 1981.

Denham, Scott. *Visions of War.* Bern: Peter Lang, 1992.

Denkler, Horst and Prümm, Karl, eds. *Die Deutsche Literatur im Dritten Reich.* Stuttgart: Reclam, 1976.

Dillmann, Michael. *Heinz Hilpert. Leben und Werk.* Berlin: Akademie der Künste, Edition Hentrich, 1990.

Eksteins, Modris. *Rites of Spring: The Great War and the Birth of the Modern Age.* Boston: Houghton Mifflin, 1989.

Feigl, Susanne and Elisabeth Pable, eds. *Väter Unser. Reflexionen von Töchtern und Söhnen.* Wien: Staatsdrückerei, 1988.

Feldman, Gerald D. *The Great Disorder. Politics, Economics, and Society in the German Inflation, 1914–1924.* New York/Oxford: Oxford University Press, 1993.

Ferguson, Niall. *The House of Rothschild.* 2 vols. New York: Penguin 1998.

Friedländer, Henry. *The Origins of Genocide.* Chapel Hill: University of North Carolina Press, 1995.

Friedländer, Saul. *Reflections of Nazism: An Essay on Kitsch and Death.* New York: Harper & Roe, 1984.

Fritzsche, Peter. *A Nation of Flyers. German Aviation and the Popular Imagination.* Cambridge, MA: Harvard University Press, 1992.

Fussell, Paul. *The Great War and Modern Memory.* New York: Oxford University Press, 1975.

Gadberry, Glen W. *E. W. Möller and the National Drama of Nazi Germany. A Study of the Thingspiel and of Möller's Das Frankenburger Würfelspiel*, master's thesis, University of Wisconsin, 1972.

Geissler, Rolf. *Dekadenz und Heroismus. Zeitroman und völkisch-national-sozialistische Literaturkritik.* Stuttgart: Deutsche Verlagsanstalt, 1964.

Gerber, Barbara. *Jud Süss. Aufstieg und Fall im frühen 18. Jahrhundert.* Hamburg: Hans Christians Verlag, 1990.

Gerlach, Christian. *Kalkulierte Morde. Die deutsche Wirtschafts-und Vernich-tungspolitik in Weissrussland 1941 bis 1944*. Hamburg: Hamburger Edition, 1999.

Geyer, Michael "There Is a Land Where Everything Is Pure: Its Name Is Land of Death." *Sacrifice and National Belonging*. Edited by Greg Eghigian and Matthew Paul Berg. College Station: Texas A&M University Press, 2002.

Giles, Geoffrey. *Students and National Socialism in Germany*. Princeton: Princeton University Press, 1985.

Gilman, Sander L. *NS-Literaturtheorie*. Frankfurt: Athenäum Verlag, 1971.

Goebel, Stefan. *The Great War and Medieval Memory: War, Remembrance and Medievalism in Britain and Germany, 1914–1940*. Cambridge: Cambridge University Press, 2006.

Gollbach, Michael. *Die Wiederkehr des Weltkrieges in der Literatur*. Kronberg/Ts: Scriptor Verlag, 1978.

Grunewald, Michael, ed. *Mit dem Blick nach Deutschland. Der Schriftsteller und das politische Engagement*. München: Ellermann, 1985.

Hartung, Günter. *Literatur und Äesthetik des deutschen Faschismus*. Berlin: Akademie Verlag, 1983.

Hass, Ulrike. "Vom Aufstand der Landschaft gegen Berlin." *Literatur der Weimarer Republik 1918–1933*. München/Wien: Carl Hanser, 1995.

Hermand, Jost. *Old Dreams of a New Reich: Völkish Utopias and National Socialism*. Bloomington: Indiana University Press, 1992.

Jarausch, Konrad H., and Geyer, Michael. *Shattered Past. Reconstructing German Histories*. Princeton: Princeton University Press, 2003.

Kater, Michael H. "Generationskonflikt als Entwicklungsfaktor in der NS-Bewegung vor 1933." *Geschichte und Gesellschaft* 11 (1985): 217–43.

———. *Das "Ahnenerbe" der SS 1935–1945. Ein Beitrag zur Kulturpolitik des Dritten Reiches*. Studien zur Zeitgeschichte herausgegeben vom Institut für Zeitgeschichte. Stuttgart: Deutsche Verlags-Anstalt, 1974.

———. *Hitler Youth*. Cambridge, MA: Harvard University Press, 2004.

Keegan, John. *The First World War*. New York: Knopf, 1999.

Ketelsen, Uwe-K. *Von Heroischen Sein und Völkischen Tod. Zur Dramatik des Dritten Reiches*. Bonn: Bouvier, 1970.

———. *Völkisch-nationale und nationalsozialistische Literatur in Deutschland 1890–1945*. Stuttgart: Metzler, 1976.

———. *Literatur und Drittes Reich*. Vierow bei Greifswald: SH-Verlag, 1994.

Koepke, Wulf, and Winkler, Michael, eds. *Deutschsprachige Exilliteratur*. Bonn: Bouvier, 1984.

Koonz, Claudia. *The Nazi Conscience*. Cambridge, MA: Harvard University Press, 2003.

Leed, Eric J. *No Man's Land. Combat and Identity in World War I*. Cambridge: Cambridge University Press, 1979.

Lepenies, Wolf. *The Seduction of Culture in German History*. Princeton: Princeton University Press, 2006.

Liulevicius, Vejas Gabriel. *War Land on the Eastern Front. Culture, National Identity and German Occupation in World War I*. Cambridge: Cambridge University Press, 2000.

Loewenberg, Peter. "The Psychohistorical Origins of the Nazi Youth Cohort." *American Historical Review* 76 (December 1971): 1457–1502.

Longerich, Peter. *Die braunen Bataillone.Geschichte der SA.* München: Beck, 1989.

Lower, Wendy. *Nazi Empire Building and the Holocaust in Ukraine.* Chapel Hill: University of North Carolina Press, 2005.

Mabire, Jean. *Die SS-Panzer Division "Wiking."* Preussisch Oldendorf: K. W. Schütz, 1983.

Mallmann, Marion. *Das Innere Reich. Analyse einer konservativen Kulturzeitschrift im Dritten Reich.* Bonn: Bouvier, 1978.

Marchand, Suzanne. *Down from Olympus. Archeology and Philhellenism in Germany, 1750–1970.* Princeton: Princeton University Press, 1996.

Marks, Sally. "Black Watch on the Rhine: A Study in Propaganda, Prejudice, and Prurience." *European Studies Review* 13 (July 1983): 297–334.

Martin, Bernhard. *Dichtung und Ideologie. Völkisch-nationales Denken im Werk Rudolf G. Bindings.* Frankfurt: Peter Lang, 1986.

Mechtel, Angelika. *Alte Schriftsteller in der Bundesrepublik.* München: Piper, 1972.

Meinl, Susanne. *Nationalsozialisten gegen Hitler. Die nationalrevolutionäre Opposition um Friedrich Wilhelm Heinz.* Berlin: Siedler, 2000.

Mosse, George L. *Masses and Man. Nationalist and Fascist Perceptions of Reality* New York: Howard Fertig, 1980.

_____. *The Nationalization of the Masses.* New York: Howard Fertig, 1975

_____. *Fallen Soldiers: Reshaping the Memory of the World Wars.* New York/Oxford: Oxford University Press, 1990.

Mouchard, Renate. *Der Dramatiker und Ideologe Eberhard Wolfgang Möller.* Master's thesis, Universität Köln, 1967.

Müssener, Helmut. "Becher und Dwinger." *Kürbiskern. Literatur, Kritik, Klassenkampf* 4 (February 1982): 125–33.

_____. "Edwin Erich Dwingers Roman 'Zwischen Weiss und Rot – Die russische Tragödie'." In *Deutschsprachige Exilliteratur.* Edited by Wulf Koepke and Michael Winkler. Bonn: Bouvier, 1984.

Müller, Hans. "Der pseudoreligiöse Charakter der nationalsozialistischen Weltanschauung," *Geschichte in Wissenschaft und Unterricht* 12 (1961): 337–52.

Norton, Robert E. *Secret Germany. Stefan George and His Circle.* Ithaca: Cornell University Press, 2002.

Pfeiler, Wm. K. *War and the German Mind.* New York: Columbia University Press, 1941.

Plewnia, Margarete. *Auf dem Weg zu Hitler. Der "völkische" Publizist Dietrich Eckart.* Studien zur Publizistik, Bremer Reihe, Deutsche Presseforschung, no. 14. Bremen: Schünemann Universitätsverlag, 1970.

Piper, Ernst. *Alfred Rosenberg. Hitlers Chefideologe.* Munich: Karl Blessing, 2005.

Rachamimov, Alon. *POWs and the Great War. Captivity on the Eastern Front.* Oxford/New York: Berg, 2002.

Richards, Donald Ray. *The German Bestseller in the 20th Century.* Bern: H. Lang, 1963.

Schnell, Ralf. *Dichtung in finsteren Zeiten*. Reinbek bei Hamburg: Rowohlt, 1998.

Schoeps, Karl-Heinz. *Literature and Film in the Third Reich*. Rochester: Camden House, 2004.

Schulte-Sasse, Linda. *Entertaining the Third Reich*. Durham: Duke University Press, 1996.

Slezkine, Yuri. *The Jewish Century*. Princeton: Princeton University Press, 2004.

Steigmann-Gall, Richard. *The Holy Reich. Nazi Conceptions of Christianity, 1919–1945*. New York: Cambridge University Press, 2003.

Stoehr, Ingo R. *German Literature of the Twentieth Century: From Aestheticism to Postmodernism*. Camden House History of German Literature, no. 10. Rochester, NY: Camden House, 2001.

Strassner, Peter. *Europäische Freiwillige. Die Geschichte der 5. SS Panzer-Division Wiking*. Osnabrück: Munin, 1968.

Tenfelde, Klaus. *Proletarische Provinz. Radikalisierung und Widerstand in Penzberg/Oberbayern 1900–1945*. Kollwitz über Regensburg: Michael Lassleben, 1969.

Thunecke, Jörg. *Leid der Worte. Panorama des literarischen Nationalsozialismus*. Bonn: Bouvier, 1987.

Verweht sind die Spuren. Bilddokumentation SS-Panzerregiment 5 "Wiking." Coburg: Nation Europa, 1998.

Vondung, Klaus. *Magie und Manipulation. Ideologischer Kult und politische Religion des Nationalsozialismus*. Göttingen: Vandenhoeck & Ruprecht, 1971.

Waite, Robert. *Vanguard of Nazism. The Free Corps Movement in Postwar Germany, 1918–1923*. Cambridge, MA: Harvard University Press, 1952.

Watanabe-O'Kelly, Helen. *The Cambridge History of German Literature*. Cambridge: Cambridge University Press, 1997.

Welch, David. *Nazi Propaganda*. London: Croom Helm, 1983.

———. *Propaganda and the German Cinema 1933–1945*. Oxford: Clarendon Press, 1983.

Weyergraf, Bernhard, ed. *Literatur der Weimarer Republik 1918–1933*. Hansers Sozialgeschichte der deutschen Literatur vom 16. Jahrhundert bis zur Gegenwart. no. 8. München/Wien: Carl Hanser, 1995.

Whalen, Robert Weldon. *Bitter Wounds. German Victims of the Great War, 1914–1939*. Ithaca: Cornell University Press, 1984.

Willett, John. *The Theater of the Weimar Republic*. New York: Holmes & Meier, 1988.

Winter, Jay. *Sites of Memory, Sites of Mourning*. Cambridge: Cambridge University Press, 1995.

Wohl, Robert. *The Generation of 1914*. Cambridge, MA: Harvard University Press, 1979.

Wulf, Joseph. *Literatur und Dichtung im Dritten Reich. Eine Dokumentation*. Gütersloh: Sigbert Mohn, 1963.

Index